Running the Numbers

Running the Numbers

A Practical Guide to Regional Economic and Social Analysis

John Quinterno

M.E.Sharpe
Armonk, New York
London, England

Library of Congress Cataloging-in-Publication Data

Quinterno, John.
  Running the numbers : a practical guide to regional economic and social
analysis / by John Quinterno. — First Edition.
     pages cm
  Includes bibliographical references and index.
  ISBN 978-0-7656-4104-5 (cloth : alk. paper) — ISBN 978-0-7656-4105-2
(pbk. : alk. paper) 1. Regional economics—United States. 2. Economic
development—United States. 3. Social sciences—Research—Methodology. I.
Title.

HT388.Q95 2013
330.973–dc23   2013025356

Printed in the United States of America

The paper used in this publication meets the minimum requirements of
American National Standard for Information Sciences
Permanence of Paper for Printed Library Materials,
ANSI Z 39.48-1984.

~

GP (c) 10 9 8 7 6 5 4 3 2 1
GP (p) 10 9 8 7 6 5 4 3 2 1

In memory of my grandparents,

Rose Marie Francesca (1918–2008) and Louis Facinelli (1909–2000)
Juliet Cifuni (1919–2012) and John Quinterno (1918–2010)

Contents

List of Illustrations

TABLES

FIGURES

MAPS

Boxes

Preface and Acknowledgments

A book about regional analysis in the United States began in Europe.

In the spring of 2010, I had the opportunity to spend a month in Europe as part of the Marshall Memorial Fellowship Program sponsored by the German Marshall Fund of the United States, a philanthropic organization that promotes transatlantic cooperation. The fund annually selects a group of young American and European fellows to travel to their nonnative region to gain exposure to a broad array of issues related to public affairs.

After the fellowship ended, I spent a few days on holiday in Innsbruck, Austria, an Alpine city where I spent time during college and that lies some 100 miles northeast of the small town in the Italian Tyrol where my grandfather was born. While hiking in the Alps and dining with local friends, I thought a great deal about my fellowship experience and realized that so many of the conversations I had with the 13 Americans with whom I had the privilege to travel focused on regional rather than national issues. Through those discussions, I recognized that many of the projects with which I have been involved professionally have provided me with perspectives of interest to regional leaders—perspectives that could enrich their abilities to address real problems. That insight sparked this book.

ACKNOWLEDGMENTS

I was extremely fortunate to benefit from the support of many friends and colleagues while writing the book, although, of course, the responsibility for any errors and omissions rests solely with me. Lara Raisanen read the very first pages and encouraged me to proceed with the project. Lawrence DiRe, a classmate from graduate school at the University of North Carolina at Chapel Hill and a dedicated professional public servant, provided early encouragement and took the time to read several chapters, as did Will Alexander, another friend from graduate school.

William Rivenbark, my former graduate advisor at the School of Government of University of North Carolina at Chapel Hill, read several of the earlychapters, provided constructive feedback, and helped me navigate the publishing process. Mark Roche, the former dean of the College of Arts and Letters of the University of Notre Dame, offered both practical insights into the publishing process and needed encouragement at several critical junctures.

Many other individuals generously critiqued chapters and shared ideas for how to improve the text. Anne Bacon of the North Carolina Department of Commerce read the chapter on labor markets. Gordon Whitaker, professor emeritus at the School of Government of the University of North Carolina, reviewed the chapter on data sources, concepts, and calculations and provided feedback regarding the introductory and concluding chapters. Ferrel Guillory, a professor of the practice of journalism at the School of Journalism and Mass Communication of the University of North Carolina, examined several chapters and offered advice on how to make the work more relevant to working journalists and elected officials.

John Infranca, a close friend since high school and an assistant professor of law at Suffolk University Law School in Boston, reviewed the chapter on data sources, concepts, and calculations and provided feedback on the chapters focused on business structure and theories of regional economic development. Shawn Fremstad of the Center for Economic and Policy Research in the District of Columbia undertook a close reading of the chapter on income distribution, inequality, and deprivation—a reading informed by his extensive work on issues of poverty measurement. Risto Raivio, an official with the Directorate-General for Education and Culture of the European Commission, critiqued the same chapter while he was a visiting scholar at the University of North Carolina at Chapel Hill.

Another European friend and colleague, José Alberto Lemos, a journalist based in Porto, Portugal, who writes regularly about American policy issues, provided both a helpful international perspective and needed encouragement at various times during the writing process. Much closer to home, Colin Austin, a senior program director at MDC, Inc., read the chapter about income distribution, inequality, and depravation and brainstormed a number of ideas over assorted breakfasts at Foster's Market in Chapel Hill.

Other insightful comments were provided by Jason Jurjevich, the assistant director of the Population Research Center at Portland State University in Oregon, who provided advice about the overall scope of the book and the discussion of regional demographics, and Mark Price, a labor economist at the Keystone Research Center in Harrisburg, Pennsylvania, who commented on the chapter about regional economic output. That same chapter benefited from input from T. William Lester, an assistant professor in the Department of City and Regional Planning at the University of North Carolina at Chapel Hill and an occasional collaborator on research projects.

Sean Brandon, a classmate from graduate school who is a senior manager with the City of Savannah, Georgia, provided ideas about how to make the work volume more relevant to practicing public administrators. Barbara Edwards Delsman, the former executive director of The HOPE Program, a social service agency in New York City, offered suggestions on how to connect the work to the daily concerns of executives in nonprofit organizations.

Thanks also are due to William High, a graduate student in the Department of City and Regional Planning at the University of North Carolina at Chapel Hill, for preparing the maps that appear throughout the book.

Rebecca Clendenin, a longtime friend and frequent collaborator, read the entire manuscript and improved the prose. Diane Morris, a former colleague at the North Carolina Justice Center, helped improve the text in several chapters. Elizabeth Jordan, a friend since graduate school, helped to prepare the end matter, while her three young children—Jack, Maddux, and Ellis—provided wonderful distractions from the world of facts and figures.

Greg Schrock of Portland State University deserves special mention for exceeding any expectations that an author rightly could have of a friend. Greg and I met on one of the first days of freshman orientation at the University of Notre Dame and have been friends ever since. I never have quite figured out if it is extremely fitting or extremely odd that two people with similar well-formed interests in regional economic and social affairs met at such a relatively young age, but that is a topic for another book. Besides critiquing the manuscript, Greg provided constant encouragement, connected me to resources, and championed the project in his classes and within the urban planning field. Greg and his wife, Leigh, also provided gracious hospitality during assorted visits to Portland.

I am grateful for the courteous and professional assistance provided by the people of M.E. Sharpe, Inc. Harry Briggs, executive editor for management, marketing, and public administration, immediately recognized the potential of this work and understood exactly what this first-time book author was hoping to accomplish. Elizabeth Parker, associate editor, Stacey Victor, production editor, and their colleagues on the M.E. Sharpe production team played active roles in preparing the manuscript and bringing the book to market. The manuscript also benefited from the copyediting skills of Molly Morrison.

Finally, I wish to acknowledge my parents, Barbara and John; my siblings, Barbara and Matthew; my brother-in-law, Stephen; my soon-to-be sister-in-law, Beth, and my nieces, Charlotte and Caroline, all of whom reside on Long Island, where I grew up before wandering south.

John Quinterno
Chapel Hill, North Carolina

Running the Numbers

Introduction

Bringing Order from Chaos

Economic and social data are seemingly everywhere. Each month, organizations of all kinds release torrents of information pertaining to such topics as output, employment, prices, income, and poverty. Because these numbers hold the power to move markets, drive elections, and shape public policies, they receive extensive scrutiny from analysts, executives, politicians, journalists, and citizens. During booms, business and political leaders hold up positive data—deservedly or not—as proof of their collective wisdom, but during busts, critics point to negative data—deservedly or not—as evidence of corporate and governmental failures. Especially during severe recessions like the recent one from which the United States slowly has been recovering since 2009, every major data release serves as a referendum on the state of the union.

Given the sheer size and diversity of the United States, the collection and analysis of economic and social data is an expensive, complex endeavor. In fiscal year 2011, the three major federal statistical agencies—the U.S. Census Bureau, the U.S. Bureau of Economic Analysis, and the U.S. Bureau of Labor Statistics (BLS)—had a combined budget authority of $1.8 billion.[1] State governments, meanwhile, funded the analytical capacities housed in agencies like commerce, agriculture, and workforce departments. Private-sector actors ranging from banks to trade associations to consultants also invested in data collection and analysis, as did universities, think tanks, and nongovernmental organizations.

To a casual observer, the quantity of available economic and social data must be overwhelming—an impression related in no small part to the lack of a central national statistical agency in the United States. Consider this: the BLS alone released an average of 15 employment-related reports each month in 2012.[2] Even a crucial statistic like the national unemployment rate is more complicated than it first appears: the monthly employment report actually presents two versions of the official rate—one adjusted for seasonal factors, a second that is not—and five alternate calculations.[3] Exacerbating the confusion is the dry, technical style of writing favored in government reports. And while major statistics like the unemployment rate, the Gross Domestic Product (GDP), and the poverty rate receive national media attention, the coverage tends toward simplistic "up-or-down" stories that are highly susceptible to obfuscation and misrepresentation.

Navigating the labyrinth of national economic and social data is a difficult process, but the maze is even more disorienting at the state, regional, and local levels. At the subnational level, there exists considerably less information owing to the practical difficulties and costs associated with collecting relevant data. What data exist often appear well after the fact. The Bureau of Economic Analysis, for instance, releases national GDP estimates quarterly, but publishes state figures annually.[4] Reductions in local media coverage of economic affairs tied to the downsizing of local media outlets further limit the dissemination of what data are available.

What, then, should public officials, business executives, and community leaders responsible for state, regional, or local affairs do? Can social and economic analysis help civic leaders, most of whom are laypeople wrestling with highly technical issues, identify public problems and design effective solutions? Is it even possible for regional leaders to bring a seemingly chaotic flow of facts to bear on matters of pressing local importance?

PURPOSE AND METHODS

"Yes" is the answer offered by this practical guide to regional economic and social analysis. Quality data analysis can yield rich insights into how communities function, but for leaders to benefit, they must adjust their thinking. Too often, individuals afford data more credit than they deserve and mistakenly view analysis as a process leading to the identification of a single correct solution. In reality, economic and social analysis is no more likely to yield one right answer than theological inquiry is to resolve which religion is the one true faith. Instead of asking the impossible, leaders should see analysis for what it is: a systematic framework for documenting regional realities, understanding underlying dynamics, identifying potential responses, weighing possible choices, and making rational decisions. Think of economic and social data as the raw materials to which an observer can apply analytical techniques to craft specific regional stories, such as how an area's industrial profile changed over the course of a business cycle.

To facilitate a shift in thinking, this book strives to demystify economic and social analysis through an explanation of fundamental concepts, sources, and methods. Three assumptions inform the discussion. First, regional economic and social analysis is a powerful tool for community advancement, yet the power rests not in the analyses themselves but in an observer's ability to find meaning in them. Second, a basic computer connected to the internet usually is all that a regional leader needs to access extensive amounts of economic and social data at minimal financial cost. Finally, fundamental analytical tools and techniques lie within the comprehension of any curious, educated individual willing to invest some time in learning about essential data sources and basic mathematical and statistical concepts and techniques.

That last point merits elaboration. Perhaps owing to the ineffective ways in which quantitative disciplines such as mathematics, statistics, and economics frequently are taught, many individuals harbor an intense fear of numbers—a fear that causes people either to avoid numbers altogether or to grant them a precision they seldom possess. In truth, all data are rough approximations of reality. The fact that quantitative information frequently appears in forms that are logical to experts yet baffling to laypersons only compounds misunderstandings. This book consequently employs math selectively and neither assumes a nuanced understanding of quantitative techniques nor employs techniques beyond basic arithmetic. The emphasis is on explaining core concepts, so the approach is a narrative one in which most chapters revolve around an extended analysis of an actual metropolitan region.

ORGANIZATION AND STRUCTURE

Running the Numbers contains three sections. The first section introduces fundamental concepts encountered in regional analyses. Chapter 1 considers what defines a region and introduces basic regional geography. Chapter 2 asks what "economic growth" is and how to measure it. The only theoretical part of the book, chapter 3, sketches major models that attempt to explain why regions grow and develop over time. Chapter 4 discusses basic data concepts, sources, and calculations and provides a review of basic statistics.

The second section applies these concepts and theories to selected topics of regional economic and social significance: chapter 5 explains demographics, chapter 6 explores business structure, and chapter 7 describes how labor markets function. To demonstrate the applicability of the data sources and analytical tools, each chapter contains an extended example based on real data for an actual American metropolitan area. The examples generally rely on data available at the time of writing, which typically means 2011, although in a few instances older information appears. Regardless, readers should avoid becoming fixated on specific dates because the goal of the book is to explain fundamental concepts, not individual values or long-term trends. Seen that way, grasping how the BLS defines and measures unemployment is more important than knowing the unemployment rate for a particular year; after all, a reader who has mastered the concept of unemployment should be able to interpret specific calculations derived from the idea.

The final section addresses issues linked to income and living standards: chapter 8 considers income and wealth as measures of living standards, while chapter 9 examines income distribution, income inequality, and income deprivation. The concluding chapter identifies seven mental habits that can help regional leaders "run the numbers."

This organizational structure ideally will draw readers into topics unfairly dismissed as inaccessible. Because each chapter builds logically and incrementally upon the preceding ones, a sequential reading will foster an understanding of individual subjects and their interconnections. At the same time, each chapter functions independently, so readers can jump directly to topics of personal interest. Perhaps the best way to profit from the book is to read it once from start to finish and then to revisit specific chapters in accordance with individual needs and tastes.

AUDIENCES AND TIMELINESS

Running the Numbers hopefully will enrich any curious reader, but the primary audience consists of regional elected officials, public administrators, business executives, and journalists—not to mention the staff members and senior managers of nongovernmental, civic, and philanthropic organizations—seeking a concise guide to economic and social analysis. Another important audience is students in multiple disciplines related to public affairs: public policy, urban and regional planning, public administration, social work, law, and journalism, to name but a few. The practical nature of the subjects covered in this volume nicely complements the more theoretical treatments of the same matters common in research methods classes, especially those offered at the graduate level. The book also functions as a handy one-volume reference work that can aid in the preparation of reports, theses, and dissertations.

Readers should understand that this volume is not a comprehensive textbook. Other excellent works explore individual topics in greater depth; discuss subjects mentioned only briefly in these pages, such as housing data; and pay much greater attention to theory. Readers with particular interests should consult the chapter notes and bibliography for more information. Nevertheless, the author's experiences as a researcher specializing in economic and social policy indicate that the topics included in this book are of frequent interest to regional leaders.

Ideally, readers will find the work a timely one. The problems that have afflicted the economy in the wake of the "Great Recession" have heightened public interest in statistical data and have led the statistical agencies to modify their programs to better capture current conditions, as the BLS did when it altered how it measures the duration of unemployment.[5] Federal statistical agencies also have become entangled in political controversies, as occurred during the 2012 presidential campaign when some critics alleged that the BLS was manipulating unemployment data for partisan purposes.[6] Meanwhile, federal budget reductions have led to the elimination of popular statistical products and the proposed termination of other programs, including several valued highly by the business community.[7]

Adding to the timeliness of the book is the ongoing release of data from the 2010 Decennial Census of Population and Housing, an enumeration of the American population. The Census Bureau published the first results in December 2010, and will continue to release data in the coming years.[8] Another milestone was reached in late 2010, when the Census Bureau completed implementation of the American Community Survey, which provides yearly information about population characteristics for every community in the country; the annual availability of data previously collected once per decade is a boon to regional analysis. The Census Bureau also recently finished releasing data from the 2007 Economic Census and launched the 2012 version of that important enumeration of business establishments. Furthermore, the growth of the internet has led federal statistical agencies to overhaul their websites and endeavor to use information technologies to disseminate data more widely and conveniently: in 2012, for example, the Census

Bureau released the "America's Economy" mobile application to provide instant access to key economic indicators.[9]

ASSUMPTIONS AND OUTCOMES

Although *Running the Numbers* is a dispassionate introduction to regional data and data analysis, some readers may try to attribute political or ideological views to the author based on the selection of topics. Such ideological questions are not particularly pertinent to a reference work like this one, but they may be asked and so deserve an upfront answer.

As the founder and principal of South by North Strategies, Ltd., a small research consultancy specializing in economic and social policy, the author recognizes that a market system is a powerful, often elegant means for organizing human relationships in pursuit of higher material living standards. The book consequently strives to deepen understanding of economic issues as they pertain to regions. Unless regional leaders grasp how an economy works, recognize strengths, perceive weaknesses, and appreciate the challenges facing local firms, entrepreneurs, and workers, their communities will not thrive. If support of market mechanisms represents a conservative worldview, at least in the American sense of the term, so be it.

Yet a respect for markets in no way implies an uncritical acceptance of market outcomes. Markets frequently fail and produce results that, even if efficient, are inequitable or offensive to popular conceptions of fairness and justice. Only common efforts can inoculate markets against their self-destructive tendencies, foster a more egalitarian community, and advance social equity. This is especially true in regard to the mechanism through which most individuals participate in the larger economy, that is, the labor market.

Much of this book follows the traditional approach of measuring living standards in relation to economic variables like output and income. The reduction of human well-being to a few factors measured solely in terms of money, however, obscures many other things that people value, such as happiness, health, education, security, and sustainability. Recall Senator Robert Kennedy's famous description of the Gross National Product as a statistic that "measures everything in short, except that which makes life worthwhile."[10] Cognizant of that shortcoming, this book notes the defects of a number of statistics and discusses alternate approaches that have attracted interest in recent years, particularly in Europe. The purpose in referencing international approaches is not to assert that they are inherently superior to American ones, but to expose readers to the diversity of thought that surrounds concepts of fundamental social importance and to illustrate how other wealthy nations have grappled with the same questions.

The correct standard against which to judge this volume, then, is not in terms of politics, but in terms of effectiveness. If the book explains regional economic and social analysis to nonexpert regional leaders in ways that improve their abilities to bring order out of a seemingly chaotic flow of information for the benefit of individual communities, it will have succeeded in achieving its goals.

NOTES

1. U.S. Department of Commerce, *Fiscal Year 2013: Budget in Brief* (Washington, DC, n.d.), 37 and 48, http://www.osec.doc.gov/bmi/budget/FY13BIB/fy2013bib_final.pdf (accessed October 26, 2012); and U.S. Department of Labor, *Fiscal Year 2013: Budget in Brief* (Washington, DC, n.d.), 57, http://www.dol.gov/dol/budget/2013/PDF/FY2013BIB.pdf (accessed October 26, 2012). The federal fiscal year runs from October 1 to September 30.

2. U.S. Bureau of Labor Statistics, "2012 Release Calendar," news release, last revised September 20, 2012, http://www.bls.gov/schedule/news_release/2012_sched.htm.

3. For an example, see U.S. Bureau of Labor Statistics, "Employment Situation, September, 2012," news release, October 5, 2012, http://www.bls.gov/news.release/archives/empsit_10052012.pdf.

4. U.S. Bureau of Economic Analysis, "2012 Release Schedule," news release, last revised October 26, 2012, http://bea.gov/newsreleases/2012rd.htm.

5. Caitlin Kenney, "BLS Changes Survey to Record Longer Periods of Unemployment," National Public Radio, December 28, 2010, http://m.npr.org/news/front/132411278.

6. John Quinterno, *Where Do National Employment Numbers Come From?* (Chapel Hill, NC: South by North Strategies, 2012), http://www.sbnstrategies.com/archives/12139.

7. For information about funding debates related to the U.S. Census Bureau, see Robert Groves, "A Future without Key Social and Economic Statistics for the Country," U.S. Census Bureau Director's Blog (blog), May 11, 2012, http://directorsblog.blogs.census.gov/2012/05/11/a-future-without-key-social-and-economic-statistics-for-the-country/; and Catherine Rampell, "The Beginning of the End of the Census?" *New York Times,* May 19, 2012, http://www.nytimes.com/2012/05/20/sunday-review/the-debate-over-the-american-community-survey.html.

8. U.S. Census Bureau, "2010 Census Data Products: United States, at a Glance, Version 2.2," http://www.census.gov/population/www/cen2010/glance/ (accessed October 26, 2012).

9. As of October 25, 2012, information about the "America's Economy" mobile application, including links for downloading the tool, was available at http://www.census.gov/mobile/.

10. Robert Kennedy, remarks at the University of Kansas, March 18, 1968, John F. Kennedy Presidential Museum and Library, http://www.jfklibrary.org/Research/Ready-Reference/RFK-Speeches/Remarks-of-Robert-F-Kennedy-at-the-University-of-Kansas-March-18–1968.aspx (accessed August 31, 2011). Gross National Product (GNP) was the primary measure of economic production used in the United States prior to the adoption of the concept of Gross Domestic Product (GDP) in 1991.

1 Regional Geography

Chapter 1

The Research Triangle region of North Carolina stretches south from the tobacco fields along the Virginia border into the ancient dunes of the Sandhills, east from the hilly Piedmont onto the flat Atlantic coastal plain. With 1.8 million residents in 2011, the Research Triangle was the 27th-most populous consolidated metropolitan region in the United States and the second-most populous one in North Carolina.[1]

Besides inhabiting a distinct physical space, residents of the Research Triangle share economic, social, political, and cultural ties that shape the patterns of daily life. For despite the capabilities of communications and transportation technologies to link people across the globe, humans remain physical, time-bound beings who are likely to define themselves in relation to the communities in which they live and work. Put simply, place matters.

People may grasp intuitively the idea of a region, but popular understandings typically lack the precision necessary for economic and social analysis. Think of all the ways of viewing the Research Triangle region: The area encompasses eight counties and four sizable cities, Raleigh (pop. 412,000), Durham (pop. 232,000), Cary (pop. 139,000), and Chapel Hill (pop. 58,000). Seven of the counties belong to one of two metropolitan statistical areas, and the remaining county is an individual micropolitan statistical area (see Map 1.1). Collectively the eight counties form a larger combined statistical area, which itself sits in a larger 13-county state economic development region. That region, in turn, functions as a single labor market containing six workforce development areas and five community college service districts. And the broad Research Triangle region is home to at least 64 incorporated municipalities, some of which are rural in character, others urban or suburban.[2]

What, then, is the Research Triangle, and which version of the region should a civic leader consider when attempting to reach decisions on behalf of the common good? A definition that is too narrow in scope will exclude relevant parts of a region, but a definition that is too broad will include extraneous areas. One solution is to beg the question and concentrate on governmental geographies like cities and counties, even though economic and social phenomena seldom follow political lines. A labor market study of Durham County

7

Map 1.1 Principal Cities and Component Counties of Raleigh-Durham-Cary, NC Combined Statistical Area, 2009 Delineation

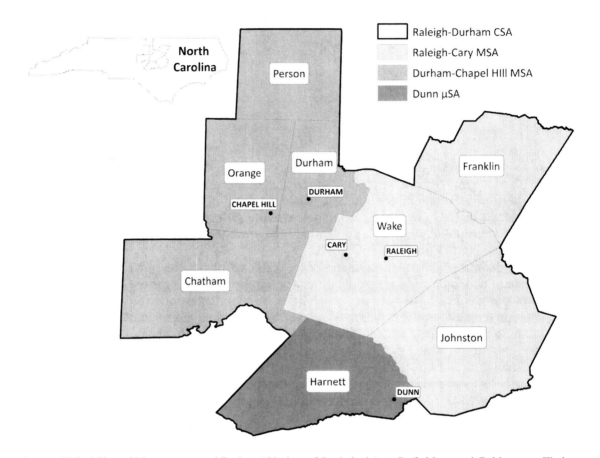

Source: U.S. Office of Management and Budget, "Update of Statistical Area Definitions and Guidance on Their Uses (OMB Bulletin No. 10-02)," December 1, 2009, http://www.whitehouse.gov/sites/default/files/omb/assets/bulletins/b10-02.pdf. Map prepared by William High.

that only included working-age residents of the county would miss the fact that, on average, half of the people who worked in the county between 2006 and 2008 commuted from other counties.[3] When it comes to the labor market, the county lines are of little importance.

Such definitional problems are hardly unique to the Research Triangle. A threshold step in any study of regional economic and social issues therefore is defining the area of interest precisely enough for analytical purposes. To assist regional leaders in that task, this chapter introduces essential concepts related to regions and regional geography. The chapter begins by summarizing three ways of viewing regions, proceeds to describe the system of regional geography developed by the U.S. Census Bureau, and concludes with a discussion of practical considerations associated with defining regions. As a way of illustrating the topics, the chapter offers examples drawn from data for the Research Triangle region.

THREE WAYS OF PERCEIVING REGIONS

Scholars, developers, journalists, planners, and politicians frequently invoke "regions" and "regionalism" as justifications for any number of public policies and investments. Perhaps one reason the term enjoys such popularity is because it lacks a clear definition. Observers of a region indeed may "know it when [they] see it," to misapply Supreme Court Justice Potter Stewart's famous definition of obscenity, but such an elastic understanding is inappropriate for regional economic and social analysis.[4]

Few residents of the Research Triangle would deny that it is a region of some sort, but many would contest its boundaries and its degree of interconnectedness. The Research Triangle nevertheless is a *region* in that it is "an area within the national economy that is sufficiently comprehensive in structure that it can function independently, although of course in most practical circumstances it has strong links with the rest of the economy."[5] Yet even that definition is vague, and in response, observers tend to view regions from one of three perspectives: territorial, functional, or administrative.

Before describing each perspective, it is important to acknowledge that each one is more complex than its description implies. An exhaustive account is beyond this book's scope, and the intention here is to provide a basic orientation to common ways of understanding regions. In practice, most regional studies blend the functional and administrative perspectives for reasons of feasibility and because civic leaders tend to think in terms of administrative structures. The exact mix of perspectives, however, hinges on the particular research questions and the availability of pertinent data.

TERRITORIAL PERSPECTIVE

The *territorial perspective* envisions a region as a "historically evolved, contiguous society that possesses a physical environment, a socioeconomic, political, and cultural milieu, and a spatial structure distinct from the other major territorial units, city, and nation."[6] The strength of this view is its recognition of the interplay between the physical environment and social dynamics. Regions are not simply discrete physical spaces, but rather the intricate products of economic and social interactions. Economic factors are particularly important in differentiating regions, as evidenced in the journalist Tom Wolfe's observation about how when traveling by road in the United States "the only way you could tell you were leaving one community and entering another was when the franchises started repeating, and you spotted another 7-Eleven, another Wendy's, another Costco, another Home Depot."[7]

More seriously, besides separating regions from one another, economic factors structure social relationships among different segments of the population. Look at how

Map 1.2 Average Per Capita Income by County as a Share of Average per Capita Income in the Raleigh-Durham-Cary, NC Combined Statistical Area, 2006–2010

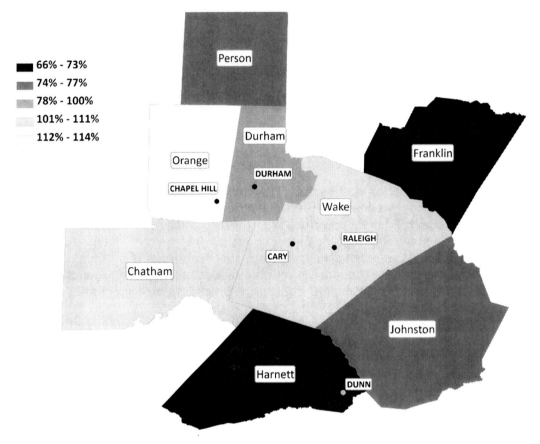

Source: Author's analysis of U.S. Census Bureau, American Community Survey, Five-Year Estimates, 2006–2010; and U.S. Office of Management and Budget, "Update of Statistical Area Definitions and Guidance on Their Uses (OMB Bulletin No. 10-02)," December 1, 2009, http://www.whitehouse.gov/sites/default/files/omb/assets/bulletins/b10-02.pdf. Map prepared by William High.

the dominance of the automotive industry in Detroit long shaped not just the region's economic activities, but also its local labor practices and social norms about what constituted—and who was entitled to—a middle-class lifestyle. The auto industry's dominance further influenced other aspects of regional life, such as local politics, due to trade union activism, and the cultural scene, thanks to corporate and personal philanthropy.[8] A similar dynamic has occurred in the Research Triangle region over the past half century in response to the growth, evolution, and decline of the technology and life science firms operating in the Research Triangle Park, a centrally located research campus.[9]

When viewing a region in terms of territory, it is important to remember three things. First, a territorial region may or may not possess a distinct political identity. The Research Triangle region, for example, has neither an independent political existence nor any binding form of regional government. Second, territorial regions are dynamic in nature and change over time in response to economic and social forces. Finally, despite being located in the same general physical area, places within a region are not homogenous in character: intraregional differences exist because economic and social forces seldom exert uniform influences across an entire territory. During the period spanning 2006 to 2010, for instance, average per capita income in Wake County (Raleigh) was 11.5 percent higher than the level posted in the entire Research Triangle, but average per capita income in neighboring Franklin County (Louisburg) was 27 percent lower than the regional figure (see Map 1.2).[10]

FUNCTIONAL PERSPECTIVE

A second way of viewing a region is from a *functional perspective*. Central to this view is the notion that regions contain certain dominant cities or places (sometimes called *nodes*) that are tied to other, less dominant places within the area. A region therefore is a discrete spatial area containing interconnected places of differing sizes and types (e.g., town and country, farms and cities, central business districts and suburbs, residential communities and office parks). While the parts of a region may differ in terms of characteristics and functions, they share links that "can be identified through observation of flows of people, factors, goods, and communication."[11]

Commuting patterns are one manifestation of the functional relationships that exist within a region. Compare the typical commuting patterns of the residents of two counties in the Research Triangle—Orange (Chapel Hill) and Wake (Raleigh)—between 2006 and 2008 (see Map 1.3). During that period, Orange County was home to an average of 62,405 working residents, of whom 58.7 percent commuted to worksites within the county and the remaining 41.3 percent to jobs in other counties. The most common destination was neighboring Durham County (Durham), to which 59.9 percent of all commuters traveled, followed by Wake County, which was where 15.4 percent of commuters headed. During the same three-year period, Wake County was home to an average of 427,259 working residents, of whom 81.6 percent worked within the county. Of the 18.4 percent of county residents who worked elsewhere, 59.3 percent journeyed to Durham County while 7.4 percent commuted to Orange County. In both communities, the overwhelming majority of commuters traveled alone in private automobiles.[12]

These commuting patterns reveal some of the functional relationships that exist among places within the Research Triangle. While Orange and Wake counties share commuting ties, those links are not as strong as those that exist between each county and Durham County, which clearly is a regional employment center. Similarly, given that Interstate 40 is a major thoroughfare connecting Durham, Wake, and Orange counties, it is unsurprising that multiple retail centers have emerged along a corridor that carries sizable numbers of people to and from work.

Map 1.3 Share of Working-Age Residents Commuting for Work to Durham County, NC, Counties in the Raleigh-Durham-Cary, NC Combined Statistical Area, 2006–2008

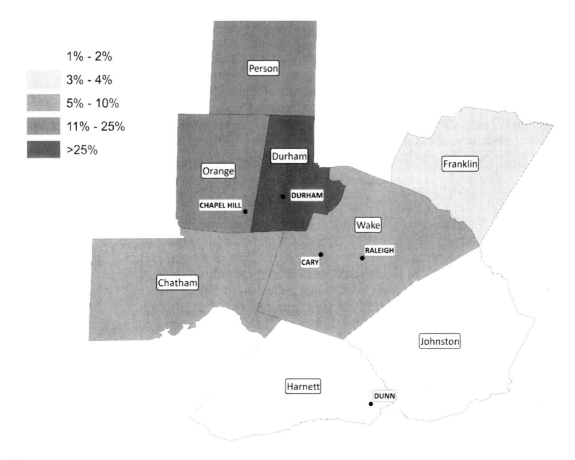

Source: Author's analysis of U.S. Census Bureau, American Community Survey, Three-Year Estimates, 2006–2008; and U.S. Office of Management and Budget, "Update of Statistical Area Definitions and Guidance on Their Uses (OMB Bulletin No. 10-02)," December 1, 2009, http://www.whitehouse.gov/sites/default/files/omb/assets/bulletins/b10-02.pdf. Map prepared by William High.

Despite its emphasis on the actual relationships among different parts of a region, the functional perspective suffers from weaknesses. Because regional boundaries frequently are blurry, it can be difficult to determine which peripheral areas belong to a region and which ones fall outside of it; this choice may prove especially vexing when regional functions spill across administrative and political borders. Another difficulty occurs when dealing with an area with multiple large population or economic centers, as it can be difficult to determine when one region has evolved into two or more regions. Lastly, because regions are dynamic in nature, intraregional functional relationships may change over time.

ADMINISTRATIVE PERSPECTIVE

An *administrative perspective* understands a region in relation to the organizational and political structures used to deliver public services, such as counties, cities, planning boards, and transportation districts. These entities are spatial areas "over which economic decisions and policy instruments apply."[13] As bureaucratic structures, administrative agencies tend to collect extensive information about their activities, and these records are robust sources of regional data.

Like most states, North Carolina has created counties to deliver certain governmental services in specific areas. Each Research Triangle county, for instance, must administer "state and federal-state social service programs for the benefit of county residents."[14] Because county agencies oversee the programs, they tend to collect data only for the county for which they are responsible. That explains why studies of social services in North Carolina typically center on counties. Research into workforce training, in contrast, regularly employs data compiled by the local workforce boards legally responsible for coordinating training within discrete, often multicounty areas (see Map 1.4).

Look beyond its apparent simplicity, and the administrative perspective suffers from practical problems such as inconsistent and incomparable data collection. More important, social and economic phenomena seldom follow administrative lines due to the mobility of individuals and the fact that the drawing of administrative lines often occurred years earlier for reasons unrelated to contemporary conditions. North Carolina established most of its counties in the nineteenth century in response to jockeying between the eastern and western parts of the state for control of the statehouse; when a new county was formed in the west, legislators would split an eastern county into two in an effort to offset the new western one.[15] That solution may have fit the times, but it has no relationship to the realities facing today's Research Triangle—a region that effectively did not exist until decades after the creation of North Carolina's most recently formed county.

CENSUS GEOGRAPHY: A POWERFUL BUT CONFUSING FRAMEWORK

The U.S. Census Bureau doubtlessly is the nation's best-known public statistical agency thanks to its responsibility for conducting the Decennial Census of Population and Housing, an enumeration of the population that is constitutionally required to occur every 10 years for the purposes of allocating congressional seats and electoral votes among the states.[16] The census started as a loosely organized affair that grew in size and scope along with the county, and in 1902, the complexity of the task led the U.S. Congress to establish a permanent Census Bureau, which today is an agency within the U.S. Department of Commerce.[17]

The mission of the Census Bureau is to be "the leading source of quality data about the nation's people and economy."[18] A challenge associated with that task is how best to organize the vast amounts of information that the agency collects, and to that end the Census Bureau has developed a geographical framework that enables the tabulation of data from the level of individual housing units to the entire nation.[19] The system is

Map 1.4 Workforce Development Boards in the Raleigh-Durham-Cary, NC Combined Statistical Area, 2009 Delineation

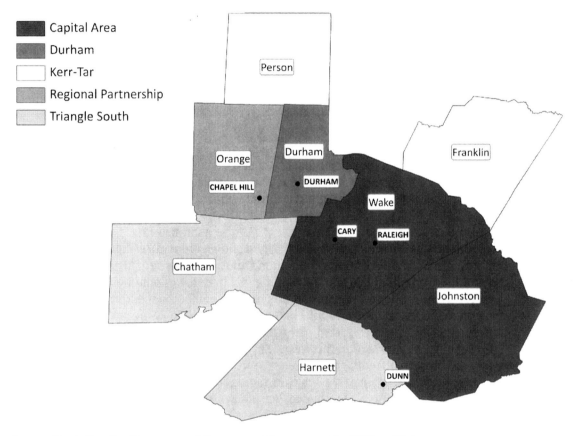

Source: North Carolina Department of Commerce. Map prepared by William High.

a practical way of organizing regional data, but the structure and terminology appear, at first glance, to be rather complicated.[20]

In essence, the Census Bureau's geographic framework is a hierarchical structure "derived from the legal, administrative, or areal relationships" that exist among governmental and statistical units.[21] Governmental units such as cities, counties, and states are familiar to most people, but statistical units such as census tracts and metropolitan statistical areas are less well understood. Statistical units often strike people as unreal because they "are created by the Census Bureau and do not exist as independent governmental units."[22] In reality, even governmental units are artificial constructs: counties and cities, after all, are "created by the state and derive their authority and power solely from the state."[23] Nevertheless, people perceive governmental units as being more tangible, perhaps because it is easy to conflate them with communities.

When interpreting geographical data from the Census Bureau, consumers of the information should heed a few practical suggestions. First, data users should remember that it is essentially impossible to obtain information about individual persons and households from census products since federal law treats all responses as confidential. One way in which the Census Bureau ensures personal privacy is by aggregating individual data into progressively larger groupings called *summary levels*. Summary data for a city encompasses information for all of the smaller geographies that constitute the city. A basic step in performing any analysis, then, is to select the appropriate summary level. Second, it is important to check for consistency across summary levels to ensure the accuracy of any comparisons that are drawn. It would be inappropriate, say, to employ state-level data in a city-level study. Third, because the composition of a summary level may change over time, data users should confirm that a given level actually contains the geography of interest.[24] Finally, for reasons outlined in chapter 4, data users should note whether the information originates in an enumeration, a survey, or a set of administrative records.

The following sections describe the Census Bureau's geographical framework. The first part explains the agency's basic hierarchy, the second part the extended geographical hierarchy, and the final part state-specific geographies sometimes encountered in regional studies.

THE BASIC GEOGRAPHICAL HIERARCHY

Housing units are the basic building blocks of census data. A *housing unit* is "a house, an apartment, a mobile home, a group of rooms, or a single room that is occupied (or if vacant, intended for occupancy) as separate living quarters"; separate living quarters are "those in which the occupants live and eat separately from any other persons in the building and which have direct access from outside the building or through a common hall."[25] The Census Bureau's Master Address File contains the addresses and geographical locations of every housing unit in the country. When administering mail-based programs like the decennial census, the agency sends questionnaires to addresses in the file. Federal law requires occupants to complete and return the forms, which the Census Bureau then codes to ensure confidentiality. The agency further organizes the responses in a geographical framework that aggregates individual observations into increasingly larger geographies.

Figure 1.1 shows the basic geographical hierarchy as it applies to a generic neighborhood in Chapel Hill, North Carolina. The indentations indicate the hierarchical relationships among the geographies. Observe how most lower-level geographies are statistical units, and most of the higher-level ones are governmental units.

The first summary level in the census framework is a *census block*, a small area that has about 85 residents and that is "bounded by visible features such as streets, roads, streams, and railroad tracks, and by nonvisible boundaries, such as selected property lines and city, township, school district, and county limits and short line-of-sight extensions of streets and roads."[26] A census block is ideally a compact area like the one formed by four intersecting roads, but a rural block may span hundreds of square miles. All American territory belongs to a census block.

Figure 1.1 The Basic Geographical Hierarchy of the U.S. Census Bureau

Generic Hierarchy

United States
  Region
    Division
      State (including District of Columbia)
        County
          County subdivision
            Place
              Census tract
                Block group
                  Census block

Sample Hierarchy for a Neighborhood in Chapel Hill, North Carolina

United States
  South
    South Atlantic
      North Carolina
        Orange County
          Chapel Hill Township (nonfunctioning unit)
          Town of Chapel Hill
            Census tract (no name; unique numerical identifier)
              Block group (no name; unique numerical identifier)
                Census block (no name; unique numerical identifier)

Source: U.S. Census Bureau, "Appendix A: Geographic Terms and Concepts," in *2010 Redistricting Data (Public Law 94-171) Summary File* (Washington, DC: U.S. Department of Commerce, 2011), A-4.

The second summary level is a *block group*. Block groups are intact clusters of (typically) contiguous census blocks. A block group contains between 600 and 3,000 people with an ideal population of 1,500. The Census Bureau generally establishes block groups, which may not cross the boundaries of census tracts or counties, in consultation with local residents. Block groups are the smallest geographical units for which data obtained through statistical sampling are available (see chapter 4).

Census tracts, the third summary level, are "small, relatively permanent statistical subdivisions of a county or equivalent entity" formed from adjoining block groups.[27] Tracts contain between 1,200 and 8,000 people but have an ideal size of 4,000. Counties with fewer than 1,200 residents have one census tract. Because census tracts resemble neighborhoods, they should remain constant over time, yet population growth periodically requires the division of a tract. For practical reasons, census tracts often are the smallest units with which analysts work.

Census tracts constitute *counties* and *county equivalents*, which are the first governmental units in the Census Bureau's basic hierarchy. Counties ("parishes" in Louisiana) are the main administrative units in every state except Alaska. Maryland, Missouri, Nevada, and Virginia, meanwhile, grant *independent cities* like Richmond, Virginia, and St. Louis, Missouri, the powers of counties. As with all governmental units, the Census Bureau imposes no population thresholds on counties: Loving County, Texas (pop. 94) and Los Angeles County, California (pop. 9.9 million) both are counties. [28] Counties and their equivalents consist of adjacent, intact census tracts. County lines are quite stable, though they occasionally change.[29] Connecticut, Massachusetts, and Rhode Island, for instance, have abolished some or all of their counties.

County subdivisions are "the primary divisions of counties and county equivalents."[30] County subdivisions may be either governmental or statistical units. Some 29 states divide counties into *minor civil divisions* that enjoy a distinct legal status; in 12 of those states, the divisions serve as general purpose governmental units along the lines of townships in Michigan. In a few states, areas that fall outside of minor civil divisions belong to *unorganized territories.* Twenty states have no legal county subdivisions and rely on statistical units known as *census county divisions.* The remaining state, Alaska, uses a statistical unit called a *census subarea.*[31]

Some counties contain *places* that are statistical or governmental units. Counties must provide services to all inhabitants of an area, but every state except Hawaii permits the formation of *incorporated places* to "provide governmental functions for a concentration of people as opposed to a minor civil division, which generally is created to provide services or administer an area without regard, necessarily, to population."[32] Incorporated places such as cities, boroughs, towns, and villages may cross county lines but not state ones. Not all cities and towns are incorporated places. In New York, Wisconsin, and the New England states, "towns" are minor civil divisions, while the independent cities of Maryland, Missouri, Nevada, and Virginia actually are counties. When a concentration of people exists in an unincorporated place with a recognized name, the statistical unit *census designated place* applies.

Groups of counties or county equivalents form *states*, which are the primary governmental divisions of the United States (the Census Bureau treats the District of Columbia as a state). Each state belongs to one of nine *census divisions* that collapse into four *census regions*, which collectively constitute the United States of America (see Map 1.5).

The census framework accommodates much of the variation and diversity found in one of the largest nations in the world. Yet no single system can reflect every nuance. In fact, the Census Bureau applies a parallel geographical framework to federally recognized American Indian, Alaskan Native, and Native Hawaiian areas.[33] Modified geographical systems also apply to the Commonwealth of Puerto Rico and the insular territories of American Samoa, Guam, the Northern Mariana Islands, and the U.S. Virgin Islands. (As a general overview, this book presents the most common geographies, and individuals with special interests should consult the sources cited in the notes and bibliography.)

Map 1.5 Census Regions and Divisions of the United States

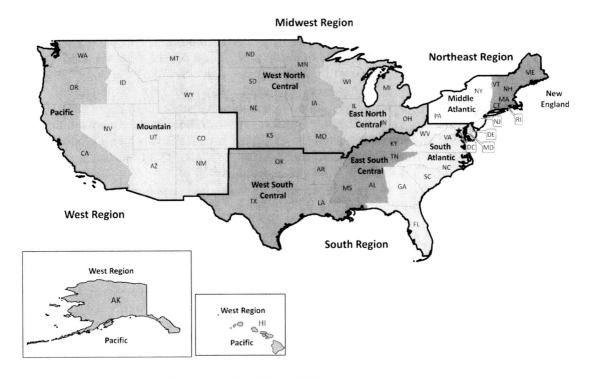

Source: U.S. Census Bureau. Map prepared by William High.

THE EXTENDED GEOGRAPHICAL HIERARCHY

Despite its usefulness, the Census Bureau's basic geographical hierarchy fails to capture all of the interconnections found within a region. The Census Bureau therefore has developed an extended geographical hierarchy that layers special units—some of which are governmental in nature, some statistical, and some a combination of the two—over the basic framework (see Figure 1.2). Places are part of the extended hierarchy, as are *special-purpose districts*, such as school districts, legislative districts, congressional districts, voting districts, ZIP code tabulation areas, and traffic analysis zones. Special-purpose districts comprise various combinations of census blocks, block groups, and census tracts. For the purposes of this book, two elements of the extended hierarchy deserve consideration: metropolitan and micropolitan statistical areas and urban and rural areas.

Metropolitan and Micropolitan Statistical Areas

Metropolitan and micropolitan statistical areas are types of *core based statistical areas* (CBSAs). These are counties or county equivalents or sets of counties or county

Figure 1.2 The Basic and Extended Geographical Hierarchies of the U.S. Census Bureau

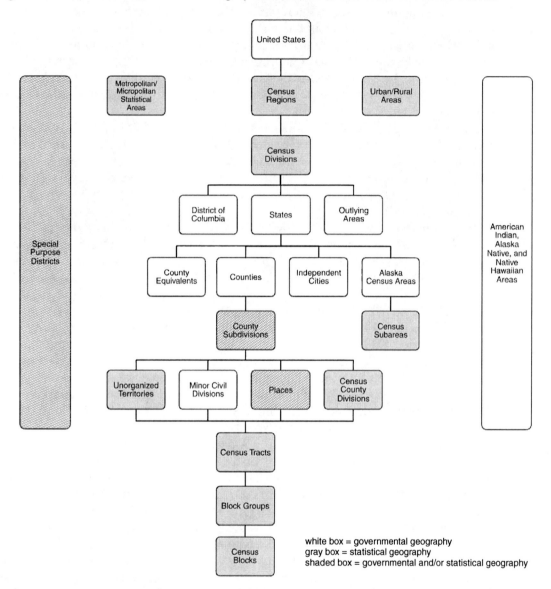

white box = governmental geography
gray box = statistical geography
shaded box = governmental and/or statistical geography

Sources: Alan Peters and Heather MacDonald, *Unlocking the Census with GIS* (Redlands, CA: Esri Press, 2004), 26; and U.S. Census Bureau, "Appendix A: Geographic Terms and Concepts," in 2010 *Redistricting Data (Public Law 94-171)* Summary File (Washington, DC: U.S. Department of Commerce, 2011), A-27, http://www.census.gov/prod/cen2010/doc/pl94-171.pdf.

equivalents with at least one urbanized area of 10,000 or more residents and a high degree of economic and social interconnectedness as measured by commuting ties to the core. A CBSA takes its name from an area's principal city—the largest, preferably incorporated, place with at least 10,000 residents—and any additional places that satisfy size and functional requirements. Examples of CBSAs and the official style of writing the names include the Casper, WY Metropolitan Statistical Area, the Charlotte-Gastonia-Salisbury, NC-SC Consolidated Statistical Area, and the Clovis, NM Micropolitan Statistical Area.

Responsibility for defining CBSAs rests with the U.S. Office of Management and Budget (OMB), a unit within the Executive Office of the President. The office undertakes an extensive review of the definitions and delineations following each decennial census.[34] While OMB prefers the term CBSA, the Census Bureau favors the term "Metropolitan and/or Micropolitan Statistical Area."[35] *Nonmetropolitan areas* refer to counties outside of CBSAs.

A *metropolitan statistical area* (MSA) is a CBSA containing a county or county equivalent or a set of counties or county equivalents with at least one urbanized area of 50,000 or more residents and a high degree of economic and social interconnectedness as measured by commuting links to the core. An MSA with a population core of at least 2.5 million inhabitants may contain smaller areas called *metropolitan divisions*. The San Francisco-Oakland-Freemont, CA MSA, for example, has two divisions: the Oakland-Freemont-Haywood, CA Metropolitan Division and the San Francisco-San Mateo-Redwood City, CA Metropolitan Division. Because counties have limited authority in the six New England states (Connecticut, Rhode Island, Massachusetts, Vermont, New Hampshire, and Maine), there exist supplemental sets of *New England City and Town Areas* and *New England City* and *Combined New England City and Town Areas* that are defined using criteria similar to those applied to county-based areas. In 2011, the country had 366 MSAs that collectively contained 83.8 percent of the national population, or 261.1 million Americans (see Figure 1.3).[36]

In 2003, OMB created a new type of CBSA: a *micropolitan statistical area* (μSA). Typically a small population center such as a town or exurb, a μSA possesses at least one urban cluster encompassing between 10,000 and 49,999 residents. Examples of μSAs are the Elko, NV μSA and the Concord, NH μSAs. As of 2011, 10 percent of the American population—some 31 million persons in all—lived in the country's 576 μSAs.[37]

Also in 2003, the OMB established a type of CBSA called a *combined statistical area* (CSA), which consists of adjacent MSAs or μSAs that have substantial economic ties as measured by employment patterns, though the linkages are weaker than those found within an MSA or μSA. The component parts therefore retain distinct identities. A simple example of a CSA is Midland-Odessa, TX, which spans two MSAs: the Midland, TX MSA and the Odessa, TX MSA. As of 2011, the country had 128 CSAs.[38]

North Carolina's Research Triangle neatly illustrates the relationships among various kinds of CBSAs (see Map 1.1, p. 8). The Raleigh-Durham-Cary CSA spans eight counties (Chatham, Durham, Franklin, Harnett, Johnston, Orange, Person, and Wake), of which seven counties belong to either the Durham-Chapel Hill MSA (Chatham, Durham, Orange, and Person counties) or the Raleigh-Cary MSA (Franklin, Johnston, and Wake counties). The last county, Harnett, is coterminous with the Dunn μSA.[39]

Figure 1.3 Distribution of Population of the United States by Metropolitan and Micropolitan Status, 2011

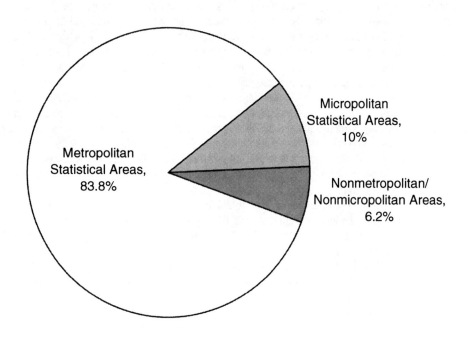

Source: U.S. Census Bureau, Population Estimates Program, 2011.

As with most components of the Census Bureau's basic and extended geographic hierarchies, MSAs and μSAs have official names and unique numerical identifiers. The American National Standards Institute coding system, which is the successor to the older Federal Information Processing Standards framework, allows advanced data users to analyze geographical data with geospatial information systems (see Box 1.1).

Urban and Rural Areas

The difference between rural and urban areas is one aspect of the extended geographical hierarchy that often confuses new users of census information. Perhaps due to the historical role that rural life long played in American society, it—or at least a romanticized idea of it—exerts a powerful hold over the popular imagination. In reality, the distinctions between rural and urban areas are not as clear as they are in the movies, and the two types of areas often blend together.

Box 1.1 Geographic Coding Systems

All of the governmental and statistical units contained in the U.S. Census Bureau's basic and extended geographical hierarchies carry unique numerical identifiers. Such numerical coding improves the organization of information and facilitates analysis with advanced statistical software packages and geospatial information systems. Because all but the lowest-level geographical units (census blocks, block groups, and census tracts) have individual names, the codes rarely appear in reports prepared for regional leaders. Nevertheless, a basic familiarity with the coding system is useful for the times when an official encounters a code or wishes to access information directly from a public statistical agency.

The Federal Information Processing Standards (FIPS) long were the main system used in Census Bureau products. Every state, county, congressional district, core based statistical area, place, county subdivision, and consolidated city received a unique code. In 2005, the federal body responsible for the FIPS codes discontinued the series, which was replaced by a similar coding structure developed under the auspices of the American National Standards Institute (ANSI), a nonprofit organization. As with FIPS standards, the ANSI codes form a uniform system that ensures consistent identification of geographical units. ANSI codes exist for the same governmental and statistical units that had FIPS identifiers.

Under the ANSI and FIPS systems, each geographical unit receives a numerical code containing a fixed number of digits. The identifier for a particular place is the combined code for the relevant geographies. Consider the formation of the unique identifier for the main quadrangle of the University of North Carolina at Chapel Hill, which is located in Orange County.

As the table below illustrates, the ANSI system assigns each state a two-digit code, which is "37" for North Carolina. Within a state, each county receives a three-digit code. The identifier for Orange County, North Carolina, then, is "37135," with the "37" denoting North Carolina, "135" the county.

No ANSI or FIPS codes exist for regions, divisions, census tracts, block groups, census blocks, and certain other geographies. To extend the reach of the ANSI and FIPS systems down to the level of census blocks, additional codes, which are revised following each decennial census, are appended to the ANSI and FIPS values. Returning to the example from the University of North Carolina at Chapel Hill, the census tract containing the campus's main quadrangle carries the six-digit value "011601," so the full identifier for the census tract is 37135011601." That tract contains three block groups, each of which has a one-digit code, and each census block within the group carries a three-digit code. The full identifier down to the block level for the university's main quadrangle therefore is 371350116011001.

American National Standards Institute (ANSI) Codes for the Main Quadrangle of the University of North Carolina at Chapel Hill, 2010 Census

Unit	Code	Value	Combined Code
State	Two digits	37	37
County	Three digits	135	37+135
Census Tract	Six digits	011601	37+135+011601
Block Group	One digit	1	37+135+011601+1
Census Block	Three digits	001	37+135+011601+1+001

Sources: Alan Peters and Heather MacDonald, *Unlocking the Census with GIS* (Redlands, CA: Esri Press, 2004), 24–25; and U.S. Census Bureau, "American National Standards Institute (ANSI) Codes," last revised December 1, 2011, http://www.census.gov/geo/www/ansi/ansi.html.

The Decennial Census of Population and Housing classifies territory as "urban" or "rural" based on the population densities of individual block groups or census blocks. In 2010, the Census Bureau called *urban* "all territory, population, and housing units located within *urbanized areas* (UAs) and *urban clusters* (UCs), both defined using the same criteria."[40] A UA "consists of densely developed territory that contains 50,000 or more people," while a UC, a geographical unit created as part of the 2000 Census, "consists of densely developed territory that has at least 2,500 people but fewer than 50,000 people."[41] A *rural area* is territory, population, or housing units that fall outside of a UA or UC. According to the 2010 Census, 19.3 percent of the American population lived in rural areas, the remaining 80.7 percent in urban areas; of urban residents, 88.2 percent were in UAs and the rest in UCs.[42]

Because the determination of rural and urban status occurs at the level of census blocks and block groups, which are statistical units, it is possible for rural areas to exist within the borders of governmental units popularly regarded as urban in character. In 2010, the population of the Research Triangle community of Durham County was overwhelmingly urban, yet 5.7 percent of the county's inhabitants lived in rural areas.[43] Statistical units like MSAs, CSAs, and µSAs also may contain rural and urban areas; of the 1.7 million people residing in the Raleigh-Durham-Cary, NC CSA at the time of the 2010 Census, 21.9 percent lived in rural areas.[44]

Analysts interested in understanding the functional relationships among rural and urban areas often look to definitions other than those used by the Census Bureau. The Economic Research Service (ERS) of the U.S. Department of Agriculture has developed at least five different coding systems that reflect factors such as population size, metropolitan status, and commuting patterns.[45] Because a place's rural status hinges on the selected definition, it is possible for a place to be deemed "rural" in one analysis and "urban" in another.[46]

Many studies take a simple approach to the matter and treat all nonmetropolitan counties as rural. Yet this method fails to reflect variations found within counties or among nonmetropolitan areas. A nonmetropolitan county on the edge of a major MSA like the Washington-Arlington-Alexandria, DC-VA-MD-WV MSA may differ greatly from one that is adjacent to a small MSA like the Danville, VA MSA. When such distinctions matter, two other classification schemes may prove more helpful.

The *rural-urban continuum* developed by the ERS categorizes individual counties as rural or urban based on a combination of population size and metropolitan status. Metropolitan counties fall into one of three groups: counties with at least 1 million residents, counties with between 250,000 and 1 million residents, and counties with fewer than 250,000 residents. The categorization of nonmetropolitan counties occurs through a two-step process. First, counties are broken into three population classes: counties with more than 20,000 residents, counties with between 2,500 and 19,999 residents, and counties with fewer than 2,500 residents. Next, counties are sorted into those that are adjacent to a metropolitan county and those that are not.[47]

When dealing with data from states with numerous metropolitan areas of differing sizes, the *urban influence codes* used by the ERS also may prove helpful. This scheme illustrates the role that geographic location plays in an area's development by considering both population size and geographical proximity to larger economies. Metropolitan counties are broken into two groups: those with one million or more residents and those with fewer inhabitants. The system further sorts nonmetropolitan counties according to population size and proximity to a metropolitan county. Under this scheme, a nonmetropolitan county that is not adjacent to a metropolitan area and lacks a town with more than 2,500 residents receives a different classification than a county that has a small population but adjoins a large metropolitan county.[48]

Interestingly, the Census Bureau's extended geographical hierarchy provides no definition of a *suburb*. Remember that the Census Bureau's categories reflect population densities, and many "suburbs" actually satisfy the requirements of urbanized areas or urban clusters. Suburban places may exist within metropolitan or micropolitan counties. To reflect the popular conception of suburbs—a perception rooted in the functional ties between low-density, residential communities and neighboring places—some analysts isolate suburbs based on commuting patterns, ERS typologies, or customized frameworks.

State-Specific Geographies

The Census Bureau's basic and extended geographical hierarchies are the foundations of most regional economic and social analyses, but other geographies occasionally appear. These often are state-established statistical or governmental units that build upon or complement the Census Bureau's framework. North Carolina, for one, has established seven economic development regions that feature prominently in analyses commissioned by the state Department of Commerce.[49] States also may deliver services through regional structures like transportation districts. Similarly, some federal funds, like those provided under the Workforce Investment Act of 1998, pass through special local entities. While no definitive listing of such state-specific geographies exists, they may prove analytically useful in some circumstances. Regional leaders therefore should develop a passing familiarity with those that are common in their states.

CONSIDERATIONS WHEN DEFINING A REGION

Appropriately defining a region is an essential part of economic and social analysis, and the first step in any study. The task is more complicated than it seems due to the differences among governmental and statistical geographies. Specific governmental entities tied to political constituencies typically commission research, but economic and social phenomena rarely respect political boundaries.

Selecting a region ultimately hinges on the exact research questions under consideration and the availability of pertinent data. Assuming the use of data compiled by public statistical agencies, the summary level for the available information will play an important role in the selection process. Information collected at the state level would not be useful for a county-level analysis. In many ways, the selection of a region reflects the art of the possible rather than a clear-cut scientific process.

As a rule of thumb, MSAs, CSAs, and μSAs are well-suited to regional economic and social analyses because they represent coherent, functional areas. An MSA, CSA, or μSA typically is large enough to capture the complexity and diversity of the relationships among individuals, households, firms, and communities, but small enough to be distinct places. Think of how residents of the Research Triangle have dubbed Cary, a community with many transplants from northern states, a "Containment Area for Relocated Yankees." Naturally, the exact choice of units depends upon local realities. The stretch of the Mississippi Delta reaching from Jackson, Mississippi, to Memphis, Tennessee, for example, contains no MSAs, so a study built around that statistical unit would be impossible; however, as the same area possesses six μSAs, a fruitful study could center on those geographies.[50]

The main shortcoming associated with using MSAs, CSAs, and μSAs is that the definitions frequently change, sometimes significantly. Prior to 2003, North Carolina's Research Triangle was a single six-county MSA known as the Raleigh-Durham-Chapel Hill, NC MSA. The 2003 revision to the CBSA system split the area into two MSAs: the Durham-Chapel Hill, NC MSA and the Raleigh-Cary, NC MSA. While the two regions belonged to the larger Raleigh-Durham-Cary, NC CSA, that area included an additional metropolitan county and a one-county μSA. The official name also changed, with Cary, a large community near Raleigh, replacing the less-populous but better-known Chapel Hill.[51]

Such revisions have little impact when looking at data for recent years, but they may prove consequential when studying regions over time. Strictly speaking, an MSA-based comparison of the Research Triangle region between 1993 and 2003 would not involve the same region. Furthermore, because the classification system is revised in the years following each decennial census, the definitional criteria tend to evolve.[52] The result is a paradox: the more accurate and refined the definitions of metropolitan and micropolitan areas become, the harder it is to conduct historical research. To circumvent such problems, many analysts organize studies around counties because county boundaries are more stable.

Regardless of which geography serves as the basic building block of a study, an analyst must ensure that the selected geography actually contains the places of interest. Think of how misleading the results would be if a study concerned with the physical location of jobs in a region omitted an employment hub. At a minimum, logical coherence is the standard that should guide the definition of a region for analytical purposes. When in doubt, a region should embody an economically functional area, as economic growth typically is an overarching concern for regional citizens and leaders.

REGIONAL GEOGRAPHY: A SUMMARY

Place matters when it comes to economic and social affairs. While people intuitively grasp the importance of place, defining the concept precisely enough for analytical purposes is a more complicated exercise. There is little agreement about what constitutes a region. The threshold step in any analysis is establishing a working definition of a region of interest—a process made easier thanks to the existence of the Census

Bureau's sophisticated geographical framework. With a working understanding of essential concepts related to regions and regional geography, civic leaders can begin to explore systematically the economic and social dimensions of the places they call home.

NOTES

1. U.S. Census Bureau, "Annual Estimates of the Population of Combined Statistical Areas: April 1, 2010 to July 1, 2011 (CBSA-EST2011-02)," http://www.census.gov/popest/data/metro/totals/2011/tables/CBSA-EST2011-02.xls.

2. U.S. Office of Management and Budget, "Update of Statistical Area Definitions and Guidance on Their Uses (OMB Bulletin No. 10-02)," December 1, 2009, 31, 46, and 108, http://www.whitehouse.gov/sites/default/files/omb/assets/bulletins/b10-02.pdf; Division of Employment Security, "North Carolina Economic Development Regions and Workforce Development Boards, 2010," last revised February 2012, http://www.ncesc1.com/lmi/publications/maps/Economic_Development_Regions_&_Workforce_Development_Board_Areas.pdf; Anna Lea, e-mail message to author, July 2011; John Quinterno, "Community Colleges in North Carolina: What History Can Tell Us About Our Future," *North Carolina Insight,* May 2008, 68–71; North Carolina Office of State Budget and Management, "Municipal Estimates by County: July 2011," http://www.osbm.state.nc.us/ncosbm/facts_and_figures/socioeconomic_data/population_estimates/demog/muniestbycounty_2011.html (accessed January 8, 2013); and North Carolina Office of State Budget and Management, "Municipal Estimates by Municipality, July 2011," http://www.osbm.state.nc.us/ncosbm/facts_and_figures/socioeconomic_data/population_estimates/demog/muniestbymuni_2011.html (accessed January 8, 2013).

3. Author's analysis of U.S. Census Bureau, American Community Survey, Three-Year Estimates, 2006–2008, Special Tabulation for Census Transportation Planning Projects.

4. *Jacobellis v. Ohio,* 378 U.S. 184 (1964).

5. Harry Richardson, *Regional and Urban Economics* (New York: Penguin, 1978), 18–19.

6. Ann Markusen, *Regions: The Economics and Politics of Territory* (Totowa, NJ: Rowman & Littlefield, 1987), 16–17.

7. Tom Wolfe, *A Man in Full* (New York: Farrar, Strauss & Giroux, 1998), 157.

8. For a detailed discussion of how economic forces shape regions, see Markusen, *Regions,* 140–155.

9. Emil Malizia and Edward Feser, *Understanding Local Economic Development* (Rutgers, NJ: Center for Urban Policy Research, 1999), 205–207.

10. Author's analysis of U.S. Census Bureau, American Community Survey, Five-Year Estimates, 2006–2010.

11. Richardson, *Regional and Urban Economics,* 21.

12. Author's analysis of U.S. Census Bureau, American Community Survey, Three-Year Estimates, 2006–2008.

13. Richardson, *Regional and Urban Economics,* 23.

14. John Saxon, *Social Services in North Carolina* (Chapel Hill: University of North Carolina School of Government, 2008), 104.

15. William Powell, *North Carolina: A History* (Chapel Hill: University of North Carolina Press, 1988), 67 and 106–107.

16. The constitutional provision authoring the decennial census is U.S. Const. art. I § 2, cl. 3, and the current laws pertaining to the Census Bureau are found in 13 U.S.C. (2011).

17. Jason Gauthier, *Measuring America: The Decennial Censuses from 1790 to 2000* (Washington, DC: U.S. Census Bureau, 2002), 125–127, http://www.census.gov/prod/2002pubs/pol02marv.pdf.

18. U.S. Census Bureau, "Mission Statement," http://www.census.gov/aboutus/# (accessed September 2, 2011).

19. The framework discussed in this section is the one used in the Decennial Census of Popula-

tion and Housing, the American Community Survey, and other studies of demographic and housing topics. Other Census Bureau products, notably the quinquennial Economic Census, employ different geographic frameworks.

20. The subsequent discussion of census geography is drawn from Heather MacDonald and Alan Peters, *Urban Policy and the Census* (Redlands, CA: Esri Press, 2011), 10–12; Alan Peters and Heather MacDonald, *Unlocking the Census with GIS* (Redlands, CA: Esri Press, 2004), 21–30; U.S. Census Bureau, "Appendix A: Geographic Terms and Concepts," in *2010 Redistricting Data (Public Law 94-171) Summary File* (Washington, DC: U.S. Department of Commerce, 2011), https://www.census.gov/prod/cen2010/doc/pl94-171.pdf; and U.S. Census Bureau, "Chapter 5: Geographic Shapefiles Concepts Overview," in *TIGER/Line Files: Technical Documentation* (Washington, DC: U.S. Department of Commerce, 2012), http://www.census.gov/geo/www/tiger/tgrshp2012/TGRSHP2012_TechDoc_Ch5.pdf.

21. U.S. Census Bureau, "Appendix A: Geographic Terms and Concepts," A-4.

22. Peters and MacDonald, *Unlocking the Census*, 21.

23. Charles D. Liner, "Introduction," in *State and Local Government Relations in North Carolina: Their Evolution and Current Status,* ed. Charles D. Liner, 2d ed. (Chapel Hill, NC: Institute of Government, 1995), xiii.

24. As of January 17, 2013, a listing of substantial changes to counties and county equivalents from 1970 onward was available at http://www.census.gov/geo/www/tiger/ctychng.html.

25. U.S. Census Bureau, "American Community Survey and Puerto Rico Community Survey 2011 Subject Definitions," 7, https://www.census.gov/acs/www/Downloads/data_documentation/SubjectDefinitions/2011_ACSSubjectDefinitions.pdf (accessed January 17, 2013).

26. U.S. Census Bureau, "Appendix A: Geographic Terms and Concepts," A-10.

27. Ibid., A-12.

28. U.S. Census Bureau, "Population, Population Change, and Estimated Components of Population Change: April 1, 2010 to July 1, 2011 (CO-EST2011-alldata)," http://www.census.gov/popest/data/counties/totals/2011/files/CO-EST2011-Alldata.csv.

29. As of January 17, 2013, a listing of substantial changes to counties and county equivalents from 1970 onward was available at http://www.census.gov/geo/www/tiger/ctychng.html.

30. U.S. Census Bureau, "Appendix A: Geographic Terms and Concepts,"A-17.

31. Ibid., A-17–A-18. The 29 states with minor civil divisions are Arkansas, Connecticut, Illinois, Indiana, Iowa, Kansas, Louisiana, Maine, Maryland, Massachusetts, Michigan, Minnesota, Mississippi, Missouri, Nebraska, New Hampshire, New Jersey, New York, North Carolina, North Dakota, Ohio, Pennsylvania, Rhode Island, South Dakota, Tennessee, Vermont, Virginia, West Virginia, and Wisconsin. The nine states with minor civil division that also have unorganized territories are Arkansas, Indiana, Iowa, Maine, Minnesota, New York, North Carolina, North Dakota, and South Dakota. The 20 states with census county divisions are Alabama, Arizona, California, Colorado, Delaware, Florida, Georgia, Hawaii, Idaho, Kentucky, Montana, Nevada, New Mexico, Oklahoma, Oregon, South Carolina, Texas, Utah, Washington, and Wyoming.

32. U.S. Census Bureau, "Appendix A: Geographic Terms and Concepts,"A-21.

33. For additional information on the American Indian, Alaska Native, and Native Hawaiian areas hierarchy, see U.S. Census Bureau, "Appendix A: Geographic Terms and Concepts,"A-5–A-10.

34. On February 23, 2013, the U.S. Office of Management and Budget released revised delineations of core based statistical areas based on data from the 2010 Decennial Census of Population and Housing and the five-year American Community Survey Estimates for 2006–2010; the new definitions are available at http://www.whitehouse.gov/sites/default/files/omb/bulletins/2013/b-13-01.pdf. Because the writing of this book was completed prior to the issuance of the new definitions, it relies on the definitions that were in effect at the time of writing, which were based on the 2000 Census.

35. U.S. Census Bureau, "Appendix A: Geographic Terms and Concepts," A-15.

36. Author's analysis of U.S. Census Bureau, Population Estimates Program, 2011; and U.S. Office of Management and Budget, "Update of Statistical Area Definitions and Guidance on Their Uses,"

2. The revisions to the definitions of core based statistical areas released in 2013 and discussed in note 34 increased the number of metropolitan statistical areas in the United States to 381 from 366.

37. Author's analysis of U.S. Census Bureau, Population Estimates Program, 2011; and U.S. Office of Management and Budget, "Update of Statistical Area Definitions and Guidance on Their Uses," 2. The revisions to the definitions of core based statistical areas released in 2013 and discussed in note 34 reduced the number of micropolitan statistical areas in the United States to 536 from 576; the change was due in part to revisions to the definition.

38. U.S. Office of Management and Budget, "Update of Statistical Area Definitions and Guidance on Their Uses," 2–3 and 100. The revisions to the definitions of core based statistical areas released in 2013 and discussed in note 34 increased the number of combined statistical areas in the United States to 169 from 128; the change was due in part to revisions to the definition.

39. The most recent revisions to the definitions of core based statistical areas contained several changes relevant to North Carolina's Research Triangle. First, the name of the Raleigh-Cary, NC Metropolitan Statistical Area was change to the Raleigh, NC Metropolitan Area. Second, the name of the Raleigh-Durham-Cary, NC Combined Statistical Area was changes to the Raleigh-Durham-Chapel Hill, NC Combined Statistical Area. Third, the boundaries of the combined statistical areas were expanded to include three one-county micropolitan statistical areas: the Henderson, NC Micropolitan Statistical Area (Vance County), the Oxford, NC Micropolitan Statistical Area (Granville County), and the Sanford, NC Micropolitan Statistical Area (Lee County). While not previously part of the combined statistical area, the Henderson and Sanford micropolitan areas existed prior to the most recent revisions to the federal definitions. The Oxford micropolitan area, however, is a new one.

40. U.S. Census Bureau, "Appendix A: Geographic Terms and Concepts,"A-25; emphasis added.

41. Ibid., A-25.

42. Author's analysis of U.S. Census Bureau, 2010 Census Summary File 1.

43. Ibid.

44. Ibid.

45. Economic Research Service, "Rural Classifications: Overview," http://www.ers.usda.gov/topics/rural-economy-population/rural-classifications.aspx (accessed January 19, 2013); and Economic Research Service, "Rural Classifications: What Is Rural?" http://www.ers.usda.gov/topics/rural-economy-population/rural-classifications/what-is-rural.aspx (accessed January 19, 2013).

46. As of January 19, 2013, state-level maps illustrating the definitions of "rural" were available at http://www.ers.usda.gov/data-products/rural-definitions.aspx.

47. Economic Research Service, "Rural-Urban Continuum Codes: Documentation," http://www.ers.usda.gov/data-products/rural-urban-continuum-codes/documentation.aspx (accessed January 19, 2013).

48. Economic Research Service, "Urban Influence Codes: Documentation," http://www.ers.usda.gov/data-products/urban-influence-codes.aspx (accessed January 19, 2013).

49. Division of Employment Security, "North Carolina Economic Development Regions and Workforce Development Boards, 2010."

50. U.S. Census Bureau, "Mississippi Core Based Statistical Areas, Counties, and Independent Cities," last revised November 2004, http://ftp2.census.gov/geo/maps/metroarea/stcbsa_pg/Nov2004/cbsa2004_MS.pdf.

51. William Frey et al., *Tracking Metropolitan America into the 21st Century: A Field Guide to the New Metropolitan and Micropolitan Definitions* (Washington, DC: Brookings Institution, 2004), 11, http://www.psc.isr.umich.edu/dis/census/freybrookings.pdf.

52. As of March 15, 2013, historical listings of core based statistical areas and the associated definitions from 1950 onward were available at http://www.census.gov/population/metro/data/pastmetro.html.

2 | Regional Economic Growth

Chapter 2

Economic growth looms large in the thinking of regional leaders. For good or bad, the concept functions as an end to pursue, a yardstick for measuring progress, and a rationale for policy choices. Building transit networks, recruiting industries, training workers—these are but some of the public investments justified as means of enhancing a region's capability to produce goods and services and, by extension, raising the living standards of local residents. When robust growth occurs, a region has the potential to thrive, but when growth lags, social and economic problems are likely to mount.

Despite its importance, economic growth is a nebulous concept. Economists agree that growth matters, yet they argue fiercely over exactly what growth is and what exactly causes it. Disagreements arise because the definition of growth is inseparable from specific theories: the choice of a theory, in effect, sets the terms of debate. When policy discussions overlook this reality, they tend to unfold in ways unlikely to produce informed decisions.

Vague understandings of economic growth are problematic given the high stakes surrounding the concept. Growth influences living standards, business success, and community prosperity. Moreover, fostering growth is a complex, costly undertaking. Consider how almost every governmental unit of any size operates some type of economic growth agency. Without a precise understanding of economic growth, it is difficult to distinguish wise investments from those that are wasteful or sheer giveaways.

When regional leaders speak of economic growth, what they typically mean, albeit often unconsciously, is increasing the aggregate level of some economic variable, such as employment or income. More often than not, regional leaders are interested in expanding economic output, meaning the total quantity of goods and services produced by a local economy, relative to a larger reference region.

To improve understanding of regional economic growth, this chapter defines the concept, contrasts it to the concept of economic development, presents a model of how regional economies are structured, and introduces the system of regional economic accounting maintained by the U.S. Bureau of Economic Analysis. As a way of demonstrating the analytical usefulness of

29

Map 2.1 Principal Cities and Component Counties of Atlanta-Sandy Springs-Marietta, GA MSA, 2009 Delineation

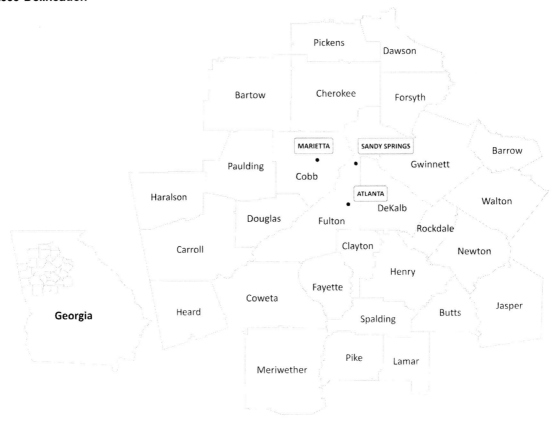

Source: U.S. Office of Management and Budget, "Update of Statistical Area Definitions and Guidance on Their Uses (OMB Bulletin No. 10-02)," December 1, 2009, http://www.whitehouse.gov/sites/default/files/omb/assets/bulletins/b10-02.pdf. Map prepared by William High.

regional economic accounting, the chapter offers several examples drawn from data for the Atlanta-Sandy Springs-Marietta, GA Metropolitan Statistical Area (MSA), a 28-county region with 5.4 million residents in 2011 (see Map 2.1).[1] Chapter 3 then builds upon these concepts and explores theories that attempt to explain how and why regional economies grow over time.

ECONOMIC GROWTH AS ECONOMIC OUTPUT

Understanding growth and its causes is perhaps the central issue with which economists wrestle. Most would say that growth originates in "increases in labor, increases in capital, and increases in the efficiency with which these two factors are used," but few would agree about what causes those factors to change or what other elements (e.g., human capital, technological progress, social institutions) affect growth.[2] And discussions of growth normally ignore regions. Macroeconomic studies typically center on national or international economic systems, while microeconomic analyses concern themselves with the behaviors of individual households and firms.

A prerequisite to any discussion of economic growth is the establishment of a working definition. One approach is to view growth in terms of changes in an economy's total output of finished goods and services, usually expressed in monetary terms; put differently, total output is the sum of the products obtained by multiplying the quantities of finished goods and services produced within an economy in a certain period by their respective final prices. To identify real changes in economic output, an analyst must control for changes in population size—after all, unless regional output grows at least as fast as the local population, per capita output will fall despite an overall increase—and strip away any shifts in the aggregate price level to reveal actual changes in the quantity of goods and services produced by an economy (see Box 2.1).

At the national level, the standard measure of output is Gross Domestic Product (GDP), which is "the market value of all final goods and services produced within a country over a given year."[3] When estimating GDP, the central challenge is to isolate the value added to a product at each stage of the production process to avoid counting the same output more than once. There are three ways of doing this. First, an analyst can calculate all the value added to all goods and services by taking their final sales prices and subtracting the costs of all inputs excluding labor. Second, because final sales prices incorporate the value added throughout the production process, the total amount of final expenditures should equal total output. Finally, as every dollar spent on final goods and services represents income received by another party, total income should be the same as total output.[4]

Measuring aggregate market production was the original reason for the development during the first half of the twentieth century of the system of national economic accounting to which GDP belongs.[5] Over time, output measures acquired a secondary status as indicators of economic well-being, despite the objections of many experts. Acting on the assumption that "growth in real GDP per capita comes hand in hand with improvements in the way people are able to live," national political leaders have come to embrace the maximization of real GDP per capita as an overarching policy goal.[6]

GDP statistics are imperfect, and the original architects of the system of national economic accounting did not design the data to serve as indicators of well-being. As measures of the market value of goods and services, GDP statistics exclude or undervalue items lacking clear prices, especially public goods such as safety, and ignore externalities not captured in market prices, such as pollution. GDP measures further fail to account for quality improvements in goods and services, sustainable uses of resources, social concerns like inequality, and structural changes to the economy. As Nobel laureate Joseph Stiglitz noted, "[t]he focus on GDP creates conflicts: political leaders are told to maximize it, but citizens also demand that attention be paid to enhancing security, reducing air, water, and noise pollution, and so forth—all of which might lower GDP growth."[7] In recent years, an awareness of the deficiencies of GDP measures has led international bodies to experiment with new statistics that

Box 2.1 Changes in the Price Level

In a market economy, the prices of individual goods and services constantly change in relation to one another. From the perspective of an economy as a whole, fluctuations in the prices of individual items are much less important than changes in the average price of all goods and services. Shifts in the aggregate price level matter more because they influence how much consumers and firms pay for goods and services and how much money is worth.

When analyzing changes in economic output, it is necessary to control for changes in the price level. Consider an economy that produces nothing other than wine and cheese. If, in a given year, the economy produced 200,000 bottles of wine that carried a final price of $15 per bottle and 100,000 wheels of cheese that carried a final price of $10 per wheel, annual output would total $4 million. If, in the next year, the quantities of wine and cheese produced held steady, but the final unit prices rose to $16 and $12, respectively, *nominal output* would equal $4.4 million, an amount 10 percent greater than that of the prior year. *Real output,* however, would be unchanged. The economy would have produced identical quantities of wine and cheese in each year. In the long run, economic growth hinges on increases in the quantity of goods and services produced by an economy, not growth in prices.

Changes to the price level occur through the processes of inflation and deflation. *Inflation* refers to periods when the average price of all goods and services is increasing. A rising price level erodes the purchasing power of a dollar and drives down the value of money. In other words, a dollar received tomorrow will purchase less than will one received today. Inflation also erodes the value of debts by enabling borrowers to repay their creditors with less valuable future dollars. While some degree of inflation tends to occur over time in any economy, extreme periods can be economically ruinous.

Deflation, in contrast, refers to periods when the average price of all goods and services is dropping. A falling price level raises the purchasing power of a dollar and the value of money. Put differently, a dollar received tomorrow will buy more than one received today. Despite boosting the value of money, deflation seriously harms an economy by depressing overall levels of economic activity and increasing the cost of servicing debts, as borrowers will have to repay their creditors with more expensive future dollars.

While the concepts of inflation and deflation are straightforward, they are difficult to measure, and over the years public statistical agencies have developed various analytical methods, each of which has strengths and weaknesses. Consistent with its role as the nation's "economic accountant," the U.S. Bureau of Economic Analysis (BEA) calculates three different price indicators for use in measuring economic output: the *gross domestic product (GDP) price deflator,* the *gross domestic purchases deflator,* and the *deflator for personal consumption expenditures.* Each statistic tracks changes in the price level of a specific bundle of goods and services purchased by a particular set of actors within the American economy. The deflator for personal consumer expenditures, for example, follows developments in the average price of a basket of goods and services purchased by individuals.

Perhaps the best-known measure of changes in the price level is the *Consumer Price Index* (CPI). Compiled by the U.S. Bureau of Labor Statistics (BLS) regularly since 1921, the CPI measures the changes in the average retail prices paid by urban consumers for a basket of essential goods and services. Each month, the BLS tracks the prices paid by urban households in 38 geographic areas—a sampling frame that covers some 87 percent of the American population—for 211 different items. Those items, in turn, cluster into eight broad categories: housing, food and beverages, transportation, medical care, apparel, recreation, education and communication, and other goods and services. After compiling data for each item in each geographic area, the BLS aggregates the information across categories to generate assorted higher-level averages for various geographic regions, including urban America as a whole.

CPI figures are *index numbers,* or scores that combine the values of different items into one amount that equals a percentage of a specified base value. The base for the CPI equals 100 and represents the market value of the CPI basket of consumer goods and services in 1982–1984. A hypothetical rise in the CPI value from 190 to 200 over the span of a year would translate into a 5.3 percent jump in the aggregate price level; by extension, the bundle of goods and services would cost twice as much as it did in 1982–1984.

The BLS prepares several data series under the CPI program, but the most expansive is the *CPI for All Urban Consumers* (CPI-U). Data appear monthly with a lag of one month, and the monthly report contains seasonally adjusted and seasonally unadjusted values. Moreover, the report contains a "headline" measure of change that includes shifts in the prices of food and energy and a "core" measure that excludes the historically volatile prices of food and energy. The core measure more clearly identifies underlying economic trends, but the "headline" measure better captures the actual conditions facing urban consumers.

As with any statistic, the CPI suffers from various limitations. Contrary to popular perception, the CPI is not a true cost-of-living index, as it only captures items with market prices and ignores items that lack prices yet matter to the well-being of households, such as safety and environmental quality. Another weakness is that the CPI is not a gauge of differences in living costs across regions even though it contains geographic estimates; rather, the statistic simply compares the relative differences in changes in prices across regions. And, as with any statistical product, the CPI is prone to various kinds of methodological and computational errors.

A final weakness of the CPI is inherent in its design. The CPI is a fixed-weight index that aims to show how much it would cost at current market prices to obtain the same basket of goods and services purchased in 1982–1984. This approach, however, ignores the fact that consumers can obtain the same standard of living by substituting relatively less expensive items for ones that have risen in price, as might happen if people buy more cereals following a jump in the price of bread. Furthermore, a fixed-weight index overlooks quality improvements to goods and services, such as the development of more reliable cars, and the advent of new products like cell phones.

One way to control for the substitution bias is through use of a *chained price index.* A chained index continuously updates the weights assigned to the items in the reference basket and compares changes to the prior period rather than against a set base year. In 2002, the BLS released a chained price index called the *Chained CPI for All Urban Consumers* (C-CPI-U). While chained measures are more difficult to calculate than those that are fixed-weight and require the passage of more time before they can be computed, they may yield more precise, not to mention lower, estimates of changes in the price level.

Note that the BEA also uses chained measures of inflation in its data products. The deflator for personal consumer expenditures is a chained measure that typically generates somewhat lower rates of increases in consumer prices than does the CPI. Similarly, the BEA currently reports estimates of GDP at the national, state, and metropolitan regions in chained 2005 dollars. When interpreting such output data, a rule of thumb is to use nominal values to assess economic structure or draw comparisons within the same year and to use chained values for time series analysis.

Sources: Bernard Baumohl, *The Secrets of Economic Indicators: Hidden Clues to Future Economic Trends and Investment Opportunities*, 2d ed. (Upper Saddle River, NJ: Wharton School Publishing, 2008), 114–116 and 271–276; David Moss, *A Concise Guide to Macroeconomics: What Managers, Executives, and Students Need to Know* (Boston: Harvard Business School Press, 2007), 36–41; and U.S. Bureau of Labor Statistics, "Consumer Price Index," in *BLS Handbook of Methods* (Washington, DC: U.S. Department of Labor, 1997), 1–7, last revised June 2007, http://bls.gov/opub/hom/pdf/homch17.pdf.

Box 2.2 Moving "Beyond GDP"

The system of national economic accounting to which gross domestic product (GDP) belongs is a framework for measuring market-based economic activities. GDP simply is an estimate of the market value of all the final goods and services produced within a nation during a certain period. While originally created as a gauge of market output, GDP has acquired a secondary status as an indicator of social well-being and progress. The maximization of GDP consequently has become an overarching—some would say the overriding—economic goal pursued by public leaders in numerous countries.

The interest in using GDP as a proxy measure of social well-being is understandable. The statistic is easily comprehended, regularly calculated, and reasonably related to living conditions. The residents of countries with high levels of GDP per capita tend to enjoy higher living standards than those who live in countries with lower GDP figures. That said, even the original architects of national economic accounting recognized that their statistics provided little perspective into social welfare. Among other limitations, GDP counts as productive activities things that actually detract from well-being, such as financial speculation and spending on personal security; ignores the harmful, nonmarket consequences of economic activities, especially pollution and the depletion of natural resources; and excludes the value of nonmarket activities (e.g., parenting) and public services (e.g., social insurance). Furthermore, as measures of aggregate market output, GDP measures offer no insights into questions of economic distribution and fairness.

Experts long have recognized the limits of GDP as an indicator of social welfare, and recently recognition of the statistic's flaws has become more widespread. The shift is attributable in large part to the widening divergence between economic growth as measured by GDP and the stagnation in the living standards experienced by average households in many wealthy countries—a divergence that has called into question the legitimacy of public statistics and the public sector itself. Heightened concern about environmental sustainability also has fueled interest in crafting better measures of well-being at the same time that advances in economic and statistical methods have opened the door to improved measurement.

A major step toward moving "beyond GDP" occurred in 2009 with the release of the report of the Commission of Economic Performance and Social Progress, an international panel convened by former French President Nicolas Sarkozy and led by noted economists Joseph Stiglitz, Amartya Sen, and Jean-Paul Fitoussi. The commission strove to identify the limitations of GDP as a measure of economic activity and social well-being and to propose improvements and alternate indicators. Suggested actions included adapting systems of economic measurement to reflect current realities, emphasizing the measurement of household well-being over aggregate economic production, and incorporating indicators of sustainability—particularly environmental sustainability—into statistical frameworks. The panel further called for tracking well-being in a multidimensional way instead of relying on one summary statistic.

The work of the Stiglitz-Sen-Fitoussi Commission attracted international attention and sparked policy action. In 2011, for instance, the Organization for Economic Cooperation and Development, an international policy forum to which most wealthy nations belong, launched a "Better Life Initiative." This ongoing research program aims to measure individual well-being in relation to material living conditions, quality of life, and sustainability. Similarly, the European Commission, the executive arm of the European Union, has been striving since 2007 to develop indicators of environmental sustainability and social well-being that can complement traditional systems of economic accounting.

In the United States, the U.S. Bureau of Economic Analysis, the federal agency responsible for national economic accounting, has considered ways of expanding and supplementing national and regional accounts to paint a more detailed portrait of social well-being. At the regional level, the agency has mooted the idea of adjusting estimates of real household incomes to reflect regional differences in price levels. Under that approach, real per capita income levels would rise in less urbanized states with lower living costs, such as West Virginia, and fall in more urbanized states with relatively higher living costs, such as New York. The agency also has suggested altering measurements of pension income—alterations that would boost income levels in states with large numbers of retirees, like Florida, and reduce them in states with large numbers of workers contributing to pension plans, like Virginia.

Another method for moving beyond GDP is through the use of a *genuine progress indicator* (GPI). With intellectual roots stretching back to the 1970s, the GPI framework attempts to adjust GDP to account for the financial values associated with various positive and negative contributions to social well-being. For instance, the framework adjusts GDP by quantifying the social cost of crime and subtracting it from GDP, while adding the value of the social benefits associated with higher education to GDP. One recent attempt to apply the GPI framework at the subnational level occurred in Maryland, which, since 2009, has maintained a state-level GPI. The Maryland model modifies GDP by state to account for 26 indicators tied to economic performance, environmental quality, and social well-being. As is the case with national GPI estimates, Maryland's historical scores rose in tandem with GDP until the 1980s, at which point the two began to diverge, with GPI growing more slowly than GDP. This suggests that continued growth in GDP alone has not improved the living standards of average households.

Despite the problems that constrain the usefulness of GDP as a measure of social welfare, no alternate indicator or set of indicators has yet to acquire widespread acceptance owing to a variety of methodological, measurement, and conceptual shortcomings. GDP therefore remains the standard, albeit darkly clouded, lens through which to view social progress. Nevertheless, interest in moving beyond GDP is mounting in much of the developed world. This new awareness highlights the need for public leaders to think more purposefully about social well-being, consider the issue more holistically, and measure well-being through the use of multiple indicators rather than relying upon a single number.

Sources: Commission of the European Communities, *GDP and Beyond: Measuring Progress in a Changing World* (Brussels: European Union, 2009), http://eur-lex.europa.eu/LexUriServ/LexUriServ.do?uri=COM:2009:0433:FIN :EN:PDF; Lew Daly and Stephen Posner, *Beyond GDP: New Measures for a New Economy* (New York: Dēmos, 2011), http://www.demos.org/publication/beyond-gdp-new-measures-new-economy; J. Steven Landefeld, Brent Mooulton, Joel Platt, and Shaunda Villones, "GDP and Beyond: Measuring Economic Progress and Sustainability," *Survey of Current Business,* April 2010, http://www.bea.gov/scb/pdf/2010/04%20April/0410_gpd-beyond.pdf; OECD, *How's Life? Measuring Well-Being* (Paris: OECD Publishing, 2011); State of Maryland, "Maryland's Genuine Progress Indicator: An Index for Sustainable Prosperity," http://www.green.maryland.gov/mdgpi/index.asp (accessed December 28, 2012); and Joseph Stiglitz, Amartya Sen, and Jean-Paul Fitoussi, *Mismeasuring Our Lives: Why GDP Doesn't Add Up* (New York: New Press, 2010).

"shift emphasis from measuring economic production to measuring people's well-being" (see Box 2.2).[8]

USES AND LIMITATIONS OF OUTPUT MEASURES

First developed to describe national economies, output concepts and measures frequently are adapted for use at the state and metropolitan levels. As explained later in the chapter, the federal government estimates economic output for each state and metropolitan statistical area in the country.[9] Other entities calculate regional output as well. The nonprofit Brookings Institution computes the "gross metropolitan product" of the 100 most populous metropolitan areas, while Moody's Analytics, a for-profit firm, estimates output for individual states and metropolitan areas.[10]

Yet it simply is wrong to think of a region as "little more than a mini-nation, with the implication that economic performance of a region can be understood in terms of traditional macroeconomics while interregional systems are comprehensible as analogues to international systems."[11] Even in a large country like the United States, it is easier for economic transactions to occur across regional lines than international borders. Another difference is that regional policy makers lack many of the tools available to their national counterparts, such as control of monetary policy and the power to regulate trade and immigration. Viewing a region like a nation in miniature also minimizes the importance of place-specific and intraregional factors.

Tracking changes in output nevertheless can illuminate regional economic and social realities. The key is to recognize what is—and what is not—being measured. Consider how increased output is not the only end valued by community residents. People frequently care about goals like "the long-run economic development of the region, an efficient and acceptable intra-regional distribution of population and economic activity, and the preservation of environmental quality."[12] Regional leaders who ignore the full spectrum of community concerns do so at their own risk.

FROM GROWTH TO DEVELOPMENT

As conventionally understood, economic growth is "best defined as simple quantitative increase" in total output or similar factors like total employment.[13] Growth policies, then, are those that aim to maximize the aggregate level of a particular factor. As mentioned previously, however, local residents often are concerned about noneconomic aspects of regional well-being. Residents may judge progress not just in terms of output, but also in regards to "economic development," a concept that is more qualitative and structural in nature.[14] Regional scholars Emil Malizia and Edward Feser explain, "[g]rowth increases output by mobilizing more resources and utilizing them more productively; development changes the output mix by devoting local resources to doing different kinds of work."[15]

Popular conceptions of growth and development often depict the two concepts as existing in opposition to one another, especially when matters of environmental sustainability and social equity are involved. A common criticism of such development-focused actions as the enactment of environmental regulations is that they slow growth, while growth-centered actions like unregulated resource extraction frequently attract criticism for ignoring the health of the natural environment. Over time, however, growth and development often complement one another. Even if the two conflict, citizens may place more value on developmental ends, so regional leaders must respect those preferences.

Unfortunately, a lack of precise terminology clouds discussions of regional growth and development. Regional leaders frequently invoke the term "economic development" when what they actually mean is "economic growth." Similarly, most public economic development departments are named improperly because they exist to maximize the aggregate growth in specified economic variables like output and employment rather than developmental ends, even those suited to quantitative measurement, such as reductions in the poverty rate or improvements in median income.[16] An agency mandated simply to boost the number of jobs in a region often will assume that all jobs are equal and that any job is a "good" job, while an agency committed to developmental goals will pay attention to the quality of jobs as measured in terms of wages, benefits, and working conditions. A poor use of language therefore may cause confusion and lead to policy choices inconsistent with the values and desires of a community.

BALANCING GROWTH AND DEVELOPMENT

Developmental ends seldom feature in standard theories or measures of economic growth. The emphasis instead is on documenting and explaining quantitative changes in output. Custom contributes to this mind-set, as does the fact that output seems comparatively easier to measure, at least at first glance. So how should a concerned regional leader think about growth and development?

One approach is to view regional progress as the byproduct of interactions between an area's resources and its capacities. Resources include the traditional production factors of land, labor, and capital, and capacity refers to the social, political, and organizational factors that enable the wise, efficient use of resources.[17] After all, without capacities, resources may sit idle: think of the waste that occurs in places rich in resources but cursed by corruption.

Thinking in terms of capacities and resources allows leaders to evaluate potential policies and investments in relation to their effects on a region's resource base, capacities, or some combination of the two. The resource element frequently attracts attention—an attraction consistent with a growth mentality—at the expense of the capacity component, even though true improvements in regional well-being flow from the interaction of the two. In fact, strong capacities can allow a region with relatively few natural resources to become more prosperous than one with a greater endowment of resources, as illustrated by the relatively small stocks of natural resources found in some of the world's most economically vibrant cities.

No single analytical framework accounts for growth and development, just as there is no single formula for maximizing regional well-being. Careful analysis of a region's resources and capacities may inform discussions, but actual policy choices require the best judgments of civic leaders who, at the end of the day, must place their bets and take their chances. A mind-set that values economic growth and economic development can improve the process of reaching informed decisions and boost the odds of making good choices for the community at large.

A Model of a Regional Economy

Economic output does not originate in a vacuum; instead, it emerges from interactions among different actors within a regional economy. Even the smallest region contains many complex, interconnected parts. Take the Carson City, NV MSA, a one-county region that, with 55,439 residents, was the nation's least populous MSA in 2010.[18] That year, Carson City produced an estimated $2.8 billion in final goods and services.[19] Irrespective of size, every metropolitan economy, ranging from Carson City to New York City, emerges from the exchanges among five groups: households, firms, financial institutions, governments, and nonlocal actors.

One way of depicting the ties binding the five groups is with a *circular flow model,* which "is a stylized picture of some important linkages and money flows."[20] Fundamentally descriptive in nature, circular flow models provide the foundations of several of the growth theories detailed in chapter 3. For the purposes of this discussion, Figure 2.1 provides a generic, regional version of a circular flow model.[21]

The institutions of the household and the firm stand at the heart of the model and interact in two ways. First, there is a *resource market* in which households provide firms with factors of production such as land, labor, and capital in exchange for money paid in the form of wages, rental income, interest, and profits. The labor market is perhaps the best example of the resource market. Second, firms and households participate in a *commodity market* in which businesses produce and sell goods and services in exchange for money. To create the items offered in the commodity market, businesses purchase intermediate products from other firms via the *interfirm market.*

In a closed market in which households spend all of their incomes and businesses retain none of their profits, total regional expenditures and total regional income are equal. In reality, households often prefer to save part of their incomes for future use. The normal method is to place those savings in financial institutions like banks, which channel the funds into the *investment market.* Financial institutions connect savers hoping to earn a return on their funds with firms seeking financing. A local bank, for example, accepts deposits from savers, agrees to pay a specified rate of interest on deposited funds, and loans deposits to credit-worthy firms that agree to repay the funds with interest at a future date.

Because local households and firms desire public services and goods such as schools and roads, governmental entities levy taxes on households and businesses. The *public-sector market* uses tax collections to transact in the resource and commodity markets in order to provide the goods and services demanded by citizens. To that end, a government might purchase items from a firm or employ a member of a household. A government also might expand the size of the investment market by placing temporarily uncommitted funds in financial institutions or by borrowing the funds needed for certain investments.

Figure 2.1 A Regional Circular Flow Model

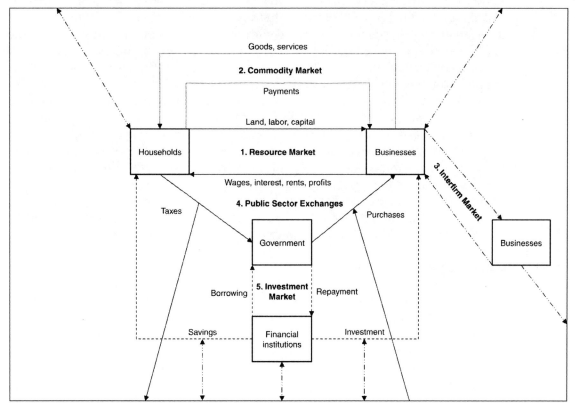

Sources: John Blair, *Local Economic Development: Analysis and Practice* (Thousand Oaks, CA: Sage Publications, 1995), 120–123; and Edwin Dolan and Kevin Klein, *Survey of Economics*, 4th ed. (Redding, CA: BVT Publishing, 2010), 232–238.

The *nonlocal market* represents a final set of economic exchanges. Regions rarely are self-contained economic units and instead participate in larger economies. Local households and businesses therefore interact with "the rest of the world." A business may purchase supplies from nonlocal firms and sell to nonlocal customers; similarly, a household may provide resources to a business in another region or invest savings with nonlocal financial institutions. Households and firms also pay taxes to nonlocal units of government, which may return some of those funds to the area through transactions in the resource and commodity markets.

Participation in larger economies means that a region's well-being is influenced by "the difference between the size of monetary inflows and outflows."[22] Inflows boost aggregate regional levels of employment and income by expanding the amount of money circulating within an economy or the speed at which money is spent. Outflows lower aggregate levels of employment and income by reducing the total amount of money circulating in an economy or the speed at which money is spent. When assessing levels of inflows and outflows, the key factor is the net level, or the difference between the two. When inflows exceed outflows, aggregate employment and income levels may rise, but when outflows exceed inflows, aggregate levels may fall.

Monetary inflows matter because they exert a *multiplier effect*, in which an increase of one dollar in regional income produces more than a dollar's worth of economic activity. Consider a local business that sells to nonlocal consumers. Those sales increase the firm's income, thereby prompting the firm to hire additional employees to meet increased demand. Those employees then might spend their pay at local businesses, causing the cycle to repeat. The exact impacts of the change hinge upon such factors as the propensity of economic actors to spend money within the affected region and the permanency of the monetary inflow. Of course, not all money will remain in the community, as some proportion will "leak" away to other communities through the nonlocal market in the form of taxes, savings, and imports, but the process of spending and responding will boost regional output, employment, and income levels.[23]

REGIONAL ECONOMIC ACCOUNTING

The main advantages of the circular flow model are how it illustrates the relationships among economic actors and demonstrates how the "market" is not a natural institution but a human one rooted in the relationships among individual households and firms. Those relationships are dynamic in nature, but circular flow models are static and unable to capture the dynamism. The model's main limitation, then, is its inability to provide "a detailed snapshot of the myriad transactions that make up the economy—buying and selling goods and services, hiring of labor, investing, renting property, paying taxes, and the like."[24] For insights into actual economic activities, analysts turn to the regional accounting system maintained by the U.S. Bureau of Economic Analysis (BEA). That system of regional accounts, in turn, derives from the larger set of national economic accounts maintained by the BEA.

NATIONAL ECONOMIC ACCOUNTING

Developed during the late 1920s and early 1930s, national economic accounting "presents a coherent, comprehensive, and consistent picture of U.S. economic activity."[25] The system's central component is the *National Income and Product Accounts* (NIPAs), "a set of economic accounts that provide[s] information on the value and composition of output produced in the United States during a given period and on the distribution and uses of the income generated by that production."[26] The best-known NIPA element is GDP, which is an estimate of the "market value of the goods and services produced by labor and property located in the United States."[27] In 2011, the nation's GDP totaled $15.1 trillion.[28]

As explained earlier, GDP is a measure of an economy's total output expressed in dollars (quantity multiplied by price). Analysts can measure GDP in one of three ways: by computing the value added at each stage in the production process, by measuring

Table 2.1 Summary Information About National Income and Product Accounts

Number	Name	Description	Left-hand account entry	Right-hand account entry
1	Domestic Income and Product Account	Total final output produced in the United States	Gross domestic product by income	Gross domestic product by expenditure
2	Private Enterprise Income Account	Uses and sources of private enterprise income	Uses of private enterprise income	Sources of private enterprise income
3	Personal Income and Outlay Account	Uses and sources of personal income	Personal taxes, outlays, and savings	Sources of personal income
4	Government Receipts and Expenditures Account	Uses and sources of governmental receipts	Government current expenditures and net savings	Sources of government current receipts
5	Foreign Transactions Current Account	Current transactions between the United States and the rest of the world	Current receipts from the rest of the world (exports from the United States)	Current payments to the rest of the world (imports to the United States) and balance on current account
6	Domestic Capital Account	Relationship between savings and investment in the economy of the United States	Gross domestic investment, capital account transactions, and net lending	Gross savings and statistical discrepancy
7	Foreign Transactions Capital Account	Counter-entries for items in "Domestic Capital Account"	Balance on current account, national income and product accounts	Capital account transactions (net) and net lending, national income and product accounts

Source: Stephanie McCulla and Shelly Smith, *Measuring the Economy: A Primer on GDP and the National Income and Product Accounts* (Washington, DC: U.S. Bureau of Economic Analysis, 2007), 8–13, http://bea.gov/national/pdf/nipa_primer.pdf.

total income, or by estimating total expenditures. The three totals theoretically should equal each other. At the national level, the income and expenditure methods typically are used. Total expenditures reflect aggregate spending by households, private investors, governmental units, and foreigners (the difference between exports and imports).[29]

At its core, NIPA is a specialized form of double-entry accounting that connects production and the income generated by that production. Think of the total value of all goods and services sold in a year as forming one side of the journal entry; the income generated by sales balances the spending on the opposite side of the ledger sheet.[30] The different NIPA components drill down into each side of the ledger to trace how production and income flow across sectors. At the national level, the NIPA contains seven interconnected summary accounts that follow the output and income associated with different aspects of production, investment, foreign transactions, personal income and outlays, and government taxation and spending (see Table 2.1).[31] A related system of balance-of-payments accounts supplements the product accounts by offering more detailed information about international transactions.[32]

Casual users of NIPA data should remember three things. First, the statistics are extremely difficult to compile and undergo numerous revisions over a period of years. Quarterly GDP estimates are prepared three different times over a three-month span before being subjected to multiple periodic revisions of varying degrees of comprehensiveness. Second, reports featuring NIPA data normally present dollar values and annualized rates of change, which "show how the economy would perform if that quarterly pace were maintained for a full year."[33] Other rates may also be present, so an observer must be mindful of which rate is under consideration. Lastly, as the purpose of national economic accounting is to identify real changes in economic production, the effects of changes in prices must be isolated. Data users interested in tracing changes over time therefore should concentrate on real or inflation-adjusted values (see chapter 4).

Regional Economic Accounting

Over the years, the BEA has developed a regional accounting framework that extends the basic NIPA framework to subnational geographies including states, counties, MSAs, and BEA economic areas (an agency-specific geography).[34] These regional accounts are prepared less frequently than the national figures and cover fewer topics, yet they are powerful tools for understanding "the process, structure, and outcomes of regional growth and development."[35] The regional accounting data also influence the distribution of federal funds. For the purposes of this book, three regional accounting tools deserve consideration: GDP by state and by metropolitan area, state and local area personal income and employment, and the Regional Input-Output Modeling System (RIMS).

GDP by State and Metropolitan Area

Subnational output estimates did not exist until 1985, when the BEA released an experimental calculation of GDP by state for selected years. Originally termed "Gross State Product," this series has evolved into an annual estimate that is "the state counterpart of gross domestic product and as such, provides a comprehensive measure of a state's production."[36] State-level estimates currently are available in two series: one covering 1997 onward, another spanning 1963 to 1997. Due to methodological differences, the two series are discontinuous.[37]

Estimates of GDP by state derive from an industry-based income approach. For each of 21 industrial sectors, income is the sum of the compensation paid to employees, the amount paid in production taxes minus the value of subsidies, and the income earned on capital (gross operating surplus). The total dollar value for all industries is available in both current (nominal) and inflation-adjusted (real) dollars. To provide a rough approximation of state living standards, the BEA divides statewide GDP totals by the statewide population to yield a per capita value.

Consider the state of Georgia. In 2011, the state's GDP totaled $418.9 billion in nominal terms—an amount equal to 2.8 percent of the country's total output in 2011. Private-sector industries generated 85.9 percent of the state's GDP. Manufacturing generated 13.1 percent of that amount, followed by real estate at 12.4 percent and finance and insurance at 8.7 percent.[38] Measured on a per capita basis, real GDP in Georgia totaled $37,270—an amount equal to 88.6 percent of the national figure of $42,070.[39]

The BEA estimates GDP by state on an annual basis and normally releases advance estimates six months after the end of the calendar year. These estimates undergo revisions as more information becomes available. For example, the advance 2011 estimates released in June 2012 contained revisions for the years 2008, 2009, and 2010 and historical revisions stretching back to 1997.[40]

In 2007, the BEA expanded its subnational data offerings by releasing estimates of GDP by metropolitan area. The estimates represent "the sum of the value added originating in all of industries in the metropolitan area."[41] Estimates of GDP by metropolitan area are based on an income approach. The BEA uses earnings data to distribute statewide output in 21 industrial sectors to specific counties, and the data for the counties that form a metropolitan area then are summed together.[42] Estimates are compiled on an annual basis and, as of 2013, appear 14 months following the end of the reference year (e.g., 2011 data appeared in February 2013).[43]

As an example, consider GDP data from the Atlanta-Sandy-Springs-Marietta, GA MSA for 2010, which was the last year for which information was available at the time of this writing. That year, the Atlanta region's GDP totaled $272.4 billion in nominal terms, meaning the 26 counties in the Atlanta area accounted for 67.5 percent of Georgia's economic output. Private-sector industries generated 90.8 percent of the area's GDP, with service-sector activities responsible for 86.7 percent of total private-sector output.[44] On an inflation-adjusted basis, per capita GDP in Atlanta totaled $46,725, which was 2.6 percent greater than the level recorded in the metropolitan United States as a whole. Furthermore, real GDP per capita in 2010 in metropolitan Atlanta metro was 8.6 percent below the value logged in 2007, a fact that illustrates the local impact of the most recent recession.[45]

As with all estimates, subnational GDP data suffer from limitations. The state series, for instance, assumes that sales occur at uniform national price levels. Similarly, the metropolitan series assumes that "the factors of production for each industry are similar between counties and their parent state."[46] Despite those limitations, the GDP series is a valuable source of regional economic data.

State and Local Area Personal Income and Employment

A second source of regional economic information is the BEA's series of estimates of state and local personal income and employment. The data product documents the income and employment related to an area's production of goods and services and changes in income and employment levels over time. Calculated on an industry basis, the data offer a comprehensive, consistent measure of employment levels and the income received by local persons.[47]

Three definitional issues commonly confuse new users of regional personal income and employment data. First, the definition of "person" includes not just actual individuals, but also such "quasi-individuals" as nonprofit organizations serving individuals, private welfare funds, and private trust funds.[48] Second, the concept of "personal income" is broader than money or taxable income (see chapter 8). Personal income is "the sum of wage and salary disbursements, supplements to wages and salaries, proprietors' income, dividends, interest, and rent, and personal current transfer receipts, less contributions for government social insurance."[49] Finally, because employment data reflect positions or jobs on employer payrolls, not employed persons, and are compiled based on the employer's location rather than an individual's place of residence, the BEA must adjust the data accordingly to reflect place of residence.[50]

The BEA has tabulated state-level estimates of personal income dating back to 1929 and local estimates from 1969 onward. These data series have evolved over time to keep pace with changes in the larger economy. Today, BEA produces two sets of state-level estimates: a quarterly series and an annual series. Quarterly estimates appear approximately three months after the end of a quarter. The first annual estimates appear three months after the end of the year, with revisions released six months later.[51] Preparation of estimates for metropolitan areas happens annually, with the release of data occurring 11 months after the end of the year.[52]

Returning to the example of the Atlanta MSA, the region's personal income totaled $212.8 billion in nominal terms in 2011, which was the latest estimate available at the time of writing. Net earnings accounted for 72.4 percent of that amount ($154 billion); dividends, interest, and rent 13.9 percent ($29.7 billion); and transfer payments like unemployment insurance and Social Security 13.7 percent ($29.2 billion). On a per capita basis, average personal income in the Atlanta MSA equaled $39,713.[53]

The Atlanta MSA had 3.1 million payroll jobs in 2011, virtually all of which were nonfarm positions. Wage and salary positions accounted for 75.9 percent of the total number of jobs. In terms of specific sectors, 89.2 percent of the region's jobs were in private firms, the remainder in the public sector. The greatest share of private-sector payroll employment was in administrative and waste management services (10 percent), followed by health care and social assistance (9.7 percent), and professional, scientific, and technical services (9.5 percent). In 2011, the average wage per job in the Atlanta MSA was $52,340.[54]

An advantage of the personal income series is its consistency with the national accounts, which allows the data to aggregate upward. So the Atlanta area's 2011 total personal income of $212.8 billion contributed to Georgia's statewide total of $353.1 billion, which, in turn, formed part of the national total of $12.9 trillion. Additionally, the consistency of the data permits the drawing of meaningful geographic comparisons; for instance, personal per capita income in the Atlanta region exceeded both the statewide and national figures ($35,979 and $41,560, respectively).[55]

Regional Input-Output Modeling System

The final regional accounting product that civic leaders periodically encounter is the *Regional Input-Output Modeling System* (RIMS). This type of information features prominently in economic impact analyses prepared by the professional employees of public agencies and independent consultants, including those involved with industrial recruitment and site selection. Regional officials therefore should possess a basic familiarity with the model.

Input-output analysis is a tool for "analyzing the impacts of small changes in a regional economy."[56] The underlying premise is that "an initial change in economic activity results in diminishing rounds of new spending."[57] This cycle of spending and responding happens because different economic actors are connected in the ways illustrated in circular flow models. Indeed, the technique of input-output analysis builds upon the circular flow model and considers how an increase in final demand is transmitted backward through the linkages among assorted regional industries and end users.

The process of input-output analysis involves the use of *input-output (I-O) multipliers,* which "represent ratios of total to partial changes in economic activity."[58] The process of constructing I-O multipliers involves three steps beginning with the construction of industry-specific transaction tables that show "sales and purchases for each sector in a regional economy during a year."[59] The next step is to convert the transaction tables into a table of trade coefficients that indicates the proportion of goods and services that a particular industry must purchase from other industries to produce an addition dollar in output, assuming that the proportion captured in the transaction table holds constant. Finally, the trade coefficients provide the basis for computing regional I-O multipliers, which indicate how an industry's decision to produce an additional one dollar of output might ripple out to other parts of the economy in four forms: output or sales, value added or GDP, earnings, and employment.

In theory, the cycle of spending and responding caused by an increase in output could extend indefinitely, but in practice analysts focus on the first three rounds of changes. *Direct effects* are the changes caused by an industry's decision to increase its output. *Indirect effects* are the changes caused by firms purchasing from one another in response to the direct change. *Induced effects* are the changes that occur when households respond to the first two sets of effects.[60] After several rounds of spending, any remaining economic activity is assumed to have "leaked" away from the regional economy through imports, taxes, and savings.[61]

In the 1970s, the BEA developed RIMS, which is a set of "national input-output (I-O) accounts that show the goods and services produced by each industry and the use of these goods and services by industries and final users."[62] RIMS contains six multipliers that can be used to estimate final demand output, final demand earnings, final demand employment, final demand value-added, direct effect earnings, and direct-effect employment.[63] With the multipliers, which are available for purchase from the BEA, an analyst can estimate the employment, output, GDP, and earnings effects associated with a small change to a regional economy. It would be possible, for instance, to assess the decrease in employment associated with the closing of a military base or the increase in earnings linked to the opening of a new manufacturing plant.

RIMS is hardly the only system of regional modeling. Numerous private vendors have created proprietary products, notably Impact Analysis for Planning (IMPLAN) developed by MIG, Inc. Proprietary software packages like IMPLAN typically are robust and contain more information than what is captured in RIMS. The downside is they tend to be expensive. Moreover, highly sophisticated data users could calculate their own multipliers from industrial data.

Bear in mind that the decision to employ I-O modeling is an endorsement of a particular theory of regional economic growth: economic base theory (see chapter 3). By opting for I-O modeling, an analyst essentially adopts a distinct view of regional economic growth and inherits the strengths and weaknesses that come along with it.

Due to the popularity of economic base theory, I-O modeling features prominently in regional studies. The technique is imperfect, however. Perhaps the most important limitation is the core assumption that there exists "only one recipe for producing the output of each sector; inputs cannot be substituted."[64] The model further assumes that local producers use the exact same mix of inputs as their national counterparts, which is an assumption that may or may not hold. I-O modeling also hinges on several unrealistic assumptions, such as an absence of production constraints, the nonexistence of economies of scale, and a lack of interregional feedback effects. Moreover, the approach pays no attention to time and the temporal aspects of economic change.[65] Finally, the results may vary greatly depending on the skill and intelligence of the analyst; I-O modeling consequently is no substitute for a nuanced understanding of the key economic features and characteristics of the region under consideration.

REGIONAL ECONOMIC GROWTH: A SUMMARY

Regional leaders interested in growing their economies require a basic understanding of what economic growth is, what it entails, how it differs from economic development, and how it is measured. Despite important limitations, the standard approach is to define economic growth in terms of quantitative increases in output. Circular flow models provide a way of conceptualizing how different regional actors like households and firms interact economically. The downside of such models is that they overlook the dynamic nature of regional economies.

Fortunately, the BEA's system of regional economic accounts fills that gap by illuminating the actual activities occurring within an economy. Yet while these concepts and tools are valuable, they are fundamentally descriptive in nature and provide no insights into why regions grow, which is the subject of the next chapter.

NOTES

1. U.S. Census Bureau, "Annual Estimates of the Population of Metropolitan and Micropolitan Statistical Areas: April 1, 2010 to July 1, 2011 (CBSA-EST2011-01)," last revised April 2012, http://www.census.gov/popest/data/metro/totals/2011/tables/CBSA-EST2011-01.xls.

2. David Moss, *A Concise Guide to Macroeconomics: What Managers, Executives, and Students Need to Know* (Boston: Harvard Business School Press, 2007), 19.

3. Moss, *Concise Guide,* 9.

4. Ibid., 8–9.

5. A useful historical overview of the development of national economic accounting in the United States is Rosemary Marcuss and Richard Kane, "U.S. National Income and Product Statistics: Born of the Great Depression and World War II," *Survey of Current Business,* February 2007, 32–46, http://www.bea.gov/scb/pdf/2007/02%20February/0207_history_article.pdf.

6. Partha Dasgupta, *Economics: A Very Short Introduction* (New York: Oxford University Press, 2007), 117.

7. Joseph Stiglitz, "The Great GDP Swindle," *The Guardian,* September 13, 2009, http://www.guardian.co.uk/commentisfree/2009/sep/13/economics-economic-growth-and-recession-global-economy.

8. Joseph Stiglitz, Amartya Sen, and Jean-Paul Fitoussi, *Mismeasuring Our Lives: Why GDP Doesn't Add Up* (New York: New Press, 2010), xlvi.

9. U.S. Bureau of Economic Analysis, "Regional Economic Accounts Overview," http://www.bea.gov/regional/pdf/overview/regional_intro.pdf (accessed September 4, 2011).

10. As of November 24, 2012, information about the Brookings Institution's calculation of gross metropolitan product as part of its "Metro Monitor" series of reports was available at http://www.brookings.edu/research/interactives/metromonitor#overall. As of November 24, 2012, information about the state and regional data products prepared by Moody's Analytics was available at http://www.economy.com/home/products/us-states-metros.asp.

11. Harry Richardson, *Regional and Urban Economics* (New York: Penguin, 1978), 25.

12. Ibid., 27.

13. Emil Malizia and Edward Feser, *Understanding Local Economic Development* (Rutgers, NJ: Center for Urban Policy Research, 1999), 21.

14. Ibid.

15. Ibid.

16. For a discussion of the growth-oriented mind-set that characterizes public economic development agencies, see John Quinterno, *When Any Job Isn't Enough: Jobs-Centered Development in the American South* (Winston-Salem, NC: Mary Reynolds Babcock Foundation, 2009), 14–18, http://www.sbnstrategies.com/2009/10/02/jobs-centered-development-in-the-american-south/.

17. Edward Blakely and Ted Bradshaw, *Planning Local Economic Development: Theory and Practice* (Thousand Oaks, CA: Sage Publications, 2002), 55–57.

18. U.S. Census Bureau, "Annual Estimates of the Population of Metropolitan and Micropolitan Statistical Areas: April 1, 2010 to July 1, 2011 (CBSA-EST2011-01)."

19. Author's analysis of U.S. Bureau of Economic Analysis, "GDP by Metropolitan Area: Carson City, NV, 2010," last revised September 29, 2011.

20. John Blair, *Local Economic Development: Analysis and Practice* (Thousand Oaks, CA: Sage Publications, 1995), 120.

21. This discussion of the circular flow model draws from Blair, *Local Economic Development,* 120–123; and Edwin Dolan and Kevin Klein, *Survey of Economics,* 4th ed. (Redding, CA: BVT Publishing, 2010), 232–238.

22. Blair, *Local Economic Development,* 123.

23. Ibid., 124–126.

24. Stephanie McCulla and Charles Ian Mead, *An Introduction to the National Income and Product Accounts* (Washington, DC: U.S. Bureau of Economic Analysis, 2007), 2, http://bea.gov/scb/pdf/national/nipa/methpap/mpi1_0907.pdf.

25. Ibid.

26. Stephanie McCulla and Shelly Smith, *Measuring the Economy: A Primer on GDP and the National Income and Product Accounts* (Washington, DC: U.S. Bureau of Economic Analysis, 2007), 1, http://bea.gov/national/pdf/nipa_primer.pdf.

27. McCulla and Mead, *Introduction,* 2.

28. Author's analysis of U.S. Bureau of Economic Analysis, "National Income and Product Accounts: Table 1.1.5. Gross Domestic Product," last revised October 26, 2012.

29. Moss, *Concise Guide,* 11.

30. Bernard Baumohl, *The Secrets of Economic Indicators: Hidden Clues to Future Economic Trends and Investment Opportunities,* 2d ed. (Upper Saddle River, NJ: Wharton School Publishing, 2008), 117.

31. McCulla and Smith, *Measuring the Economy,* 6–13.

32. Moss, *Concise Guide,* 115.

33. Baumohl, *Secrets of Economic Indicators,* 110.

34. As of November 24, 2012, a complete list of the 179 BEA economic areas was available at http://bea.gov/regional/docs/econlist.cfm.

35. Malizia and Feser, *Understanding Local Economic Development,* 71.

36. George Downey, *Gross Domestic Product by State Estimation Methodology* (Washington, DC: U.S. Bureau of Economic Analysis, 2006), 1, http://www.bea.gov/regional/gsp/help/.

37. Ibid., 2.

38. Author's analysis of U.S. Bureau of Economic Analysis, "GDP by State: Georgia, 2011," last revised June 5, 2012.

39. Author's analysis of U.S. Bureau of Economic Analysis, "Per Capita Real GDP by State: Georgia and the United States, 2011," last revised June 5, 2012.

40. U.S. Bureau of Economic Analysis, "Widespread Economic Growth across States in 2011," news release, June 5, 2012, 3–4, http://bea.gov/newsreleases/regional/gdp_state/2012/pdf/gsp0612.pdf.

41. Sharon Panek, et al., "Gross Domestic Product by Metropolitan Area," *Survey of Current Business,* October 2011, 97, http://www.bea.gov/scb/pdf/2011/10%20October/1011_gdp_metro_text.pdf.

42. Sharon Panek, Frank Baumgardner, and Matthew McCormick, "Introducing New Measures of the Metropolitan Economy," *Survey of Current Business,* November 2007, 85–86, http://bea.gov/scb/pdf/2007/11%20November/1107_gdpmetro.pdf.

43. U.S. Bureau of Economic Analysis, "Note on Future Regional Statistical Releases," news release, August 1, 2012, http://www.bea.gov/regional/docs/releasenote.cfm.

44. Author's analysis of U.S. Bureau of Economic Analysis, "GDP by Metropolitan Area: Atlanta-Sandy Springs-Marietta, GA Metropolitan Area, 2010," last revised September 29, 2011; and author's analysis of U.S. Bureau of Economic Analysis, "GDP by State: Georgia, 2010," last revised June 5, 2012.

45. Author's analysis of U.S. Bureau of Economic Analysis, "Per Capita Real GDP by Metropolitan Area: Atlanta-Sandy Springs-Marietta, GA Metropolitan Area, 2007 and 2010," last revised September 29, 2011.

46. Panek, Baumgardner, and McCormick, "Introducing New Measures of the Metropolitan Economy," 86.

47. Robert Brown, "BEA's State and Local Area Personal Income," presentation to Pacific Northwest Regional Economic Analysis Project, Reno, NV, September 29, 2009, http://workshops.reaproject.org/2009/Reno-Nevada/presentations/Brown-BEA-Income.ppt.

48. U.S. Bureau of Economic Analysis, *Local Area Personal Income and Employment Methodology* (Washington, DC: 2012), I-1, http://www.bea.gov/regional/pdf/lapi2010.pdf.

49. Ibid.

50. Ibid., I-3.

51. Ibid., I-11.

52. U.S. Bureau of Economic Analysis, "Note on Future Regional Statistical Releases."

53. Author's analysis of U.S. Bureau of Economic Analysis, "Table CA1-3: Personal Income Summary: Atlanta-Sandy Springs-Marietta, GA Metropolitan Statistical Area, 2011"; and U.S. Bureau of Economic Analysis, "Table CA04: Personal Income and Employment Summary: Atlanta-Sandy Springs-Marietta, GA Metropolitan Statistical Area, 2011."

54. Author's analysis of U.S. Bureau of Economic Analysis, "Table CA25N: Total Full-Time and Part-Time Employment by NAICS Industry, Atlanta-Sandy Springs-Marietta, GA Metropolitan Statistical Area, 2011"; and U.S. Bureau of Economic Analysis, "Table CA34: Wage and Salary Summary: Atlanta-Sandy Springs-Marietta, GA Metropolitan Statistical Area, 2011."

55. Author's analysis of U.S. Bureau of Economic Analysis, "Table CA1-3: Personal Income Summary: Atlanta-Sandy Springs-Marietta, GA Metropolitan Statistical Area, 2011"; and U.S. Bureau of Economic Analysis, "Table SA1-3: Personal Income Summary: Georgia and United States, 2011."

56. Zoë Ambargis, "Regional Input-Output Modeling System," presentation, Pacific Northwest Regional Economic Analysis Project, Reno, NV, September 29, 2009, http://workshops.reaproject.org/2009/Reno-Nevada/presentations/Ambargis-RIMS.ppt.

57. U.S. Bureau of Economic Analysis, *RIMS II: An Essential Tool for Regional Developers and Planners* (Washington, DC: U.S. Department of Commerce, 2012), 1–2, http://www.bea.gov/regional/pdf/rims/RIMSII_User_Guide.pdf.

58. Rebecca Bess and Zoë Ambargis, "Input-Output for Impact Analysis: Suggestions for Practitioners Using RIMS II Multipliers," presentation, Southern Regional Science Association Conference, New Orleans, LA, March 2011, 5, http://www.bea.gov/papers/pdf/WP_IOMIA_RIMSII_020612.pdf.

59. Blair, *Local Economic Development,* 159.

60. Ibid., 162.

61. U.S. Bureau of Economic Analysis, *RIMS II: An Essential Tool for Regional Developers and Planners,* 1–2.

62. Ibid., 2.

63. Ibid., 2–11.

64. Blair, *Local Economic Development,* 160–161.

65. U.S. Bureau of Economic Analysis, *RIMS II: An Essential Tool for Regional Developers and Planners,* 2-1–2-4.

3 | Theories of Regional Economic Development

Economic growth is a foundation of regional progress and well-being, which is a major reason why public leaders demonstrate a keen interest in nurturing, maintaining, and increasing economic activities. To that end, all units of American government engage in "economic development," defined as "the intersection of public policy and commerce for creating jobs, prosperity, business, and wealth."[1] Such efforts have transpired since the nation's founding, yet they were too sporadic to form a discrete area of public policy. It was not until the Great Depression that the modern practice of state and local economic development emerged, driven largely by the attempts of southern states to improve their comparatively lagging economies.[2]

Today, virtually every state and local government of any size sponsors economic development efforts—efforts typically coordinated by public agencies or authorities with the support of various quasigovernmental and nongovernmental organizations. These entities control sizable amounts of public funds and possess the authority to expend those dollars for the benefit of private firms. While no definitive estimates of public spending on economic development exist, one analysis found that state governments alone appropriated $10 billion for that purpose in 2008–2009, with billions more spent through assorted tax breaks.[3]

Despite the importance of economic development and the sizable sums of public monies involved, regional leaders frequently act without any solid understanding of why regions grow. The lack of a theoretical basis for action creates a bias toward short-term, technique-based "deal making" devoid of any larger vision of regional well-being.[4] In fairness, this tendency is attributable less to myopia on the part of civic leaders and more to the fact that economic development is a young field that is "currently more of a movement rather than a strict economic model specifying a uniform approach."[5]

To help civic leaders think systematically about why regions grow, this chapter begins by discussing the extent to which economic development is a "practice in search of a theory." Attention then shifts to a consideration of the essential theoretical aspects of economic development. The chapter concludes by profiling four sets of theoretical models that attempt to explain how and why regions grow and develop: economic base models, location models, innovation and entrepreneurship models, and production models. While civic leaders may not know these models by name, they actually are quite familiar with the basic theories, given the extent to which they underpin most policy and political debates about economic development.

ECONOMIC DEVELOPMENT: A PRACTICE IN SEARCH OF A THEORY

The relationship between the practice and theory of economic development resembles the joke in which a French scholar wonders aloud, "Well yes, it works in practice, but will it work in theory?" In the United States, economic development originated as a practical response to actual economic conditions, with scientific and theoretical inquires occurring later. The practical and theoretical understandings of regional economic development consequently have unfolded along two tracks that only occasionally have intersected.

THE PRACTICE OF ECONOMIC DEVELOPMENT

The modern practice of state and local economic development originated in the American South during the Great Depression. Southern states of that era trailed well behind the rest of the country on every major indicator of economic and social well-being, as evidenced by a federal report from the 1930s that found that "the richest state in the South ranks lower in per capita income than the poorest State outside of the region."[6] As a tool for bridging the economic gap that separated it from the rest of the country, Mississippi opted in 1936 to establish a statewide subsidy program designed to entice businesses to relocate to the state. Under the "Balance Agriculture with Industry" program, certain local governments could issue tax-exempt bonds and spend the proceeds to purchase land and build facilities for relocating firms that met certain criteria; the firms would lease the properties at a nominal cost, with any new tax revenues generated by the firm and its employees used to repay the debt.[7]

While local communities in Mississippi and elsewhere had provided subsidies to private sector firms before 1936, those efforts were ad hoc in nature. It was the systematic and centralized nature of the Balance Agriculture with Industry program that distinguished it from past initiatives and that "lifted the curtain on an era of more competitive subsidization and broader state and local government involvement in industrial development efforts."[8] The program further introduced many of the features still common to the practice of economic development: the idea that communities must "compete" for economic activities; a belief that the way to compete is by offering factors of production as cheaply as possible; a negotiating stance that privileges the interests of firms over the community at large; an acceptance of the need to "buy" economic activities; and a willingness to support private enterprises with public resources in the hope of benefiting society at large.

In the course of creating their initiative, the architects of the Balance Agriculture with Industry program articulated what remain as the two most commonly cited rationales for the involvement of the public sector in private sector activities. First, economic development supposedly is an appropriate governmental function because successful efforts will increase the number of jobs present in the community, both directly and through associated "spillover" effects. Public aid to private industry ideally will increase the amount of private investment in a community, which will expand the number of jobs available. More jobs, in turn, will raise local incomes and reduce economic hardships, thereby boosting the demand for goods and services. Satisfying the new demand will require firms to invest more, which will cause the cycle to repeat, resulting in even more jobs.[9]

The second argument holds that economic development is an appropriate governmental function because successful efforts will generate the resources needed to finance public investments and improve the community. Viewed this way, public aid to private firms will increase the amount of private investment in a community, which will expand the local tax base. The enlarged tax base, in turn, will yield higher tax revenues, which can finance improvements in public services and amenities. An improved community will lead private firms to invest more, leading to a repeat of the cycle. (Alternately, a jurisdiction could use the larger tax base to reduce tax rates, which also would lead private firms to invest more and cause the cycle to repeat.)[10]

These two rationales have underpinned each of the three waves of economic development practice that have occurred since the 1930s.[11] Drawing their inspiration from efforts like those in Mississippi, first-wave initiatives sought to recruit firms from one part of the country to another, typically from northern states to southern ones. Sometimes called "Smokestack Chasing," first-wave models enjoyed their heyday from the late 1940s through the mid-1970s. Second-wave efforts emerged in response to the economic slowdown of the 1970s and the beginnings of northern deindustrialization and centered on the cultivation of internal sources of growth through improving educational opportunities, investing in higher education, funding scientific research, and commercializing innovations. The third wave in the practice of economic development formed in the 1990s and sought to blend elements of the first two waves with a deeper understanding of business processes and local economies to shape how firms, industries, and local economies operate; perhaps the most prominent third-wave model is cluster development.

As this brief sketch of the evolution of the practice of economic development suggests, the adoption and rejection of particular strategies hinged on shifts in the larger economic and political environments. The driving force, in other words, was a practical sense of what could work given existing political realities rather than any insights gleaned from theoretical or empirical research. Furthermore, the shift from one wave of practice to another never involved a clean break with the past. New ideas instead settled upon old ones regardless of whether the new and old ideas actually were compatible or even intellectually consistent or coherent.

The Theory of Economic Development

To reduce complex human interactions into forms suitable for analysis, scholars fashion theoretical models that attempt to describe and predict actions and their consequences. These models contain "assumptions about a situation and a series of deductions about what behavior will flow from the assumptions."[12] Models that assume that people primarily seek to maximize their own profit, for example, predict outcomes different from those anticipated by models that posit altruism as the central human motivation. Even in a practical field like economic development, models matter because they "determine, either explicitly or implicitly, how . . . developers understand economic development, the questions they ask about the process, the information they collect to analyze development, and the development strategies they pursue."[13]

Consider the two rationales for public support of private enterprise commonly cited by working economic developers: job growth and community development. Both justifications sound appealing yet suffer from internal contradictions. Job growth, for one, may be desirable, but an influx of residents in search of the new jobs may require more spending on public services than is generated in added tax revenues.[14] In the same way, an increase in business investment may not result in more jobs if firms intensify their capital stocks and become more productive without adding positions.[15] Similarly, a narrow focus on job growth may detract from community development, especially if the jobs are of a poor quality.[16] Another flaw is that job growth is a means for creating wealth, not an end in itself, so efforts that foster job growth but detract from the efficient use of scarce resources can be detrimental.[17]

Theoretical models can help to identify such shortcomings in practical thinking, yet scholarly inquiry into subnational economic development in the United States has trailed behind actual practice. One reason is the relative youth of the field. Additionally attention has tended to gravitate to the challenges facing the world's poorest places or the processes that have led to the development of the industrialized world. Finally, the practice of economic development emerged during a time of extensive federal support for regional development (approximately 1955–1978), so scholarly interest focused on the actions of the federal government. It was only after the federal government stepped back in 1978 that the role of states and localities in economic development became more pronounced and, therefore, of greater research interest, heightened by the process of industrial restructuring that started in northern states around the same time.[18]

None of this implies that scholars were uninterested in regional development. Prior to World War II, a group of academics connected to the University of North Carolina at Chapel Hill developed a comprehensive (if dated) account of the reasons for the relative economic and social underdevelopment of the South.[19] During the 1950s and 1960s, other scholars began to analyze the forces that drive regional growth, such as the role of exporting, the impact of import replacement, and the significance of locational factors. In the 1970s and 1980s, questions related to deindustrialization and the expansion of the service sector came to the fore, while more recently, researchers have occupied themselves with questions of business practices and processes, interfirm relationships, entrepreneurship, and human capital.

A key insight that has emerged from academic inquiries—an insight that differentiates scholarship from practice and often is a source of contention between scholars and practitioners—is that economic development is not the same as economic growth. In the opinion of many practitioners, the end they are pursuing is economic growth, defined as quantitative increases in the overall levels of economic variables such as total employment. Seen this way, any increase in the employment base is an accomplishment. Researchers, however, tend to stress development, or "a qualitative increase in collective well-being," as the overriding goal.[20] Viewed that way, the simple addition of new jobs is not necessarily a desirable outcome; after all, a gain in employment in low-wage jobs would boost overall employment yet contribute little to the developmental goal of increasing per capita income.

THEORETICAL ASPECTS OF ECONOMIC DEVELOPMENT

The models that guide the practice and theory of economic development—both experiential models formed by practitioners and formal ones crafted by scholars—have a direct bearing on public policy and regional well-being. Regardless of their differences, each model attempts to explain economic development in relation to certain basic categories and core concepts—all of which demonstrate important strengths and limitations and have practical applications.[21] At the same time, the models are not mutually exclusive. One way to appreciate the similarities and differences is to consider five theoretical aspects of each model: theory focus, analytical unit, driving dynamic, theoretical lens, and policy applications.[22]

The first aspect to consider is the focus of each theory. As mentioned previously, practitioners and scholars frequently conceptualize the goals of economic development differently. Economic developers often focus on short-term growth and researchers on long-term development. The difference matters for theoretical reflection. If growth is the goal, related theories will attempt to explain why growth occurs and how it might be cultivated. If long-term development is the goal, the associated theories will center on the causes of development. A theory of growth therefore would account for changes in, say, regional income levels over a short period of time, while a theory of development would offer an explanation of changes in income levels that unfold over years. A theory of development would be likely to consider questions of income stability and distribution in addition to growth.

A second aspect to note is the unit or level of analysis. Microeconomic accounts of economic development concern themselves with individual economic units and matters such as "how households and firms make decisions and how they interact in markets."[23] Macroeconomic explanations of economic development, in contrast, consider the region as the unit of analysis and study how the regional economy operates within larger, open, market-based national and international economies ones. Lastly, meso-level theories concern themselves with units larger than households and firms but smaller than national or global economies, and often attempt to draw connections between microeconomic and macroeconomic forces. For example, a meso-level theory might try to explain how certain technological advances affect the competitive position of a specific industry.

Box 3.1 Neoclassical Economics

Neoclassical economics feature prominently in media stories and policy debates about economic development. In fact, neoclassical ideas are so common that observers often take them as being synonymous with the entire discipline of economics, even though they are just one framework for explaining economic interactions.

Neoclassical models represent ongoing attempts to update the economic ideas of the eighteenth and nineteenth centuries for modern conditions. Rooted in microeconomics, neoclassical models build from the level of individual households and firms upward. Specifically, six assumptions underpin these models:

- Economic actors are rational and have clear, logical preferences.
- Individuals seek to maximize their satisfaction, firms their profits.
- Individuals are constrained by their incomes, firms by their costs.
- Economic actors possess full information and are free to behave as they see fit.
- Markets are perfectly competitive, so economic actors are price takers.
- Economic exchanges only occur when the marginal benefit exceeds the marginal cost.

If these assumptions hold, so proponents argue, market forces will yield socially optimal outcomes. Neoclassical models envision markets as naturally inclined toward states of equilibrium in which the quantities of specific goods that buyers demand and can afford match the quantities of those goods that firms wish to supply and can provide. Price is the mechanism that reconciles supply and demand. If prices fluctuate freely, they should converge on a market-clearing level that balances supply and demand. The attainment of equilibrium signals the optimal allocation of scarce resources and the maximization of social welfare. Maximum welfare results because, provided conditions hold constant, it is impossible to deviate from equilibrium without leaving some party worse off.

This state of "Pareto optimality," named after Vilfredo Pareto, a nineteenth-century Italian economist, refers to efficiency and is silent to questions of distribution or fairness. A Pareto optimum could exist when one person controls 99 percent of the food in a region while the rest of the population possesses the remaining 1 percent. Assuming the food supply is finite and that the dominant person objects to any reduction in his or her share, any move that altered the status quo would be Pareto inefficient; of course, the have-nots could attempt to entice the person controlling the food supply to agree to a change by offering something of compensating value.

The factors influencing the abilities of firms to supply goods and services, such as the availability of land, labor, and capital, are the primary concern in neoclassical inquires. Demand-side factors receive limited attention on the assumption that supply will create its own demand. Furthermore, public sector involvement in markets is opposed except in rare circumstances. The role of government ideally is limited to smoothing inefficiencies in markets, providing pure public goods like public safety, precluding economic actors from controlling prices as under monopolies, and preventing market actions that impose costs on third parties, such as pollution. Government also may have some role in encouraging the formation of supply-side capacities, such as by funding infrastructure, education, and scientific research.

When it comes to regions, neoclassical models view them as abstract economic entities rather than particular places. If supplies of capital and labor can move freely, market forces should direct resources toward the regions offering the greatest returns. Capital therefore should flow from relatively high-cost to low-cost areas. Regional growth, in short, flows from a place's ability to attract supply-side factors, chiefly capital. At the same time, any comparative regional cost advantages are temporary since, over time, interregional prices, costs, and profits should converge. Neoclassical models further posit that capital must flow "naturally," implying that governmental actions that attempt to direct capital flows will fail.

Advantages of neoclassical models include their intuitive appeal and their ability to generate testable predictions about economic behavior. At the same time, the simplicity and ubiquity of neoclassical models obscure important limitations. Perhaps the most serious shortcoming is the inherent unreality of the models' assumptions. Neoclassical models may exhibit a logical elegance, but their basic conditions seldom apply to daily life: human beings are not omniscient, dispassionate calculators of rational utility, perfect competition rarely exists, and markets frequently fail. Another flaw is that neoclassical models evince little interest in questions of distribution, fairness, and nonmarket concerns despite their social importance. Moreover, neoclassical models offer no compelling explanations for why some regions thrive and others fail. Such flaws explain why economics writer John Cassidy refers to neoclassical economics as "utopian economics."

When it comes to regional economic development, neoclassical thinking manifests itself in calls to nurture the "business climate" so that the region can attract inflows of capital. Some preferred actions—streamlining bureaucracies, say—indeed may yield benefits, as might steps to improve supply-side factors like the quality of the workforce. Yet arguments for business climate sometimes are mere justifications for policies that enrich businesses and investors at the expense of the public. Regional leaders therefore must scrutinize such proposals to ensure they benefit the entire region.

Sources: Edward Blakely and Ted Bradshaw, *Planning Local Economic Development: Theory and Practice*, 3d ed. (Thousand Oaks, CA: Sage Publications, 2002), 58; John Cassidy, *How Markets Fail: The Logic of Economic Calamities* (New York: Farrar, Strauss, and Giroux, 2009), 8 and 53–56; Emil Malizia and Edward Feser, *Understanding Local Economic Development* (Rutgers, NJ: Center for Urban Policy Research, 1999), 40 and 125–130; and N. Gregory Mankiw, *Principles of Microeconomics* (Fort Worth, TX: Dryden Press, 1998), 3–14, 25, 76–78, and 150.

The third theoretical aspect to consider is the source of change in regional economic activity. Some theories hold that regions grow in response to exogenous or external factors, such as the demand by people in other regions for the goods and services produced within a local economy. Other theories hold that changes in economic activity result from endogenous or internal factors, such as improvements in human capital, scientific research, and business innovation. Theories that emphasize exogenous factors will differ in key respects, including their policy applications, from those that stress endogenous sources of growth.

A fourth aspect to consider is the theoretical lens through which economic activity is viewed. Neoclassical economics doubtlessly is the theoretical lens most often encountered, but there also exist numerous so-called heterodox perspectives (see Box 3.1). For instance, the institutional school of economics that traces its roots to the work of early twentieth-century economists such as Thorstein Veblen holds that economic forces are intertwined inextricably with social, legal, and political structures and that these institutions influence economic outcomes. Similarly, Marxian economics, named after the nineteenth-century intellectual Karl Marx, emphasizes, among other things, the interdependence of regions, the role that social class plays in a capitalist economy, the consequences associated with the mobility of capital, and the extent to which economic choices privilege some classes over others.

A final aspect to contemplate when studying theories of regional economic development is the type of policy responses supported by each theory. In other words, the selection of a model determines the scope of practical policy actions. Models that assume an economy has a natural tendency toward a state of equilibrium—a hallmark of the neoclassical perspective—envision a limited role for public intervention. Meanwhile, disequilibrium models that see no inherent tendency for economies to move toward a state of balance perceive a broader scope for policy action and the need for more active management of an economy.

Theoretical Models of Economic Development

In the course of exercising their duties, regional leaders responsible for economic development encounter numerous arguments in support of or in opposition to proposed actions. While the arguments may seem overwhelming at times, almost all of them originate in one of four broad sets of theoretical models: economic base models, location models, innovation and entrepreneurship models, and production models. To shed light on those models, the following sections profile each set, paying special attention to the five theoretical aspects of economic development discussed earlier in the chapter.

Economic Base Models

Economic base models dominate the practice of economic development in the United States. Such models hold that the growth of a region is "directly related to the demand for its goods, services, and products from areas outside its local economic boundaries."[24] As a result, these growth-centered, macroeconomic, disequilibrium theories attribute economic changes to exogenous factors and are rooted in "a Keynesian theory of regional income."[25]

The central premise of economic base theory is that "in a trade-integrated world, regions outside of one's own are superior producers of many goods and services locally consumed, and in order to pay for these imports, the region must specialize in exportable goods and services for which they have a competitive advantage."[26] Given the extent to which "the export base plays a vital role in determining the level of absolute and per capita income in a region," the aim is to maximize the inflow of money into a region.[27] Exports are central to this end because nonlocal sales draw in new money that ripples through the local economy. Export firms may use the higher incomes derived from nonlocal sales to raise the wages of employees, who spend the money locally. Local firms, in turn, pass along some of their increased incomes in the forms of higher wages and purchases from other businesses, thereby causing the cycle to repeat. This process of increasing specialization improves economic efficiency and boosts levels of output, employment, and income, at least in the short term.[28]

Economic base theory conceptualizes a regional economy as having two segments: a traded (export) sector and a nonbasic (local) sector. The traded sector comprises all of the industries and firms that produce goods and services for nonlocal markets, while the nonbasic sector encompasses the industries and firms that serve local residents. Note the nonbasic sector is not synonymous with the service sector because some services are tradable; health care, for one, is a service that can attract nonlocal money into a region, as often happens in places with top-tier medical institutions. The core distinction, then, is the source of economic demand rather than the type of economic activity.

One popular tool for identifying a region's export strengths is the *location quotient*. This technique identifies relative strengths by comparing an aspect of a regional economy to that of a larger reference economy (see Box 3.2). For instance, one way of illustrating the local concentration of an industry is to take that industry's share of total regional employment and divide it by the corresponding national figure. Quotients greater than 1 suggest a regional advantage; for lower values, the opposite is true.[29]

A limitation of location quotients is that they provide snapshot information for one moment and yield few insights into how a region's economic structure and competitive position change over time, especially relative to changes in a larger reference economy. To capture such trends, analysts frequently employ another, albeit more complicated, analytical tool called *shift-share analysis* (see Box 3.3). By comparing the rate of change in an aspect of the regional economy to that of a larger economy, shift-share analysis is "a way to isolate the effect of local influences on growth from effects that operate industry-wide or at a national level" and is "especially useful for noting variations in the local effect across industries that may signal strengths and weaknesses of the local economy."[30]

The policy prescriptions that emerge from economic base theory "emphasize the priority of aid to and recruitment of businesses that have a national or international market over aid to local nonexport firms."[31] Preferred actions include the provision of technical and marketing assistance to export-oriented firms, the awarding of preferential tax treatment or subsidies to traded industries, and the recruitment of export-oriented firms. Because economic base theory holds that a region's nonbasic sector "will develop automatically either because of locational advantages of materials-oriented industry or as a passive reflection of growing income in the region resulting from the success of its exportable commodities," practitioners tend to pay little attention to nonbasic industries, even those with large numbers of employees.[32]

Despite their ubiquity, economic base models suffer from multiple weaknesses. First, as short-term, demand-side theories, they are unable to account for the drivers of long-term growth and development; in short, "the concept of the export base may be useful in describing regional income growth, but this need not be considered the same problem as general economic development."[33] Second, the single-minded focus on exports obscures other possible sources of regional growth, such as the process of import replacement (substitution) and other types of endogenous growth. Third, the division of an economy into traded and nonbasic sectors is arbitrary and ignores the fact that "the consumption base—goods and services that are locally produced and locally consumed—can also be a source of regional job growth and stability."[34] Fourth, economic base models often confuse supporting export industries with assisting politically favored industries. Finally, the models tend to break down at geographic levels smaller than a metropolitan area, though in reality smaller geographies are too small to be functional economies in their own right.

Box 3.2 Location Quotients

A common tool for identifying industries in which a regional economy appears to possess a relative advantage, the *location quotient* compares the contribution of one industry to a local economy to the same industry's contribution to a larger reference economy. While numerous economic variables are suitable for analysis with location quotients, the one most commonly used is employment because of its overall importance and the ready availability of high-quality, geographically detailed data.

Below is a version of a location quotient formula intended for comparing the regional share of employment in a certain industry to the corresponding national level:

$$LQ_i = \frac{(re_i / re_t)}{(NE_i / NE_t)}$$

where

LQ_i = Location quotient for industry i
re_i = Regional employment in industry i
re_t = Total regional employment
NE_i = Total national employment in industry i
NE_t = Total national employment

The value of the location quotient indicates how the region performs on the variable of interest relative to the reference economy. When applied to employment levels, a location quotient of 1.0 indicates that the share of regional employment in an industry matches the share of national employment in the same industry. A location quotient value greater than 1.0 indicates that the share of regional employment in an industry exceeds the national share of employment in that industry, while a value of less than 1.0 indicates the opposite. In the context of economic base theory, regional industries with location quotients greater than 1.0 generally belong to the export sector, those with quotients less than 1.0 to the local sector.

For a practical application of the location quotient technique, consider the following example that compares payroll employment levels in the information industry (supersector) in 2011 in the Austin-Round Rock-San Marcos, TX Metropolitan Statistical Area (MSA) to the nation as whole through use of the formula described previously:

$$LQ_i = \frac{(re_i / re_t)}{(NE_i / NE_t)}$$

$$= \frac{(20,236 / 616,065)}{(2,674,852 / 108,184,795)}$$

$$= 1.33$$

This relatively high location quotient of 1.33—a value 33 percent higher than would be expected—suggests that the Austin area enjoys a relative advantage in the information industry, which encompasses such fields as software publishing, motion pictures, sound recording, and wireless telecommunications. Of course, while Austin enjoys an advantage in these fields, the advantage is not as strong as in, say, the Los Angeles-Long Beach-Santa Ana, CA MSA, which has a location quotient of 1.9 (a level 90 percent greater than expected); given the Los Angeles area's strengths in entertainment fields, such a high location quotient is not surprising.

Location quotients require careful interpretation. External shocks, such as a major plant closing, sometimes may produce an illusion of competitiveness, as might region-specific factors (like climate) that create local demand for particular industries. Similarly, for the technique to work, analysts must rely on a number of assumptions—for example, that the local and reference regions belong to a closed economy, that the demand for goods and services is constant across the local and reference economies, that firms produce identical products, that labor productivity is uniform across the local and reference economies, and that a region never imports any of what it exports—all of which may prove problematic or unfounded in reality.

Sources: Author's analysis of U.S. Bureau of Labor Statistics, *Quarterly Census of Employment and Wages, 2011;* John Blair, *Local Economic Development: Analysis and Practice* (Thousand Oaks, CA: Sage Publications, 1995), 106–112; and Mary McLean and Kenneth Voytek, *Understanding Your Economy: Using Analysis to Guide Local Strategic Planning*, 2d ed. (Chicago: American Planning Association, 1992), 61–66.

LOCATION MODELS

An important shortcoming of economic base models and, more generally, theories rooted in a neoclassical perspective, is that they ignore the role of place in regional growth. Such models instead conceptualize regions in abstract and dualistic terms— there simply is the region and the rest of the world—and ignore intraregional differences by assuming regional uniformity. In response, scholars active between the 1950s and 1970s proposed various location models that conceived of regional growth "as a process that involves changing industrial structure and spatial structure, both between and within labor market areas."[35] By incorporating spatial concerns, researchers are better able to craft more nuanced accounts of how a regional economy functions, how its components interact, and how it develops over time.

Location theory emerged during an era of muscular domestic policy making in the United States and was concerned not merely with describing how regions grow, but also with closing the gaps between lagging regions and prosperous ones. Consequently, location theories envision an active role for the public sector in promoting "the spread of growth across space" and, in the more aggressive variants of the theory, regional and social equity.[36] Location models further provided the rationale for the federal government's few modern forays into regional development, notably the Tennessee Valley Authority and the Appalachian Regional Commission.

Despite the ambitious aims of certain types of location theories, the resulting policy strategies have yielded more failures than successes. This stems from the tendency of practitioners to confuse a place's need for growth with its capacity to sustain growth and a bias toward one-shot growth efforts over comprehensive investments in social and human capital. More recently, globalization has scrambled the assumptions upon which location models rest. Not only have improvements in transportation and communication reduced the importance of place, but the increasing importance of

---

Box 3.3 Shift-Share Analysis

Shift-share analysis is an analytical tool for comparing changes in a region's economic structure over a period of time to the changes experienced in a larger reference economy over the same period. Many economic variables are suitable for shift-share analysis, but the technique is most often applied to employment data. When used to study changes in employment, the shift in regional employment is the sum of the changes recorded in three different component parts:

- The *share* is the overall rate of employment change in all industries in the reference economy.
- The *industrial shift* is the difference between the rate of employment change in a given industry in the reference economy and the rate of employment changes in all industries in the reference economy.
- The *differential shift* is the difference between the rate of employment change in a given industry in the regional economy and the rate of employment change in the same industry in the reference economy.

When interpreting the results of a shift-share analysis, observers typically focus on the differential shift and treat it as an indicator of a region's competitive advantages or disadvantages. A positive differential shift means that employment in a given regional industry is growing at a faster rate than the same industry within the reference economy. A negative differential shift means that a regional industry is declining; however, if the rate of decline is slower than the national one, the region has a relative advantage.

The results of shift-share analyses require careful interpretation. One limitation is that the technique offers no insights into why a regional industry is growing or contracting, yet it is impossible to advance effective development strategies without an understanding of root causes. A second shortcoming is that shift-share analysis has limited predictive value. A third difficulty is that the results obtained through a shift-share analysis may change greatly depending on the level of industrial detail included in a calculation. A final problem is that observers often mistakenly assume that a region's performance should match that of the reference region, but there is no reason why that should be the case, so an inordinate focus on national comparisons may preclude consideration of factors specific to a region.

Sources: John Blair, *Local Economic Development: Analysis and Practice* (Thousand Oaks, CA: Sage Publications, 1995), 145–149; Edward Blakely and Ted Bradshaw, *Planning Local Economic Development: Theory and Practice*, 3d ed. (Thousand Oaks, CA: Sage Publications, 2002), 127–131; and Mary McLean and Kenneth Voytek, *Understanding Your Economy: Using Analysis to Guide Local Strategic Planning*, 2d ed. (Chicago: American Planning Association, 1992), 67–71.

---

human resources and interpersonal networks also challenges some of the assumptions underpinning location models.[37]

While all location models consider the importance of place in regional development, the various theories differ in regard to the five theoretical aspects discussed previously. Four variants of location theory merit consideration: attraction models, central place models, growth pole models, and cumulative causation models. Of these, the first two are equilibrium theories, while the second two are disequilibrium theories.

Equilibrium Theories: Attraction Models

Attraction models are growth-centered, microeconomic, equilibrium ones that attribute economic changes to exogenous forces and are rooted in a neoclassical perspective that views factors of production, such as labor and capital, as being highly mobile. The models emphasize the forces that draw and anchor rational, utility-maximizing firms, workers, and households to particular places. When applied to firms, the assumptions of rationality and utility maximization hold that businesses seek "to minimize their costs by selecting locations that maximize their opportunities to reach the marketplace."[38] In other words, firms negotiate trade-offs between locations that offer low production costs and those that allow for the effective servicing of customers, as when manufacturing firms select locations where they cheaply and efficiently can receive inputs from suppliers and ship finished products to market.

By and large, attraction models are neoclassical in their basic assumptions, causal mechanisms, and policy prescriptions. In this view, "communities are products" that "must be 'packaged' and appropriately displayed."[39] The associated policy agenda therefore calls for communities to tailor their cost structures to the needs of particular industries and firms and to recruit them aggressively, in part by providing the information that firms require to reach rational decisions in their best interest. While normally applied to firms, the same mentality may inform any effort to recruit resources to an area, such as campaigns to attract well-educated workers, highly skilled immigrants, or affluent retirees.

Among other weaknesses, the emphasis on community marketing and presentation common to attraction models sometimes devolves into simple boosterism that ignores pressing community problems, such as underperforming school systems. Further, there is a real risk that the use of public funds to attract firms, workers, and households will lead to redistribution of community resources from the public at large to private actors, resulting in little actual economic development. For example, the use of tax subsidies to attract firms that pay low wages actually may harm a community by siphoning away resources that could ameliorate social problems or promote long-term prosperity. Such efforts may leave a place worse off than it was before the intervention.

Equilibrium Theories: Central Place Models

Central place models are growth-centered, macroeconomic, equilibrium ones that attribute economic changes to exogenous factors and share the same basic perspective as economic base theory. Specifically, central place models explain intraregional differences in terms of the urban hierarchy formed by the "spatial ranges" over which sales of specific goods and services occur. Such models envision a major urban center as "being supported by a series of smaller places that provide resources (industries and raw materials) to the central place, which is more specialized and productive."[40] A small town, for instance, may offer basic economic services (e.g., grocery stores) targeted at local residents and those in nearby rural areas, just as a larger city may offer more services (e.g., a shopping mall) that draw business from the inhabitants of the small town. Thanks to the highly specialized economic activities offered by its firms (e.g., professional services), a major metropolitan area will succeed in drawing business from all of the smaller places within its orbit.

The policy applications originating from central place models involve strengthening the ties between the central place and locations lower in the urban hierarchy. These strategies suffer from many of the limitations of location models mentioned previously. Central place models are also hindered by their static nature, an inability to explain why regions change over time, and a failure to account for developments in postindustrial economies.

Disequilibrium Theories: Growth Pole Models

Growth pole models are growth-centered, microeconomic, disequilibrium ones that attribute economic changes to a mix of endogenous and exogenous factors and stand in opposition to the neoclassical claim that growth flows to regions with comparative cost advantages. The models hold that regional economic activity is "stimulated by cutting-edge industries, firms, or other actors who are dominant in their field."[41] Once growth poles form, they quickly overpower other firms, industries, and places "due to their large size, market power, high growth rate, and high degree of linkage."[42] While growth poles draw in resources from other places, they also may devolve activities back to peripheral areas, with that devolution fueling growth in the periphery.

While the growth pole model originally focused on specific industries and considered space in abstract economic terms, it eventually developed connections to geographic-based growth efforts. Instead of propulsive industries, there could be, some theorists suggested, propulsive regions that drew in resources from a larger area and would eventually devolve other functions to the periphery. That presents a potential role for public policy to influence the flows of economic activities between a core and its periphery and in building linkages between growth poles and smaller, linked regions. This tantalizing idea has provided the justification for attempts to tie growing metropolitan areas to smaller, adjacent places. In North Carolina, for instance, the state has attempted to boost the presence of the life science industry by connecting the research capabilities present in the Research Triangle to affordable manufacturing locations in adjoining rural places. Firms ideally will be able to conduct research in the metropolitan area while placing production facilities nearby, thereby sparking growth in both places.[43]

Despite the appeal of growth pole theories, their practical applications have yielded few successful cases of economic growth diffusing from a core region to a peripheral one. Just because a region is in need of economic growth in no way implies that it can support growth. And the investments that peripheral places undertake to attract economic activities from core regions frequently bind those places too closely to the fortunes of one industry; consume resources that might have gone to other, more productive economic and social purposes; or saddle communities with idle resources, a fact to which the scores of empty industrial shell buildings that litter small towns throughout the Southeast attest. Another problem is that it has proven challenging to adopt growth pole models, which were developed for an industrial economy, to the characteristics of postindustrial economies like those now found in much of the developed world.[44]

Disequilibrium Theories: Cumulative Causation Models

Cumulative causation models are growth-centered, microeconomic, disequilibrium ones that attribute economic changes to a mix of endogenous and exogenous factors and stand in opposition to the neoclassical claim that the free movement of capital eventually will eliminate interregional disparities. On the contrary, growing regions may draw resources from less vibrant areas and exacerbate regional disparities. Left unchecked, a downward spiral may lead to the permanent impoverishment of the peripheral region. An extension of this idea, core periphery theory, argues that the way to ameliorate the unbalanced relationship among growing and peripheral regions is through governmental efforts to steer industrial growth to struggling areas "by concentrating infrastructure investments and direct business investments at selected locations that possess growth potential."[45] Unfortunately, practical attempts to apply both of these models have encountered the same basic problems as have applications of growth pole models.

A recent variation of cumulative causation models called new markets theory seeks to channel resources, particularly investment capital, to places with untapped potential to spark growth and development.[46] This idea gained currency in the 1990s and manifested itself in concentrated efforts to invest in distressed places such as inner cities. Similarly, the growth of community development finance institutions like the nonprofit Center for Community Self-Help, based in Durham, North Carolina, and the Southern Good Faith Fund in Little Rock, Arkansas, reflects an interest in extending capital to places where traditionally it has been unavailable.

INNOVATION AND ENTREPRENEURSHIP MODELS

Innovation and entrepreneurship models consider the role played by the skills and abilities of individual human beings in fostering economic growth. After all, economic activity is a direct result of human efforts, and without people there would be no such thing as an economy, nor any need for one. While human skills are necessary to the success of a broad range of endeavors, innovation and entrepreneurship models tend to stress the role of human capabilities in the formation of new businesses and the process of innovation. Two models that have become especially popular in recent years relate to entrepreneurship and creativity.

Entrepreneurship Models

Entrepreneurship models are development-centered, microeconomic, disequilibrium ones that attribute economic changes to endogenous factors and fall outside of the neoclassical perspective. These models conceive of regional growth as the product of a particular set of individual actors: entrepreneurs, or "people who carry out the venture-creation functions that, in turn, generate development through innovation."[47] To tap this potential, regions often attempt to foster entrepreneurship by offering direct support to business owners or creating an environment that supports entrepreneurial activity.

While Americans long have romanticized entrepreneurs as visionary risk takers who create wealth-producing enterprises, major economic theories actually pay little attention to them. Neoclassical economics holds that the attainment of market equilibrium precludes entrepreneurship. After all, if equilibrium signals a perfect allocation of resources and the satisfaction of all individual preferences, there are no gaps for entrepreneurs to fill or inefficiencies to exploit. Entrepreneurs exist, of course, but many models respond to this inconvenient truth by ignoring it.[48]

Writing in the early twentieth century, Austrian economist Joseph Schumpeter sketched the first comprehensive account of entrepreneur-led development. Schumpeter saw capitalist economies as marked by a continual process of "creative destruction." Established firms engaged in routine production favor stability and order, but entrepreneurs imagine new possibilities. When backed by adequate capital, entrepreneurs can wield their ideas to disrupt the status quo. The disruption triggers a wave of innovation that ripples through the economy and propels growth. Once a cycle exhausts itself, a recession normally follows during which market actors reorganize, exchange places, and begin building toward the next disruptive wave.[49]

The appeal of entrepreneurship models has sparked numerous regional efforts to promote entrepreneurship (see Box 3.4). One practical approach is to cultivate a regional environment that is supportive of entrepreneurship and offers the resources—such as skilled labor, first-rate physical infrastructure, and vibrant social spaces—that entrepreneurs require. A second method is to provide direct aid to entrepreneurial firms.

Despite their popularity, entrepreneurship strategies are problematic. One difficulty is that theories of entrepreneurship emphasize the attributes of individual entrepreneurs, but the policy prescriptions aimed at encouraging entrepreneurship stress the attributes of individual places. Another shortcoming is that responsible officials typically fail to differentiate entrepreneurial businesses from businesses in general. Few enterprises truly are entrepreneurial, and most regional businesses simply are iterations of established types (e.g., restaurants, professional service firms, and retail stores). These businesses matter greatly to their owners, employees, and communities, but they are not sources of disruptive innovations. Finally, even when aid is targeted at entrepreneurial firms, it often flows to the firms most likely to succeed, or it arrives too late to alter the odds of success.[50]

Creativity Models

In recent years, creativity models have attracted considerable interest, thanks mainly to the work of Richard Florida, a scholar at the University of Toronto who has popularized the idea of the "creative class." Florida argues that regional growth hinges upon a place's ability to nurture, attract, and retain creative individuals. These individuals fall into two main groups: supercreative professionals in "science and engineering, architecture and design education, arts, music and entertainment, whose economic function is to create new ideas, new technology, and/or new creative content" and a supporting cast of "creative professionals in business and finance, law, health care and related fields."[51] Florida further claims that creatives tend to concentrate in metropolitan areas with educated populations, strong technological infrastructures, and high degrees of social toleration.

Box 3.4 Entrepreneurship

There has been a recent surge of interest in entrepreneurship as a regional development strategy, both in the United States and abroad. Despite the increased attention, entrepreneurship remains an ill-defined phenomenon.

The Organization for Economic Cooperation and Development (OECD), an international policy forum to which most wealthy nations belong, defines *entrepreneurial activity* as "the enterprising human action in pursuit of the generation of value, through the creation or expansion of economic activity, by identifying and exploiting new products, processes, or markets." Entrepreneurial activities can occur in various settings. Employees working within a large multinational corporation can behave entrepreneurially, as can self-employed persons working alone. Similarly, entrepreneurship may involve the creation of new products or improvements to existing products or production processes. And entrepreneurial activities may generate monetary value like business profits, social value like improved public health, or a combination of the two. Practically speaking, analysts tend to define entrepreneurship as the creation of new products or services by profit-seeking business enterprises that have employees.

While every individual has the potential to be an entrepreneur, the ability to launch and sustain an entrepreneurial venture hinges on multiple factors. According to the OECD, entrepreneurial performance depends on six broad determinants: the regulatory framework surrounding a venture, the market conditions facing a venture, the ability of a venture to access financing, the availability of needed knowledge, the entrepreneurial capabilities of a venture's principals, and the extent to which a larger society encourages entrepreneurship. These factors influence the creation rates, survival rates, employment levels, and financial successes of entrepreneurial firms. Entrepreneurial performance, in turn, may bring about such desirable economic and social effects as job creation and poverty reduction.

The OECD attempted in 2011 to measure in a standardized manner the determinants, performance, and impacts of entrepreneurship across 25 countries, including the United States. The research found that businesses with fewer than 10 employees accounted for the majority of businesses in every country studied. There also existed a significant degree of "churn" among enterprises, as new firms start and existing ones close. Furthermore, most firms appeared not to grow much in terms of employment size, but a subset of fast-growing firms was a significant source of job creation. The research further concluded that societies differed widely in their opinions of entrepreneurship, with Americans and the residents of the Nordic countries holding the most favorable views.

The complexity of entrepreneurship has hindered the development of regional economic development policies aimed at boosting entrepreneurship. A 2008 study by the Ewing Marion Kaufman Foundation divided regional entrepreneurship strategies into three broad categories: "serendipity" strategies that nurture entrepreneurial activities that have developed organically; "build-it-and-they-will-come" strategies that seek to boost the odds of serendipity striking; and development strategies that try to jump-start entrepreneurial ventures in targeted industries. To a large degree, "build-it-and-they-will-come" strategies are consistent with the traditional responsibilities of regional and local governments: investing in education, minimizing crime, building physical infrastructure, nurturing a favorable quality of life, and administering efficient regulatory systems. As an added bonus, these undertakings produce lasting community benefits even when serendipity fails to strike.

Sources: Zoltan Acs et al., *Entrepreneurship and Urban Success: Toward a Policy Consensus* (Kansas City, MO: Ewing Marion Kauffman Foundation, 2008), 4–5, http://www.kauffman.org/uploadedfiles/state_local_road-map_022608.pdf; and OECD, *Entrepreneurship at a Glance 2011* (Paris: OECD Publishing, 2011), 9, 14–16, and 104.

Strip away the aspirational language, and creativity models, at least as explained by Florida, emerge as growth-centered, microeconomic, disequilibrium ones that attribute economic changes to endogenous factors and reflect ideas about human capital consistent with the neoclassical perspective. In that regard, they really are little different from the location models discussed earlier in the chapter. Florida's writings and speeches nevertheless have attracted considerable attention, due to his engaging style of communication and, more alarmingly, "the profound policy vacuum that has characterized the neoliberalized urban realm" coupled with a desire for quick policy fixes.[52] Yet these ideas have resonated with civic leaders around the world and have influenced greatly policy discussions about the ties among creativity, place, and economic development.

Almost every state and region seems to have a creativity agenda. Some places have reoriented attraction strategies in attempts to lure "creatives," such as by providing certain forms of affordable urban housing or by investing in cultural amenities. Michigan, for one, sponsored a "Cool Cities" initiative that provided cities with grant funds to build the amenities thought necessary to attract and retain creative people.[53] Other communities have pursued more of an industry-based development approach targeted at "the enterprises and people involved in producing and distributing goods and services in which the aesthetic, intellectual, and emotional engagement of the consumers gives the product value in the marketplace."[54] For instance, places in Appalachia have tried to tap the economic potential of the area's excellent folk arts and handicrafts.[55]

Recent creativity models have attracted extensive criticism. One objection is that the idea of a "creative class" is a fuzzy one that misrepresents the concepts of both creativity and class, not to mention the politics of class. Another criticism is that the category of the creative class is meaningless and simply lumps together everyone with a college degree, even though "talent, skill, and creativity are not synonymous with higher education."[56] Lastly, there exists little empirical evidence that efforts to attract the creative class are a "substitute for traditional strategies such as investing in quality education, upgrading the skills of the workforce, creating new businesses, or expanding existing industries."[57]

This is not to say that creativity is unimportant, just that the current popular creativity model is weak. In fact, research focused more narrowly on the economic contributions of certain types of artists—actors, painters, musicians, photographers, and writers, among others—has found that regions with high concentrations of persons engaged in such occupations earn an "artistic dividend" in the forms of current income streams and returns on past investments in the artistic infrastructure.[58] Artists also possess certain traits, such as extensive levels of formal education, high rates of self-employment, and a strong propensity to spend their incomes locally, that may significantly boost "regional growth by providing import-substituting consumption activities and through direct export of their work."[59]

At best, creativity models represent intriguing yet unproven pathways for regional development. The threshold question for interested regional leaders, then, is to define just what terms like creativity, creative industries, and the creative class mean and to craft policies that support creativity without detracting from traditional strategies that produce known outcomes.

PRODUCTION MODELS

Production models differ from the other categories of models discussed in this chapter. While other theories conceive of economic progress as originating from some combination of economic processes, place, and talent, production models consider how "work is organized and managed between and within firms."[60] In short, economic development results from the ways in which firms and industries organize their internal processes and interact with other local enterprises and institutions. In this respect, meso-level production models focus on regional development. At the same time, they frequently blend elements of the other four sets of models discussed earlier in the chapter, and so tend not to fall into clear-cut theoretical categories.

Product Cycle Models

Product cycle models consider "the relationships between innovation, structural change, and economic development outcomes."[61] This firm-centered and industry-centered approach analyzes the factors that allow an enterprise or industry located in a particular place to create new goods and encourage the diffusion of those goods and their production to linked places. Regional growth and development proceed from this recurring, reinforcing cycle of creation and diffusion.

Product cycle models acknowledge that places differ in terms of their endowments and assert that innovation occurs "in areas with greater wealth and capital to invest in the process of inventing and developing new products, supported by local markets that can pay higher prices for products that have not yet been standardized."[62] When the item becomes popular enough to enter into routinized production, assembly can shift from the innovation center to less costly places (e.g., branch plants). Once the good becomes a commodity, production may move overseas to reap even greater cost advantages. During the cycle, the original firm should use part of its earnings to seed the next round of innovation, while the linked communities should direct some of their increased incomes to fund development. Ideally, all of the places linked through the innovation will prosper; there is no guarantee, however, that this will happen.[63]

The policy implications of product cycle models include support for private research and development activities; investment in the creation and commercialization of university-based research, especially science, engineering, and technology; and funding for technical education. More recently, product cycle models have inspired efforts at technology-oriented regional development, which typically takes the form of building research parks. Yet with the notable exceptions of the Boston's Route 128 corridor, California's Silicon Valley, and North Carolina's Research Triangle Park, most such efforts in the United States have failed. The technology parks that have survived generally function as branch production sites that generate process rather than product innovations.[64]

Over the years, critics have questioned numerous aspects of product cycle theory. One concern is that the theory focuses solely on the production of tangible manufactured and industrial goods, although the provision of services has become the dominant activity in most advanced economies. Innovation indeed occurs in the service sector, sometimes in ways consistent with product cycle theories, sometimes differently. Additionally, product cycle theory ignores both globalization and the fact that large firms are not as place-bound as they once were, so production now can involve numerous combinations of places spanning the globe. Finally, there is little evidence that the policy strategies originating in product cycle theory actually benefit less-developed places.[65]

Cluster Development Models

Popularized by Michael Porter, a scholar at Harvard Business School who built upon earlier research pertaining to economies of agglomeration and industrial districts, cluster development models reflect the idea that regions possess specific concentrations of interconnected enterprises. A cluster is a "geographically bounded concentration of similar, related, and complementary businesses with active channels for business transactions, communications, and dialogue, that share specialized infrastructure, labor markets and services, and that are faced with common opportunities and threats."[66] Clusters provide a lens for viewing regional economic strengths, the ties among firms, and the resources required to cultivate regional strengths.[67]

Clusters generate economic activity by increasing the productivity of existing firms or industries found within the cluster, boosting the innovative capacities of organizations within the cluster, and stimulating the formation of new businesses related to the cluster.[68] These gains occur through the formation of specialized labor markets, the emergence of highly sophisticated supply chains, and the transfer of knowledge among participants in the cluster. Altogether, such factors enable firms within a specific cluster to "gain higher productivity through accessing external economies of scale or other comparative advantages and the trading of this higher quality and lower cost output with other places."[69] The benefits of specialization accrue to the host community in the forms of higher wages and profits, increased economic activity involving local businesses outside of the cluster, the formation of new companies that spin out of the cluster, and the attraction of new investments, firms, and residents.

While clusters may form and thrive without policy interventions, public involvement can nurture the growth of clusters. One approach is to cultivate the building blocks essential to cluster growth, such as the preparation of appropriately skilled workforces. A second approach is to encourage collaborations among the members of specific clusters, such as by creating venues for knowledge exchanges and providing smaller suppliers with the assistance needed to sell successfully to larger firms. A final approach is to use a cluster framework to analyze the local economy, identify existing strengths, and better tailor existing economic development efforts to enhance the competitiveness of key clusters.

Compared to other theories, production models like cluster development paint a detailed portrait of how regional economies organize themselves and the factors that allow specific industries to compete. Successful application of such models requires regional leaders to think deeply about a broad range of subjects relevant to the vitality of local enterprises. This process, however, is information intensive, and many regions lack the resources needed to generate, analyze, and use the requisite data. Moreover, implementing the models frequently requires significant departures from traditional economic development strategies, and changing the mind-sets of practitioners often is difficult. Lastly, the popularity of production models, and of cluster development in particular, has led it to being "applied so widely that its explanation of causality and determination becomes overly stretched, thin, and fractured," and at an extreme, the basic ideas have come to resemble consumer brands rather than explanatory models of regional growth and development.[70]

THEORIES OF REGIONAL GROWTH AND DEVELOPMENT: A SUMMARY

Considerations of theory traditionally have played a minor role in the practice of regional economic development, thereby depriving leaders of "a logical tool for thinking about development, as well as an independent basis on which to build the local consensus needed for effective action."[71] Absent theory, the practice of economic development revolves around some combination of business recruitment, business expansion, and business formation.[72] The recruitment function is typically dominant and receives the greatest amount of resources. Yet various studies have found little proof that current practices materially influence the behavior of firms and yield tangible benefits for communities; in fact, such efforts actually may starve communities of the investments needed for long-term development.[73]

By incorporating theoretical insights into their efforts, regional leaders can overcome some of these limitations. An appreciation of theories, their key aspects, and their relationship to practice prepares regional leaders to understand how local economies function, identify relative advantages, appreciate industrial challenges, and target public strategies and resources. While helpful, none of the models profiled in this chapter are complete or all-encompassing, and each one suffers from serious limitations. Civic leaders ultimately must weigh the relative advantages of each model and favor those that best fit with regional needs, goals, and values. Unfortunately, no perfect formula exists, but sincere efforts to understand the complex forces that drive short-term regional growth and long-term regional development can facilitate the adoption of policies and practices that foster broad-based prosperity.

NOTES

1. Jesse White, "Economic Development in North Carolina: Moving Towards Innovation," *Popular Government*, Spring/Summer 2004, 5, http://ncinfo.iog.unc.edu/pubs/electronicversions/pg/pgspsm04/article1.pdf.

2. James Cobb, *The Selling of the South: The Southern Crusade for Industrial Development* (Baton Rouge: Louisiana State University Press, 1982), 12; and Peter Eisinger, *The Rise of the Entrepreneurial State* (Madison: University of Wisconsin Press, 1988), 91 and 93.

3. John Quinterno, *Strengthening State Economic Development Systems: A Framework for Change* (Chevy Chase, MD: The Working Poor Families Project, 2010), 2–3, http://www.workingpoorfamilies.org/pdfs/WPFP_policybrief_winter2010.pdf.

4. Emil Malizia and Edward Feser, *Understanding Local Economic Development* (Rutgers, NJ: Center for Urban Policy Research, 1999), 8.

5. Edward Blakely and Ted Bradshaw, *Planning Local Economic Development: Theory and Practice,* 3d ed. (Thousand Oaks, CA: Sage Publications, 2002), 55.

6. National Emergency Council, "Report on Economic Conditions of the South," in *Confronting Southern Poverty in the Great Depression*, eds. David Carlton and Peter Coclanis (Boston: Bedford Books, 1996), 54.

7. Cobb, *The Selling of the South,* 11–19.

8. Ibid., 5.

9. Eisinger, *The Rise of the Entrepreneurial State,* 34–36.

10. Ibid.

11. John Quinterno, *When Any Job Isn't Enough: Jobs-Centered Development in the American South* (Winston-Salem, NC: Mary Reynolds Babcock Foundation, 2009), 16–17, http://mrbf.org/sites/default/files/docs/resources/when_any_job_isnt_enough.pdf.

12. John Blair, *Local Economic Development: Analysis and Practice* (Thousand Oaks, CA: Sage Publications, 1995), 2.

13. Malizia and Feser, *Understanding Local Economic Development,* xii.

14. Eisinger, *The Rise of the Entrepreneurial State,* 36–37.

15. Ibid., 41.

16. Ibid., 38.

17. Malizia and Feser, *Understanding Local Economic Development,* 15.

18. Eisinger, *The Rise of the Entrepreneurial State,* 67–69.

19. David Carlton and Peter Coclanis, "Introduction," in *Confronting Southern Poverty in the Great Depression*, eds. David Carlton and Peter Coclanis (Boston: Bedford Books, 1996), 5–7.

20. Eisinger, *The Rise of the Entrepreneurial State,* 39.

21. Malizia and Feser, *Understanding Local Economic Development,* 23.

22. This section is an outgrowth of numerous conversations with Greg Schrock of the Nohad A. Toulan School of Urban Studies and Planning at Portland State University in Oregon. The explanations and interpretations, however, are the author's.

23. N. Gregory Mankiw, *Principles of Microeconomics* (Fort Worth, TX: Dryden Press, 1998), 25.

24. Blakely and Bradshaw, *Planning Local Economic Development,* 58.

25. Malizia and Feser, *Understanding Local Economic Development,* 52.

26. Ann Markusen and Greg Schrock, "Consumption-Driven Economic Development," *Urban Geography* 30, no. 4 (2009): 346.

27. Douglass North, "Theory and Regional Economic Growth," *Journal of Political Economy* 63, no. 3 (1955): 250.

28. Blair, *Local Economic Development,* 127–128.

29. Joseph Cortright and Andrew Reamer, *Socioeconomic Data for Understanding Your Regional Economy* (Washington, DC: U.S. Department of Commerce, 1998), 8.

30. Mary McLean and Kenneth Voytek, *Understanding Your Economy: Using Analysis to Guide Local Strategic Planning,* 2d ed. (Chicago: American Planning Association, 1992), 67.

31. Blakely and Bradshaw, *Planning Local Economic Development,* 59.

32. North, "Theory and Regional Economic Growth," 254.

33. Charles Tiebout, "Exports and Regional Economic Growth," *Journal of Political Economy* 64, no. 2 (1956): 164.

34. Markusen and Schrock, "Consumption-Driven Economic Development," 344.

35. Harry Richardson, *Regional and Urban Economics* (New York: Penguin, 1978), 154.

36. Malizia and Feser, *Understanding Local Economic Development,* 104.

37. Ibid., 114–117.

38. Blakely and Bradshaw, *Planning Local Economic Development,* 62.

39. Ibid., 66.

40. Ibid., 64.

41. Ibid., 63.

42. Malizia and Feser, *Understanding Local Economic Development*, 105.

43. Quinterno, *When Any Job Isn't Enough*, 37–38.

44. Malizia and Feser, *Understanding Local Economic Development*, 114–117.

45. Blakely and Bradshaw, *Planning Local Economic Development*, 61.

46. Ibid., 64.

47. Malizia and Feser, *Understanding Local Economic Development*, 196.

48. Ibid., 195–197.

49. Ibid., 209–213.

50. Ibid., 202–205.

51. Richard Florida, *The Rise of the Creative Class* (New York: Basic Books, 2002), 8.

52. Jamie Peck, "Struggling with the Creative Class," *International Journal of Urban and Regional Research* 29, no. 4 (2005): 767.

53. Ibid., 751–752.

54. Regional Technology Strategies et al., *Creativity in the Natural State: Growing Arkansas's Creative Economy* (Carrboro, NC: Regional Technology Strategies, 2007), 8.

55. Quinterno, *When Any Job Isn't Enough*, 41.

56. Ann Markusen, "Urban Development and the Politics of a Creative Class: Evidence from a Study of Artists," *Environment and Planning* A 38 (2006): 1921.

57. Mary Donegan et al., "Which Indicators Explain Metropolitan Economic Performance Best?" *Journal of the American Planning Association* 74, no. 2 (2008): 192.

58. Ann Markusen and Greg Schrock, "The Artistic Dividend: Urban Artistic Specialization and Economic Development Implications," *Urban Studies* 43, no. 10 (2006): 1662–1663.

59. Markusen, "Urban Development and the Politics of a Creative Class," 1921.

60. Malizia and Feser, *Understanding Local Economic Development*, 239.

61. Ibid., 178.

62. Blakely and Bradshaw, *Planning Local Economic Development*, 59.

63. Malizia and Feser, *Understanding Local Economic Development*, 175–178.

64. Ibid., 180 and 193–194.

65. Ibid., 185–186.

66. Brian Bosworth, "Regional Economic Analysis to Support Job Development Strategies," in *Jobs and Economic Development: Strategies and Practice*, ed. Robert Giloth (Thousand Oaks, CA: Sage Publications, 1998), 96.

67. Jonathan Morgan, "Clusters and Competitive Advantage: Finding a Niche in the New Economy," *Popular Government*, Spring/Summer, 2004, 53, http://ncinfo.iog.unc.edu/pubs/electronicversions/pg/pgspsm04/article6.pdf.

68. Michael Porter, "Location, Competition, and Economic Development: Local Clusters in a Global Economy," *Economic Development Quarterly* 14, no. 1 (2000): 21.

69. Jonathan Potter, "Policy Issues in Clusters, Innovation, and Entrepreneurship," in *Clusters, Innovation, and Entrepreneurship*, eds. Jonathan Potter and Gabriela Miranda (Paris: OECD Publishing, 2009), 26.

70. Ron Martin and Peter Sunley, "Deconstructing Clusters: Chaotic Concept or Policy Panacea?" *Journal of Economic Geography* 3 (2003): 28–29.

71. Malizia and Feser, *Understanding Local Economic Development*, xii.

72. White, "Economic Development in North Carolina," 7.

73. Quinterno, *When Any Job Isn't Enough*, 17–18.

4 | Data Sources, Concepts, and Calculations

Data presentations are staples of public hearings. In a typical situation, an analyst of some stripe—a government employee, an industry representative, a nongovernmental advocate, an academic expert—stands at a podium and cycles through a series of information-rich presentation slides. When controversial matters are under discussion, dueling analysts may appear and use seemingly identical slides to argue radically opposing positions. A question-and-answer period normally follows during which public officials pose questions that presenters frequently answer indirectly, electing instead to emphasize methodological limitations and computational concerns.

Such exchanges often foster confusion rather than clarity. Exasperated civic officials may react by discounting the data and unfairly dismissing the role of analysis in informing public policy. Befuddled presenters, meanwhile, may wonder why public leaders seem unable to grasp information that, to the experts at least, appears straightforward. And puzzled citizens may doubt the impartiality of decision makers and view data presentations as pieces of performance theater designed to justify a predetermined course of action—a course of action that may not be in the public interest.

These outcomes are unfortunate and unnecessary since economic and social analysis can illuminate how regions function. Many times the confusion stems not from the analysis, but from experts, public leaders, and citizens talking past one another. Researchers too often fail to present their work in the concise, actionable forms that civic leaders need, while civic leaders frequently lack the basic familiarity with data and analytical techniques needed to critique the studies they commission.

To help prevent public leaders and analysts from talking past one another, this chapter introduces the essential data sources, concepts, and calculations needed to profit from economic and social research. The chapter begins by profiling three major public sources of regional economic and social data and then explains the basic techniques needed to manipulate them. Lastly, the chapter provides an overview of essential statistical concepts for readers who have never taken a course in statistical methods or who wish to refresh their knowledge. Bear in mind that the chapter is not an exhaustive account of quantitative data analysis, so readers desiring more information should consult the works cited in the references and bibliography.[1]

SOURCES OF REGIONAL ECONOMIC AND SOCIAL DATA

The information that regional leaders encounter in economic and social analyses is rarely collected from scratch. Most studies obtain their raw information from data sets compiled by public statistical agencies. Such information is comprehensive, timely, credible, and free; it nevertheless can be difficult to locate, navigate, and understand. That said, the preponderance of available regional data comes from three federal agencies: the U.S. Census Bureau, the U.S. Bureau of Economic Analysis, and the U.S. Bureau of Labor Statistics.

U.S. CENSUS BUREAU

Unlike most industrialized nations, the United States lacks a centralized national statistical agency akin to Statistics Canada or the Office for National Statistics in the United Kingdom. The closest American analogue is the U.S. Census Bureau, which exists to collect "quality data about the nation's people and economy."[2] The Census Bureau's importance stems from its responsibility for conducting the Decennial Census of Population and Housing.

A constitutionally mandated count of the population, the decennial census is "both an apportionment tool and a baseline measure for American social science."[3] This mixture of politics and social science has placed the census at the center of the nation's social and political debates. Arguments over the future of slavery, the balance of political power among the states, the responses to industrialization and urbanization, and the effects of immigration and internal migration are but a few of the controversies in which census data have featured prominently.

Surprisingly, given the importance of the census, no permanent federal census agency existed until 1902.[4] The standard practice in the nineteenth century was for the U.S. Congress to create temporary offices responsible for coordinating the decennial count. The temporary offices would compile and analyze responses collected by federal marshals and their deputies. Early censuses focused on apportionment, but the count gradually evolved into a tool for governance and a broader instrument of social and economic inquiry.

Today, the Census Bureau, a branch of the U.S. Department of Commerce, collects extensive information about the American people, their economic activities, and their quality of life. The *Decennial Census of Population and Housing*, an enumeration of every person residing in the country, is the agency's premier product. Administered primarily through the mail, the 2010 Census asked 10 questions of every American household; of those questions, four applied to the household, the other six to each individual household member (see Appendix 1).[5] The results determine the allocation of congressional seats and influence the awarding of federal funds, the apportionment of state legislatures, and the division of state and local resources. In late 2010, the Census Bureau identified the need to reapportion 12 congressional seats. Due to population changes between 2000 and 2010, Texas gained four congressional seats, Florida two seats, and Arizona, Georgia, Nevada, South Carolina, Utah, and Washington one seat apiece. In contrast, New York and Ohio each lost two congressional seats, while Illinois, Iowa, Louisiana, Massachusetts, Michigan, Missouri, New Jersey, and Pennsylvania each relinquished one seat.[6]

A 1999 ruling of the U.S. Supreme Court requires the Census Bureau to conduct an actual headcount of the population for the purposes of allocating congressional seats. Statistical (survey) sampling is permissible for other ends, and the Census Bureau has employed sampling in one form or another since the 1940 Census.[7] Between the 1940 and 2000 censuses, the agency selected a subset of households to receive a supplemental "long form" containing additional questions. The long form provided accurate information down to the smallest level of census geography, but because the census occurs only once every 10 years, the data typically became outdated well before the next count.

To provide accurate and timely local information, the Census Bureau began in the 1990s to develop a new survey that would collect data each month and produce annual estimates of social, economic, and housing characteristics. The resulting *American Community Survey* (ACS), first conducted in 2005, replaced the long form beginning with the 2010 Census (see chapter 5). Fully implemented in late 2010, the ACS provides annual estimates for large governmental and statistical areas (those with at least 65,000 residents), three-year estimates for mid-sized areas (those with at least 20,000 residents), and five-year estimates for all other areas.[8]

The decennial enumeration and the ACS are not the only studies for which the Census Bureau is responsible. The *Current Population Survey* is a monthly survey of the labor force characteristics of the population conducted on behalf of the U.S. Bureau of Labor Statistics. Similarly, the *Survey of Income and Program Participation* is a longitudinal study of household income and participation in income transfer programs like the Supplemental Nutrition Assistance Program. Additionally, the bureau conducts studies related to housing and economic conditions. The quinquennial *Economic Census*, meanwhile, captures the traits of business establishments.

The Census Bureau also undertakes surveys for other public agencies. Examples include the *American Housing Survey* sponsored by the U.S. Department of Housing and Urban Development, the *Consumer Expenditure Survey* conducted for the U.S. Bureau of Labor Statistics, and the *National Crime Victimization Survey* collected for the U.S. Bureau of Justice Statistics. Table 4.1 lists census programs of interest to regional leaders and notes which chapters of this book discuss individual data products in greater depth.

U.S. BUREAU OF ECONOMIC ANALYSIS

The smallest of the major federal statistical agencies, the U.S. Bureau of Economic Analysis (BEA) is the nation's "economic accountant." Specifically, the BEA compiles the National Income and Product Accounts (NIPA), "a set of economic accounts that provide information on the value and composition of output produced

Table 4.1 Selected Data Programs of U.S. Census Bureau

Data program	Purpose	Frequency	Discussion
American Community Survey	A survey of the population designed to collect detailed demographic, economic, and housing data down to the community level.	Annual	Chapter 5
Business Dynamics Statistics	A longitudinal data set that tracks the creation and destruction of individual business establishments and associated measures of employment growth.	Annual	Chapter 6
Census of Governments	An annual study of the employment and financial characteristics of every unit of state and local government found in the United States.	Annual	Chapter 6
Current Population Survey	A survey of the labor force characteristics of the population.	Monthly with a special Annual Social and Economic Supplement fielded each March	Chapter 7
County Business Patterns	A tabulation of employment, payroll, and establishment size of all private nonfarm business establishments with paid employees at the national, state, metropolitan, county, and zip code levels.	Annual	Chapter 6
Decennial Census of Population and Housing	An enumeration of the entire population for the purpose of apportioning congressional seats among the states.	Every 10 years in years ending in "0"	Chapter 5
Economic Census	A census of nonfarm business establishments with paid employees.	Every five years in years ending in "2" or "7"	Chapter 6
Local Employment Dynamics	A national longitudinal job frame that combines information about individual business establishments with census data about individual workers.	Quarterly	Chapter 7

Nonemployer Statistics	A tabulation of business location, industrial classification, legal type, and receipts of all private business establishments with no paid employees at the state, metropolitan, and county levels.	Annual	Chapter 6
Population Estimates Program	An estimate of population size and the components of population change for states, counties, metropolitan areas, places, and county subdivisions.	Annual	Chapter 5
Small Area Health Insurance Estimates	A model-based estimate of health insurance coverage by age, sex, income, and ethnicity (state-level only) for states and counties.	Annual	Chapter 8
Small Area Income and Poverty Estimates	A model-based estimate of median household income, total persons in poverty, and total children in poverty at the national, state, county, and school district level.	Annual	Chapter 8
Statistics of U.S. Businesses	An annual compilation of information about business firms with employees.	Annual	Chapter 6
Survey of Business Owners	A periodic study of selected economic and demographic characteristics for businesses and business owners.	Every five years in years ending in "2" or "7"	Chapter 6
Survey of Income and Program Participation	A panel survey of households focused on labor force, income, demographic, and public program participation.	Panels formed every 3–4 years	Chapter 8

Source: U.S. Census Bureau.

in the United States during a given period and on the distribution and uses of the income generated by that production."[9] Almost all NIPA data come from such outside sources as the Census Bureau, the U.S. Bureau of Labor Statistics, and the Internal Revenue Service.

National economic accounting originated during the 1930s as an effort to measure the economic activities occurring within the United States. At its core, NIPA is a form of double-entry accounting that reconciles economic production with the income generated by that production. Think of the total value of all goods and services sold in a year as forming one side of a journal entry balanced by the income generated from the sales of the goods and services.[10] The different components of the NIPA drill down into each side of the ledger to show how production and income flow across sectors. The best-known NIPA element is Gross Domestic Product (GDP), which is an estimate of the "market value of the goods and services produced by labor and property located in the United States."[11]

While research into national income accounting began in the 1930s, the modern BEA emerged in 1972 following a reorganization of several departments within the U.S. Department of Commerce.[12] The agency is responsible for compiling seven interconnected summary accounts that track the output and incomes associated with different aspects of production, investment, foreign transactions, personal income and outlays, and government taxation and spending.[13] A related system of balance-of-payments accounts details international transactions.[14] At the regional level, the agency calculates GDP by state and metropolitan area, estimates state and local personal income and employment levels, and maintains the Regional Input-Output Modeling System (see chapter 2 for a discussion of these data products).

U.S. BUREAU OF LABOR STATISTICS

Established in 1884, the U.S. Bureau of Labor Statistics (BLS) is the oldest of the major federal statistical agencies. The agency's original mission was to collect "information upon the subject of labor, its relation to capital, the hours of labor and the earnings of laboring men and women, and the means of promoting their material, social, intellectual, and moral prosperity."[15]

During its early history, the BLS possessed limited funding and little more than fact-finding authority. The situation changed during the Great Depression when the BLS received the resources needed to expand its statistical programs and policy role. The 1930s was the era during which the BLS expanded its cost-of-living index, developed its family expenditure survey, created a basic family budget study that lasted until the early 1980s, and moved toward the monthly publication of wage and employment data. Additionally, the BLS joined with the Census Bureau to create modern measures of unemployment. The BLS also launched its occupational forecast studies, expanded its estimates of productivity, and refined its measurements of industrial safety and health.[16]

Today's BLS prepares information on three categories of regional interest: labor force, jobs and wages, and prices. The agency also prepares estimates of consumer expenditures, worker productivity, and workplace injuries, but unfortunately those estimates rarely are available for areas smaller than census regions. Table 4.2 lists BLS programs of special interest to regional leaders and notes which chapters discuss particular data products in greater depth.

OTHER AGENCIES

The Census Bureau, BEA, and BLS are not the only federal agencies that collect statistical information. The U.S. Small Business Administration compiles state and local information about business establishments, just as the U.S. Department of Agriculture assembles data on agricultural production and related subjects. Similarly, agencies like the U.S. Department of Education and the Internal Revenue Service generate information related to their responsibilities. No exhaustive directory of federal statistical information exists, but one useful, albeit rather dated, starting point is the website FedStats, while a more recent one with much greater functionality is Data.gov.[17] Various state agencies also post relevant information on their own websites.

DATA CONCEPTS

Public statistical agencies generally collect information in one of four ways. Some studies are actual counts of every member of a population of interest, just as the Economic Census covers every business establishment in the United States. Other studies survey a subset of a population of interest and take the results as representative of the larger group. The ACS comes from a sample of households, while the Current Employment Statistics program of the BLS focuses on a subset of individual businesses. Meanwhile, some studies, like many of those undertaken by the BEA, rely on administrative records, and others employ a mix of methods.

When interpreting results, it is important to understand the source of the data. This is because different data types are subject to different limitations. At the same time, sophisticated knowledge of data sources and techniques is not necessary to grasp quantitative information compiled by public statistical agencies. In fact, a familiarity with four concepts—absolute and relative quantities, change and growth, time effects, and financial values—typically is all that a regional leader needs to interpret analyses and perform basic calculations.

ABSOLUTE AND RELATIVE QUANTITIES

Most data sets contain an assortment of absolute and relative quantities. A Census Bureau estimate of poverty might report the number of persons in a region with incomes below the federal poverty level and the share of all persons in the region with incomes below the poverty threshold. Both numbers are meaningful, but for different reasons.

An *absolute quantity* is a value obtained by counting or measuring the number of times an item or event of interest occurs. Think of it as a total count. Examples of absolute quantities include the number of persons with incomes below the poverty

Table 4.2 Selected Data Programs of U.S. Bureau of Labor Statistics

Data program	Subjects	Geographic coverage	Frequency	Discussion
Business Employment Dynamics	A longitudinal data set that tracks job flows within individual business establishments.	Nation and census regions	Quarterly with data released eight months after the end of a quarter	Chapter 7
Consumer Expenditure Survey	Household survey focused on expenditures, income, and household characteristics.	Nation and census regions	National data released annually with a one-year lag	Chapter 8
Consumer Price Index	A study of the average change over time in the prices paid by urban consumers for a market basket of goods and services.	Nation, census regions, and 14 selected substate areas	National data released monthly; most substate data released every other month	Chapter 2
Current Population Survey	Household survey of labor force, employment, unemployment, hours of work, earnings, and demographic characteristics.	Monthly survey provides national data; Annual Social and Economic Supplement provides data for states and selected substate areas	Monthly with a special Annual Social and Economic supplement fielded each March	Chapter 7
Current Employment Statistics	Business establishment survey of employment, hours, and earnings of nonfarm workers.	Nation, states, and major metropolitan areas	Monthly	Chapter 7
Employment Projections	Periodic projections of the future size and composition of the labor force, aggregate economic growth, detailed estimates of industry production, and industry and occupational employment.	Nation (prepared by BLS), states and local areas (prepared by state labor market information agencies)	Biennial	Chapter 7

Job Openings and Labor Turnover Survey	Business establishment survey focused on employment, job openings, hires, quits, layoffs, discharges, and other separations.	Nation, census regions	Monthly	Chapter 7
Local Area Unemployment Survey	Household survey of employment and unemployment.	7,300 areas ranging from the nation to cities with 25,000 resident	Monthly	Chapter 7
National Compensation Survey	Business establishment survey of employee salaries, wages, and benefits.	Nation, census regions and divisions, states, and selected substate areas	National data released annually with a one-year lag; subnational data released gradually afterwards	Chapter 8
Occupational Employment Statistics	Business establishment survey used to compile employment and wage estimates for 8,000 occupations.	Nation, states, metropolitan areas and non-metropolitan areas	Semiannual survey with results released once per year	Chapter 7
Quarterly Census of Employment and Wages	Enumeration of the number of employees on the payrolls of companies subject to state unemployment insurance laws.	Nation, states, and core based statistical areas, including metropolitan and micropolitan statistical areas	Quarterly and annually; quarterly data appear six to seven months after the quarter ends; annual data appear nine months after the year ends	Chapter 7

Source: U.S. Bureau of Labor Statistics.

line, the number of unemployed workers in a region, and the number of homeless individuals present in a city.

While useful, knowledge of absolute quantities is insufficient for regional analysis. This is because social and economic phenomena normally are interrelated and are influenced by contextual factors. *Relative quantities* are measurements of one item in relation to another. Ratios, proportions, percentages, and percentiles all are relative quantities. A *ratio* shows a relationship between two numbers of the same kind; for instance, a ratio of poor to nonpoor persons of 95:100 means that there are 95 poor persons for every 100 nonpoor ones. A *proportion*, meanwhile, is a comparison between two quantities that equal the entire population of interest when added together. In a society with a total population of 195 people of whom 95 are poor and 100 are not poor, the proportion of poor individuals would equal 95/195. Another way of expressing a proportion is as a *percentage*, which compares one quantity to another as a fraction of 100. In a community with 95 poor persons out of a total population of 195 residents, poor individuals would constitute 48 percent of the population.

Percentiles or *percentile ranks* are forms of "norm-referenced scoring" used to compare an individual value to a larger reference group.[18] A percentile rank simply shows the percentage of the comparison group below a specified level. Percentiles feature prominently in studies pertaining to education scores and income statistics. A household with an annual income at the 90th percentile of the regional income distribution would have an income greater than that of 90 percent of all households in the comparison group, and a household with an income at the 50th percentile would have an income greater than that of half of all households in the region. Percentile scores range from 0 to 99 percent.

Relative quantities permit the standardization of data and the drawing of valid comparisons. This is especially important for regional analysis since places vary in terms of population size and gain and lose residents over time. Consider children under age 18 who live in poverty in New York State's two largest cities: New York City and Buffalo. In 2011, an estimated 520,799 New York City children lived in poverty compared to 27,303 children in Buffalo. In absolute terms, child poverty was a greater problem in New York City than in Buffalo, as New York had 19.1 times as many poor children. Yet New York City's total child population was 29.9 times greater than that of Buffalo (1.7 million versus 58,391). Relative to size, 29.8 percent of New York City's children lived in poverty compared to 46.8 percent of Buffalo's children.[19] New York City might have had more poor children, but a larger share of Buffalo's children lived in poverty (Figure 4.1). In a situation like this, a failure to consider relative quantities would produce a flawed understanding of the differences in child poverty between the two cities.

Regional studies generally express relative quantities as percentages, but some studies use another relative measure known as an *index number*. An index combines different items into a single value that equals "a percentage of a single base figure," typically the value 100.[20] Index numbers have no units associated with them to better focus attention on the actual values. An example of an index is the Consumer Price Index discussed in chapter 2. Similarly, an analyst could use index values to measure the number of poor persons in a region. If the number of poor persons residing in

Figure 4.1 Child Poverty in the Cities of Buffalo and New York, 2011

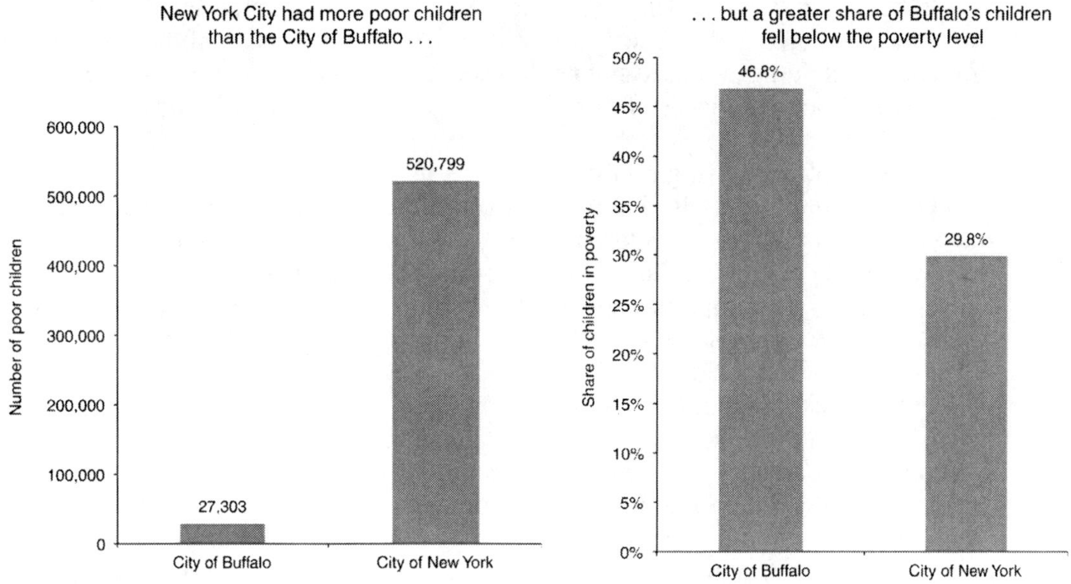

New York City had more poor children
than the City of Buffalo . . .

... but a greater share of Buffalo's children
fell below the poverty level

Source: U.S. Census Bureau, American Community Survey, One-Year Estimates, 2011.

Buffalo in 2009 were indexed to 100, an index value of 110 in 2010 would mean that poverty had increased over the year. If the value dropped to 95 in 2011, poverty would have fallen relative to the 2010 level and would be below the 2009 level.

A final consideration when interpreting quantities is differentiating between stocks and flows. A *stock* represents a quantity of a given item at a particular moment in time, and a *flow* is a change in the quantity of a variable over time. Stocks and flows feature prominently in studies of economic, financial, and accounting subjects. To grasp the difference, think of the number of persons with incomes below the poverty level on the first day of the year as a stock and the total number of people moving into and out of poverty during the year as a flow. If more people move above the poverty line than fall below it during the course of the year, the stock of poor residents will be lower at the end of the year. The actual number of people who experienced a spell of poverty during the year, however, would exceed the total stock on the last day of the year.

CHANGE AND GROWTH

A common concern in many economic and social analyses is how specific phenomena have changed over time. A study of regional childhood poverty, for instance, typically will offer snapshots of poverty at different moments and trace the trend over a span of years. As with quantities, changes may be expressed in absolute and relative terms.

Absolute change shows the difference between two values observed at two different points in time. Take child poverty in the City of Buffalo. In 2011, Buffalo had 27,303 poor children, up from 25,510 in 2007. The absolute increase over the period was 1,793 children. While useful, knowledge of absolute change often is insufficient for analytical purposes because it neither accounts for contextual factors nor permits comparisons among places of differing sizes. Measures of relative change are more telling.

One way of expressing relative change is as a *rate*, which is a comparison between two quantities. Child poverty in Buffalo could be shown as the number of poor children per 1,000 children. Viewed that way, the city's child poverty rate rose to 476.8 per 1,000 children in 2011 from 417.3 per 1,000 children in 2007. An advantage of rate comparisons is that they control for changes in size; this matters in the Buffalo example because the total number of children living in the city fell over the four-year period.[21]

Perhaps the most common way of presenting relative movements is as a *percentage change,* which expresses the size of a change relative to 100. This approach provides "a consistent yardstick for interpreting change."[22] Returning to the Buffalo example, the number of children living in poverty grew by 7 percent between 2007 and 2011, while the total child population declined by 4.5 percent.[23] While Buffalo had fewer children in 2011 than in 2007, more of the children residing in the city lived in poverty.

When interpreting percentage changes, analysts and readers should avoid four crucial errors:[24]

- *Mixing units:* When calculating percentage changes, the reference units must remain constant. A study of the child population, for instance, should not involve data for adults. This avoids the proverbial problem of "mixing apples and oranges."

- *Confusing types of changes:* Percentage changes and percentage point changes are not the same thing and are not interchangeable. In the Buffalo example presented earlier, the number of children living in poverty increased by 7 percent between 2007 and 2011, but the share of all children living in poverty grew by 5.1 percentage points, rising from 41.7 percent to 46.8 percent during that period.[25]

- *Overlooking starting levels:* The absolute effect of a percentage change depends on the starting level. Consider that a 10 percent rise in the poverty rate in a city with 50,000 poor children translates into an absolute increase of 5,000 children, yet a 10 percent jump in a city with 25,000 poor children equals an absolute increase of 2,500 children.

- *Forgetting "up and back":* A percentage increase followed by an equal percentage decrease does not return a quantity to its starting level; rather, it reduces the quantity below the starting level. A 10 percent jump in child poverty in a city with 25,000 poor children followed by a 10 percent drop would bring the total number of poor children to 24,750, not 25,000. This happens because the decline occurs from the higher starting point brought about by the initial increase.

Similar confusion may occur when measuring relative changes using index values. An absolute change in an index is not the same as a percentage change. If the starting level is 100, a 50-point jump equates to a 50 percent increase, but if the starting level is 150, a 50-point jump translates into a rise of 33 percent. An additional issue is the problem of illusionary convergence. Because index series share a base value (typically 100), they always converge at the base. The way in which the base is shown therefore may lead to a misleading impression; this mistake is likely when viewing graphical representations of an index. Consumers of index data consequently always should check where the base levels are set.[26]

Another way of presenting change is as a *growth rate*. This involves taking an observed rate of growth in a given period and projecting the change over a longer period. As anyone who ever has had a simple interest-bearing savings account knows, growth compounds over time.

Assuming no additional deposits or withdrawals of money, a savings account that pays interest of 1 percent per month will grow by 12.7 percent—not 12 percent—over a year. This happens because each month's interest calculation applies to the higher balance created by the addition of the previous month's interest payment. The rate of growth determines how long it will take a quantity to double. An item that grows at a monthly rate of 1 percent will double in roughly 70 months; raise the rate to 5 percent and the doubling time falls to 14 months.[27]

In the United States, analysts customarily annualize growth rates, especially economic growth rates. This shows the change that would occur if an observed rate of change were to continue for 12 consecutive months. The BEA normally reports output data on an annualized basis. For instance, national GDP grew at an annualized rate of 2 percent during the first quarter of 2012. This means that total output would grow by 2 percent if the observed rate continued for a full year.[28] Although annualized growth rates appear most frequently, analysts may calculate rates for any number of periods.

TIME EFFECTS

Time is an important dimension to consider when analyzing economic and social data. Phenomena like child poverty ebb and flow with the passage of time. Accounting for the effects of time therefore is essential to the proper interpretation of regional data. Four topics—data types, seasonality, business cycles, and financial values—require elaboration.

Regional studies typically employ two types of data: *cross-sectional* and *longitudinal*. Think of cross-sectional data as a snapshot of a subject at a particular moment in time. The number of children living in poverty in the City of Buffalo in 2011 is a cross-sectional data point. Additionally, analysts sometimes combine cross-sectional data from various years into a time series, such as one showing the child poverty rate in Buffalo over a period of years. Remember that such a time series shows the overall share of Buffalo children living in poverty rather than the poverty experiences of individual children. A longitudinal study of child poverty in Buffalo, in contrast, would follow the same group of children over time. Longitudinal studies are expensive and complicated to field. A noted example is the federally sponsored *Panel Study of Income*

Dynamics, which has tracked changes in the economic, health, and social behaviors of the same 5,000 American families since 1968.[29]

Because many economic subjects exhibit a "pattern that repeats itself over time," consideration of *seasonality* is required when evaluating economic data.[30] Employment is one topic marked by distinct seasonal patterns. Retail employment, for one, predictably rises in November and December to accommodate the holiday rush and then falls in January. Similarly, construction employment tends to be higher in the warmer months of the year than in the colder ones. Not accounting for seasonality may lead to analytical errors. Given that retail employment normally falls in January, an employment drop in that month by itself is not necessarily evidence of trouble in the retail industry. Some statistical agencies like the BLS adjust their data to control for seasonality. Yet the adjustment process is imperfect, so the resulting data are subject to periodic revisions to the benchmark data from which the seasonal adjustment factors originate (see chapter 7). Other simple ways of adjusting for seasonality include the use of moving averages and studying long-term data trends rather than single observations.

Economic data vary with the *business cycle.* In general, total economic activity fluctuates between periods of growth and contraction, or expansion and recession. A period of expansion typically builds to a peak after which activity declines until reaching a trough from which growth recovers; after growth recovers and exceeds the previous peak, an expansion occurs until a new peak is reached.[31] The stage of the business cycle influences economic matters. Unemployment, for one, typically mounts during periods of contraction and falls during expansions, so an analysis that compares employment between expansionary and recessionary period may yield a distorted understanding of actual conditions. Business cycles vary greatly in terms of duration and intensity. To illustrate those differences, Table 4.3 provides information about the dates of the 11 American business cycles that have occurred since 1945.

FINANCIAL VALUES

As with any numerical value, financial values and changes in those values may be expressed in absolute and relative terms. In some ways, relative quantities are even more important when dealing with large financial values with which people are unfamiliar, such as budget amounts. The U.S. Department of Housing and Urban Development, for example, received a total discretionary appropriation of $43.6 billion during Fiscal Year 2009–2010. This is an absolute number beyond the direct experience of virtually every American. Yet that total accounted for a mere 3.2 percent of total estimated federal discretionary spending for the year. And on a per capita basis, total spending equaled $141 for every man, woman, and child in America.[32] So while the $43.6 billion seems large in absolute terms, it actually is a modest amount relative to the size of the entire federal budget and the nation's population.

When considering financial values, two special considerations apply. First, as mentioned in chapter 2, the prices of goods and services in an economy are constantly changing, both relative to each other and at an aggregate level. Changes in the overall price level result from inflation or deflation. *Nominal (current) values* measure prices

Table 4.3 Business Cycle Contractions and Expansions in the United States, 1948–2012

Peak month	Trough month	Peak month
November 1948	October 1949	July 1953
July 1953	May 1954	August 1957
August 1957	April 1958	April 1960
April 1960	February 1961	December 1969
December 1969	November 1970	November 1973
November 1973	March 1975	January 1980
January 1980	July 1980	July 1981
July 1981	November 1982	July 1990
July 1990	March 1991	March 2001
March 2001	November 2001	December 2007
December 2007	June 2009	—

Source: National Bureau of Economic Research, "U.S. Business Cycles Expansions and Contractions," http://www.nber.org/cycles/cyclesmain.html (accessed October 16, 2012).
Note: Each business cycle contains a recession period and an expansion period. A recession period spans the period from the peak month to the trough month, and an expansion period stretches from the trough month to the following peak month.

irrespective of changes in the price level. Compare a loaf of bread with a nominal price of $0.25 in 1965 to one with a nominal price of $1.50 in 2005. In nominal terms, the price of a loaf of bread was 500 percent higher in 2005 than in 1965. Yet the overall price level as measured by the consumer price index increased during that 40-year period. By controlling for changes in the price level, *real (constant) values* allow for the drawing of fair comparisons. Because $0.25 in 1965 had the same value as $1.55 in 2005, the real price of the illustrative loaf of bread actually would have fallen by 3.2 percent over the span of four decades.[33]

Second, because the value of money changes over time, individuals and organizations exhibit time preferences for money. During periods of inflation, a dollar possessed today will buy more goods and services than a dollar received in the future. The amount that an individual would need to receive in the future for postponing current consumption is a time preference. A person willing to forgo $100 today in exchange for $110 a year from now has a time preference of 10 percent. This preference informs calculations of *present value,* which is a computation of a future sum of money "discounted" to its current value. Because complex public investments like the building of an airport involve multiyear streams of costs and benefits, present values provide a way of comparing financial costs and benefits; crudely put, projects with positive net present vales are worthwhile.[34] The concepts of time preference, discounting, and present value undergird the *financial appraisal* and *cost-benefit analysis* techniques described in Box 4.1.

Box 4.1 Financial Appraisal and Cost-Benefit Analysis

The time value of money and temporal preferences for money underpin the analytical techniques of financial analysis and cost-benefit analysis. These tools are helpful when dealing with projects involving inflows and outlays of money, or streams of benefits and costs, that stretch over a period of years. Examples include investments in infrastructure projects like the building of an airport or the funding of an early childhood education program.

Both financial appraisal and cost-benefit analysis are methods for reaching informed decisions about possible uses of public resources. Yet the two techniques differ in their objectives. Financial appraisal judges potential projects against the commercial objective of maximizing financial profit. Cost-benefit analysis, in contrast, considers broader social objectives, primarily the maximization of total social welfare. In one formulation of the social welfare criterion, a project is worth undertaking only if the resulting benefits are sufficient enough to allow the gainers to compensate the losers—at least in theory—and still be better off than they were prior to the undertaking of the project.

Another difference between the techniques is how they define and measure inflows and outflows. Financial appraisal tends to define and measure inflows and outflows in terms of accounting values and financial prices rather than economic values and measures; for instance, financial appraisal uses the narrow accounting concept of depreciation over the broader economic concept of opportunity cost. Similarly, in situations where an action creates externalities like pollution, market prices understate the true social cost of an action.

An advantage of financial appraisal is its directness, and in many ways, it is a first step in a cost-benefit analysis. Cost-benefit analysis builds off those concepts and adds to them economic ideas like opportunity cost, shadow pricing, taxation, and subsidization. This yields a richer portrait of overall economic and social costs.

Regardless of the definition of inflows and outflows, both analytical tools use the same approach when dealing with multiyear projects. An analyst calculates the values of the benefits and costs incurred in each year of a project and then "discounts" them to their present value. Such restatement of totals in current terms permits meaningful comparisons. Finally, an analyst subtracts the present costs from the present benefits to produce a net present value. Projects with positive net present values are potentially worthwhile.

Despite their utility as methods for assessing options, neither financial appraisal nor cost-benefit analysis yield a "right" decision. Both techniques hinge upon a wide array of assumptions and suffer from methodological limitations. They also are silent on ethical and moral concerns, such as the worth of a human life or fairness. Regional leaders therefore need to weigh the results of such analyses alongside other factors when attempting to reach decisions in the best interest of the community.

Source: Robert Sugden and Alan Williams, *The Principles of Practical Cost-Benefit Analysis* (New York: Oxford University Press, 1978), chapters 1, 2, 3, and 7.

STATISTICAL CALCULATIONS

Regional leaders and members of the public commonly affix the label "statistics" to any kind of quantitative information. The unemployment rate, the number of persons living in poverty, the proportion of the electorate that favors a candidate, the batting average of a baseball player, and the relationships among the factors contributing to teen pregnancy—all of these popularly are termed "statistics." Some individuals take a further step and associate statistics with a set of mathematical techniques. Researchers, however, typically mean something different when they invoke the word. For them, statistics is "a field of study that develops and uses mathematical procedures to describe data and make decisions regarding it."[35]

The differing understandings account for many of the frustrations that regional leaders and analysts experience when dealing with one another. Officials, citizens, and journalists tend to look to statistical research to provide the "right" number that will solve a problem. Researchers, however, are concerned about the methodological and practical complexities that limit a study's credibility. In other words, regional leaders look to statistical research as a way of generating answers, but researchers view it as an analytical framework. Researchers must translate their work into forms relevant to regional leaders, but those leaders will also benefit from better appreciating statistics as a process for inquiring into important subjects. At a minimum, regional officials should ask themselves the following four questions when reviewing an economic or social analysis that employs statistical techniques.

WHAT ARE THE ANALYTICAL PROBLEMS, DEFINITIONS, AND MEASURES?

Public leaders often commission studies in response to actual events. When a development attracts the attention of a regional actor like an elected official, a public agency, a trade group, or a community organization, a typical first response is to study the matter. Essential to that process is the identification of the analytical problem, the definition of key concepts, and the selection of appropriate measures.

Take the seemingly straightforward matter of whether or not poverty is rising in a region. To tackle the question, a researcher would need to answer questions such as the following: What is the region of interest? What is poverty—having an income below a certain level or something else? If poverty is defined in relation to an income level, what should the level be, and what should count as income? At what level should poverty be measured—that of an individual, a family, or a household? What is meant by rising poverty—a jump in the size of the population meeting the poverty definition or an increase in the share of the population meeting the definition? And over what period should change be measured?

As the poverty example shows, even a seemingly simple question quickly becomes complicated. Strip away the complexity, and every analysis attempts to address one of three problems: problems of description, problems of evaluation, and problems of estimation.[36] In regard to regional poverty, a descriptive analysis would focus on the size and characteristics of the population living in poverty, an evaluation on the effects of an antipoverty program, and an estimate of possible future changes in poverty levels.

After identifying the analytical problem, a researcher must define key concepts. An attempt to describe household poverty might define a poor household as one with an annual cash income below the federal poverty level. Alternately, the household poverty measurement could involve multiple factors, such as having a total cash income below the federal poverty threshold and lacking a nutritious diet. Similarly, the concept of income would require definition. Income might include all of the cash received by a household, or it might include noncash benefits like the value of employer-provided or public benefits. Investment earnings might be included, too.

Following the establishment of definitions, an analyst must assign units of measurement to the concepts. Four units of measurement exist.[37] First, there are *ratio data*, like household income, that start at zero and that can be manipulated through the arithmetic properties of addition, subtraction, multiplication, and division. Compared to a household with an annual income of $25,000, a household with a yearly income of $50,000 earns twice as much, 100 percent more, and $25,000 more. *Interval data* like temperature measurements and the consumer price index, meanwhile, have an arbitrary zero point and a uniform measurement scale, but because they have an arbitrary zero point, they can be manipulated only through addition and subtraction. Note that ratio and interval data normally are continuous, meaning they can assume any value within a range, including fractional ones.

Ordinal data, a third kind of measurement, have a logical order in which a higher value indicates that more of a specific property is present. Although ordinal data show differences in value, they offer no insight into how great the differences are. Examples include educational attainment levels and consumer confidence. Finally, *nominal data* lack any numerical meaning and use numbers merely for convenience; consider how an analyst may measure biological sex by assigning a value of "0" to males and "1" to females. Many demographic factors like marital status are nominal variables. Note that ordinal and nominal data are discrete, which means they have whole values: a household may have four members or five members, not 4.6 members.

When interpreting analytical studies, a regional leader should ask, at a minimum, what the analytical problem is, what the key definitions are, and what measurements are involved. Consider a descriptive analysis of child poverty. Because children are unable to work, they depend upon the income of their parents or guardians, so a study that defines child poverty in relation to the incomes of individual children would make little sense. In the same manner, a definition that includes households without children would paint a distorted picture. A study that measures child poverty nominally (e.g., is a child poor or not?), meanwhile, is less useful for detailed analysis than one that measures poverty with ratio data.

A second question to contemplate when evaluating regional studies is if the data measures are reliable and valid. *Reliability* refers "to how consistent or repeatable measurements are," and *validity* captures "how well a test or rating scale measures what it is supposed to measure."[38] A reliable indicator yields consistent values over time, while a valid indicator is one that fairly measures the concept of interest. Every indicator ideally should be reliable and valid, but in practice that standard is difficult to achieve. Nevertheless, consumers of a study should consider whether it accurately and consistently addresses the subjects of concern; if not, the study will be of limited use.

Which Kinds of Data Does a Study Use?

Most studies of regional economic and social issues rely on data derived from enumerations, statistical samples, and administrative records. Each data type is subject to different limitations that consumers of research reports should bear in mind.

An *enumeration*, or census, is a count of every member of a population of interest. An enumeration of the child population in a city would involve collecting information on every child. While comprehensive, enumerations are expensive and complicated to field. Perhaps the best-known enumeration is the Decennial Census of Population and Housing, a count of every American. Given that the United States contains more than 300 million people scattered from the forests of Maine to the islands of Hawaii, this is an ambitious undertaking.

For practical reasons, most social and economic studies rely on data derived from *statistical sampling*, a process by which a subset of a population of interest is selected and analyzed.[39] If each population member has an equal, nonzero chance of selection, it is possible to generate results that apply not just to the sample, but also to the entire population. This is because, in most situations, a properly drawn sample will yield results that approximate a "bell curve" or normal distribution "centered on the true value of the quantity being measured."[40] While seemingly counterintuitive, the results of statistical sampling may be less prone to error than the results obtained through an enumeration.[41]

Some studies also employ data derived from *administrative records*. As a means for providing the public services demanded by citizens, governments create bureaucratic structures responsible for particular functions. To perform their missions, these agencies collect information that may prove useful to analysts as well as public managers. Yet the research benefits are secondary to the management ones. In administering the tax code, for instance, the Internal Revenue Service compiles detailed income information from personal income tax filings. That information may enrich research into the income of households, but the data exist to help the agency enforce the tax laws.

Data generated through enumerations and statistical samples are prone to different types of errors. Because an enumeration contains every member of a population of interest, its total error equals the sum of *measurement error*, which is the difference between an observed value and the true value resulting from design and measurement flaws, and *random error*, which is the difference between an observed value and a true value resulting from pure chance. Samples are subject to additional kinds of error, notably *sampling error*, which is the difference between the sample value and the population value. Using probability theory, an analyst can compute a margin of error at a given *confidence level* for sample data. For instance, an estimate of the number of children in a state with incomes below the poverty level might total 14 percent with a standard error of +/–2 percentage points at a 95 percent confidence level. This means that if the analysis were to be repeated an infinite number of times, the true poverty rate would fall between 12 and 16 percent some 95 percent of the time. Confidence intervals may be set at any level, but levels of 90, 95, and 99 percent are common.[42]

The idea of a confidence interval is worth considering in more depth. The bulk of the information contained in regional economic and social analyses comes from statistical sampling, not enumerations. While attention normally gravitates to a *point estimate*, which is a specific "best" judgment value, the true value actually sits within a range of possible values.

Which Statistical Tools Are Being Used?

At the broadest level, researchers employ two types of statistical methods—descriptive statistics and inferential statistics—to analyze economic and social data. Descriptive statistics apply to data collected from enumerations and sampling, while inferential statistics apply solely to statistical samples.

Descriptive Statistics

Descriptive statistics involves "the use of statistical and graphic techniques to present information about the data set being studied."[43] There are three categories of descriptive statistics: measures of central tendency, measures of dispersion, and measures of association.

A measure of central tendency is "a number or score or data value that represents the average in a group of data."[44] The main measures are the *mean* (the arithmetic average), the *median* (the middle observation in an ordered set of numbers), and the *mode* (the value that appears most often). A common problem encountered when using measures of central tendency is differentiating between the mean and the median.[45] Because the mean is an average, it is subject to distortion by extreme values. Consider a community with 10 residents, nine of whom have annual incomes between $50,000 and $75,000 and one with an income of $1 million. In this community, the average will be extremely high due to the presence of the millionaire, so the median would be a better measure of the annual income of local residents (see Box 4.2).

Measures of dispersion assess "how much the data do or do not cluster around the mean."[46] Major measures include the *range* (the difference between the highest and lowest values), the *interquartile range* (the value obtained by subtracting the 25th percentile value from the 75th percentile value), and the *variance* (a measure of how much an individual value varies from the mean). Perhaps the most important measure is the *standard deviation*, which applies to interval and ratio data. The standard deviation reflects how tightly the data points cluster around the mean. When a data set falls along a normal distribution, or "bell curve," 95 percent of the observations will sit within two standard deviations of the mean.[47]

Lastly, measures of association identify relationships or patterns among variables. In a set of data with information on both the academic test scores of twelfth-grade students and the household incomes of those students, a relationship might exist among scores and income. Remember that measures of association identify relationships, not causes. In the test score example, an association between household income and test scores is not proof that income causes test scores. Different measures of association apply to various levels of measurement. One way of presenting associations is through a *cross-tabulation*, which is a "two-dimensional table that shows the conditional frequency distributions for two variables."[48]

Box 4.2 Descriptive Statistics

Descriptive statistics involves the analysis and presentation of the ways in which quantitative data cluster around a specific value. There are three kinds of descriptive statistics:

- A *measure of central tendency* captures the typical value of a variable within a data set; the key measures are the mean, median, and mode.
- A *measure of dispersion* indicates the extent to which data in a series cluster around a central value; the key measures are the range, interquartile range, and standard deviation.
- A *measure of association* assesses the relationships that exist between two variables; the key measure is the correlation coefficient.

Regional leaders commonly encounter measures of central tendency and dispersion in analytical studies. To illustrate those measures, imagine a town with 10 households that have the following annual incomes: $25,000, $30,000, $35,000, $40,000, $45,000, $50,000, $50,000, $60,000, $75,000, and $250,000.

For this set of data, the *mean* (average) annual household income equals the sum of the individual observations divided by the total number of observations. The average annual income of households in this community, then, is $66,000. The *median*, or the "middle value" that occurs when a set of data points is arranged in ascending or descending order, equals $47,500. The difference between the mean and median is due to the one household with $250,000 in income. Because the mean is sensitive to extreme values, outliers may skew the results, so the median may be a better measure. Lastly, the *mode*—the value that appears most often—is $50,000.

Shifting to measures of dispersion, the range of annual household incomes in the town is $225,000, which is the difference between the highest and lowest values. Because extreme values can distort the range, the *interquartile range*, which is the difference between the 75th percentile and the 25th percentile values, sometimes provides a more accurate picture of dispersion. In this example, the interquartile range totals $21,250.

Finally, the standard deviation reflects how tightly individual data points cluster around the mean. The *standard deviation* is "the square root of the average of the squares of the deviation of each case from the mean" and is calculated differently depending on whether the data come from a sample or a population. In the previous example of a 10-household town, the standard deviation equals $62,881.

Standard deviations are useful for comparing data sets. Imagine a second town with exactly 10 households with identical household incomes except that the top household's income is $100,000 rather than $250,000. In that situation, the standard deviation would equal $21,424, and the income spread would be narrower in the second town than in the first one.

Sources: Sarah Boslaugh and Paul Andrew Watters, *Statistics in A Nutshell* (Sebastopol, CA: O'Reilly, 2008), 54 and 57; Kenneth Meier, Jeffrey Brudney, and John Bohte, *Applied Statistics for Public and Nonprofit Administration*, 7th ed. (Belmont, CA: Thomson Wadsworth, 2009), 77 and 96; and U.S. Government Accountability Office, *Quantitative Data Analysis: An Introduction* (Washington, DC: U.S. Government Accountability Office, 1992), 45–47.

Inferential Statistics

Inferential statistics involves "the use of quantitative techniques to generalize from a sample to a population."[49] Descriptive statistics apply to populations and samples, but inferential statistics apply solely to data obtained through sampling. Probability theory forms the foundation of inferential statistics and provides a rationale for extending the results of sample observations to a population. The techniques also allow for the mathematical testing of hypotheses, which explains why inferential statistics features prominently in medical research attempting to establish the effectiveness of particular treatments.

WHAT IS THE PURPOSE OF THE ANALYSIS?

Despite their seeming complexity, all of the studies that regional leaders encounter in their work fall into one of three categories: studies of description, studies of correlation, and studies of causation. Some studies may combine multiple types, but the combination in no way changes the basic nature, strengths, and limitations of each type.

In many situations, community leaders look to social and economic analysis for a *description* of some aspect of the region, such as the population's racial composition. Sometimes leaders may be interested in how a particular factor, like the size of an area's foreign-born population, has changed over time. Descriptive studies answer such questions while establishing a baseline for further inquiry.

Other analyses move beyond description and attempt to identify correlations among different variables. *Correlation* gauges the "statistical associations between two (or more) variables" in order to identify the relationships that exist and predict outcomes.[50] Assorted statistical techniques can identify the strength and direction of the relationships among variables. A community's educational attainment and its wage income, for instance, may correlate positively, meaning that wages and educational attainment rise together. Although educational attainment and wages may correlate, that relationship in no way proves that a change in one variable causes the change in the other. To invoke the old adage, correlation is not causation.

A final kind of study attempts to prove *causation*. A causal relationship is one in which a change in one variable brings about a change in another; in short, the change in the first variable *causes* the other to change. Establishing causality is a difficult process that requires an analyst to consider the association among variables, the temporal relationship among the variables (a change in one must precede the change in the other), and the degree to which the variables have been isolated from other potential influences.[51]

Demonstrating causation is difficult, and one tool that regularly informs causation studies is *regression analysis*. This is "a statistical technique used to describe the relationship between two variables based on the principle of minimizing errors in prediction."[52] Regression shows how certain dependent variables change when other independent variables vary. A change in the dependent variable(s) proven as *statistically significant* is a change brought about by the independent variable(s), not random chance. Statistical significance is measured through a statistical formula called the "R^2" (the correlation coefficient squared), which yields values ranging between zero and one. In general, the higher the value, the more promising the relationship; the exact cutoff, however, depends on the study design and the desired level of confidence. Regression analysis alone is unable to prove causality, but it can suggest potential causal mechanisms and serve as a pivotal first step in a larger inquiry into causation.

DATA SOURCES, CONCEPTS, AND CALCULATIONS: A SUMMARY

Quantitative data, concepts, and calculations feature prominently in studies of regional economic and social issues due to their potential to illuminate how regions actually function. At the same time, regional leaders often unfairly dismiss quantitative information due in no small part to the ineffective ways in which analysts often communicate the information. This unfortunate development deprives regional leaders of powerful tools for bettering their communities. To overcome that shortcoming, this chapter sought to cultivate a basic familiarity with essential data sources, concepts, and calculations. When combined with the information about regional geography and economic growth shared in earlier chapters, this understanding prepares regional leaders to approach quantitative information critically and profitably.

NOTES

1. Useful introductions to quantitative data include: Maureen Berner, *Statistics for Public Administration: Practical Uses for Better Decision Making* (Washington, DC: ICMA Press, 2010); Sarah Boslaugh and Paul Andrew Watters, *Statistics in A Nutshell* (Sebastopol, CA: O'Reilly, 2008); Lawrence Giventer, *Statistical Analysis for Public Administration,* 2d ed. (Sudbury, MA: Jones and Bartlett, 2008); J.D. Hand, *Statistics: A Very Short Introduction* (New York: Oxford University Press, 2008); Kenneth Meier, Jeffrey Brudney, and John Bohte, *Applied Statistics for Public and Nonprofit Administration*, 7th ed. (Belmont, CA: Thomson Wadsworth, 2009); and U.S. Government Accountability Office, *Quantitative Data Analysis: An Introduction* (Washington, DC: U.S. Government Accountability Office, 1992).

2. U.S. Census Bureau, "Mission Statement," http://www.census.gov/aboutus/# (accessed September 2, 2011).

3. Margo Anderson, *The American Census: A Social History* (New Haven, CT: Yale University Press, 1988), 240.

4. Ibid., 117.

5. U.S. Census Bureau, "Census 2010 Questionnaire," http://2010.census.gov/2010census/pdf/2010_Questionnaire_Info.pdf (accessed September 17, 2011).

6. U.S. Census Bureau, "Apportionment Population and Number of Representatives, by State: 2010 Census," http://2010.census.gov/news/pdf/apport2010_table1.pdf (accessed September 17, 2011).

7. Anderson, *American Census*, 187.

8. National Research Council, *Using the American Community Survey: Benefits and Challenges,* eds. Constance Citro and Graham Kalton (Washington, DC: National Academies Press, 2007), 20–22 and 46.

9. Stephanie McCulla and Shelly Smith, *Measuring the Economy: A Primer on GDP and the National Income and Product Accounts* (Washington, DC: U.S. Bureau of Economic Analysis, 2007), 1, http://bea.gov/national/pdf/nipa_primer.pdf.

10. Bernard Baumohl, *The Secrets of Economic Indicators: Hidden Clues to Future Economic Trends and Investment Opportunities*, 2d ed. (Upper Saddle River, NJ: Wharton School Publishing, 2008), 117.

11. Stephanie McCulla and Charles Ian Mead, *An Introduction to The National Income and Product Accounts* (Washington, DC: U.S. Bureau of Economic Analysis, 2007), 2, http://bea.gov/scb/pdf/national/nipa/methpap/mpi1_0907.pdf.

12. U.S. Bureau of Economic Analysis, "Measuring National Income and Product," http://library.bea.gov/cdm4/history.php (accessed September 17, 2011).

13. McCulla and Smith, *Measuring the Economy,* 6–13.

14. David Moss, *A Concise Guide to Macroeconomics: What Managers, Executives, and Students Need to Know* (Boston, MA: Harvard Business School Press, 2007), 115.

15. Joseph Goldberg and William Moye, *The First Hundred Years of The Bureau of Labor Statistics*

(Washington, DC: U.S. Department of Labor, 1985), 4, http://www.bls.gov/opub/blsfirsthundred-years/100_years_of_bls.pdf.

16. Ibid., chapter 6.

17. As of November 6, 2012, the FedStats website was active at www.fedstats.gov, and the Data.gov website was active at www.data.gov.

18. Sarah Boslaugh and Paul Andrew Watters, *Statistics in a Nutshell*, 367–368.

19. Author's analysis of U.S. Census Bureau, American Community Survey, One-Year Estimates, 2011.

20. Economist, *Guide to Economic Indicators: Making Sense of Economics*, 6th ed. (New York: Bloomberg Press, 2006), 14.

21. Author's analysis of U.S. Census Bureau, American Community Survey, One-Year Estimates, 2007 and 2011.

22. Economist, *Guide to Economic Indicators*, 18.

23. Author's analysis of U.S. Census Bureau, American Community Survey, One-Year Estimates, 2007 and 2011.

24. Economist, *Guide to Economic Indicators*, 20.

25. Author's analysis of U.S. Census Bureau, American Community Survey, One-Year Estimates, 2007 and 2011.

26. Economist, *Guide to Economic Indicators*, 17–18.

27. Ibid., 23.

28. U.S. Bureau of Economic Analysis, "Table 1.1.1. Percent Change from Preceding Period in Real Gross Domestic Product, Seasonally Adjusted at Annual Rates," last revised September 27, 2012, http://www.bea.gov/iTable/iTable.cfm?ReqID=9&step=1.

29. Patricia Andreski et al., PSID Main Interview User Manual: Release 2011.1 (Anne Arbor, MI: Institute for Social Research, 2011), 11, http://psidonline.isr.umich.edu/data/Documentation/User-Guide2009.pdf.

30. Economist, *Guide to Economic Indicators*, 25.

31. Baumohl, *The Secrets of Economic Indicators*, 18–19.

32. Center for Economic and Policy Research, "Online Budget Calculator," last accessed September 17, 2011, http://www.cepr.net/calculators/calc_budget.html; Congressional Budget Office, *The Budget and Economic Outlook: Fiscal Years 2010 to 2020* (Washington, DC: Congress of the United States, 2010), 8, http://cbo.gov/ftpdocs/108xx/doc10871/01-26-Outlook.pdf; and U.S. Department of Housing and Urban Development, *Investing in People and Places: FY 2011 Budget* (Washington, DC: U.S. Department of Housing and Urban Development, 2010), 39, http://hud.gov/budgetsummary2011/full-budget-2011.pdf.

33. Baumohl, *The Secrets of Economic Indicators*, 20–21, and the U.S. Bureau of Labor Statistics, "Online Consumer Price Index Calculator," http://data.bls.gov/cgi-bin/cpicalc.pl (accessed September 17, 2011).

34. Robert Sugden and Alan Williams, *The Principles of Practical Cost-Benefit Analysis* (New York: Oxford University Press, 1978), 13–16.

35. Boslaugh and Watters, *Statistics in a Nutshell*, xii.

36. Lawrence Giventer, *Statistical Analysis for Public Administration*, 2d ed. (Sudbury, MA: Jones and Bartlett, 2008), 4–6.

37. This discussion of measurement levels is based on Boslaugh and Watters, *Statistics in a Nutshell*, 2–5; Giventer, *Statistical Analysis for Public Administration*, 14–18; and Kenneth Meier, Jeffrey Brudney, and John Bohte, *Applied Statistics for Public and Nonprofit Administration*, 7th ed. (Belmont, CA: Thomson Wadsworth, 2009), 61 and 131.

38. Boslaugh and Watters, *Statistics in a Nutshell*, 9 and 12.

39. For a useful overview of statistical sampling, see U.S. Government Accountability Office, *Using Statistical Sampling* (Washington, DC: U.S. Government Accountability Office, 1992).

40. John Allen Paulos, *Innumeracy: Mathematical Illiteracy and Its Consequences* (New York: Hill and Wang, 2001), 158.

41. U.S. Government Accountability Office, *Quantitative Data Analysis: An Introduction* (Washington, DC: U.S. Government Accountability Office, 1992), 26–27.

42. When using inferential statistics to test hypotheses, the basic concepts underlying confidence intervals are expressed in terms of "statistical significance." A statistically significant result is one unlikely to result from pure chance. So, a value found to be significant at the 95 percent level is one with only a 5 percent chance of being a completely random result.

43. Boslaugh and Watters, *Statistics in a Nutshell,* 54.

44. Meier, Brudney, and Bohte, *Applied Statistics,* 77.

45. While the arithmetic mean is the most commonly encountered average, other types exist. A weighted average, for instance, is one in which some values are adjusted to contribute more to the final average than other values. A simple moving average is a method for smoothing short-term fluctuations in time series data and involves replacing the oldest observation in a series with the newest one and computing the mean for the revised data set.

46. Meier, Brudney, and Bohte, *Applied Statistics,* 96.

47. Maureen Berner, *Statistics for Public Administration: Practical Uses for Better Decision Making* (Washington, DC: ICMA Press, 2010), 52.

48. Giventer, *Statistical Analysis,* 150.

49. Meier, Brudney, and Bohte, *Applied Statistics,* 173.

50. Boslaugh and Watters, *Statistics in a Nutshell,* 169.

51. U.S. Government Accountability Office, *Quantitative Data Analysis,* 93.

52. Meier, Brudney, and Bohte, *Applied Statistics,* 540.

5   **Demographics**

No region would exist if not for the human beings who live and work there. Without people, there would be no one to found businesses, hold jobs, buy goods, or use public services. Without people, in short, there would be no need for any of the trappings of modern life. For proof, consider the scores of small, rural towns scattered across the Great Plains that have lost so many residents they no longer can support institutions like local public schools.[1]

Ironically, the importance of real people to regional vitality often escapes notice. Debates about public policies typically unfold in isolation from their social contexts and consequences. Yet human institutions like government exist not for their own purposes but as mechanisms for progress. Even in the seemingly transactional realm of economics, thinkers from Adam Smith to John Maynard Keynes have understood economic activity not as an end in itself, but as a means for living "wisely, agreeably, and well."[2]

Any analysis of regional social and economic conditions therefore must begin with the people who call a place home. A city with a large population of recent immigrants likely will be economically and socially distinct from a community with a smaller immigrant population, just as the residents of a relatively affluent region probably will demand a mix of public services different from those desired by the inhabitants of a less prosperous place. Unless civic leaders appreciate such differences, they are likely to pursue policies inappropriate to local needs.

It is impossible, of course, to weigh the individual needs, wishes, and circumstances of each local resident. Analysts therefore approach populations as a whole and study them with tools taken from demography, a statistical field concerned with understanding population size, change, and composition or characteristics. To help regional leaders understand demographic concepts and tools, this chapter begins by differentiating demography from demographics and then describes important sources of demographic information, especially the American Community Survey, an annual product of the U.S. Census Bureau. The chapter concludes by explaining four essential demographic concepts: population size, population change,

Map 5.1 Principal Cities and Component Counties of Seattle-Tacoma Bellevue, WA Metropolitan Statistical Area, 2009 Delineation

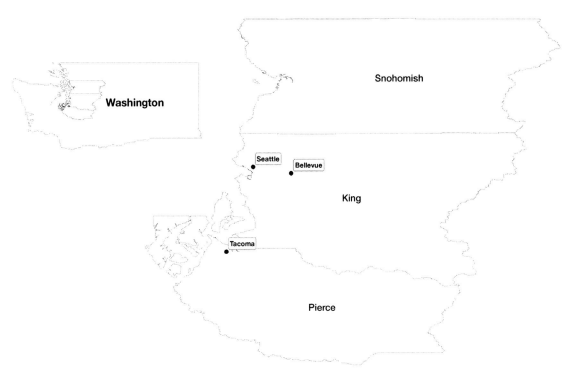

Source: U.S. Office of Management and Budget, "Update of Statistical Area Definitions and Establishments (OMB Bulletin No. 10-02)," December 1, 2009, http://www.whitehouse.gov/sites/default/files/omb/assets/bulletins/b10-02.pdf. Map prepared by William High.

population distribution, and population composition or characteristics. To illustrate the selected topics, the chapter offers practical examples drawn from data for the Seattle-Tacoma-Bellevue, WA Metropolitan Statistical Area (MSA), a three-county region that had 3.5 million residents in 2011 (see Map 5.1).[3]

Differentiating Demography and Demographics

While used interchangeably, the terms "demography" and "demographics" refer to distinct fields. *Demography* is the study "of the size, distribution, and composition of populations; the processes determining these—namely fertility, mortality, and migration; and the determinants and consequences of all of the above."[4] Central to the discipline is the use of quantitative methods to analyze populations and their characteristics as aggregate wholes.[5] Demography contains two main branches. *Formal demography*, also called "pure demography" or "mathematical demography," revolves around technical calculations of population measures. In contrast, *social demography*, which is synonymous with the terms "applied demography" and "population studies," investigates the effects of demographic processes on nondemographic variables, like those related to economic life.[6]

Despite being rooted in social demography, many regional analyses employ demography not in a strict, social scientific manner but in a broad way aimed at conveying "information and data on the size, geographic distribution, and characteristics of a population that affect its use of, its participation in, and/or its access to specific types of goods and services."[7] This wider, nontechnical approach, known as *demographics*, looks at demography in relation to other issues. This applied approach employs the tools of demography to answer practical questions.

Consistent with the practical nature of this book, demographics, not demography, is the subject of this chapter. The aim is to equip regional leaders to understand demographic information and apply it to regional issues, but the trade-off associated with this practical approach is a certain loss of technical precision.

SOURCES OF DEMOGRAPHIC DATA

Public statistical agencies like the U.S. Census Bureau collect, tabulate, and disseminate copious amounts of demographic information. Despite being freely available on the internet, the data often are difficult to find, in part because there exists no central repository. To paint a portrait of a *population*, or "the persons living in a specific area at a specific point in time," regional analysts typically must piece together data from multiple national and state sources.[8]

NATIONAL DATA SOURCES

Numerous federal agencies compile demographic information. For instance, the National Center for Health Statistics, a division of the Centers for Disease Control and Prevention is a leading source of public health information, such as records of births and deaths. The National Center for Educational Statistics, a unit of the U.S. Department of Education, meanwhile, collects education-related information. When it comes to demographic data, however, the U.S. Census Bureau is the "leading source of quality data about the nation's people and economy."[9]

U.S. Census Bureau

As chapter 4 mentioned, the U.S. Census Bureau is the closest American counterpart to the centralized national statistical agencies found in other countries. The Census Bureau plays the leading role in the collection of demographic information, thanks to the sophisticated administrative and analytical capacities the agency has cultivated in the course of conducting the Decennial Census of Population and Housing (see Box 5.1). Other important demographic data products of the Census Bureau are the Population Estimates Program, the Population Projection Program, the American Community Survey, and the Current Population Survey.

Box 5.1 Accessing Demographic Data from the U.S. Census Bureau

Much of the demographic information collected by the U.S. Census Bureau is available on the agency's website (http://www.census.gov). Casual visitors often find the site difficult to navigate due to the sheer amount of information it contains, the unintuitive ways in which the information is organized, the lack of clear instructions, and the dynamic nature of the site. One way to overcome the confusion is to conceptualize the website as containing three increasingly sophisticated resources.

Prior to 2012, the first resource consisted of reference books published by the Census Bureau. Those works included *The Statistical Abstract of the United States*, a volume first published in 1878; *The State and Metropolitan Data Book,* a supplement to the *Statistical Abstract* that provided social and economic information for every state, metropolitan statistical areas, and micropolitan statistical area in the country; and *The County and City Data Book*, a supplement to the *Statistical Abstract* that featured social and economic information for every U.S. county and for every city with 10,000 or more residents. Recent budget reductions unfortunately led the Census Bureau to discontinue the three works, but past copies are available online (http://www.census.gov/compendia/statab/ and http://www.census.gov/compendia/databooks/).

The second resource is *American FactFinder*, an online query system (http://factfinder2.census.gov). FactFinder provides structured access to data from multiple statistical programs, including, but not limited to, the Decennial Census of Population and Housing, the American Community Survey, and the Population Estimates Program. Casual visitors can view fact sheets about specific communities and narrative descriptions of individual topics, while experienced users can distill data from prepared tabulations, generate tables and maps, and download information in formats suitable for manipulation in spreadsheet and statistical software programs.

The final resource is the *Public Use Microdata Sample* (PUMS). Microdata are extracts of untabulated individual records collected through various data programs. The microdata files essentially are anonymous samples drawn from larger samples. To protect the identities of individual respondents, the Census Bureau only releases microdata for a special unit of geography called a *Public Use Microdata Area* (PUMA), which contains at least 100,000 residents located in a set of contiguous counties or census tracts. The idea is for a PUMA to mirror, as far as possible, the composition of an actual community. Because it often takes special statistical software to process microdata, only knowledgeable analysts should attempt to work with PUMS files, which are available for download through the American FactFinder.

Sources: U.S. Census Bureau, *The 2012 Statistical Abstract: The National Data Book*, 131st ed. (Washington, DC: U.S. Department of Commerce, 2011), http://www.census.gov/compendia/statab/2012edition.html; U.S. Census Bureau, *A Compass for Understanding and Using American Community Survey Data: What PUMS Data Users Need to Know* (Washington, DC: U.S. Department of Commerce, 2009), http://www.census.gov/acs/www/Downloads/handbooks/ACSPUMS.pdf; U.S. Census Bureau, *County and City Data Book: 2007*, 14th ed. (Washington, DC: U.S. Department of Commerce, 2007), http://www.census.gov/compendia/databooks/pdf_version.html; and U.S. Census Bureau, *State and Metropolitan Area Data Bank: 2010*, 7th ed. (Washington, DC: U.S. Department of Commerce, 2010), http://www.census.gov/compendia/databooks/pdf_version.html.

Decennial Census of Population and Housing. A count of every person residing in the United States on April 1 of the reference year, the *Decennial Census of Population and Housing* is the nation's definitive source of population data. That is due to the census's broad coverage and its ability to organize data within the sophisticated geographical framework explained in chapter 1. The Census Bureau also releases information stripped of individually identifiable information in raw forms from which researchers can fashion customized analyses.

The main shortcoming of the decennial census is its infrequency, a by-product of the enumeration's complexity and cost. For example, the original congressional appropriation for the 2010 Census totaled $14.7 billion spread over a 12-year period of planning, implementation, and processing The Census Bureau succeeded in conducting the count for $1.6 billion less than that amount.[10] Because of the impracticability of conducting a full census more often, the demographic findings may have short lifespans, particularly in places undergoing rapid population changes.

Population Estimates Program. To provide accurate population data in the years between enumerations, the Population Division of the Census Bureau prepares annual estimates of the resident population of the nation, states, District of Columbia, counties, incorporated places, minor civil divisions, metropolitan statistical areas, micropolitan statistical areas, census regions, census divisions, and Puerto Rico.[11] These estimates, which are the definitive intercensal counts, influence the allocation of federal funds to state and local governments.[12]

The Population Estimates Program, a joint undertaking of the Census Bureau and state partner agencies, provides population estimates of particular places as of July 1 of the reference year. In each year between decennial counts, the Census Bureau releases three sets of population estimates that appear on a rolling basis throughout the year.[13] First, the agency prepares population counts for major geographic units. Second, the Census Bureau estimates the effects of the two drivers of population change: natural increase and net migration. Finally, the program breaks out population changes by age, sex, race, and Hispanic origin, although estimates of population characteristics exist only for the nation, states, and counties.[14]

When interpreting population estimates, regional leaders should remember that the calculations are subject to various kinds of errors. As the estimates originate from secondary data such as tax returns and vital records, the limitations of those files may flow through to the population estimates. Furthermore, the Census Bureau's cohort-component population model—a forecasting model that estimates changes to various population categories defined by shared traits like age, sex, race, and Hispanic ethnicity—is imperfect. If, say, actual female fertility proves lower than the model assumes, the estimate of natural population growth may prove too high. The estimates yielded by the cohort model also "become progressively less reliable at smaller scales."[15] Nevertheless, the Population Estimates Program offers credible, annual insights into population sizes, dynamics, and characteristics.

As an example of the usefulness of the Census Bureau's Population Estimates Program to regional analysis, consider population changes from 2010 to 2011 in the Seattle-Tacoma-Bellevue, WA MSA. The 2010 Census found that the three-county region contained 3.44 million residents on April 1, 2010, a number that grew to 3.45 million by July 1, 2010. One year later, the estimated metropolitan population equaled 3.50 million. In short, the Seattle MSA netted slightly more than 60,000 residents in a span of 15 months. That overall gain of 1.8 percent translates into an annual rate of growth of 1.4 percent.[16]

When analyzing regional population growth, the *rule of 70* is a practical tool for approximating the time it will take for a population to double in size. The formula calls for dividing the number 70 by an annual growth rate. With a 1.4 percent annual rate of growth, the size of Seattle's population would double in 50 years; if the growth rate were to rise to 2.8 percent, the region's population would double in size in 25 years.[17]

Population Projections Program. In contrast to population estimates, which are based on past trends, population projections "illustrate possible courses of population change based on assumptions about future births, deaths, net international migration, and (for state-level projections) state-to-state or domestic migration."[18]

The Census Bureau's Population Division periodically prepares population projections. National projections forecasting changes for age, sex, race, and ethnicity appear approximately every four years. The most recent national projections available at the time of writing were from 2012 and covered the period from 2012 to 2060.[19] At one point in time, the Census Bureau prepared state-level population projections that forecasted changes by age and sex, but the agency has not produced any subnational population estimates since 2005 and is not planning any future releases of this data.[20] In some states, government agencies and academic research centers have assumed responsibility for developing statewide and local projections.

Census Bureau projections originate in a cohort-component population model related to the one used to prepare population estimates, so the projections are subject to similar kinds of errors. An additional source of error is that projections require analysts to make assumptions about future developments, but the assumptions may not hold. If actual net domestic migration proves lower than assumed, for example, the population total projected for a later date may prove too high. Population projections nevertheless provide a plausible basis for long-term planning.

American Community Survey. In response to limitations associated with the decennial nature of the census, the Census Bureau began in 1994 to design a replacement for the "long form," a supplemental socioeconomic survey sent to a subset of households as part of every decennial census from 1940 to 2000. Between 1995 and 2004, the Census Bureau designed, developed, and demonstrated a replacement survey capable of providing continuous information about the demographic characteristics of the population. After the tests proved successful and the U.S. Congress provided funding, the Census Bureau worked between 2005 and 2010 to implement the new data product, the *American Community Survey* (ACS). The agency further eliminated the long form from the 2010 Census, and in the future the ACS will serve as the main source of information about the demographic traits of the population.[21]

The ACS is a representative, mail-based survey of some 3 million housing units—a sample size equal to 2.5 percent of all households in the United States. Selected households receive a survey form that poses questions about demographic characteristics, housing conditions, social traits, and economic characteristics (see Appendix 2).[22] Unlike other Census Bureau data products, the ACS is a continuous survey, which means that it collects data over a rolling period of time rather than for a specific date.

Box 5.2 Understanding Data from the American Community Survey

The annual release of socioeconomic data collected through the American Community Survey (ACS) involves three different products: *one-year estimates* contain information about the demographic, housing, social, and economic characteristics of every community with at least 65,000 residents; *three-year estimates* provide the same information for every community with at least 20,000 residents; and *five-year estimates* offer that information for every community regardless of population size.

As with all data collected through statistical surveys, ACS estimates are subject to nonsampling and sampling errors. *Nonsampling error* occurs when an observed value differs from the true one owing to design and measurement flaws, while *sampling error* is when the characteristics of the survey group vary from those of the larger population of interest. Sampling error causes the true value of any ACS estimate to fall within a range bounded by a margin of error. In 2011, for example, the one-year ACS point estimate for the share of grandparents in the Seattle-Tacoma-Bellevue, WA Metropolitan Statistical Area (MSA) who lived with their grandchildren and were responsible for those children was 29.4 percent. The margin of error surrounding that estimate was +/–3.2 percentage points, which means there was a 90 percent chance that the true share of grandparents responsible for the grandchildren with whom they lived fell between 26.2 and 32.6 percent.

Another point to remember when dealing with ACS figures is that the numbers are period estimates, not point-in-time or cumulative estimates. A *period estimate* shows the average value of the variable over a specific reference period. Three-year and five-year estimates, then, show the average value of the variable over each time frame, meaning that a three-year estimate of the foreign-born population in a city would show the average number of foreign-born individuals in the community over a 36-month span.

The ACS employs multiyear values to compensate for the fact the sampling frame includes too few households to yield reliable annual estimates for small geographies and small population subgroups. Pooling data from multiple periods overcomes that problem and yields regular, usable estimates for places and population groups previously counted just once per decade.

Two cautions pertain to the use of multiyear estimates. First, observers interested in small communities and population groups generally should rely on the three-year or five-year estimates, but when drawing comparisons among places of differing sizes, it is wise to use the same data series. An analysis comparing the Seattle MSA, for which annual estimates exist, to a smaller one for which only three-year or five-year estimates exist, such as the Lewiston, ID-WA MSA, should rely on the same data set and not mix one-year and multiyear estimates. Second, it is important to pay attention to reference years when using multiyear ACS estimates as time spans may overlap. A comparison of three-year data for 2009–2011 and 2008–2010 would reveal little given how the periods share two reference years, so a better comparison might be between 2006–2008 and 2009–2011.

As a general rule of thumb, one-year ACS estimates are useful when dealing with large geographies or in situations in which the timeliness of the estimates matters more than the precision of the data. Multiyear estimates are better when dealing with smaller geographies or situations in which the precision of the estimates outweighs the timeliness of the estimates.

Source: U.S. Census Bureau, *A Compass for Understanding and Using American Community Survey Data: What General Data Users Need to Know* (Washington, DC: U.S. Department of Commerce, 2008), 9–10 and A-1–A-7, http://www.census.gov/acs/www/Downloads/handbooks/ACSGeneralHandbook.pdf.

In essence, the ACS produces a changing image of the demographic characteristics of a population instead of a portrait snapped on a particular day (see Box 5.2). While the ACS collects data almost daily, estimates appear annually in the fall of the subsequent calendar year (e.g., 2011 data appeared in 2012).

The annual ACS data release contains three products. *One-year estimates* normally appear in September and provide information for all geographies with at least 65,000 residents. *Three-year estimates* offer information for all geographies with 20,000 or more residents, and *five-year estimates* provide information for all geographies irrespective of population.[23] The Census Bureau typically releases the three-year and five-year estimates in December.

One important difference between the ACS and the decennial census is the way in which the two studies define *place of residence*. The decennial census contacts people by housing units and asks the respondent from each unit to list the number of persons who usually live and sleep in that place as of April 1 of the census year. In contrast, the ACS imposes a length-of-stay requirement, and to be included as a resident of a housing unit, an individual must have lived or intends to live in the housing unit for more than two consecutive months relative to the response date.[24] The length-of-stay requirement is a common source of confusion. College students responding from their dormitories, for instance, are residents of the community where the dorm is located, not their hometown. Similarly, the residency of "Snowbirds" depends on where they are when responding to the ACS: a person who regularly lives in New York but has a winter home in Florida would be a Florida resident if surveyed while in the Sunshine State. The ACS also counts people living in group quarters, such as nursing homes, mental health facilities, prisons, and homeless shelters, as residents of the places where the facilities are located.

While the ACS is a relatively young survey, it has become an important one. The survey matters not merely because of the rich demographic information it yields, but also because of its use in allocating federal funds to state and local governments. A 2010 study by the Brookings Institution, a nonprofit research organization, found that 184 federal programs used ACS data to award $416 billion in federal domestic assistance during federal fiscal year 2008—an amount equal to 29 percent of all federal domestic assistance awarded that year.[25] Programs that tie funding to ACS data include Medicaid, the Federal-Aid Highway Program, and Title I Grants to Local Educational Agencies; other federal programs use ACS information to set eligibility criteria, allocate formula grants, define selection preferences, and set interest rates.[26]

Regional leaders interpreting ACS data should remember three things. First, because the ACS is a survey, it is subject to the kinds of sampling and nonsampling errors explained in chapter 4. Second, because they come from a survey, ACS data are not precise counts; rather, they are estimates at a particular level of confidence (90 percent). While analysts often present point estimates of ACS data, the true values actually fall within ranges bounded by margins of error. The errors are particularly important when analyzing small populations and communities. Finally, ACS data provide *period estimates*, not point-in-time or cumulative assessments.[27] A three-year estimate of the number of persons in poverty shows neither the total number of people who experienced poverty during that span nor the number of persons in poverty on a particular date. The estimate instead reflects the average number of persons in poverty over a 36-month period.

Current Population Survey. Conducted continuously since 1943, albeit in revised forms, the *Current Population Survey* (CPS) is a monthly survey of the labor force fielded by the Census Bureau on behalf of the U.S. Bureau of Labor Statistics (BLS).[28] Each month, the Census Bureau interviews approximately 60,000 households either by telephone or in person and inquires about the labor force characteristics of each household member age 15 and older who is not in the armed forces or residing in various types of institutions; topics of interest include employment, unemployment, earnings, and hours of work.[29] A supplemental survey undertaken every March, the *Annual Social and Economic Supplement* asks more detailed questions about income, poverty, work experience, workplace benefits, and other topics, as well as about demographic characteristics such as age, sex, race, marital status, and educational attainment.[30]

The CPS is the primary source of information about the American labor force. Because the CPS is a major tool for understanding labor markets, a full discussion of the survey appears in chapter 7. Suffice it to say, the demographic data contained in the CPS are helpful for understanding the characteristics of the labor force, though the survey's relatively small size yields monthly estimates only for the nation, states, and a dozen large metropolitan areas.[31] More detailed information is found in the supplemental March survey.

State Data Sources

Various state agencies collect demographic information of regional importance. Some of those state data collection efforts unfold independently, others in conjunction with federal agencies. While the exact organization of data agencies varies from one state to another, key sources of information include health agencies, labor market information agencies, and state data centers.

State Health Agencies. State health agencies are responsible for collecting information about such health-related matters as the incidence of disease, the characteristics of health care facilities, the qualifications of health care professionals, and the conditions of public health. State health agencies matter for demographic research because they compile vital records about births, deaths, marriages, and divorces. Birth and death data are particularly important. In most states, central health agencies receive birth and death certificates and then share statistics based on vital records with the National Center for Health Statistics, a unit of the Centers for Disease Control and Prevention, which itself is part of the U.S. Department of Health and Human Services.

Labor Market Information Agencies. The Labor Market Information Program is a partnership involving the BLS and the state agencies responsible for administering unemployment insurance systems (see Appendix 3).[32] State agencies collaborate with the BLS to produce statistical studies of labor force and employment trends. Major data products include the Local Area Unemployment Statistics program, the Current Employment Statistics program, and the Quarterly Census of Employment and Wages. Chapter 7 discusses these three resources.

State Data Center Program. The State Data Center Program is another source of demographic data. Established in 1978, this collaborative program involves the Census Bureau and partners in every state. The collaboration strives "to make data available locally to the public through a network of state agencies, universities, libraries, and regional and local governments."[33] Governors appoint the lead partners in their respective states (see Appendix 4).[34] Additionally, the Census Bureau and the states agreed in 1988 to launch a Business and Industry Data Center Program to provide economic data for the benefit of local business communities.

In many states, data centers belong to a Federal-State Cooperative for Population Estimates, which develops a common system for generating reliable, consistent population estimates. Much of this partnership's work informs the Census Bureau's Population Estimates Program, and some data centers prepare state-specific estimates and projections.[35]

ESSENTIAL DEMOGRAPHIC CONCEPTS

The demographic information generated by national and state data agencies provides regional analysts with the raw materials needed to study four essential demographic concepts: population size, population change, population distribution, and population composition or characteristics. The following sections explain each concept in turn, partly by offering examples drawn from ACS data for the Seattle-Tacoma-Bellevue, WA MSA.

POPULATION SIZE

Accurate population counts are the foundation of any demographic analysis. A population count is "the absolute number of a population or any demographic event occurring in a specified area in a specified time period."[36] Examples include estimates of the total population on a specific date and the number of children born during a year. Because regions differ in size, relative quantities like rates feature prominently in demographic studies since the use of standardized values enables the drawing of meaningful comparisons among places of varying sizes (see Box 5.3).

Regional analysts may prepare population counts for an entire region or a specific population group. According to the ACS, for instance, metro Seattle had 3.5 million residents in 2011, but the region's total population of persons ages 15 to 19 was a much smaller 214,000.[37] Both values are population counts. A study focused on the region as a whole would take 3.5 million as the population count, and research concerned solely with people around high school age would start with the 214,000 number.

Households, Persons, and Families

A crucial step in any demographic study is selecting a unit of analysis. As part of the ACS, the Census Bureau collects information on three potential analytical units: households, persons, and families. While these categories appear straightforward,

---

Box 5.3 Demographic Rates

Demographic studies rely on common mathematical and statistical tools. Percentages, ratios, proportions, and rates are staples of demographic analysis, as are statistical computations ranging from basic descriptive methods to complex inferential ones. Familiarity with the data concepts and calculations discussed in chapter 4 therefore provides a foundation for understanding demographic information.

Rates play a special role in demographic studies. A *rate* is a ratio that compares two different quantities. Because regions typically differ in terms of population sizes, comparisons of absolute quantities are of limited usefulness. By placing values on a common base, the use of rates helps to control for differences in population sizes and facilitates the drawing of valid conclusions.

When applied in demographic contexts, rates measure how often an event occurs relative to the size of a reference population. A demographic rate involves two variables: a count of how many times the event of interest has occurred in a specific place during a particular time (e.g., the number of deaths in a city in a year) and the size of the reference population (e.g., the total population). The rate is the quotient obtained by dividing the first number by the second one and multiplying the result by a constant value like 100 or 1,000 to set the numbers on the same base (e.g., the number of deaths per 1,000 residents).

Three types of rates are important when dealing with demographic data. These rates differ in regard to the reference population, which is the second number (denominator) used in each calculation.

- A *crude rate* compares the total occurrence of an event to the total population. An example is the crude birth rate, which reflects the total number of births in a community in a given year divided by the total population in that year.
- A *general rate* compares the total occurrence of an event to the segment of the population that could experience the event. An example is the general birth rate, which shows the total number of births in a community in a given year relative to the total number of women.
- A *specific rate* compares the total occurrence of an event to the segment of the population most likely to experience the event. An example is the specific birth rate, which expresses the total number of births in a community in a given year in relation to the total number of women of childbearing age.

When considering demographic data, it is important to differentiate between the *incidence* of an event and the *prevalence* of that event. The rate of incidence reflects the number of new times an event occurs within a population during a given time period. So, the annual incidence of pregnancy is a measure of how many women became pregnant during the year. In contrast, the rate of prevalence reflects the total number of people within a population who experience an event in a period. The annual rate prevalence of pregnancy in a community, then, is the number of women who were pregnant at any time during the year.

Sources: Arthur Haupt and Thomas Kane, *Population Handbook*, 5th ed. (Washington, DC: Population Reference Bureau, 2004), 58 and 62, http://www.prb.org/pdf/pophandbook_eng.pdf; and Steve Murdock et al., *Demographics: A Guide to Methods and Data Sources for Media, Business, and Government* (Boulder, CO: Paradigm Publishers, 2006), 23–27.

---

they actually are quite intricate, and a failure to appreciate the differences is a common source of confusion.

The fundamental analytical unit in the ACS is the household. A *household* consists of "all the people who occupy a housing unit."[38] For the purposes of the ACS, the adult person who owns or rents a housing unit and who is named in the survey questionnaire is deemed to be the "householder" and is responsible for providing information about each individual residing in the household, including each person's relationship to the householder. The information about individual household members is the basis of counts of *persons*, or unique human beings of any age.

Since 2006, the ACS also has compiled information about the individual residents of *group quarters*, which are "places where people live or stay, in a group living arrangement that is owned or managed by an entity or organization providing housing and/or services for the residents."[39] Examples include college dormitories, nursing homes, military barracks, correctional facilities, and homeless shelters. Individual residents of group quarters are not part of the ACS household population but are included in the tally of persons.

When using ACS data pertaining to households, it is important to recognize that a household is not the same as a family. A *family household* contains "a householder and one or more other people living in the same household who are related to the householder by birth, marriage, or adoption."[40] The ACS categorizes family households according to the kind of relationships that exist among the family members and the sex of the householder. A *married-couple family* is one in which the householder and an opposite-sex spouse reside together, and a *single-parent family* is one in which the householder lives without a spouse. The ACS also tabulates data for children under age 18 according to their relationship to the householder. An *own child* is the biological child, stepchild, or adopted child of the householder, and a *related child* is one tied to the householder in another way, such as a grandchild, niece, or nephew.[41]

While a family household has only one family, the number of persons living in that household may be greater than the total number of family members. That is because a family household may contain other individuals, such as a married-couple family living with a foster child. Similarly, a *subfamily* could be present. A subfamily is one that meets the basic definition of a family but lives in a household headed by a relative or the spouse of a relative.[42] Think of a married-couple family household that has taken in the householder's elderly parents. The ACS does not count subfamilies independently from primary families.

A *nonfamily household* is one in which the householder lives alone or with no one who is related to the householder by birth, marriage, or adoption. Nonfamily households include single persons living by themselves, roommates sharing an apartment, unmarried persons who are cohabitating, and same-sex couples living together.[43]

Many of the complexities involved in classifying persons, households, and families stem from changes in Americans' living habits. Shifting social norms regarding divorce, marriage, and family life have altered basic living arrangements, thereby necessitating changes to demographic concepts and measures. Consider the rapid growth of *unmarried-partner households,* a category that barely existed a few decades ago. Such households contain a householder and another adult "who is unrelated to the householder, but shares living quarters and has a close personal relationship with the householder."[44] Confusingly, an unmarried-partner household can be either a family or nonfamily household, depending on the presence of relatives of one of the partners. Take an unmarried opposite-sex couple in which the householder has a child from a prior relationship. That would be a family household, but if no child were

Figure 5.1 Composition of Households in the Seattle-Tacoma-Bellevue, WA MSA, 2011

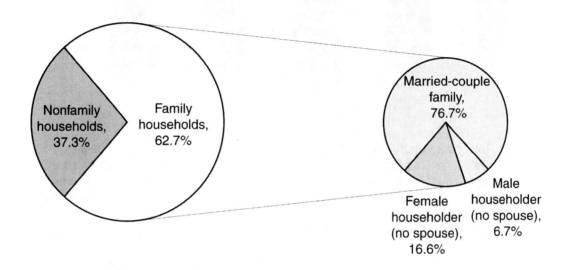

Source: U.S. Census Bureau, American Community Survey, One-Year Estimates, 2011.

present, it would be a nonfamily household. Note that the ACS counts all same-sex couples, including those that have married legally, as unmarried-partner households.

A second important change in living arrangements is the explosive rise in the number of single-person households. Between 1960 and 2012, the share of American households containing just one person more than doubled, rising to 27.4 percent from 13.1 percent. In 2012, some 33.2 million Americans lived alone, with single women responsible for 55.3 percent of the total.[45] Factors contributing to the rise in single-person households include higher divorce rates, lower marriage rates, shifting social norms, increased female independence, and lengthening lifespans that have created more chances for older people to live alone as widows or widowers.[46]

As a way of illustrating the complicated relationship between households and families, Figure 5.1 presents the 2011 distribution of households and families in the Seattle MSA. That year, Seattle had 1.4 million households, of which 855,000 were family households. Married-couple households accounted for 76.7 percent of the total number of family households, single female-headed households 16.6 percent, and single male-headed households 6.7 percent. Moreover, 6.8 percent of Seattle households were unmarried-partner households, of which 89.3 percent had opposite-sex partners. And, some 28.9 percent of Seattle households contained no one other than the householder.[47]

Population Cohorts

As a way of streamlining the process of working with population counts, analysts often divide a population into cohorts. A *cohort* is "a group of people sharing a common temporal demographic experience who are observed through time."[48] While numerous definitions of cohorts exist, age is a common criterion. For instance, a researcher might divide the population into five-year cohorts based on birth years. Dividing the population into cohorts enables analysts to compare different groups, though this process often involves other statistical adjustments.[49]

POPULATION CHANGE

Regional population sizes ebb and flow. Changes result from the interplay among the processes of fertility, mortality, and migration. Simply put, the size of a population change equals the sum of natural change (the number of births less the number of deaths) and net migration (the number of in-movers less the number of out-movers).[50]

Natural Change: Fertility and Mortality

In a population experiencing no net migration, natural processes drive all of the changes in the size of the population. For a population to grow without migration, the number of babies born in a region during a particular period would need to exceed the number of persons who died during the same span. Alternately, if the number of deaths were to exceed the number of births, the population would shrink. That dynamic is what demographers refer to as *natural change*.

Natural change depends on the relationship between fertility and mortality. *Fertility* refers "to the number of births that occur to an individual or a population" and typically is measured in relation to women of childbearing age, often defined as ages 15 to 44 or 15 to 49.[51] One common indicator is the general fertility rate, which reflects the number of births in a given year per 1,000 women of childbearing age.[52] *Mortality*, meanwhile, refers "to deaths that occur within a population" in a given period; the common way of expressing mortality is as the number of deaths that occur in a year for every 1,000 persons.[53] Fertility and mortality are not self-contained phenomena and instead are subject to external influences.

Fertility hinges on factors such as sexual practices, contraception, and physical health, and mortality hinges on such intermediate factors as advances in medical care that enable people to live longer and public health improvements that lower infant and child mortality. In the United States, average life expectancy at birth has increased sharply since 1900, climbing to 78.1 years in 2008 from 49.2 years in 1900–1902. Much of the improvement was attributable to the adoption of the germ theory of disease during the first half of the twentieth century and accompanying improvements in public health that reduced infant and child deaths. Between 1900–1902 and 1959–1961, average life expectancy at birth jumped by 20.7 years, increasing to 69.9 years from 49.2 years. Since then, average life expectancy has risen by only 10 years, due chiefly to improved treatment of diseases that affect adults.[54]

Assuming no immigration, the combination of fertility and mortality will shape a population's size and age structure. A population with high fertility levels and declining infant mortality rates will be comparatively younger than a population with low fertility levels and lengthening lifespans. Meanwhile, the size of a population will decline if its fertility rate falls below the replacement level—a level currently pegged at 2.1 children per woman in the United States and other advanced industrial countries.[55]

In general, fertility rates in the United States and other wealthy nations have been declining for decades. American fertility rates have fallen since the end of the Baby Boom that followed World War II—even though that period actually was an exception to a broader pattern of falling fertility rates—until reaching a record low of 1.74 children per woman in 1976.[56] While fertility rates subsequently rose, low fertility appears to have become an entrenched feature of American society. If not for immigration, the size of the U.S. population probably would be constant or declining, as is occurring in other industrialized countries. The Central European nation of Hungary, for example, has experienced population declines in every decennial census conducted since 1980. Between 2001 and 2011, 387,000 more Hungarians died than were born; net immigration offset 44.2 percent of the natural decline, but the excess of deaths over births reduced the country's population to 10 million from 10.2 million.[57]

Net Migration

The second source of population growth is migration, which occurs in both domestic and international variations. If more people move into an area than move away, net migration will add to population growth, but if more people move away from a place than move into it, net migration will subtract from growth.

Migration is "the geographic movement of people across a specified boundary for the purpose of establishing a new permanent or semipermanent residence."[58] *Domestic migration* reflects moves that occur within a country, such as the movement of an American family from one state to another, while *international migration* captures movements from one country to another. When it comes to international population movements, the United States long has gained more people than it has lost.

Measuring migration flows is a tricky business. In the United States, international flows are easier to track due to the existence of visa and legal entry requirements, though unauthorized entry is a problem. Domestic movements are more difficult to track since Americans are not required to register moves. To shed light on this issue, the ACS inquires about the place of residence one year ago of all persons who are at least one year of age.[59] Even though the United States has higher levels of domestic mobility than many other advanced nations, relatively few Americans move in a given year, and most moves involve short distances. In 2011, an estimated 84.8 percent of Americans lived in the same place as they did one year earlier. Among those who had moved, 60.5 percent stayed within the same county.[60]

Migration is "the most complex and volatile demographic variable." It is also highly selective.[61] When it comes to domestic migration, more educated and ambitious people are more likely to move, especially over long distances. Domestic migration is also an age-dependent process more likely to occur at certain points in life, such as during a person's early twenties. Domestic migration tends to peak when people are in their early thirties and then gradually declines before ticking up again around age 85.[62] And communities experiencing net outmigration tend to become older places with reduced stores of human capital, while communities experiencing positive net migration typically acquire younger, more skilled populations.

International migrants tend to be younger, better educated, and more ambitious than their compatriots who remain at home, but compared to the populations of the receiving countries, immigrants often are more diverse and comparatively less educated; immigrants also tend to cluster in specific communities with established social networks.[63] Receiving countries generally gain human capital via immigration, but sending countries frequently lose talented individuals.

Consider the changes in residence that occurred between 2010 and 2011 in the Seattle MSA. According to the ACS, an average of 632,516 Seattle residents changed their residences over the course of the year. Some 63.5 percent of the movers simply switched residences within the counties in which they already lived, and 14.3 percent exchanged residences in one county in Washington State for another. Another 16.7 percent of the movers came to the Seattle MSA from other states, and the remaining 5.4 percent of movers came to the region from abroad.[64]

Causes of Migration. People migrate for various reasons. Short-distance domestic moves often stem from personal considerations, such as a desire to acquire a larger residence. Long-distance domestic movers, however, tend to weigh a more complex set of calculations. Certain forces, such as the loss of a job or a change in life circumstances, may push a person away from an area, and other forces, such as a booming economy, may pull a person toward a new location. Push-pull factors are particularly relevant for international migration.

Economic theory holds that people will relocate "if they perceive that the marginal benefits of the move are greater than the marginal costs."[65] Three theories try to explain migration choices. The *human capital model* holds that people move "only if the present value of increased income in the new region is greater than the increased costs of living there."[66] In short, the decision to move reflects a calculation of how best to maximize lifetime income. Under this model, younger people are more likely to move as they have more time to recoup the investment.

A weakness of the human capital model is that people are not dispassionate income maximizers and instead value the availability of noneconomic amenities. In response, the *amenity attraction model* holds that people move to obtain certain amenities such as proximity to family or a pleasant climate. The decision to move hinges on whether the value assigned by a person to the amenities offered in the new location exceeds any combination of lost income and increased costs.[67] One recent study of the Portland–Vancouver–Hillsboro, OR–WA MSA found that the region attracts and retains college-educated adults under the age of 40 at rates above those posted in most other metropolitan regions despite the fact that well-educated young adults in Portland are more likely than their peers in other regions to be unemployed, employed part-time, engaged in occupations for which a college degree is unnecessary, and paid less. What appears to attract such people to Portland is the city's distinctive lifestyle.[68]

A final theory, the *local public goods model*, assumes that people move to obtain a preferred mix of taxes and public services. This theory, named the Tiebout model after the noted economist Charles Tiebout, assumes that people possessed of perfect information and mobility will move from higher-tax locations to lower-tax ones or from places with lower-quality public services to places with better services. This movement also influences land prices as outmigration causes land values to fall in the sending communities and rise in the receiving ones.[69] While the Tiebout model possesses explanatory power at the local level, it has limited applicability to long-distance domestic migration or international migration.

Economic considerations and push-pull factors are relevant, particularly in regard to international migration given the distances and costs associated with international moves. Poverty and limited economic prospects may "push" people to leave their homes, while job prospects, economic opportunities, and linguistic and cultural similarities may "pull" migrants toward a place. At the same time, noneconomic factors influence international flows. Political instability or religious persecution may drive people away regardless of economic conditions. Legal realities like border controls and visa requirements further mold immigration patterns. In the United States, federal immigration policies that effectively preclude the granting of visas to less-skilled workers combined with a practice of turning a blind eye to firms that employ undocumented workers have fueled the problem of unauthorized immigration.[70]

POPULATION DISTRIBUTION

Issues related to *population distribution*—"the patterns of settlement and dispersal of a population"—are just as important to regional well-being as are issues of population size and growth.[71] After all, the distribution of a population over a region influences the kinds of goods and services demanded by local residents and the ways in which public authorities furnish those services. A police department serving a rural area probably will provide monitoring services by car, but a force in an urban area might rely more heavily on foot and bicycle patrols. As with population growth, the distribution of the population across an area is dynamic.

The primary measure of population distribution is *population density* or "the number of inhabitants per square mile."[72] In 2008, the Seattle MSA had an estimated density of 567.5 persons per square land mile, making it the nation's fifteenth-most densely populated MSA.[73] Population densities varied across the three-county Seattle region. King County (Seattle) had a population density of 882.1 persons per square land mile, compared to 468 persons per square land mile in Pierce County (Tacoma) and 305.8 persons per square land mile in Snohomish County (Everett).[74] The variations are indicative of such community-level differences as total population, land size, urbanization, housing patterns, and zoning rules; they also affect the type, quality, and delivery of local public services.

Population distributions change over time due to natural increase and net migration. Between 2000 and 2008, population density in the Seattle MSA rose by 51.1 persons per square mile, climbing to 567.5 from 516.4.[75] Given that a significant part of the population increase came from net migration, the change suggests that issues linked to housing and transportation have increased in regional importance. And the rise in population density may have opened the doors to certain solutions (e.g., modes of mass transit) that are not as viable in less dense regions.

Assuming that land area holds steady, changes in population densities can transform communities. The influx of people into Seattle proper, for example, has sparked urban redevelopment and has raised problems of gentrification and displacement, just as changes in the population distribution in Great Lakes cities like Flint, Michigan, have led to neighborhood abandonment and urban contraction.[76]

POPULATION COMPOSITION OR CHARACTERISTICS

A final set of demographic concepts pertains to the composition or characteristics of a region's population. When it comes to variables like age, race, sex, marital status, and educational attainment, a population assumes a profile derived from the traits of the individual members. This section describes nine variables related to the composition of a population: age, sex, race, ethnicity, place of birth, citizenship, language, education, and disability. Discussions of other population characteristics appear elsewhere in this volume; chapter 7 covers topics related to employment, and chapters 8 and 9 explore issues of income, wealth, and deprivation.

Sex and Age

The ACS asks about the biological sex (male or female) of persons living in households and group quarters. To draw comparisons among regions, analysts often compute a *sex ratio*, which reflects "the number of males per 100 females in a population."[77] Sex ratios influence other demographic factors such as the availability of marriage partners, fertility, and family stability. In a population in which one gender greatly outnumbers the other, for example, not every member of the larger group will succeed in finding a marriage partner.

As part of the ACS, all individuals living in households or group quarters provide data about their *age* at the time when surveyed. The survey asks for an age in whole years and a date of birth. The annual ACS data releases provide aggregate age data in single-year increments and for selected age groups.[78] Age also is a key variable in many cross-tabulations like those breaking out information about educational attainment by age and sex.

Age is an essential demographic variable, as a population's age structure exerts a powerful influence over economic and social matters. A population that is relatively old likely will expect different public services than a younger population, such as fewer public schools and more health care. An older population also will have different consumer preferences, perhaps for houses that are smaller or residences that place the master bedroom on the ground floor.

A simple way of grasping a population's age structure is by considering the *median age* or "the age that divides the population into two numerically equal groups; that is, half the people are younger than this age and half are older."[79] In 2011, the median age in the Seattle MSA was 36.9 years.[80] Put differently, half of the people

Figure 5.2 Population Pyramid for the Seattle-Tacoma-Bellevue, WA MSA, 2011

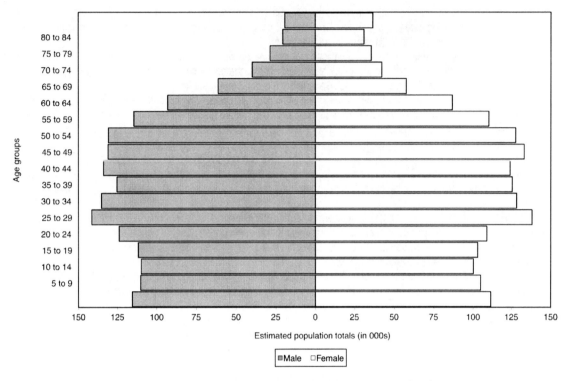

Source: U.S. Census Bureau, Population Estimates Program, 2011.
Note: Pyramid based on population totals for King, Pierce, and Snohomish counties.

in the Seattle area were younger than 36.9, half older. A more complex analytical tool is a *population pyramid*, which is "a bar chart arranged vertically that shows the distribution of a population by age and sex."[81] An advantage of population pyramids is that they provide a clear sense of the age structure. The wider the pyramid's base is, the younger the population.

Figure 5.2 is a 2011 population pyramid for the Seattle MSA that indicates Seattle's aging population. The graph shows the significant size of the so-called Baby Boom cohort (born 1946–1964, 2011 ages 47 to 65), the comparatively smaller size of Generation X (born 1965 to 1981, 2011 ages 30 to 46), and the somewhat larger size of the Millennial Generation (born 1982–1999, 2011 ages 12 to 29). Interestingly, while generational labels like Baby Boomers regularly appear in media reports, there exist no official definitions of generations (see Box 5.4).

Analysts may employ the information contained in population pyramids to construct *dependency ratios* that compare an arbitrarily defined economically dependent segment of the population to an arbitrarily defined economically productive segment of the

Box 5.4 Generations

The term "generation" features prominently in popular discussions and media accounts of social, historical, and political matters. The animating idea is that people born around the same time as one another share common experiences that lead them to perceive events and issues in similar ways.

Generational factors frequently are the causes cited for the differences in attitudes and ideas that exist among people of varying ages. For instance, some commenters have claimed that the social conflicts of the 1960s had their roots in the different values held by members of the G.I. Generation, a group commonly held up as an example of selflessness, and the members of the Baby Boom Generation, a group often portrayed as holding itself in extremely high regard. In the same way, observers have attributed workplace conflicts between people in their thirties and those in their twenties to frictions between the alleged cynicism of Generation X and the supposed idealism of the Millennial Generation.

At its best, generational analysis grounded in a careful use of sociological theory and methods may deepen understanding of complex social issues, but at its worst, the approach can devolve into a form of armchair commentary that recycles stereotypes. Yet for all the popularity of generational theory, there exist no fixed definitions of generations, and when it comes to demography, there are no generations in the common sense of the word; instead, there simply are counts of births, ranges of ages, and periods of higher or lower fertility.

To provide civic leaders with some perspective regarding the generational labels they are likely to encounter, the table below sketches one plausible generational framework and applies it to national population estimates for 2011. That year, the Millennial Generation (b. 1982–1999) was the nation's largest in absolute and relative terms, followed by the Baby Boom Generation (b. 1946–1964). Altogether, the 154.3 million members of those two generations accounted for 49.5 percent of the American population. The 69.7 million persons born during the Baby Bust of the late 1960s and 1970s—a cohort known as Generation X (b. 1965–1981)—contributed 22.4 percent of the population. Another 48.8 million Americans accounting for 15.7 percent of the population were children born since 2000, a group sometimes referred to as Generation Z or the iGeneration. Next came the 33.9 million members of the Silent Generation (b. 1926–1945), who contributed 10.9 percent of the total population. The remaining 1.5 percent of the population consisted of the 4.8 million surviving members of the G.I. Generation (b. 1925 and earlier), the youngest of whom were 86 years old.

Generational Distribution of the Population of the United States, 2011

Generation	Birth years	Age range in 2011	Total persons	Share of total population
G.I. Generation	1925 and before	86 and older	4,824,718	1.5%
Silent Generation	1926–1945	66–85	33,896,514	10.9%
Baby Boom Generation				
Early Boomers	1946–1954	57–65	32,238,540	10.3%
Late Boomers	1955–1964	47–56	44,615,313	14.3%
Generation X				
Early Xers	1965–1973	38–46	37,613,283	12.1%
Late Xers	1974–1981	30–37	32,124,774	10.3%
Millennial Generation/Generation Y				
Early Millennials	1982–1990	21–29	38,837,513	12.5%
Late Millennials	1991–1999	12–20	38,615,359	12.4%
Generation Z/iGeneration	2000 and after	11 or younger	48,825,903	15.7%
Totals			311,591,917	100.0%

Sources: Author's analysis of U.S. Census Bureau, Annual Estimates of the Resident Population by Single Year of Age and Sex for the United States: April 1, 2010 to July 1, 2011; Bruce Horovitz, "After Gen X, Millennials, What Should Next Generation Be?" *USA Today*, May 4, 2012; and William Strauss and Neil Howe, *Generations: The History of America's Future* (New York: Morrow, 1991).

Box 5.5 Population Aging

In 2011, the first surviving members of the Baby Boom generation—the roughly 77 million-person cohort born between 1946 and 1964—celebrated their sixty-fifth birthdays. By 2035, all surviving Boomers will be between the ages of 71 and 84. Due to the large size of the Baby Boom cohort, its aging will alter the nation's age structure. Projections from the U.S. Census Bureau suggest that older adults' share of the population will climb to 29.9 percent from 13 percent between 2010 and 2035.

On one level, this is a remarkable achievement. Little more than a century ago, few Americans lived to age 65, and those who did were likely to survive for just a few more years. In 1900, an American man turning age 65 was apt to live for another 11.5 years, with a 65-year-old woman living for 12.2 years. By 2008, the typical 65-year-old man would live for 17.3 years, a woman for 20 years. Furthermore, a person who reached age 65 in 1900 likely possessed few financial resources and either would work or would rely on the support of relatives. Today, older adults not only are healthier, on average, than their counterparts from a century ago, but they are generally more financially secure and able to pursue leisure activities, thanks to the existence of social insurance programs like Social Security and Medicare and the emergence of the concept of retirement.

On another level, population aging entails new challenges. Never before has the country had a population structure like the one currently taking shape. How will older adults finance their retirements? Can the health care system handle a large older population? Are social insurance programs stable? Such questions have come to occupy a prominent place in the nation's political and policy debates.

Such issues merit careful consideration, but they have become clouded in misinformation. Notably, some observers claim that population aging will impose debilitating economic and social burdens on the United States. For proof, proponents of this view frequently cite projected changes in the *old-age dependency ratio,* which the U.S. Census Bureau forecasts rising from 22 older adults per 100 working-age persons in 2010 to 35 older adults per 100 working-age persons in 2030.

Yet the old-age dependency ratio, by itself, tells little of America's ability to adapt to aging. After all, many countries have more favorable old-age dependency ratios due to a lack of the social, medical, and economic resources that allow sizable numbers of people to reach older ages. And the old-age dependency ratio is not a comprehensive measure; rather, the *total dependency ratio,* which compares the number of older adults and children to the number of working-age persons, is a more telling statistic. Because the child population should grow slowly, the total number of older adults and children per 100 working adults likely will climb from 67 to 83 between 2010 and 2030 and then stabilize at that level.

Another point to recognize is that society's ability to manage an older population is not simply a demographic numbers game. If it were, a straightforward solution would be to allow more immigration. In the long run, what matters is economic growth, a key driver of which is increasing labor productivity. If productivity were to grow at approximately the same annual rate posted between 1995 and 2012, economic output per hour per worker will be 40.8 percent higher in 2035 than in 2012. That cumulative increase would be almost five times greater than the estimated decline in productivity attributable to population aging. Put differently, rising productivity should allow fewer workers to support a larger number of dependent persons. That is hardly wishful thinking. On the contrary, it is exactly what happened in the United States between 1950 and 2000, a period marked by real increases in living standards despite a tripling in the size of the older population.

Sources: Elizabeth Arias, "United States Life Tables, 2008," *National Vital Statistics Report,* September 24, 2012, 52, http://www.cdc.gov/nchs/data/nvsr/nvsr61/nvsr61_03.pdf; Dean Baker, *Debt, Deficits, and Demographics: Why We Can Afford the Social Contract* (Washington, DC: New America Foundation, 2012), 2, http://nsc.newamerica.net/sites/newamerica.net/files/policydocs/Baker_Dean_DebtDeficitsDemographics_November2012.pdf; John Quinterno, "The Demographics of Aging in North Carolina," *North Carolina Insight,* June 2009, 11; and Grayson Vincent and Victoria Velkoff, *The Next Four Decades: The Older Population in the United States: 2010–2050* (Washington, DC: U.S. Census Bureau, 2010), http://www.census.gov/prod/2010pubs/p25-1138.pdf.

population. In the Seattle MSA, the *old-age dependency ratio* in 2011 equaled 15.8; in sum, there were 15.8 people ages 65 and older for every 100 working-age adults (ages 15 and 64). Similarly, the *total dependency ratio*, which compares the total number of adults ages 65 and older and children under age 15 to the total number of people ages 15 to 64 was 42.6 in 2011; in short, there were almost 43 children and older adults for every 100 working-age adults.[82] While dependency ratios feature prominently in social policy debates like those surrounding the long-term future of Social Security, it is important to recognize that "demography is not destiny."[83] Demographic projections are merely that, and a society's ability to adapt to demographic change hinges largely on nondemographic factors such as economic growth (see Box 5.5).

Race and Ethnicity

The demographic concepts of race and ethnicity are regular sources of confusion. Many of the misunderstandings originate in the fact that these concepts are flexible social constructs rather than immutable scientific facts.

The history of the decennial census mirrors American society's shifting understanding of race. The same constitutional provision that mandates the census requires, albeit in a roundabout way, specific counts of what today would be labeled the White, African-American, and American Indian populations.[84] The first question pertaining to individuals with ties to an Asian country, China, appeared in the 1870 Census. Over the years, the census questionnaires added and removed other racial categories. Interestingly, prior to the 1960 Census, it was the responsibility of census enumerators to assign a racial classification to individuals.[85]

Today, the Census Bureau defines *race* in a manner consistent with "a social definition of race recognized in this country and not an attempt to define race biologically, anthropologically, or genetically."[86] The ACS asks for the self-reporting of racial information for individuals living in households or group quarters. Respondents may choose from six broad categories: White, Black or African American, American Indian or Alaskan Native, Asian, Native Hawaiian or Other Pacific Islander, and Some Other Race. For some racial categories, like Asian, there exist subcategories like Vietnamese or Filipino. Respondents also may select multiple races, with the ACS containing 57 possible racial combinations.[87] Relatively few people, however, report multiple races, and in 2011, just 2.8 percent of Americans identified as multiracial, though the number of such persons is rising, particularly among the child population.[88]

The ACS inquires into the *ethnicity* of individual persons. For the Census Bureau's purposes, ethnicity differs from race. A person therefore belongs to a racial group(s) and an ethnic group. The basic ethnic division is between persons of Hispanic or Latino origin and persons of non-Hispanic or non-Latino origin. *Hispanic* or *Latino* ethnicity applies to persons who trace their origin or descent to Mexico, Puerto Rico, Cuba, the Dominican Republic, the Spanish-speaking Central and South American countries, and other Spanish cultures; everyone else is *non-Hispanic/non-Latino*.[89] The question of how best to define and measure Hispanic ethnicity has vexed the census agency since the 1850 Census, which was the first enumeration to occur following the granting of statehood to Texas and

Table 5.1 Racial and Ethnic Composition of the Population of the Seattle-Tacoma-Bellevue, WA MSA, Ranked by Share of Total Population, 2011

Category	Number	Share
White, Non-Hispanic	2,364,952	67.6%
Asian	403,958	11.5%
Hispanic	323,177	9.2%
Black or African American	186,145	5.3%
Multiracial	160,364	4.6%
Native Hawaiian and Other Pacific Islander	28,437	0.8%
American Indian and Alaskan Native	27,871	0.8%
Some Other Race	5,122	0.1%
Total	3,500,026	100.0%

Source: Author's analysis of U.S. Census Bureau, American Community Survey, One-Year Estimates, 2011.

the acquisition of extensive amounts of Mexican territory as a consequence of the War of 1848; the current census definition of Hispanic ethnicity, however, dates only from the 1980 Census.[90]

The difference between ethnicity and race is a source of misunderstanding since many Americans think of Hispanics as forming a racial group even though Hispanics may be of any race. Countries like Cuba have sizable numbers of people who speak Spanish as a first language and are descended from Africans originally brought to the island as slaves. An Afro-Cuban resident of Florida therefore would be ethnically Hispanic and racially Black. Due to the overlap between Hispanic origin and race, tabulations showing Hispanic data alongside racial data should filter the data by non-Hispanic ethnicity (e.g., non-Hispanic White) to avoid counting persons twice.

Table 5.1 presents race and ethnic data for the Seattle MSA in 2011. That year, 67.6 percent of the region's 3.5 million residents classified themselves as Non-Hispanic Whites, 11.5 percent as Asians, 9.2 percent as Hispanics, and 5.3 percent as African Americans. Another 4.6 percent of area residents identified as multiracial. The remaining 1.7 percent of the population consisted of people who were Native Hawaiian and Other Pacific Islander, American Indian and Alaskan Native, and Some Other Race. Of the 323,177 persons who identified as Hispanic, 74.5 percent were of Mexican origin.[91]

To complicate the situation, the Census Bureau also tracks ancestry, which is distinct from race and ethnicity. The basic ancestry question came into being in 1980 as a replacement for an older question about the birthplace of a person's parents.[92] The ACS asks for self-reported, open-ended ancestry information for all persons living in the household and group quarters populations. Sample responses include "Arab," "Ethiopian," "French Canadian," and "German." Ancestry counts are independent from those pertaining to race and ethnicity.[93]

Place of Birth and Citizenship

While the United States is a country of immigrants, demographers have struggled with how to measure immigration, and today two concepts are used: place of birth and citizenship status.

The ACS inquires about the *place of birth* of all individuals living in households or group quarters. The questionnaire asks respondents to indicate whether each person was born inside or outside of the United States and to list the state or country of birth. A second question asks if the reference person is a citizen of the United States, and, if so, how the person acquired citizenship, by birth or through naturalization. For naturalized citizens, the ACS questionnaire asks for the year of naturalization.[94]

With that combination of information, it is possible to sort respondents by nativity. The *native-born population* comprises persons who obtained citizenship at birth. The native-born population further divides into four groups: individuals living in the state where they were born; individuals living in states other than the one of birth; individuals born in Puerto Rico or an island area like Guam, American Samoa, the Northern Mariana Islands, and the U.S. Virgin Islands; and individuals born abroad to a citizen parent. The *foreign-born population* encompasses everyone who was not a citizen at birth, including those who later acquired citizenship through the process of naturalization.[95]

The ACS further classifies people as *citizens* or *noncitizens*. Citizens are anyone who has acquired citizenship through birth or naturalization, and all other persons are noncitizens. Note that the ACS does not ask about immigration status, thereby rendering it impossible to use ACS data to differentiate individuals legally present in the country from those who are not.[96]

In 2011, the Seattle MSA had a sizable foreign-born population, with 16.9 percent of the region's residents having been born abroad. Of those 592,526 persons, 49.5 percent had been born in Asia, 24.6 percent in the Americas, 17 percent in Europe, 7.3 percent in Africa, and 1.6 percent in Oceania. In terms of citizenship status, 50.6 percent of Seattle's foreign-born residents were noncitizens, and the remaining 49.4 percent had naturalized at some point. Meanwhile, 55.2 percent of Seattle's 2.9 million native-born residents had been born in the State of Washington.[97]

Language

Linguistic ability—the ability to speak English—is an important demographic variable associated with immigration. The ACS measures language ability through a set of questions that pertains to every household member age five and older. The questionnaire first asks respondents to indicate whether each person in the household age five and older speaks a language other than English at home. If the answer is "yes," the questionnaire prompts the respondent to name that language and to indicate how well the person in question speaks English.[98]

When the Census Bureau tabulates ACS responses, it categorizes households according to the presence of persons who speak languages other than English at home. A *non-English speaking household* is one in which any person primarily speaks a language other than English at home. This causes confusion in situations in which household members vary in their linguistic preferences and abilities, as when a householder primarily speaks Korean but the children regularly speak English. The Census Bureau also tabulates the number of households that are *linguistically isolated,* meaning that no member of the household age 14 and older speaks English without at least some difficulty.[99]

Given the sizable number of foreign-born individuals living in 2011 in Seattle, the region had a diverse linguistic mix. According to the ACS, 723,104 local residents age five and older (22.1 percent) reported speaking a language other than English at home. Of those, 41.3 percent said they spoke an Asian or Pacific Island language at home, while 28.8 percent reported primarily speaking Spanish or a Spanish creole at home. At the same time, 78.9 percent of the individuals who primarily spoke a foreign language at home reported speaking English "well" or "very well." The ACS further estimated that 5.1 percent of area households were linguistically isolated. Isolation was higher among households that spoke an Asian or Pacific Island language at home (26.4 percent) than among those that spoke Spanish (20.3 percent).[100]

Education

Education data are of great interest to regional leaders for numerous reasons, including the dominant role that public institutions play in providing education. With an awareness of school enrollment trends, for example, public leaders can ensure that enough seats are available at local community colleges. Moreover, education data matter because the federal government allocates much of its educational funding to local communities based on Census Bureau findings.

The ACS tracks two main educational variables: educational attainment and school enrollment. *Educational attainment* measures the highest degree completed or highest level of formal schooling completed by every adult person in a household. The Census Bureau reports educational attainment data for individuals 18 years of age and older. Many analysts, however, focus on data pertaining to individuals age 25 and older, as most individuals traditionally have completed all of their formal schooling by then.[101] That is changing, however. In the fall of 2010 some 27.4 percent of all American college students were 30 years of age or older, up from 15.1 percent in the fall of 1970.[102]

Census Bureau tabulations of educational attainment divide the population into six categories: individuals without a high school diploma, individuals with a high school diploma or equivalent, individuals with some college but no degree, individuals with an associate's degree, individuals with a bachelor's degree, and individuals with a graduate or professional degree. Remember, these data show the highest level of education completed by an individual, not all the credentials a person may have earned. Someone with a graduate degree, for example, would have earned a bachelor's degree, a high school degree, and, possibly, an associate's degree.

Compared to the United States as a whole, the Seattle MSA has a well-educated population. In 2011, some 46.5 percent of Seattle residents age 25 and older had earned at least an associate's degree, compared to a national figure of 36.3 percent (see Figure 5.3). Moreover, while 10.6 percent of all Americans possessed a graduate or professional degree, 13.6 percent of Seattle residents in 2011 possessed such advanced credentials.[103]

Figure 5.3 Educational Attainment of Persons Ages 25 and Older, Seattle-Tacoma-Bellevue, WA MSA, 2011

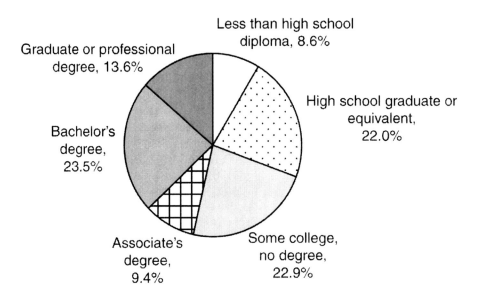

Source: U.S. Census Bureau, American Community Survey, One-Year Estimates, 2011.

On a related note, the ACS began in 2009 to ask people with at least a bachelor's degree to state the field in which they earned their first degree. In 2011, approximately 42.2 percent of Seattle residents with at least a bachelor's degree had studied a field in science or engineering (including social sciences) as a first subject, 7.7 percent a field related to science and engineering, 17.1 percent a field associated with business, 8.6 percent a field tied to education, 20.1 percent a field in the arts and humanities, and 4.3 percent some other field.[104]

Given the importance of educational attainment, it is frequently cross-tabulated with other social and economic variables. Perhaps the most common cross-tabulation is one showing income by educational attainment. As Figure 5.4 shows, the typical Seattle resident age 25 and older with a bachelor's degree in 2011 had an annual income that was 2.5 times greater than that of the typical person who had not completed high school and 1.8 times greater than that of the typical high school graduate. A person with a graduate degree typically earned 1.3 times more than an individual with a bachelor's degree. Similarly, just 3.9 percent of Seattle residents with a bachelor's degree or higher fell below the poverty level in 2011 versus 28.7 percent of those without a high school diploma.[105]

School enrollment is the second major educational variable tracked in the ACS. For each person age 3 and older in the household, the survey inquires whether the individual has attended school or college within the past 3 months and, if applicable, the grade or instructional level attended and the nature of the school (public or private).[106]

Figure 5.4 Median Annual Earnings Relative to Holders of a High School Degree or Equivalent, Persons Ages 25 and Older with Earnings, Seattle-Tacoma-Bellevue, WA MSA, 2011

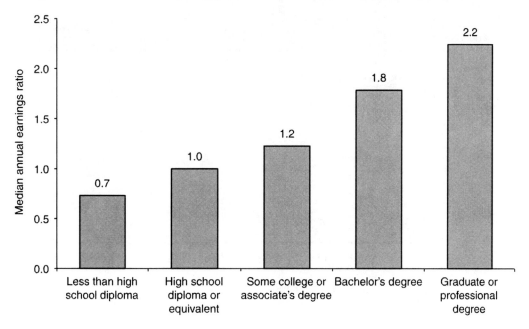

Source: U.S. Census Bureau, American Community Survey, One-Year Estimates, 2011.

Because school attendance is compulsory for children, school enrollment is nearly universal for individuals between the ages of 5 and 17. After that age, enrollment falls steadily, as illustrated in Seattle, where the school enrollment rate of adults age 35 and older equaled 3.4 percent in 2011, compared to an enrollment rate of 98.6 percent for children between the ages of 10 and 14.[107]

Disability

A final important demographic variable tracked in the ACS is disability status. Medical practice defines a *disability* as a situation in which an interaction between personal health and environmental factors result "in limitations of activities and restrictions to full participation at school, at work, at home, or in the community."[108] Unfortunately, practical limitations prevent the Census Bureau from assessing disability in such a holistic manner, so the ACS measures disability more narrowly by asking if persons have difficulties in performing specific functions.

To provide civic leaders with the information needed to serve individuals with disabilities, the ACS inquires as to whether each member of a household has a hearing difficulty, a vision difficulty, an ambulatory impairment, or a cognitive limitation. The ACS further asks if these conditions limit the person's ability to perform independently activities like bathing, dressing, or completing simple errands.[109]

Figure 5.5 Share of Population with a Disability by Age, Seattle-Tacoma-Bellevue, WA MSA, 2011

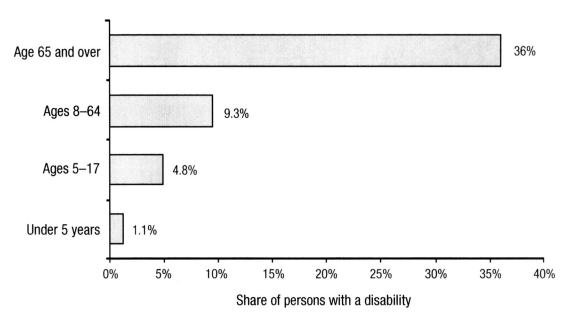

Source: U.S. Census Bureau, American Community Survey, One-Year Estimates, 2011.

In 2011, an estimated 11 percent of Seattle residents reported a disability of some sort with the share of the population with a disability increasing with age (see Figure 5.5). Among individuals between the ages of 5 and 17, some 4.8 percent had a disability, as opposed to 36 percent of individuals age 65 and older. Among younger individuals, cognitive difficulties were the most common, while older individuals were more likely to struggle with ambulatory difficulties. Similarly, only 0.7 percent of Seattle residents between the ages of 5 and 17 had a hearing difficulty, compared to 14.7 percent of individuals age 65 and older.[110]

DEMOGRAPHICS: A SUMMARY

Demographic data are the cornerstones of almost every regional economic and social analysis. When community leaders are unfamiliar with essential demographic concepts, they are more likely to misinterpret trends, overlook regional problems, or pursue ineffective solutions.

To help regional leaders profit from demographic information, this chapter differentiated demographics from demography, introduced key sources of demographic information, and explained four essential demographic concepts: population size, population change, population distribution, and population composition or characteristics. Consistent with this book's practical approach, attention focused on demographic data compiled by public statistical agencies. Besides being official, credible, frequent estimates of demographic subjects, public data are widely cited and freely available. One essential resource is the American Community Survey, a relatively new Census Bureau product that quickly has become indispensable to regional analysis.

Possessed of a basic understanding of a region's demographic profile, it is possible to analyze how regional residents interact economically with each other through institutions like businesses and the labor market, the subjects to which the next two chapters turn.

Notes

1. John Mitchell, "Change of Heartland: The Great Plains," *National Geographic,* May 2004, http://ngm.nationalgeographic.com/ngm/0405/feature1/fulltext.html; and Steven Wilson, *Population Dynamics of the Great Plains: 1950–2007* (Washington, DC: U.S. Census Bureau, 2009), http://www.census.gov/prod/2009pubs/p25-1137.pdf.

2. Quoted in Robert Skidelsky, *Keynes: The Return of the Master* (New York: Public Affairs, 2009), 55.

3. U.S. Census Bureau, "Annual Estimates of the Population of Metropolitan and Micropolitan Statistical Areas: April 1, 2010 to July 1, 2011 (CBSA-EST2011-01)," last revised April 2012, http://www.census.gov/popest/data/metro/totals/2011/tables/CBSA-EST2011-01.xls.

4. Steve Murdock et al., *Demographics: A Guide to Methods and Data Sources for Media, Business, and Government* (Boulder, CO: Paradigm Publishers, 2006), 1.

5. David Yaukey, *Demography: The Study of Human Population* (New York: St. Martin's Press, 1985), 2.

6. Yaukey, *Demography,* 10.

7. Murdock, *Demographics,* 4.

8. Ibid., 11.

9. U.S. Census Bureau, "Mission Statement," http://www.census.gov/aboutus/# (accessed September 2, 2011).

10. Ed O'Keefe, "2010 Census Was $1.6 Billion Under Budget," Federal Eye (blog), August 11, 2010, http://voices.washingtonpost.com/federal-eye/2010/08/2010_census_was_16_billion_und.html.

11. U.S. Census Bureau, "Population Estimates: Geographic Terms and Definitions," http://www.census.gov/popest/about/geo/terms.html (accessed January 2, 2013).

12. Use of Most Recent Population Data, 13 U.S.C. § 183 (2011), http://www.gpo.gov/fdsys/pkg/U.S.CODE-2011-title13/pdf/U.S.CODE-2011-title13-chap5-subchapIV-sec183.pdf.

13. As of January 2, 2013, the most recent population estimates prepared by the Census Bureau were available at http://www.census.gov/popest/data/index.html, and historical estimates were available at http://www.census.gov/popest/data/historical/index.html.

14. U.S. Census Bureau, "Current Estimates Data," last revised December 20, 2012, http://www.census.gov/popest/data/index.html.

15. Alan Peters and Heather MacDonald, *Unlocking the Census with GIS* (Redlands, CA: Esri Press, 2004), 110.

16. Author's analysis of U.S. Census Bureau, Population Estimates Program, 2011.

17. Murdock, *Demographics,* 151–152.

18. U.S. Census Bureau, "About Population Projections," http://www.census.gov/population/projections/about/ (accessed January 2, 2013).

19. As of January 2, 2013, the Census Bureau's national population projections dating back to 1996 were available at http://www.census.gov/population/projections/data/national/.

20. U.S. Census Bureau, "State Population Projections," http://www.census.gov/population/projections/data/state/ (accessed January 3, 2013). This website also archives state-level population projections prepared by the U.S. Census Bureau in 1996 and 2005.

21. U.S. Census Bureau, *American Community Survey: Design and Methodology* (Washington, DC: U.S. Department of Commerce, 2006), 2-1–2-6, http://www.census.gov/history/pdf/ACSHistory.pdf.

22. Heather MacDonald and Alan Peters, *Urban Policy and the Census* (Redlands, CA: Esri Press, 2011), 6.

23. U.S. Census Bureau, "American Community Survey: When to Use 1-Year, 3-Year, or 5-Year Estimates," http://www.census.gov/acs/www/guidance_for_data_users/estimates/ (accessed January 2, 2013).

24. U.S. Census Bureau, American Community Survey: Design and Methodology, 6-1–6-3; and U.S. Census Bureau, "Residence Rules and Residence Situations for the 2010 Census," http://www.census.gov/population/www/cen2010/resid_rules/resid_rules.html (accessed January 2, 2013).

25. Andrew Reamer, *Surveying for Dollars: The Role of the American Community Survey in the Geographic Distribution of Federal Funds* (Washington, DC: Brooking Institution Press, 2010), 1, http://www.brookings.edu/~/media/Files/rc/reports/2010/0726_acs_reamer/0726_acs_reamer.pdf.

26. Reamer, *Surveying for Dollars,* 5 and 8–9.

27. National Research Council, *Using the American Community Survey: Benefits and Challenges* (Washington, DC: National Academies Press, 2007), 61–66.

28. Pat Doyle, "Federal Household Surveys," in *Encyclopedia of the U.S. Census,* ed. Margo Anderson (Washington, DC: CQ Press, 2000), 220–222.

29. U.S. Census Bureau, "Current Population Survey: Methodology," http://www.census.gov/cps/methodology/ (accessed January 2, 2013).

30. U.S. Census Bureau, "Current Population Survey: Supplemental Surveys," http://www.census.gov/cps/about/supplemental.html (accessed January 2, 2013).

31. U.S. Census Bureau, "Current Population Survey: Frequently Asked Questions," http://www.census.gov/cps/about/faq.html (accessed January 2, 2013).

32. As of January 2, 2013, a listing of state Labor Market Information Agencies was available at http://www.bls.gov/bls/ofolist.htm.

33. U.S. Census Bureau, "State Data Centers: Program Overview," http://www.census.gov/sdc/index.html (accessed January 2, 2013).

34. As of January 2, 2012, a listing of State Data Centers was available at http://www.census.gov/sdc/network.html.

35. U.S. Census Bureau, "Federal-State Cooperative for Population Estimates: Overview," http://www.census.gov/popest/fscpe/overview.html (accessed January 2, 2013). As of January 2, 2013, a listing of state partners was available at http://www.census.gov/popest/fscpe/contacts.html.

36. Arthur Haupt and Thomas Kane, *Population Handbook,* 5th ed. (Washington, DC: Population Reference Bureau, 2004), 2.

37. Author's analysis of U.S. Census Bureau, American Community Survey, One-Year Estimates, 2011.

38. U.S. Census Bureau, "American Community Survey and Puerto Rico Community Survey 2011 Subject Definitions," 72, https://www.census.gov/acs/www/Downloads/data_documentation/Subject-Definitions/2011_ACSSubjectDefinitions.pdf.

39. U.S. Census Bureau, "American Community Survey 2011 Subject Definitions," 8.

40. Ibid., 74.

41. Ibid., 73–76.

42. Ibid., 75.

43. Ibid., 76.

44. Ibid., 76.

45. Author's analysis of U.S. Census Bureau, "Table HH-4: Households by Size: 1960 to Present," http://www.census.gov/hhes/families/files/hh4.xls (accessed January 2, 2013); and U.S. Census Bureau, "Table A-2: Family Status and Household Relationship of People 15 Years and Over, by Marital Status, Age, and Sex, 2012," in *America's Families and Living Arrangements: 2012,* http://www.census.gov/hhes/families/files/cps2012/tabA2-all.xls (accessed January 2, 2013).

46. Sabrina Tavernise, "Married Couples Are No Longer a Majority, Census Finds," *New York Times,* May 26, 2011, http://www.nytimes.com/2011/05/26/us/26marry.html.

47. Author's analysis of U.S. Census Bureau, *American Community Survey,* One-Year Estimates, 2011.

48. Haupt and Kane, *Population Handbook,* 56.

49. Murdock, *Demographics*, 15.

50. Joseph McFalls, *Population: A Lively Introduction,* 5th ed. (Washington, DC: Population Reference Bureau, 2007), 15, http://www.prb.org/pdf07/62.1LivelyIntroduction.pdf.

51. Ibid., 4.

52. Ibid., 6.

53. Haupt and Kane, *Population Handbook,* 25.

54. Elizabeth Arias, "United States Life Tables, 2008," *National Vital Statistics Report,* September 24, 2012, 52, http://www.cdc.gov/nchs/data/nvsr/nvsr61/nvsr61_03.pdf; and Laura Shrestha, *Life Expectancy in the United States* (Washington, DC: Congressional Research Service, 2006), 3–4, http://aging.senate.gov/crs/aging1.pdf.

55. McFalls, *Population*, 19.

56. Ibid., 6–7.

57. Census Department, *Population Census 2011: Preliminary Data* (Budapest: Hungarian Central Statistical Office, 2012), 19, http://www.ksh.hu/docs/eng/xftp/idoszaki/nepsz2011/enepszelo2011.pdf.

58. Haupt and Kane, *Population Handbook,* 35.

59. U.S. Census Bureau, "American Community Survey 2011 Subject Definitions," 112.

60. Author's analysis of U.S. Census Bureau, American Community Survey, One-Year Estimates, 2011.

61. McFalls, *Population*, 12.

62. Ibid.

63. Ibid., 13–15.

64. Author's analysis U.S. Census Bureau, American Community Survey, One-Year Estimates, 2011.

65. Mary Edwards, *Regional and Urban Economics and Economic Development: Theory and Methods* (Boca Raton, FL: Auerbach Publications, 2007), 297.

66. Edwards, *Regional and Urban Economics,* 298.

67. Jason Jurjevich and Greg Schrock, *Is Portland Really the Place Where Young People Go to Retire? Migration Patterns of Portland's Young and College-Educated, 1980–2010* (Portland, OR: Portland State University, 2012), 1–2, http://mkn.research.pdx.edu/wp-content/uploads/2012/09/JurjevichSchrockMigrationReport1.pdf; and Greg Schrock and Jason Jurjevich, *Is Portland Really the Place Where Young People Go to Retire? Analyzing Labor Market Outcomes for Portland's Young and College-Educated* (Portland, OR: Portland State University, 2012), i–ii, http://mkn.research.pdx.edu/wp-content/uploads/2012/09/SchrockJurjevich_YCELaborMarket_Full1.pdf.

68. Edwards, *Regional and Urban Economics,* 304.

69. Ibid., 305–306.

70. Judith Gans, *Illegal Immigration to the United States: Causes and Policy Solutions* (Tucson, AZ: Udall Center for Studies in Public Policy, 2007), 2–3, http://udallcenter.arizona.edu/immigration/publications/fact_sheet_no_3_illegal_immigration.pdf.

71. Haupt and Kane, *Population Handbook,* 61.

72. McFalls, *Population*, 24.

73. U.S. Census Bureau, "Table B-1: Metropolitan Areas: Area and Population," in *State and Metropolitan Area Data Book: 2010,* 7th ed. (Washington, DC: U.S. Department of Commerce, 2010), http://www.census.gov/prod/2010pubs/10smadb/btables.pdf.

74. Author's analysis of U.S. Census Bureau, American Community Survey, One-Year Estimates, 2008; and U.S. Census Bureau, "Table B-1: Counties Area and Population," in *County and City Data Book: 2007,* 14th ed. (Washington, DC: U.S. Department of Commerce, 2007), http://www.census.gov/statab/ccdb/cc07_tabB1.pdf.

75. U.S. Census Bureau, "Table B-1: Metropolitan Areas: Area and Population."

76. David Streitfeld, "An Effort to Save Flint, Mich., by Shrinking It," *New York Times,* April 22, 2009, http://www.nytimes.com/2009/04/22/business/22flint.html.

77. Haupt and Kane, *Population Handbook,* 62.

78. U.S. Census Bureau, "American Community Survey 2011 Subject Definitions," 45.

79. Haupt and Kane, *Population Handbook,* 59.

80. Author's analysis of U.S. Census Bureau, *American Community Survey,* One-Year Estimates, 2011.

81. Haupt and Kane, *Population Handbook,* 61.

82. Author's analysis of U.S. Census Bureau, American Community Survey, One-Year Estimates, 2011.

83. Robert Friedland and Laura Summer, *Demography Is Not Destiny* (Washington, DC: National Academy on an Aging Society, 1999), 1, http://www.agingsociety.org/agingsociety/pdf/destiny1.pdf.

84. U.S. Const. art. I, § 2.

85. Claudette Bennett, "Race: Questions and Classifications," in *Encyclopedia of the U.S. Census,* 313–314.

86. U.S. Census Bureau, "American Community Survey 2011 Subject Definitions," 104.

87. Ibid., 105–109.

88. Author's analysis of U.S. Census Bureau, American Community Survey, One-Year Estimates, 2011; and Susan Saulny, "Census Data Presents Rise in Multiracial Population of Youths," *New York Times,* March 24, 2011, http://www.nytimes.com/2011/03/25/us/25race.html.

89. U.S. Census Bureau, "American Community Survey 2011 Subject Definitions," 70.

90. Jorge Chapa, "Hispanic/Latino Ethnicity and Identifiers," in *Encyclopedia of the U.S. Census,* 243–245.

91. Author's analysis of U.S. Census Bureau, American Community Survey, One-Year Estimates, 2011.

92. Margo Anderson, *The American Census: A Social History* (New Haven, CT: Yale University Press, 1988), 226–227.

93. U.S. Census Bureau, "American Community Survey 2011 Subject Definitions," 47–50.

94. Ibid., 51–53 and 99–100.

95. Ibid., 100.

96. Ibid., 52.

97. Author's analysis of U.S. Census Bureau, American Community Survey, One-Year Estimates, 2011.

98. U.S. Census Bureau, "American Community Survey 2011 Subject Definitions," 92–93.

99. Peters and MacDonald Peters, *Unlocking the Census,* 99–100.

100. Author's analysis of U.S. Census Bureau, American Community Survey, One-Year Estimates, 2011.

101. U.S. Census Bureau, "American Community Survey 2011 Subject Definitions," 58.

102. National Center for Educational Statistics, "Table 200. Total Fall Enrollment in Degree-granting Institutions, by Sex, Age, and Attendance Status, Selected Years, 1970 through 2020," in Thomas Snyder and Sally Dillow, *Digest of Education Statistics: 2011* (Washington, DC: U.S. Department of Education, 2012), http://nces.ed.gov/programs/digest/d10/tables/dt10_199.asp.

103. Author's analysis of U.S. Census Bureau, American Community Survey, One-Year Estimates, 2011.

104. Ibid.

105. Ibid.

106. U.S. Census Bureau, "American Community Survey 2011 Subject Definitions," 114–116.

107. Author's analysis of U.S. Census Bureau, American Community Survey, One-Year Estimates, 2011.

108. U.S. Census Bureau, "American Community Survey 2011 Subject Definitions," 55.

109. Ibid., 56–58.

110. Author's analysis of U.S. Census Bureau, American Community Survey, One-Year Estimates, 2011.

6 | Business Structure

Every inhabitant of a region possesses a mix of needs and desires, skills and talents, likes and dislikes, advantages and handicaps. Because no one is truly self-sufficient, the most practical way for individuals to satisfy their needs and wants while putting their talents to optimal use is by joining together in institutions.

The "arrangements that govern collective undertakings," institutions are the structures though which people interact.[1] Families, communities, churches, governments, markets, households, and firms—all these institutions structure human dealings to help people improve their economic and social well-being. Institutions range in size and complexity from international corporations to families, but regardless of type, every institution revolves around a combination of trust, rules, culture, and authority. In short, institutions shape the ways in which the individuals united in a common undertaking deal with each other and with persons external to the institution.

Institutions are indispensable to economic life. One theory of economic history, in fact, argues that the emergence of inclusive political and economic institutions is what has enabled wealthy nations to prosper.[2] Markets are perhaps the best-known economic institutions, although they actually encompass two smaller institutions: households and firms. A household is "a unit of housekeeping or consumption," while a firm is an entity "whose sole purpose is to produce goods and services for the market."[3] As described in chapter 2, regional economies originate from the dealings of households and firms in multiple markets. A household may provide labor to a firm in exchange for wages; the firm then may sell the products to other businesses while the household uses its wages to purchase assorted goods and services.

Chapter 5 introduced the institution of the household, and this chapter considers the institution of a business. To facilitate the analysis of a region's business structure, the chapter explores essential questions related to businesses and the associated concepts, as well as sources of regional business data, most of which are derived from the U.S. Census Bureau's quinquennial

Map 6.1 Principal Cities and Component Counties of Milwaukee-Waukesha-West Allis, WI MSA, 2009 Delineation

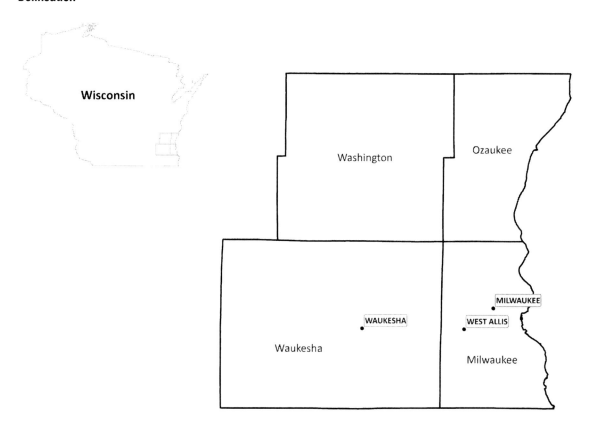

Source: U.S. Office of Management and Budget, "Update of Statistical Area Definitions and Guidance on Their Uses (OMB Bulletin No. 10-02)," December 1, 2009, http://www.whitehouse.gov/sites/default/files/omb/assets/bulletins/b10-02.pdf. Map prepared by William High.

Economic Census. The usefulness of the concepts and data sources is demonstrated in a description of the business structure of the Milwaukee-Waukesha-West Allis, WI Metropolitan Statistical Area (MSA), a four-county region with 1.6 million residents in 2011 (see Map 6.1).[4]

TAKING CARE OF BUSINESS: QUESTIONS AND CONCEPTS

Despite the importance of the institution of the firm in regional economies, it is poorly understood by policy makers and members of the general public who often invoke terms like "firm," "enterprise," "industry," and "small business" without regard for their actual meanings.

Consider the oft-cited research finding of the U.S. Small Business Administration (SBA) that small businesses accounted for almost two-thirds of all the net new jobs created between 1993 and 2008.[5] This sounds impressive until one realizes that the SBA defines a small business as one with 500 or fewer employees: a definition that covered 99.7 percent of all American firms with employees in 2010.[6] Few people other than researchers would consider a firm with a few hundred employees as "small." And what about the 22.1 million businesses without employees?[7] They are indeed small, yet they normally are excluded from small business statistics.

A failure to define business terms like "small business" leads to ill-informed public debates and ineffective or wasteful public policies. Take an economic development strategy aimed at promoting small business growth through the provision of tax subsidies to firms. If the subsidies overwhelmingly benefit firms with a few hundred employees, are they really benefiting small businesses? Perhaps, if that was consistent with what regional leaders understood a small business to be. But if not, taxpayer resources would be flowing to the wrong kinds of firms. One way to concentrate thinking about business issues is to reflect on four core questions: what a business is, how big a business is, what a business does, and how a business does what it does. Answering each question requires familiarity with a related set of concepts.

What Is a Business? Establishments, Enterprises, and Firms

The first issue encountered when discussing businesses is defining just what a "business" is. Most economic statistics fail to answer the question directly and instead shift fluidly among the three related concepts of establishments, enterprises, and firms.

An establishment is the basic analytical unit featured in most data sets compiled by public statistical agencies. An *establishment* is "a single physical location where business is conducted, or where services are performed."[8] An *enterprise*, meanwhile, spans "all of the establishments under common ownership or organizational structure, regardless of where they are located."[9] Finally, a *firm* (sometimes called a company) is "a business organization or entity consisting of one or more domestic establishments in the same state and industry that were specified under common ownership or control."[10] Think of an establishment as a distinct place of business, an enterprise as a grouping of all jointly owned establishments, and a firm as a regional or industry-specific manifestation of an enterprise. Furthermore, while the number of establishments will sum to the number of enterprises, the number of firms will exceed the number of enterprises.

Imagine a pizzeria with a single owner who controls no other restaurants. That pizzeria would be an establishment, a firm, and an enterprise. If the owner controlled seven other pizzerias, all in the same state, each pizzeria would be a separate establishment, but the eight stores collectively would form one enterprise and one firm. If the eight pizzerias were located in two states, there would be eight establishments, two firms (one in each state), and one enterprise. The difference between firms and enterprises matters primarily when dealing with larger businesses active in multiple states and industries.

Table 6.1 Nonfarm Employer Statistics: Firms, Establishments, and Employment, by Size of Firm, 2010

A. Data by Detailed Firm Size Class

Employment size of firm	Number of firms	Number of establishments	Ratio of establishments to firms	Total employment	Share of total employment (%)
Total	5,734,538	7,396,628	1.29	111,970,095	100.00
0–4†	3,575,240	3,582,826	1.00	5,926,452	5.29
5–9	968,075	982,019	1.01	6,358,931	5.68
10–14	407,404	425,641	1.04	4,767,288	4.26
15–19	209,685	227,021	1.08	3,521,097	3.14
20–24	120,787	137,465	1.14	2,635,563	2.35
25–29	80,526	95,098	1.18	2,161,156	1.93
30–34	58,557	72,882	1.24	1,865,736	1.67
35–39	42,860	56,323	1.31	1,580,717	1.41
40–44	33,697	46,334	1.38	1,410,309	1.26
45–49	26,529	38,467	1.45	1,242,981	1.11
50–74	76,223	125,214	1.64	4,582,829	4.09
75–99	35,946	76,603	2.13	3,075,081	2.75
100–149	35,590	97,513	2.74	4,312,353	3.85
150–199	18,195	66,780	3.67	3,139,298	2.80
200–299	16,184	87,806	5.43	3,914,153	3.50
300–399	7,449	56,843	7.63	2,567,426	2.29
400–499	4,355	45,371	10.42	1,935,310	1.73
500–749	5,681	75,291	13.25	3,452,042	3.08
750–999	2,808	50,248	17.89	2,420,696	2.16
1,000–1,499	2,801	64,098	22.88	3,410,858	3.05
1,500–1,999	1,489	46,947	31.53	2,577,221	2.30
2,000–2,499	872	39,603	45.42	1,947,272	1.74
2,500–4,999	1,761	124,386	70.63	6,165,819	5.51
5,000+	1,824	775,849	425.36	36,999,507	33.04

B. Cumulative Data

Employment size of firm	Cumulative number of firms	Cumulative share of all firms (%)	Cumulative number of establishments	Cumulative employment total	Cumulative share total employment (%)
<10	4,543,315	79.23	4,564,845	12,285,383	10.97
<25	5,281,191	92.09	5,354,972	23,209,331	20.73
<50	5,523,360	96.32	5,664,076	31,470,230	28.11
<75	5,599,583	97.65	5,789,290	36,053,059	32.20
<100	5,635,529	98.27	5,865,893	39,128,140	34.95
<500	5,717,302	99.70	6,220,206	54,996,680	49.12
<1,000	5,725,791	99.85	6,345,745	60,869,418	54.36
<5,000	5,732,714	99.97	6,620,779	74,970,588	66.96
All sizes	5,734,538	100.00	7,396,628	111,970,095	100.00

Source: Author's analysis of U.S. Small Business Administration, "Employer Firms, Establishments, Employment, and Annual Payroll Small Firm Size Classes, 2010," http://www.sba.gov/advocacy/849/12162 (accessed February 15, 2013).

†Because employment is measured in March, new, closing, and seasonal firms will report no employment and some payroll.

Figure 6.1 Businesses by Legal Form of Organization, 2008

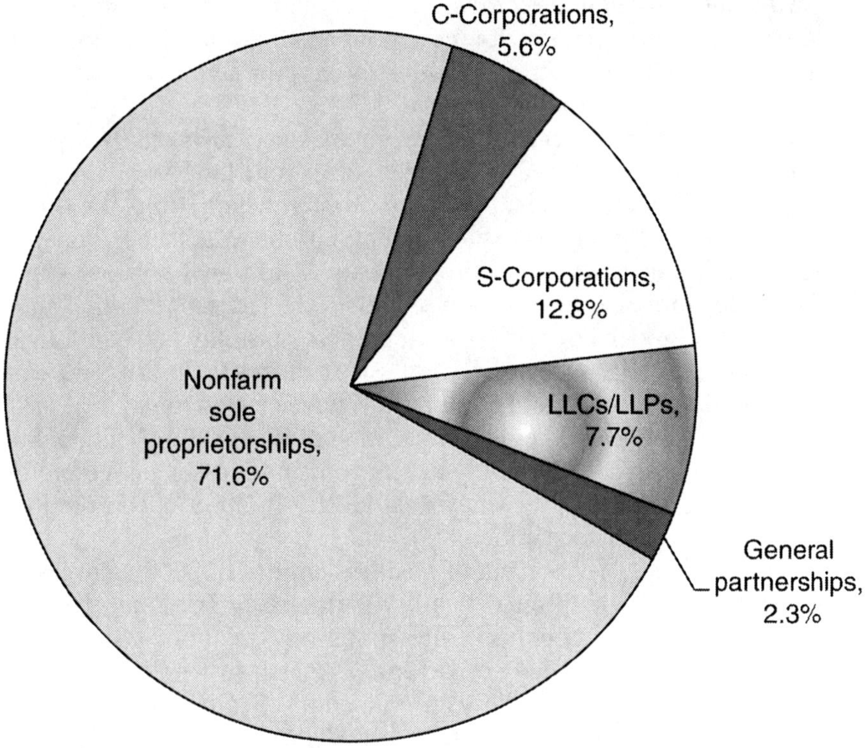

C-Corporations, 5.6%
S-Corporations, 12.8%
LLCs/LLPs, 7.7%
General partnerships, 2.3%
Nonfarm sole proprietorships, 71.6%

Source: Analysis of U.S. Internal Revenue Services, "Table 1: Number of Returns, Total Receipts, Business Receipts, Net Income (less deficit), Net Income, and Deficit by Form of Business, Tax Years 1980–2008," http://www.irs.gov/pub/irs-soi/80ot1all.xls (accessed February 15, 2013).

Because firms may operate more than one establishment, the aggregate number of establishments in an area typically will exceed the total number of firms. In 2010, the United States contained 5.7 million firms with paid employees but 7.4 million establishments with employees. Observe the relationship between firm size, as measured by the number of employees, and the ratio of establishments to firms (see Table 6.1). The smallest firms (those with four or fewer employees) demonstrated an almost 1-to-1 correspondence between the number of establishments and firms; among firms with 5,000 or more employees, the ratio of establishments to firms was 425-to-1.[11]

Legal Organization and Tax Status

The definition of a business is distinct from its legal organization or tax status. According to the Internal Revenue Service, 71.6 percent of all business entities (including those with and without employees) in 2008, the latest year for which data were available at time of writing, were nonfarm sole proprietorships and another 2.3 percent were general partnerships (see Figure 6.1).[12] Sole proprietorships and general partnerships are unincorporated business entities with owners who potentially face unlimited personal liability for the actions and financial obligations of their businesses; moreover, all business profits and losses pass through to the proprietors and partners and are taxed at the individual level.[13]

Corporations represented 18.4 percent of American businesses in 2008.[14] A *corporation* is a distinct legal entity organized under state law. An incorporated firm acquires a legal identity independent from its owners, which limits their legal liabilities. As long as the corporation satisfies legal requirements and acts properly, its owners can lose nothing more than their investments. Traditional taxable corporations—called C-corporations after the relevant section of the federal tax code—must pay corporate income tax, and the owners or shareholders must pay personal income taxes on any dividends and gains received.[15] Ever since changes to the tax code were made in 1982, many smaller, closely held corporations have elected to pay taxes as S-corporations, named in reference to the relevant section of the federal tax code. Such firms are not subject to corporate taxation, and all profits and losses pass directly to the owners, who must pay taxes at the individual level.[16] In 2008, S-corporations accounted for 69.3 percent of all corporations.[17]

The remaining 7.7 percent of business entities in 2008 were limited liability corporations (LLCs) or limited liability partnerships (LLPs).[18] These hybrid business structures blend the benefits of incorporation—mainly the limits on personal liability—with the tax simplicity of general partnerships—notably the ability to avoid the corporate income tax.[19] A 2009 report by the U.S. Government Accountability Office found hybrid business partnerships and S-corporations to be the two fastest growing business types between tax years 2000 and 2006.[20]

Employer and Nonemployer Businesses

The defining characteristic of a business, at least in the popular mind, is employees, yet the vast majority of American firms—79.4 percent in all—have no paid employees.[21] Given that, how should regional leaders think about such nonemployer firms, or should they think of them at all?

Most business statistics distinguish between nonemployer and employer businesses. A *nonemployer business* is "one that has no paid employees, has annual business receipts of $1,000 or more ($1 or more in the construction industry), and is subject to federal income taxes."[22] An *employer business* is one "with payroll and paid employees."[23] Even though nonemployer firms accounted for the vast majority of businesses in 2007, the last year with complete data at the time of writing, they generated just 3.2 percent of all business receipts.[24] Owing to the modest receipts of nonemployer firms and their lack of employees, researchers often exclude them from studies.

This exclusion is a rational choice but hardly an inconsequential one. First, the exclusion of nonemployers pushes a great deal of business activity out of sight because, though small, nonemployer firms deliver goods and services to their clients, provide income for their owners, and generate sales for their vendors. Second, recent research suggests that the role of nonemployer firms is evolving. The stereotypical example of a nonemployer business is a home-based, hobby-related endeavor, but start-up rates for nonemployer businesses actually are high in a range of industries, especially in the service sector.[25] Third, rates of formation of nonemployer businesses have been increasing, at least prior to the most recent recession. Fourth, by providing people with an important, if small, income, nonemployer businesses may play an important role in economically distressed regions like Appalachia. Finally, nonemployer businesses may provide many Americans, especially those from socially disadvantaged groups, with economic opportunities that otherwise would be unavailable.[26]

None of this implies that a focus on employer businesses is inappropriate. Such firms matter greatly, but nonemployer firms also are part of the regional economy and a failure to consider them may cause civic leaders to overlook a sizable section of the economic landscape. Fortunately, government agencies like the U.S. Census Bureau and SBA, along with philanthropic organizations like the Ewing Marion Kaufmann Foundation in Kansas City, Missouri, recently have taken a heightened interest in nonemployer businesses and are striving to improve research understanding of the contributions of nonemployer businesses to the larger economy.[27]

How Big Are Businesses? Business Size

Americans revere business, as there is something deeply appealing in the notion that anyone with a good idea and work ethic can strike out and create something new. Small businesses are particularly valued since a small venture is conceivably within the grasp of any individual. That may explain why calls to aid small business are staples of political and policy speeches. As President Barack Obama wrote in a 2011 proclamation, "[f]rom the family businesses that anchor Main Street to the high-tech startups that keep American on the cutting edge, small businesses are the backbone of our economy and the cornerstone of America's promise. . . . Small businesses embody the promise of America: that if you have a good idea and are willing to work hard enough, you can succeed in our country."[28]

Because there exists no accepted definition of a small business, "smallness" lies in the eye of the beholder. Even the SBA, an organization that seemingly should have one, lacks a meaningful definition, as made obvious by the fact that 99.7 percent of all American firms with employees qualify under their guidelines. How then should an observer assess firm size?

When it comes to size, researchers commonly classify firms based on three variables: total employment, total payroll, and total sales. *Total employment* refers to the number of people employed by a business on a specific date; *total payroll* is the cumulative amount of gross wages, salaries, tips, and selected benefits paid to all employees during a specified period; and *total sales* reflects the amount of money received for goods sold or services rendered during a particular time frame.[29] Because most public statistical agencies compile information for business establishments, data may not capture the full extent of an enterprise's activities.

All dimensions of business activity are pertinent, but total employment tends to attract the most interest, even though an exclusive focus on total employment is myopic in at least four ways. First, such a focus excludes all nonemployer firms—and a significant amount of regional business activity—from consideration. Second, a single-minded focus on the number of jobs obscures the fact that some jobs add more value than others, and it is the value added that fuels regional growth. Third, an emphasis on job quantity often blinds people to questions of job quality: a business may employ many people, but if the wages are low and benefits nonexistent, the jobs may detract from regional well-being. Finally, the pressure to increase total employment may lead regional officials to adopt shortsighted development strategies that deliver few long-term benefits and impose steep costs on the public.

WHAT DO BUSINESSES DO? INDUSTRIES AND PRODUCTS

The importance of businesses to an economy ultimately rests not in their organizational structure or size, but in the goods and services that they provide. Any attempt to understand a regional economy therefore must consider what local businesses do—a task easier said than done in a globalized economy in which enterprises engage in diverse activities.

Take the extreme example of Wal-Mart Stores, Inc. Is Wal-Mart a retailer, a wholesaler, a grocer, a logistics firm, a warehouser, a financial firm, a bank, a real estate company, a photography studio, an import-export firm, a travel agency, a corporate office, or something else? The corporation engages in all of these activities. Wal-Mart was the world's largest company in terms of revenue in 2011, but the same analytical problems apply to many smaller firms.[30]

Between the late 1930s and late 1990s, American public statistical agencies categorized businesses according to a framework called the *Standard Industrial Classification* (SIC). This system categorized business establishments "by [the] type of activity in which they are primarily engaged."[31] The SIC placed establishments into four hierarchical levels according to their primary business activities. At the broadest level, every establishment belonged to one of ten industrial divisions (e.g., construction).[32] By the early 1990s, the SIC framework was proving inadequate to the statistical needs of a service-based economy. In response, the major public statistical agencies in the United States, Canada, and Mexico joined together to create a new classification scheme.

Unveiled in 1997, the *North American Industry Classification System* (NAICS) is the standard classification typology used in North America's three largest countries. Like the SIC, the NAICS takes establishments as the basic unit of analysis, but, unlike the SIC, the NAICS classifies establishments not by their business activities but by "the similarity of their production processes."[33] The NAICS is a hierarchical framework, and in the 2007 version of the system the 1,175 NAICS industries ultimately collapsed into 20 economic sectors. Table 6.2 lists the 20 NAICS sectors and illustrates how the 2007 NAICS hierarchy applied to two industries: envelope manufacturing and greeting card publishers.

The NAICS represents a significant advance over the SIC because the new system allows "for greater detail, logical groupings of industries, and international compatibility with NAFTA [North American Free Trade Agreement] trading partners."[34]

Table 6.2 North American Industrial Classification System, 2007

A. Listing of NAICS Sectors (Two-Digit Level)

Code	Name	Code	Name
11	Agriculture, Forestry, Fishing, and Hunting	53	Real Estate and Rental and Leasing
21	Mining, Quarrying, and Oil and Gas Extraction	54	Professional, Scientific, and Technical Services
22	Utilities	55	Management of Companies and Enterprises
23	Construction	56	Administrative and Support and Waste Management and Remediation Services
31–33	Manufacturing	61	Educational Services
42	Wholesale Trade	62	Health Care and Social Assistance
44–45	Retail Trade	71	Arts, Entertainment, and Recreation
48–49	Transportation and Warehousing	72	Accommodation and Food Services
51	Information	81	Other Services (except Public Administration)
52	Finance and Insurance	92	Public Administration

B. General NAICS Hierarchy (2007)

Sector [2-digit] (20 categories in total)
    Sub-Sector [3-digit] (99 categories in total)
        Industry Group [4-digit] (313 categories in total)
            NAICS Industry [5-digit] (721 categories in total)
                National Industry [6-digit] (1,175 categories in total; 505 same as 5-digit level + 670 unique categories)

C. Examples of NAICS Classifications

Envelope Manufacturing		Greeting Card Publishers	
Code	Title	Code	Title
32	Manufacturing	51	Information
322	Paper Manufacturing	511	Publishing Industries (except Internet)
3222	Converted Paper Product Manufacturing	5111	Newspaper, Periodical, Book, and Directory Publishers
32223	Stationary Product Manufacturing	51119	Other Publishers
322232	Envelope Manufacturing	511191	Greeting Card Publishers

Source: U.S. Office of Management and Budget, *North America Industry Classification System, 2007* (Lanham, MD: Bernan, 2007).

Compared to the SIC, the NAICS is better able to classify service industries and keep current with economic changes since the sponsoring governments require revisions at five-year intervals. In fact, the international agencies responsible for the NAICS already have completed three revisions (in 2002, 2007, and 2012), with a fourth slated for 2017. Revisions to the SIC, in contrast, occurred only six times in its roughly 60-year lifespan.[35] Limitations of the NAICS include a lack of historical continuity and the confusion caused by public agencies adopting the system at different times.[36]

Perhaps the major strength of the NAICS is its nature as a production-based classification scheme. The core idea is to group establishments by their production processes rather than by their products. This view of an industry as a grouping of production units facilitates the integration of economic data about "inputs and outputs, industrial performance, productivity, unit labor costs, employment, and other statistics and structural changes."[37] In sum, the NAICS approach offers a coherent framework for tracking the entire production process.

As with the SIC, the NAICS is subject to confusion since the industry classification is determined for establishments rather than firms or enterprises. This is not problematic when an establishment, firm, and enterprise are one in the same, but it is vexing when dealing with a company with multiple establishments engaged in different industries.[38] Returning to the Wal-Mart example, a Wal-Mart retail store, distribution center, and corporate office would have different NAICS codes. What, then, is the industry of Wal-Mart as a whole? As an establishment-centered system, the NAICS passes over such questions in silence.

The establishment-level, production-based NAICS framework has become the standard way of classifying what business establishments do, but other categorizations are possible. For instance, the American, Canadian, and Mexican governments currently are crafting a hierarchical *North American Product Classification System* (NAPCS) that will integrate the collection of data about the actual goods and services produced by business establishments. The development of NAPCS is ongoing, and so far the focus has been on service industries. When implemented, the demand-side NAPCS structure will complement the supply-side NAICS.[39]

HOW DOES A BUSINESS DO WHAT IT DOES? BUSINESS OPERATIONS

When it comes to business structure, regional leaders typically confine their interest to broad topics like the number of establishments in an area, the industrial composition of a regional economy, the total value of local business revenues, and the aggregate levels of employment. On occasion, regional leaders, particularly economic development officials, must look more closely at business operations and consider how establishments produce their goods and services.

Although the specifics are beyond the scope of this volume, public statistical agencies collect a vast amount of information about business inputs (e.g., materials, labor, capital needs) and outputs (e.g., value added, shipments, foreign sales). The U.S. Bureau of Labor Statistics, for instance, prepares quarterly estimates of employer costs for employee compensation and a separate set of productivity measures that tracks how much employees produce per hour worked (see chapter 8). As noted in chapter

2, the U.S. Bureau of Economic Analysis calculates regional output and models business ties among industries. And this chapter discusses the U.S. Census Bureau's Economic Census, which is a rich source of information about business operations.

A familiarity with business operations is beneficial in several respects. First, an understanding of production processes and the linkages among industries is the building block of economic cluster analysis (see chapter 3). Second, recognition of the workforce skills demanded by specific industries enables workforce development officials and educators to prepare trained workers. Lastly, an appreciation of business costs can equip public agencies to think deliberately about the effects of regulatory and tax policies and to target more effectively business assistance and industrial recruitment efforts.

Sources of Regional Business Data

In contrast to demographic and social data, statistical agencies collect economic indicators more often and by more methods. Keeping abreast of these reports could be a full-time job.

Individuals interested in regional business issues can find answers to common questions in data sets maintained by a handful of federal agencies like the Census Bureau, the SBA, and the Internal Revenue Service. State-level counterparts to those agencies also may be rich sources of information, but perhaps the most important resource is the national Economic Census and the various data products derived from it.

Regardless of the information source, users of business data should remember two things. First, more times than not, business establishments, not firms or enterprises, are the basic analytical units. Second, because businesses are constantly changing, business activities may be measured using either static or dynamic data. Static data capture a snapshot of an activity on a specific date. A firm that has 12 employees one day might have more or fewer employees the next day. Dynamic data, meanwhile, capture changes in a business activity over time, such as the changes in payroll levels during the course of a year.

U.S. Census Bureau

The U.S. Census Bureau plays an essential role in the generation of business statistics by conducting the quinquennial Economic Census. Yet that hardly is the only business-related statistical product prepared by the agency's Economic Directorate. Other important data products in regional economic analysis include Nonemployer Statistics, County Business Patterns, Statistics of U.S. Businesses, Survey of Business Owners, the Census of Governments, and Business Employment Dynamics (see Table 6.3). Many of these products originate in data collected through the Economic Census.

Economic Census

The *Economic Census* serves as "the foundation for the nation's system of statistics about the functioning of the American economy."[40] While the collection of economic

Table 6.3 Economic Data Products with Regional Information by Level of Coverage, U.S. Census Bureau, 2012

Data Product	Latest version	Level of geography					
		U.S.	States	Metro areas	Counties	Cities	Zip codes
Economic Census	2007	X	X	X	X	X	X
Nonemployer Statistics	2010	X	X	X	X		
County Business Patterns	2010	X	X	X	X		X
Statistics of U.S. Businesses	2009	X	X	X	X		
Survey of Business Owners	2007	X	X	X	X	X	
Census of Governments	2010	X	X		X	X	
Business Dynamics Statistics	2010	X	X				

Source: U.S. Census Bureau, "Economic Data for States, Metros, Counties, Cities, and ZIP Codes," revised May 21, 2012, http://www.census.gov/econ/geo-compall.html.

data by the Census Bureau dates to the 1810 Census, the modern Economic Census originated in 1954. That enumeration was the first to provide "comparable census data across economic sectors, using consistent time periods, concepts, definitions, classifications, and reporting units."[41] Starting in 1967, a census of economic activity has occurred every five years in those ending in a "2" or "7." Despite its long history, the Economic Census lacked wide name recognition, partly because the Census Bureau labeled the study by its component parts. In 1997, the agency rebranded the census as a single product.[42]

An enumeration of business establishments in the United States, the Economic Census generates information about the physical location of establishments, their total employment, their total payrolls, and their total sales, as well as about industry-specific topics. As with the population count, the Economic Census employs a mail-based questionnaire that respondents must answer.[43] The Census Bureau treats all responses as confidential and suppresses the release of information that would permit the identification of individual establishments. When combined with the associated Census of Governments, the Economic Census captures some 96 percent of the economic activity that occurs within the United States.[44] Note that since the 1990s the agriculture industry is not included in the Economic Census. Congress shifted responsibility for the Census of Agriculture, which also occurs every five years in those ending in a "2" or "7," from the Census Bureau to the National Agricultural Statistics Service, an agency within the U.S. Department of Agriculture (see Box 6.1).

Data from the Economic Census are available for levels of geography down to individual zip codes. Depending on the topic, data exist for the nation, states, census regions, census divisions, counties, places, core-based statistical areas, and zip codes, though less information is available for smaller geographies than larger ones.[45] Data from the Economic Census is available via the American FactFinder website.[46]

Box 6.1 Agricultural Statistics

Most of the data products discussed in this book exclude topics related to agriculture. This is not because agriculture is unimportant. In 2007, the nation's 2.2 million farms grew crops and raised livestock and poultry that sold at market for almost $300 billion. Additionally, approximately 1 million people in addition to self-employed farm operators and their immediate family members work in agriculture. Nevertheless, agriculture is a complex field with unique characteristics that statistical data programs focused on the nonfarm economy are not designed to measure or measure poorly.

The federal government long has compiled agricultural data. The 1790 Census, the nation's first, collected basic information about farms, with additional information gathered the next year through a special study—a study developed by George Washington himself. Modern statistics trace their roots to 1840, when the first Census of Agriculture occurred. The next development occurred in the early 1860s when the U.S. Department of Agriculture and an associated public statistical agency were established. Today, the agricultural statistical system used in the United States tracks agricultural production, prices received and paid by farmers, farm labor and wages, farm income and finances, chemical use, and demographic characteristics.

The most important source of agricultural information is the quinquennial *Census of Agriculture*, responsibility for which rests with the National Agricultural Statistics Service, a unit of the U.S. Department of Agriculture. The enumeration occurs in years ending in a "2" or "7" and counts farms, defined as places "from which $1,000 or more of agricultural products were produced and sold, or normally would have been sold, during the census year." Detailed census data are available for the nation, states, outlying areas, Puerto Rico, counties, congressional districts, and individual zip codes.

To shed light on the conditions of agricultural work, the National Agricultural Statistics Service fields a quarterly *Farm Labor Survey*, a representative, telephone-based survey of 12,000 farm establishments and 600 agricultural service establishments that provide contract labor to farms. The survey draws its samples from all farm establishments with at least $1,000 in sales and every agricultural service establishment. Survey questions pertain to the number of farm workers hired, the hours worked by farm workers, and the wage rates paid to farm workers. The survey publishes data for the nation and 15 geographic regions four times each year; the October release contains annual estimates. Apart from some information for California and Florida, the Farm Labor Survey produces no state or regional estimates.

Another data product related to farm labor is the *National Agricultural Workers Survey*, an initiative of the U.S. Department of Labor. Launched in 1988, the study is "an employment-based, random survey of the demographic, employment, and health characteristics of the U.S. crop labor force." Each year, researchers personally interview between 1,500 and 4,000 workers and collect confidential information pertaining to the demographic characteristics of individual workers, the demographic characteristics of the households of the workers, the recent employment and migration profiles of workers, the earnings and benefits of workers, and the characteristics of individual worksites. The survey further inquires into issues related to health, safety, housing, income, assets, legal status, and social services. Unfortunately, the survey is not designed to produce state and regional estimates.

A final resource of interest to regional leaders is the *Economic Research Service*, a unit of the U.S. Department of Agriculture. This office undertakes applied economic and policy research into issues related to agriculture and rural development. In effect, the Economic Research Service synthesizes data from numerous sources into a portrait of rural America. The service's website is a useful source of regularly updated information available at varying levels of geographic detail.

Sources: Economic Research Service, "Farm Labor," http://www.ers.usda.gov/Briefing/LaborAndEducation/farmlabor. htm (accessed February 17, 2013); National Agricultural Statistics Service, *2007 Economic Census*, vol. 1, United States Summary and State Data (Washington, DC: U.S. Department of Agriculture, 2009), 7, http://www.agcensus. usda.gov/Publications/2007/Full_Report/Volume_1,_Chapter_1_U.S./usv1.pdf; National Agricultural Statistics Service, *An Evolving Statistical Service for American Agriculture* (Washington, DC: U.S. Department of Agriculture, 2005), 3–4, http://www.nass.usda.gov/About_NASS/evolving_nass.pdf; National Agricultural Statistics Service, "Farm Labor Survey," http://www.nass.usda.gov/Surveys/Guide_to_NASS_Surveys/Farm_Labor/index.asp (accessed February 17, 2013); and U.S. Department of Labor, "The National Agricultural Workers Survey," http://www.doleta.gov/agworker/ naws.cfm (accessed February 17, 2013).

Results appear gradually, following the census year, in different formats including the following:

- The *Core Business Statistics Series* contains industrial data for the nation and some states.
- The *Industry Series* presents national information about industries and their products.
- The *Geographic Area Series* offers data about individual industries for the nation, states, counties, places, and Metropolitan Statistical Areas.
- The *Subject and Summary Series* provides industry-specific information about product lines, establishment and firm size, and special topics for the nation, and in some cases, states.
- The *ZIP Code Statistics Series* lists counts of establishments by sales-size ranges by industry; these data exist only for the retail trade industry and some service industries.[47]

Additionally, the Census Bureau maintains a series of continuously updated *Economy-wide Key Statistics* as part of the Economic Census. The series provides industry-specific information about establishment counts, sales value, payroll amounts, and employment levels for every covered level of geography. Of course, the Census Bureau may suppress some information to ensure confidentiality, as happens frequently with small areas. As part of the 2007 Economic Census, this Economy-wide Key Statistics series expanded to include counts of nonemployer establishments and sales.[48] Data users interested in regional issues can find much of the information they require by accessing the information in the Economy-wide Key Statistics and Geographic Area series. But bear in mind that while the Economic Census has collected standardized business information since the 1950s, the shift to the NAICS has limited the ability to compare changes over time since older enumerations employed the SIC framework.

Nonemployer Statistics

Since 1998, the Census Bureau has released annual estimates of the number, legal forms, and receipts of nonemployer businesses. Such businesses must pay federal taxes, have no paid employees, and have annual receipts of at least $1,000 ($1 in construction). Data are available by industry and are broken out for the nation, states, counties, metropolitan statistical areas, and combined statistical areas.[49]

As mentioned previously, nonemployer firms—businesses that have no paid employees and rely entirely on the labor provided by their owners—account for almost 80 percent of all businesses but 3.2 percent of all business receipts. Nevertheless, nonemployer firms contribute to the regional economy and are important sources of income for their owners. Prior to 1998, the gathering of information about nonemployer firms occurred irregularly, and the resulting data were not necessarily consistent with other economic information. The standardization of the data and its collection through the Economic Census provides a basis for better understanding the full extent of business activities in a regional economy.

The Census Bureau bases its nonemployer statistics on administrative records, primarily tax data furnished by the Internal Revenue Service. While this process eliminates certain kinds of errors, it is not immune to shortcomings like the improper inclusion or exclusion of nonemployer establishments. Results normally appear 18 months following the end of the reference year and are available on the internet through the American FactFinder website.[50] Specifically, the site provides information about the number of nonemployer establishments and their business receipts broken out by industry and geography. A second data series covers the legal form (sole proprietorship, partnership, or corporation) of nonemployer establishments disaggregated by industry, but that information is available solely for the nation and states.

County Business Patterns

Every year since 1964, the Census Bureau has released estimates of the total number of business establishments with employees, their total employment levels, and their total payroll values for every county in the United States. Arranged by industry, the data in the annual *County Business Patterns* (CBP) report are available for the nation, states, Puerto Rico, and metropolitan areas.[51]

The Census Bureau bases the CBP series on administrative and statistical records contained in its Business Register, which is created as part of the Economic Census. Estimates for total employment and payroll come from records for the pay period that includes March 12 of the reference year. Because the CBP series is not the result of a survey, it is not subject to sampling errors, but it does suffer from nonsampling errors like the undercounting of establishments that belong to multi-unit companies. Moreover, while the CBP series has occurred continuously since 1964, the shift to the NAICS system has limited the historical comparability of the information as older versions employed the SIC framework.[52]

CBP data normally appear 18 months following the end of the reference year and are available on the internet through the American FactFinder website. Specifically, the site provides information about the number of employer establishments, quarterly and annual payroll information, and employment counts during the week containing March 12. The data are grouped by NAICS industry—though public administration, certain agricultural industries, and a few other industries are omitted—and by employment size class. A series of ZIP Code Business Pattern data sets extends the industry-level count of establishments down to individual zip codes.

Statistics of U.S. Businesses

The business establishment, not the enterprise, is the basic unit of analysis encountered in most economic statistics. For an enterprise with only one establishment, the distinction is immaterial, yet it matters greatly when considering an establishment that is part of a larger firm.

Based on the same underlying data as the CBP series, the *Statistics of U.S. Businesses* (SUSB) is the only source of annual, complete, and consistent enterprise-level data for all establishments with paid employees. Data are available by NAICS code and for the nation, states, and metropolitan statistics areas. The SUSB focuses exclusively on firms with employees, and produces data about the annual number of firms in an area, the annual number of establishments in the area, the total annual employment levels, the total annual payroll levels, and the total annual business receipts. The data are disaggregated by industry, although public administration, certain agricultural industries, and a few other industries are excluded, and by employment size classes.[53]

The Census Bureau has prepared annual SUSB data since 1989 with the results appearing 24 months following the end of the reference year. Because SUSB originates from the data set used to generate the CBP series, it relies upon the same basic methodology and suffers from the same general limitations. SUSB data are available on dedicated websites maintained by the Census Bureau and SBA.[54]

Survey of Business Owners

The *Survey of Business Owners* (SBO) is a second data series compiled on the basis of firms rather than establishments. The SBO differs from the SUSB in two respects. First, SBO data come from a survey administered to a sample of nonfarm businesses—both employers and nonemployers—with annual receipts of at least $1,000. Second, the SBO focuses not on the firm itself, but "on selected economic and demographic characteristics for businesses and business owners by gender, ethnicity, race, and veteran status."[55] In short, the SBO documents the characteristics of the individuals who own firms.

Fielded in the same years as the Economic Census, the SBO generates estimates of firm size, sales, receipts, payrolls, and employment. Data are disaggregated by NAICS industry—although public administration, certain agricultural industries, some transportation industries, and others are excluded—and by selected demographic traits of business owners, or those persons who possess 51 percent or more of a business's stock or equity. SBO information appears for the nation, states, Metropolitan and Micropolitan Statistical Areas, counties, and places.[56] Unfortunately, survey limitations and the need to ensure confidentiality may limit the amount of information available for smaller geographies.

The SBO is a survey, so the results are subject to both sampling and nonsampling errors. Because the data derive from a survey, they contain a margin of error, and the true value of an observation actually falls within a range bounded by a specified level of confidence. Another concern is that SBO data reported on the basis of race and ethnicity may not sum. This can happen because, as explained in chapter 5, the Census Bureau treats race and ethnicity as separate concepts. Also, a firm may fall into multiple racial categories if a multiracial individual owns it or if people of differing racial or ethnic backgrounds share ownership.[57]

The Census Bureau has fielded the SBO in conjunction with the Economic Census since 1972. Results appear gradually over the years following the reference years and are accessible via a dedicated website and the American FactFinder internet portal.[58]

Census of Governments

Technically part of the Economic Census, the *Census of Governments* is in many respects a stand-alone product due to the distinctive structure, organization, and operations of the public sector. This enumeration is the only regular source of standardized information about the employment and financial characteristics of state and local governments.

The Census of Governments covers every unit of state and local government found in the United States. Local governments include those responsible for counties, cities, townships, school districts, and such special districts as library and water authorities. The questionnaire inquires into how governments are organized, what their total employment levels and payrolls are, and how they finance their operations. All data pertain to October of the year preceding the census year.[59]

Findings from the Census of Governments appear gradually over the years following the census year. As information becomes available, it appears on a dedicated website maintained by the Census Bureau.[60] An interactive query system enables data users to generate tabulations of selected variables grouped by level of government, geography, and governmental function. Note that the website contains no information that identifies specific local governments. Depending on the applicable state and local laws, such information may be a public record available upon request, or it may be available in published financial documents or regulatory filings.

Business Dynamics Statistics

All of the Census Bureau products discussed so far in this chapter rely upon static data and offer a snapshot of some phenomenon at a moment in time. Yet businesses are dynamic entities that constantly change. Over the course of a year, an establishment may open its doors, add employees, shed employees, and cease operations. Static data fail to capture such churn despite its importance in understanding the underlying dynamics of business activities.

In response, the Census Bureau launched its *Business Dynamics Statistics* (BDS) program in 2008. By combining data contained in economic statistical programs like the Economic Census with other administrative records and data sources, BDS aims to track net employment changes at individual establishments over time. The longitudinal data set currently covers the period spanning 1976 to 2010. The BDS provides information about the creation and destruction of individual establishments, as well as measures of employment growth and contraction. Data are available by the employment size class of business establishments and the age of business establishments.[61] Unfortunately, the BDS currently provides no information below the state level; all BDS data are accessible via a dedicated website.[62]

U.S. Small Business Administration

Created in 1953 as an independent agency of the federal government, the *U.S. Small Business Administration* (SBA) exists to "aid, counsel, assist, and protect the interests of small business concerns."[63] Perhaps the agency's best-known programs are the financial assistance it provides to small businesses, notably loan guarantees, and the counseling services it provides to small firms through Small Business Development Centers, operated jointly by the SBA, state governments, and institutions of higher education.[64]

The SBA's Office of Advocacy is responsible for compiling statistics relevant to the small business economy and for sponsoring research. Rather than generating its own data, the SBA draws heavily from products prepared by the Census Bureau. The SBA also commissions original studies of small business issues. While the SBA relies extensively on data collected by other organizations, the agency maintains a comprehensive research website that provides "one-stop" access to key information and publications.[65] Additionally, the office publishes an annual series of state economic profiles that contain a mix of static and dynamic data.[66]

Internal Revenue Service

The *Internal Revenue Service* (IRS) also provides information about businesses. The Statistics of Income Division prepares various data sets related to aspects of the federal tax code, such as summary data about corporate tax returns and tax filings by sole proprietorships. A listing of major IRS data products is available on the agency's website.[67] Though the IRS publicly releases relatively little data for state and local areas for reasons of practicality and confidentiality, the agency's data are fed into many of the Census Bureau's economic programs, such as Nonemployer Statistics, CBP, and SUSB. Note that many state tax agencies publish tax statistics that often contain county-level data.

Piecing the Puzzle Together: The Business Structure of the Milwaukee MSA

Nestled on the shore of Lake Michigan and centered on the City of Milwaukee, the Milwaukee-Waukesha-West Allis, MSA is the nation's 39th-most-populous metropolitan area.[68] In 2010, the 1.6 million inhabitants of the four-county region powered a regional economy that produced $84.6 billion in goods and services; put differently, 27.4 percent of Wisconsin's residents generated 34.5 percent of the state's economic output.[69]

Aggregate estimates of economic output offer few insights into how that output is produced. Researchers and regional leaders interested in gaining a deeper understanding of an area's business structure consequently must consult the statistical resources described earlier in this chapter. To illustrate how such information can illuminate a region's business structure, this section employs public data products to analyze aspects of the economy of metropolitan Milwaukee.[70] The discussion revolves around the four core questions previously raised: what a business is, how big a businesses is, what a business does, and how a business does what it does.

What Is a Business? Defining the Business Universe of the Milwaukee MSA

Despite the importance of businesses to regional economies, there exists no standard definition of what a business is. Individuals commonly think of businesses in terms of "companies," but as explained previously, most economic statistics take business establishments—actual worksites—as the basic analytical unit. This approach works well when dealing with single-establishment enterprises, but it becomes confusing in situations in which a multijurisdictional business entity owns several establishments. Another complication arises from the fact that some businesses have employees while others do not. The first step in any economic analysis, then, is to define the universe of relevant businesses.

Nonemployers and Employers

A threshold issue to weigh in any analysis is whether to focus on employer firms, nonemployer firms, or both. According to data drawn from the Census Bureau's County Business Patterns and Nonemployer Statistics series, the Milwaukee MSA contained an estimated 125,578 business establishments in 2010, of which 69.4 percent had no employees. Metropolitan Milwaukee's share of nonemployer establishments was slightly lower than that of the State of Wisconsin (70.4 percent) and considerably lower than the national figure (74.9 percent).[71] As will be seen, these results are intertwined with Milwaukee's industrial composition.

As expected, the distribution of nonemployer establishments in 2010 exhibited an industry-based pattern. Some 89.8 percent of Milwaukee's nonemployer establishments belonged to a service-producing industry. Moreover, nonemployer establishments accounted for a larger share of total establishments in some industries than in others. More than three-fourths of all establishments in the professional services sector and nearly nine-tenths of real estate establishments had no paid employees. In contrast, almost three-quarters of establishments in the accommodation and food service industry had employees.[72] These differences reflect the ways in which industries are organized. Construction and real estate, for example, rely on independent contractors, while many kinds of professional services lend themselves to sole practitioners acting as consultants. Also, the mix of establishments in an industry may change over time, as has occurred in the retail industry as chain stores have replaced independent "mom-and-pop" operations.

While nonemployer businesses accounted for the bulk of all establishments found in the Milwaukee region, they generated relatively few business receipts: the estimated annual sales of nonemployer establishments in 2010 amounted to a mere $3.8 billion. Of total nonemployer receipts, the largest amount was attributable to establishments in the real estate sector (31.9 percent), followed by the professional, scientific, and technical services sector (12.9 percent), and the construction sector (10.3 percent).[73] By definition, nonemployers were responsible for none of the region's 737,279 payroll jobs.[74]

Employer Firms and Establishments

Because regional leaders typically are interested in issues of employment and payrolls, most regional studies exclude nonemployer business establishments and focus on employer establishments. That choice, however, raises concerns about how to handle situations in which one business entity owns multiple establishments.

In 2009, the most recent year for which complete data were available at the time of writing, the Milwaukee region was home to 31,367 employer firms that controlled 38,989 individual business establishments. The professional, scientific, and technical services sector had the largest concentration of employer firms (11.9 percent), followed by the health care and social assistance sector (11.8 percent). Moreover, the broad service-producing sector contained 83.4 percent of local firms.[75]

In regard to employment size, most Milwaukee employer firms are small. Some 51 percent of firms had four or fewer employees, and 67.9 percent of firms had fewer than 10 employees. The data further suggest that firm size varies by industry. For example, only 5.8 percent of all Milwaukee firms in the art, entertainment, and recreation sector had 100 or more employees, compared to 72.2 percent of businesses in the management sector.[76] Such findings offer insights into the nature of a region's economy. The Milwaukee MSA, for instance, hosts the headquarters of 16 *Fortune 1000* companies, which may explain the sizable number of management firms based in the area.[77]

Specific demographic information about the owners of firms in the Milwaukee area is available through the Survey of Business Owners. In 2007, the latest year for which data exist, the Milwaukee MSA possessed 26,507 employer firms and 80,957 nonemployer firms classifiable by the owners' gender, race, ethnicity, or veteran status. Men owned 62.3 percent of employer firms and 48.1 percent of nonemployer firms; women, in contrast, owned 17.1 percent of the region's employer firms and 34.5 percent of its nonemployer firms (men and women jointly owned the remaining firms in both categories).[78]

When viewed through the lenses of race and ethnicity, Hispanic individuals owned just 2.1 percent of the businesses in the Milwaukee area and African Americans 7.5 percent. Altogether, members of racial and ethnic minority groups owned or co-owned 14.1 percent of all businesses in metropolitan Milwaukee, with—as was the case for women—their rates of ownership being higher for nonemployer firms than employer ones (15.6 percent versus 9.5 percent). This suggests that nonemployer businesses provide members of traditionally disadvantaged groups with business opportunities that otherwise might be unavailable. Additionally, veterans owned or co-owned 14.1 percent of the area's businesses, with their ownership rates being somewhat higher for nonemployer than employer firms (14.4 percent versus 13.3 percent).[79]

HOW BIG ARE BUSINESSES? BUSINESS SIZE IN THE MILWAUKEE MSA

As mentioned earlier, there exists no standard definition of business size, and instead, the concept typically is measured in relation to three variables: total employment, total payroll, and total sales.

Most of the business firms in metropolitan Milwaukee are small when measured in terms of employment. Nonemployer firms obviously have no employees, while 51 percent of employer firms in 2009 had fewer than five employees. By extension, such small firms (sometimes called "microenterprises") had relatively small payrolls and generated relatively few sales; in fact, employer establishments with fewer than nine employees were responsible for only 3.3 percent of the region's wages and 7.1 percent

Table 6.4 Ranking of Industry Size (Employer Establishments) by Total Employment, Payrolls, and Receipts, Milwaukee-Waukesha-West Allis, WI MSA

NAICS code (2-digit)	Sector name	Total employment (2009)		Annual payroll (2009)		Estimated annual receipts (2007)	
		Number of payroll positions	Rank (1 = largest)	Dollar amount (in 000s)	Rank (1 = largest)	Dollar amount (in 000s)	Rank (1 = largest)
11	Agriculture, Forestry, Fishing, and Hunting	100	18	$2,097	18	$6,727	18
21	Mining	398	17	$34,693	17	$172,561	17
22	Utilities	No Data	–	No Data	–	No Data	–
23	Construction	25,758	13	$1,396,819	8	$7,861,968	6
31–33	Manufacturing	115,989	2	$5,899,067	1	$42,956,596	1
42	Wholesale Trade	39,132	8	$2,127,734	6	$37,805,665	3
44–45	Retail Trade	81,174	3	$1,860,015	7	$19,144,163	4
48–49	Transportation and Warehousing	26,121	12	$967,361	12	$3,212,665	11
51	Information	19,215	14	$1,161,520	10	$5,394,921	8
52	Finance and Insurance	57,005	5	$4,079,671	3	$41,970,367	2
53	Real Estate and Rental and Leasing	9,620	16	$335,551	16	$1,817,686	15
54	Professional, Scientific, and Technical Services	41,116	7	$2,354,412	5	$5,642,697	7
55	Management of Companies and Enterprises	31,590	10	$2,508,162	4	$2,504,684	13
56	Administrative and Support and Waste Management and Remediation Services	45,883	6	$1,311,934	9	$3,403,724	10
61	Educational Services	30,607	11	$1,117,175	11	$2,819,438	12
62	Health Care and Social Assistance	120,706	1	$5,137,193	2	$11,357,409	5
71	Arts, Entertainment, and Recreation	13,716	15	$452,507	15	$1,134,338	16
72	Accommodation and Food Services	58,310	4	$739,162	14	$2,477,836	14
81	Other Services (except Public Administration)	34,776	9	$901,973	13	$3,452,833	9

Source: Author's analysis of U.S. Census Bureau, Statistics of U.S. Businesses, 2007 and 2009.
Note: Data for total employment and annual payrolls are collected annually, but data on estimated annual receipts are collected only in years ending with a "2" or a "7."

of its business receipts. Establishments with 500 or more employees, in contrast, represented 4.8 percent of the area's firms with employees yet accounted for 58.3 percent of total employer payrolls and 65.7 percent of total employer business receipts.[80]

Regardless of the measure of size selected for the purposes of analysis, the sizes of employer businesses vary by industry. The corporate management sector, for example, is skewed heavily toward the very largest firms (500 or more employees), while the construction sector is skewed toward the very smallest (fewer than five employees).[81] In the Milwaukee region, manufacturing is the largest industry in terms of annual receipts and payroll, and it is the second-largest employer (see Table 6.4). Meanwhile, the health care and social assistance sector is the region's largest employer but the fifth-largest industry in terms of annual receipts. The manufacturing sector may employ slightly fewer people than the health care and social assistance sector, yet each manufacturing employee generates almost four times as much in receipts. It is unsurprising, then, that the average wage paid to manufacturing employees is 19.5 percent higher than that paid to employees in the health care and social assistance sector.[82]

What Do Businesses Do? The Industrial Composition of the Milwaukee MSA

There are many ways to classify businesses based on what they do, but the standard typology used in the United States is the NAICS, a hierarchical framework that groups business establishments according to similarities in their production processes.

When measured as a share of total establishments, the two largest NAICS sectors in 2009 in the Milwaukee MSA were health care and social assistance (12.5 percent) and retail trade (12.1 percent). More broadly, 80.2 percent of local business establishments belonged to the service-providing sector. The construction sector accounted for an additional 8.5 percent of the area's establishments, the manufacturing sector another 6.7 percent.[83]

One way to assess a region's industrial profile and identify potential strengths is through the use of the location quotient technique described in chapter 3. Applying that technique to Milwaukee's universe of employer establishments suggests that, compared to the nation as a whole, the area may enjoy competitive advantages in the manufacturing, corporate management, educational services, and finance and insurance sectors (see Table 6.5). Conversely, the region appears to be relatively weak in the construction, real estate, professional services, and accommodation and food services sectors.[84]

From a regional development perspective, not all industries contribute equally to growth. Some industries tend to employ more individuals than others, while some generate higher levels of sales or payrolls. In the Milwaukee region, for example, there were 1.8 times more retail trade establishments than manufacturing ones in 2009, but total employment in the retail sector was 42.3 percent lower. Besides offering fewer positions compared to manufacturers, the retail sector had a lower total annual payroll than did manufacturing ($1.9 billion versus $5.9 billion). Retailers also sold much less: an estimated total of $19.1 billion in annual receipts compared to $43 billion in manufacturing receipts.[85] (Of course, retailers generally serve local markets while manufacturers often sell globally.)

Table 6.5 Industry Location Quotients for Milwaukee-Waukesha-West Allis, WI MSA, 2009

NAICS code (2-digit)	Sector name	Location quotient	Percent difference from expected value (%)
23	Construction	0.65	−34.5
31–33	Manufacturing	1.51	51.2
42	Wholesale Trade	1.02	1.8
44–45	Retail Trade	0.83	−16.8
48–49	Transportation and Warehousing	0.95	−4.8
51	Information	0.89	−11.4
52	Finance and Insurance	1.40	40.1
53	Real Estate and Rental and Leasing	0.72	−28.4
54	Professional, Scientific, and Technical Services	0.80	−20.5
55	Management of Companies and Enterprises	1.68	67.9
56	Administrative and Support and Waste Management and Remediation Services	0.77	−23.2
61	Educational Services	1.45	45.0
62	Health Care and Social Assistance	1.04	4.4
71	Arts, Entertainment, and Recreation	1.03	3.5
72	Accommodation and Food Services	0.77	−22.7
81	Other Services (except Public Administration)	1.00	0.2

Source: Author's analysis of U.S. Census Bureau, Statistics of U.S. Businesses, 2009.
Notes: Calculations are based on employment data for establishments with employees. Limited or no data were available for NAICS sectors 11, 21, and 22, so they are excluded from the table. Due to rounding of the location quotients, the percent difference from expected value will differ slightly from the results obtained by using the stated location quotients.

The bottom line, then, is this: Milwaukee may have more retailers than manufacturers, but the manufacturers produce comparatively more valuable products that command higher sales prices, and so, manufacturers pay better wages. Yet the wage premium is not the product of charity on the part of employers: manufacturing workers receive a premium because they produce high value-added goods. (Skill levels and institutional arrangements like unionization and minimum wages matter as well.) Each manufacturing employee in 2009 in Milwaukee generated some $327,000 in receipts compared to an annual per employee payroll cost of $50,628. In contrast, each employee in the region's retail sector contributed an average $220,748 in sales with annual payroll per employee amounting to $21,759.[86] Such differences matter because, as explained in chapter 2, improvements in regional well-being hinge on real changes in output. Industries that add more value therefore are apt to have a greater influence on regional prosperity. Seen that way, Milwaukee's large manufacturing sector is an economic strength.

How Do Businesses Do What They Do? Business Operations in the Milwaukee MSA

In some situations, regional leaders may be interested not merely in the size and industrial structure of business firms in the regional economy, but also in the operations of those firms. This interest may manifest itself in an attempt to understand the processes used to transform inputs into finished outputs or a desire to comprehend the cost pressures facing firms and the practical consequences of tax and regulatory policies. Furthermore, an awareness of the ties among firms may enrich regional economic development issues, particularly when cluster-based strategies are under consideration.

Public statistical agencies indeed compile information about business operations, but those products are beyond the scope of this volume. The amount of information available at the level of a metropolitan region often is limited as well; nevertheless, some information is available. In metropolitan Milwaukee, for instance, an economic development official could use regional input-output tools prepared by the Bureau of Economic Analysis or private vendors to model the consequences of a business decision on other local industries (see chapter 2). Similarly, the results of a supply-chain analysis could help local leaders connect firms thinking about locating in the area to a local firm that produces needed inputs, thereby creating opportunities for both firms.

Business Structure: A Summary

Businesses are vital economic institutions that facilitate and structure the ways in which regional residents interact to produce and consume goods and services. Well-functioning businesses enable the productive uses of resources and contribute to a region's material advancement. Yet for all its importance, the institution of a business lacks a standard definition. This chapter attempted to provide individuals interested in understanding a region's business structure with two things: a grounding in the major data products complied by public statistical agencies and a framework for thinking about regional business issues. Additionally, the extended example based on data for the Milwaukee MSA demonstrated how to tie together the two strands to generate analytical insights. Against that backdrop, it is possible to consider another institution vitally important to the long-term prospects of businesses, individuals, and entire regions, not to mention the one to which most individuals devote most of their lives: the labor market.

Notes

1. Partha Dasgupta, *Economics: A Very Short Introduction* (New York: Oxford University Press, 2007), 27.

2. For a theoretical and historical discussion of the relationship between economic and political institutions and prosperity, see Daron Acemoglu and James Robinson, *Why Nations Fail: The Origins of Power, Prosperity, and Poverty* (New York: Crown Publishing, 2012).

3. Dasgupta, *Economics,* 100 and 113.

4. U.S. Census Bureau, "Annual Estimates of the Population of Metropolitan and Micropolitan

Statistical Areas: April 1, 2010 to July 1, 2011 (CBSA-EST2011-01)," last revised April 2012, http://www.census.gov/popest/data/metro/totals/2011/tables/CBSA-EST2011-01.xls.

5. Brian Headd, *An Analysis of Small Business and Jobs* (Washington, DC: U.S. Small Business Administration, 2010), 9, http://www.sba.gov/sites/default/files/files/an%20analysis%20of%20small%20business%20and%20jobs(1).pdf.

6. Author's analysis of U.S. Small Business Administration, "Employer Firms, Establishments, Employment, and Annual Payroll Small Firm Size Classes, 2010," http://www.sba.gov/sites/default/files/files/static_us.xlsx (accessed February 15, 2013).

7. Author's analysis of U.S. Small Business Administration, "Nonemployer Firms and Receipts by Industry, 1992–2010," http://www.sba.gov/sites/default/files/files/static_ne.xlsx (accessed February 15, 2013).

8. U.S. Census Bureau, "2007 Economic Census: Definitions," last revised April 13, 2011, http://www.census.gov/econ/census07/www/definitions.html.

9. Jennifer Boettcher and Leonard Gaines, *Industry Research Using The Economic Census: How to Find It, How to Use It* (Westport, CT: Greenwood Press, 2004), 40.

10. U.S. Census Bureau, "Statistics of U.S. Businesses: Definitions," http://www.census.gov/econ/susb/definitions.html (accessed February 15, 2013).

11. Author's analysis of U.S. Small Business Administration, "Employer Firms, Establishments, Employment, and Annual Payroll Small Firm Size Classes, 2010."

12. Author's analysis of U.S. Internal Revenue Service, "Table 1: Number of Returns, Total Receipts, Business Receipts, Net Income (less deficit), Net Income, and Deficit by Form of Business, Tax Years 1980–2008," http://www.irs.gov/pub/irs-soi/80ot1all.xls (accessed February 15, 2013).

13. Kelly Luttrell, Patrice Treubert, and Michael Parisi, "Integrated Business Data, 2003," *Statistics of Income Bulletin,* Fall 2006, 47, http://www.irs.gov/pub/irs-soi/03intbus.pdf.

14. Author's analysis of U.S. Internal Revenue Service, "Table 1: Number of Returns, Total Receipts, Business Receipts, Net Income (less deficit), Net Income, and Deficit by Form of Business, Tax Years 1980–2008."

15. Lutrell, Treubert, and Parisi, "Integrated Business Data, 2003," 47.

16. Congressional Budget Office, *Taxing Businesses through the Individual Income Tax* (Washington, DC: Congress of the United States, 2012), 6, http://www.cbo.gov/sites/default/files/cbofiles/attachments/43750-TaxingBusinesses2.pdf.

17. Author's analysis of U.S. Internal Revenue Service, "Table 1: Number of Returns, Total Receipts, Business Receipts, Net Income (less deficit), Net Income, and Deficit by Form of Business, Tax Years 1980–2008."

18. Ibid.

19. Luttrell, Treubert, and Parisi, "Integrated Business Data, 2003," 51.

20. U.S. Government Accountability Office, *Tax Gap Actions Needed to Address Noncompliance with S Corporation Tax Rules* (Washington, DC: U.S. Government Accountability Organization, 2009), 43, http://www.gao.gov/new.items/d10195.pdf.

21. Author's analysis of U.S. Small Business Administration, "Employer Firms, Establishments, Employment, and Annual Payroll Small Firm Size Classes, 2010"; and U.S. Small Business Administration, "Nonemployer Firms and Receipts by Industry, 1992–2010."

22. U.S. Census Bureau, "Nonemployer Statistics: Definitions," http://www.census.gov/econ/nonemployer/definitions.htm (accessed February 15, 2013).

23. Ibid.

24. Author's analysis of U.S. Small Business Administration, "Employer Firms, Establishments, Employment, and Annual Payroll Small Firm Size Classes, 2010"; and U.S. Small Business Administration, "Nonemployer Firms and Receipts by Industry, 1992–2010."

25. Zoltan Acs, Brian Headd, and Hezekiah Agwara, *Nonemployer Start-up Puzzle* (Washington, DC: U.S. Small Business Administration, 2009), 8, http://archive.sba.gov/advo/research/rs354tot.pdf.

26. Brian Headd and Radwan Saade, *Do Small Business Definition Decisions Distort Small Business*

Research Results? (Washington, DC: U.S. Small Business Administration, 2008), 7 and 11, http://ftp. sbaonline.sba.gov/advo/research/rs330tot.pdf.

27. The Ewing Marion Kaufmann Foundation is a philanthropic organization dedicated to advancing entrepreneurship and is a major funder of research into entrepreneurship in domestic and international contexts. As of February 15, 2013, much of the foundation's published research was available at http:// www.kauffman.org/Section.aspx?id=Research_And_Policy.

28. Barack Obama, *Presidential Proclamation: Small Business Week* (Washington, DC: White House, 2011), http://www.whitehouse.gov/the-press-office/2011/05/12/presidential-proclamation-small-business-week (accessed January 6, 2012).

29. Boettcher and Gaines, *Industry Research Using the Economic Census,* 44.

30. "2011 Global 500," *Fortune,* accessed February 15, 2013, http://money.cnn.com/magazines/fortune/global500/2011/full_list/.

31. U.S. Office of Management and Budget, *North American Industry Classification System: United States, 2007* (Lanham, MD: Bernan, 2007), 13.

32. As of February 15, 2013, the Occupational Safety and Health Administration, a division of the U.S. Department of Labor maintained a historical online version of the SIC hierarchy at http://www. osha.gov/pls/imis/sic_manual.html.

33. U.S. Office of Management and Budget, *North American Industry Classification System,* 14.

34. Boettcher and Gaines, *Industry Research Using the Economic Census,* 51.

35. Ibid., 52.

36. The problem of historical data continuity can be a serious issue for researchers. Some public agencies like the U.S. Bureau of Economic of Analysis have recalculated parts of older data sets to reflect the NAICS. The U.S. Census Bureau also has published "crosswalk" tables that allow analysts to adjust data recorded on an SIC basis to an NAICS basis and vice versa. While the Census Bureau stopped publishing crosswalk tables in 2002, past tables were available, as of February 15, 2013, at http://www.census.gov/eos/www/naics/concordances/concordances.html.

37. U.S. Office of Management and Budget, *North American Industry Classification System,* 16.

38. Boettcher and Gaines, *Industry Research Using the Economic Census,* 54.

39. U.S. Census Bureau, "Frequently Asked Questions about NAPCS," http://www.census.gov/eos/www/napcs/faqs.html (accessed February 15, 2013).

40. Paul Zeisset, "Economic Census," in *Encyclopedia of the U.S. Census,* ed. M.J. Anderson (Washington, DC: CQ Press, 2000), 187.

41. Boettcher and Gaines, *Industry Research Using the Economic Census,* 4.

42. Ibid., 4–5.

43. As of February 16, 2013, copies of the questionnaires in use for the 2012 Economic Census were available at http://bhs.econ.census.gov/ec12/php/census-form.php. The first results from the enumeration will appear in December 2013, with additional data releases occurring through mid-2016. As of February 16, 2013, a schedule of key dates was available at http://www.census.gov/econ/census/schedule.html.

44. U.S. Census Bureau, *2007 Economic Census User Guide* (Washington, DC: U.S. Census Bureau, 2009), 39, http://www.census.gov/econ/census07/pdf/econ_user_guide.pdf.

45. Ibid., 31–36.

46. As of February 13, 2013, the dedicated website for the Economic Census was http://www.census.gov/econ/census/index.html, and the American FactFinder site was available at http://factfinder2.census.gov/faces/nav/jsf/pages/index.xhtml.

47. U.S. Census Bureau, *2007 Economic Census User Guide,* 17.

48. Ibid., 17–18.

49. U.S. Census Bureau, "Nonemployer Statistics: About the Data," http://www.census.gov/econ/nonemployer/overview.htm (accessed February 5, 2013).

50. U.S. Census Bureau, "Nonemployer Statistics: How the Data Are Collected," http://www.census.gov/econ/nonemployer/methodology.htm (accessed February 15, 2012).

51. U.S. Census Bureau, "County Business Patterns: About the Data," http://www.census.gov/econ/cbp/overview.htm (accessed February 15, 2013).

52. U.S. Census Bureau, "County Business Patters: Coverage and Methodology," http://www.census.gov/econ/cbp/methodology.htm (accessed February 15, 2013).

53. U.S. Census Bureau, "Statistics of U.S. Businesses: About the Data," http://www.census.gov/econ/susb/about_the_data.html (accessed February 15, 2013).

54. As of February 15, 2013, the dedicated SUSB websites were www.census.gov/econ/susb/ and www.sba.gov/advocacy/849/12162#susb.

55. U.S. Census Bureau, "Survey of Business Owners: About the Survey," http://www.census.gov/econ/sbo/about.html (accessed February 15, 2013).

56. Ibid.

57. U.S. Census Bureau, "Survey of Business Owners: How the Data Are Collected," http://www.census.gov/econ/sbo/methodology.html (accessed February 15, 2013).

58. As of February 15, 2013, the dedicated website was available at www.census.gov/econ/sbo/.

59. U.S. Census Bureau, "Census of Governments: About the Survey," http://www.census.gov/govs/cog2012/about_the_data.html (accessed February 15, 2013).

60. As of February 15, 2013, the dedicated website was http://www.census.gov/govs/cog2012/.

61. U.S. Census Bureau, "Business Dynamics Statistics: Overview," https://www.census.gov/ces/dataproducts/bds/overview.html (accessed February 15, 2013).

62. As of February 15, 2013, the dedicated website was https://www.census.gov/ces/dataproducts/bds/.

63. U.S. Small Business Administration, "Mission Statement," http://www.sba.gov/content/mission-statement-0 (accessed February 15, 2013).

64. Small Business Development Centers currently operate in every state, the District of Columbia, Guam, Puerto Rico, American Samoa, and the U.S. Virgin Islands. As of February 15, 2013, an online directory of local offices was available at http://www.sbdcnet.org/find-your-local-sbdc-office.

65. As of February 15, 2013, the website of the Office of Advocacy was available at http://www.sba.gov/category/advocacy-navigation-structure/about-us.

66. As of February 15, 2013, the SBA State Economic Profiles were available at www.sba.gov/advocacy/848.

67. As of February 15, 2013, the dedicated IRS data website was http://www.irs.gov/uac/Tax-Stats-2.

68. U.S. Census Bureau, "Annual Estimates of the Population of Metropolitan and Micropolitan Statistical Areas: April 1, 2010 to July 1, 2011 (CBSA-EST2011–01)."

69. Author's analysis of and U.S. Bureau of Economic Analysis, "GDP by Metropolitan Area: Milwaukee-Waukesha-West Allis, WI MSA, 2010"; U.S. Bureau of Economic Analysis, "Gross Domestic Product by State: Wisconsin, 2010"; and U.S. Census Bureau, "Annual Estimates of the Resident Population: April 1, 2010 to July 1, 2011."

70. Readers interested in a more in-depth consideration should see Center for Economic Development, *The Economic State of Milwaukee, 1990–2008* (Milwaukee, WI: University of Wisconsin-Milwaukee, 2010), http://www4.uwm.edu/ced/publications/milwecon_2010.cfm, and various publications of the Center on Wisconsin Strategies, which, as of February 16, 2013, were available at http://www.cows.org/.

71. Author's analysis of U.S. Census Bureau, County Business Patterns, 2010; and U.S. Census Bureau, Nonemployer Statistics, 2010.

72. Ibid.

73. Author's analysis of U.S. Census Bureau, Nonemployer Statistics, 2010.

74. Author's analysis of U.S. Census Bureau, County Business Patterns, 2010.

75. Author's analysis of U.S. Census Bureau, Statistics of U.S. Businesses, 2009.

76. Ibid.

77. CNN Money.com, "2009 Fortune 1000," accessed January 6, 2012, http://money.cnn.com/magazines/fortune/fortune500/2009/states/WI.html.

78. Author's analysis of U.S. Census Bureau, Survey of Business Owners, 2007.

79. Ibid.
80. Author's analysis of U.S. Census Bureau, Statistics of U.S. Businesses, 2007 and 2009.
81. Author's analysis of U.S. Census Bureau, Statistics of U.S. Businesses, 2009.
82. Author's analysis of U.S. Census Bureau, Statistics of U.S. Businesses, 2007 and 2009.
83. Author's analysis of U.S. Census Bureau, Statistics of U.S. Businesses, 2009.
84. Ibid.
85. Author's analysis of U.S. Census Bureau, Statistics of U.S. Businesses, 2007 and 2009.
86. Author's analysis of U.S. Census Bureau, Survey of Business Owners, 2007.

7 | Labor Markets

For most American households, the labor market is the most important part of the economy. Between 2007 and 2011, households collectively derived an average of 75 percent of their annual income from the wages and salaries earned through paid employment.[1] Participation in the labor market is what enables households to satisfy their material needs, save for the future, and contribute their talents to the larger economy. For those reasons, the health of local labor markets matters greatly to regional well-being. When jobs are plentiful, an economy booms and households thrive, but when jobs are scarce, an economy slumps and households struggle to make ends meet.

"The great American jobs machine," the labor economists Lawrence Mishel, Jared Bernstein, and Heidi Shierholz wrote, "arguably is the most powerful mechanism in our economy for achieving broadly shared prosperity."[2] The collection and analysis of information about labor markets therefore is an important statistical function performed best by the public sector. The federal government initiated the regular collection of labor market information in the 1930s, but the statistical framework that has evolved is "decentralized, complex, and idiosyncratic, involving multiple federal agencies and sets of state government partners."[3] In short, the system is not user-friendly.

Created for the purposes of top-down policy making and social scientific research, the federal labor market information system is difficult to grasp. Think of how often the unemployment rate—perhaps the only labor force indicator with broad name recognition—is misrepresented and misinterpreted. To improve understanding of labor market information, this chapter explains three types of labor market data: static data, like the unemployment rate; dynamic data, like worker flows; and projection data, like forecasts of occupational employment. The chapter begins by identifying the core components of the labor force and essential data sources. Attention then shifts to matters related to occupational structure, labor market dynamics, and labor market forecasting.

A shortcoming of the current labor market information system is that it contains limited regional information, so unlike other chapters in this book, this one illustrates core concepts through an extended state-level example rather than a regional one. Specifically, the chapter presents data for the state of North Carolina—a state that in 2011 was home to 9.7 million people of whom 7.6 million were of working age—supplemented, as appropriate, with information for individual metropolitan statistical areas within the state.[4]

DEFINING THE LABOR FORCE

Because most people work for a living, they possess a general sense of the labor market and concepts like unemployment. These intuitive understandings, however, are too imprecise for statistical purposes. Public statistical agencies therefore have established rigorous definitions of core subjects—definitions that often differ from popular notions. If they are to profit from labor market studies, civic leaders must grasp how statistical agencies define the labor force.

Figure 7.1 shows the model of the labor force used for statistical purposes in the United States; each cell contains the seasonally unadjusted, annual average value recorded for the variable in 2011 in North Carolina.[5] This model applies to any unit of geography found in the country (e.g., states, counties, and metropolitan areas), and the values in the chart provide the basis for understanding basic labor force concepts and measures of labor utilization.

LABOR FORCE CONCEPTS

Public statistical agencies base all measures of the labor force on data drawn from the *civilian noninstitutional population*.[6] This group encompasses every person age 16 and older except military personnel on active duty and residents of institutions like prisons and nursing homes. The reason for excluding young people, active military personnel, and institutional residents is that they are unable to work in the civilian economy. Of course, a person's status can change, as happens when a member of the armed forces leaves the service. In 2011, the average size of the civilian noninstitutional population in North Carolina was 7.4 million.

Just because a person can work in no way implies that the person wishes to work. The civilian noninstitutional population therefore encompasses two groups: individuals *not in the labor force* and individuals in the *civilian labor force*. Retired persons and stay-at-home parents, for example, could hold jobs but have elected not to work for personal reasons. As will be discussed later in the chapter, the population not in the labor force embraces two groups of *marginally attached workers*, or jobless individuals who fail to meet the technical definition of unemployment. In 2011, some 2.8 million North Carolinians were not in the labor force; of those individuals, 2.6 million reported not working by choice.

The civilian labor force includes all members of the civilian noninstitutional population who are *employed* or *unemployed*. Individuals in the civilian labor force are active labor market participants who hold jobs or are seeking jobs. An average of 4.6 million North Carolinians participated in the civilian labor force in 2011. The over-

Figure 7.1 Structure of the North Carolina Labor Force, 2011

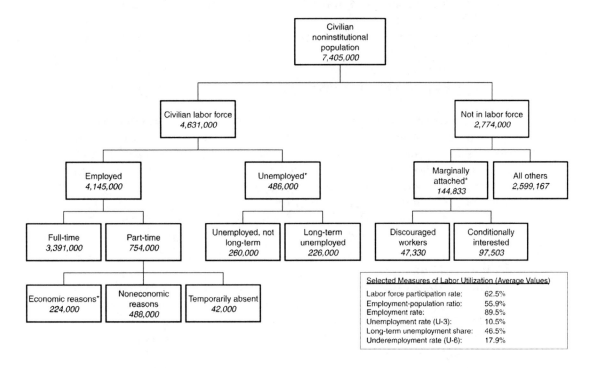

Sources: U.S. Bureau of Labor Statistics, *Geographic Profile of Employment and Unemployment, 2011*, http://www.bls.gov/opub/gp/laugp.htm (accessed January 28, 2013); and U.S. Bureau of Labor Statistics, *Alternative Measures of Labor Underutilization for States: 2011 Annual Averages*, http://www.bls.gov/lau/stalt11q4.htm (accessed January 28, 2013).
Notes: All values are seasonally unadjusted annual averages; * denotes groups included in the count of underemployed workers.

whelming majority of those individuals worked, but 486,000 people were unemployed. Some 61.1 percent of unemployed North Carolinians in 2011 were jobless due to the loss of a job, the completion of a temporary work situation, or a layoff that was temporary in nature. Another 32.1 percent of unemployed individuals were without work because they were entering or reentering the labor force, and the remaining 6.5 percent of unemployed persons had left their jobs voluntarily.

Because statistical definitions of employment and unemployment differ from popular understandings, the concepts of employment and unemployment require additional explanation. As will be explained later in the chapter, labor force estimates originate in the Current Population Survey, a monthly survey of the working-age members of individual households that refers to the week containing the 12th of the month, known as the reference week. To be "employed," an individual must meet *one* of the following three conditions:

- Performed some work for pay or profit during the reference week
- Were temporarily absent from a regular job due to illnesses, leave, bad weather, industrial action, or personal reasons, regardless of whether the person was paid for the time
- Completed at least 15 hours of unpaid work in a family-owned enterprise operated by a household member

The employed population contains two groups of workers classified according to the number of hours worked during the reference week. *Full-time workers* are persons employed for 35 or more hours during the reference week, and part-time workers are those employed for fewer than 35 hours. Some *part-time workers* prefer their schedules for a *noneconomic reason*, but others work part time for *economic reasons*, such as an inability to find a full-time job. In 2011, some 3.4 million of the 4.1 million North Carolinians with jobs worked on a full-time basis. Of the 712,000 part-time workers not temporarily absent from their jobs, 488,000 preferred part-time work, but the remaining 224,000 desired full-time employment but could not find it.

When dealing with employment data, the treatment of self-employed individuals is a frequent source of confusion. Self-employed workers fall into one of two categories: the *incorporated self-employed* and the *unincorporated self-employed*. Labor force statistics capture both kinds of workers but classify them differently. Because self-employed individuals who have legally incorporated their businesses are actually employees of those firms, they technically are wage and salary employees. Individuals who have not incorporated their businesses are considered self-employed. In 2011, the number of unincorporated self-employed individuals in the United States averaged 9.4 million, which was the equivalent of 6.8 percent of the labor force. Another 5.1 million persons representing 3.7 percent of the labor force were employed, on average, in legally incorporated businesses that they owned.[7]

The unemployed population consists of members of the civilian labor force who meet *all three* of the following criteria:

- Lacked a job during the reference week (the week in which the 12th day of the month falls)
- Were available for work
- Had made at least one active effort to find a job during the previous four weeks

Individuals on a temporary layoff (e.g., manufacturing workers idled during a plant retooling) also are counted as unemployed.

Unemployed individuals belong to one of two groups based on how long they have been unemployed. Those out of work for fewer than 26 weeks are the *unemployed*, and those unemployed for more than 26 weeks are the *long-term unemployed*. Twenty-six weeks serves as the dividing line because unemployed individuals in most states are unable to collect state-funded unemployment insurance for longer than that. In 2011, North Carolina was home to an average of 260,000 individuals who had been unemployed for fewer than 26 weeks and 226,000 individuals who had been unemployed for more than 26 weeks.

The statistical definition of unemployment has no relationship to receipt of unemployment insurance compensation. Some unemployed workers receive insurance payments, but most do not. In fact, estimates suggest that only 26 percent of unemployed Americans in 2011 received regular, state-funded unemployment insurance payments.[8] That gap happened for multiple reasons: some individuals who are potentially eligible for insurance compensation failed to apply, some individuals applied but failed to meet the eligibility criteria, and some individuals had exhausted all of the compensation for which they were eligible. Because insurance claimants are a subset of the unemployed population, it is wrong to treat data about claims for unemployment insurance as being interchangeable with unemployment data (see Box 7.1).

Not every jobless person who desires work is unemployed. As mentioned earlier, marginally attached workers are not unemployed because they are not actively seeking work. Although such *discouraged workers* have looked for work in the recent past, they have stopped looking and therefore are not considered unemployed. In the same way, *conditionally interested workers* are jobless individuals who desire work but are not seeking it for reasons other than discouragement, such as a lack of childcare. Of the 145,000 North Carolinians marginally attached to the labor force in 2011, some 98,000 were conditionally interested in work, and the remaining 47,000 were discouraged workers.

Marginally attached workers, individuals working part time for economic reasons, and the unemployed constitute the *underemployed*. The concept of underemployment provides a broad view of the degree to which labor is unused or underused. For instance, individuals working part time for economic reasons are working, but they are neither providing as much labor as they wish nor producing as much output as they could.

Besides causing confusion, the difference between unemployment and underemployment often leads to claims that the government deliberately undercounts unemployment. That criticism is unfounded. While the official measure of unemployment is narrow in scope, it clearly and accurately measures what it purports to measure. Moreover, the federal government publishes five supplemental measures of unemployment each month, including the "U-6" measure, which tracks underemployment.[9] Besides providing monthly underemployment data for the nation, the federal government releases quarterly, state-level estimates of underemployment. In 2011, an average of 855,000 North Carolinians were underemployed.

The difference between unemployment and underemployment sometimes clouds international comparisons because some advanced industrial countries, notably Germany, define unemployment in a way akin to the American concept of underemployment. When drawing international comparisons, analysts should rely on the "harmonized rates" prepared by international bodies such as the Organization for Economic Cooperation and Development, a policy forum to which most wealthy nations belong, and the International Labor Organization, an agency of the United Nations. The U.S. Bureau of Labor Statistics also prepares international estimates that adjust foreign data to domestic concepts, although that program soon may be terminated.[10]

Box 7.1 Weekly Unemployment Insurance Claims

The U.S. Bureau of Labor Statistics reports weekly on the number of new and continuing claims for unemployment insurance (UI) compensation filed during the previous week.

Established in 1935 as part of the Social Security Act, UI compensation temporarily replaces a portion of the wages lost by qualifying individuals who are jobless through no fault of their own. The insurance system is a federal-state partnership. The federal government establishes basic program guidelines, exercises program oversight, and funds state operating costs. States, in turn, set eligibility criteria, determine benefit levels, and administer statewide insurance programs. Both levels of government levy payroll taxes to generate the monies needed to finance the program.

Each weekly report lists the number of new and continuing claims for compensation filed during the prior week, known as the "reference week." Because people file claims after losing a job, the claims filed in the reference week are for compensable events that occurred the week before, which is called the "benefit week." Besides providing absolute counts of new and continuing claims, the weekly report presents the insured unemployment rate, which is the number of UI claims expressed as a share of the total number of insured workers. National data appear in seasonally adjusted and unadjusted series.

The weekly release only reports on claims for regular state-funded insurance payments, which individuals in most states may draw for no more than 26 weeks. During recessions, however, the U.S. Congress often establishes and funds, at least in part, emergency programs that provide additional weeks of insurance compensation; figures for those programs typically appear elsewhere.

State-level information is available in the weekly claims report. While local information is not provided, state Labor Market Information agencies have such data and often publish them in other formats. Because statistical agencies do not adjust state and local data for seasonal effects, analysts must draw time-series comparisons with care. A simple method for accounting for seasonal fluctuations is to calculate a four-week moving average of claims.

The weekly claims report is a regular economic indicator that reflects current trends in the labor market and is suggestive of future developments. Steady increases in the number of new filings might indicate the onset of a recession, just as steady declines might signal the beginnings of a recovery.

While useful, the weekly claims report is not a comprehensive measure of unemployment: it simply lists the number of claims for UI compensation. Yet the vast majority of unemployed Americans never collect UI. In fact, just 26 percent of unemployed individuals in 2011 received regular state-funded insurance payments. The weekly claims report therefore is not a substitute for the information about the broader universe of unemployment captured by the Current Population Survey or Local Area Unemployment Statistics programs.

Release of the weekly report typically occurs each Thursday morning at 8:30 a.m., and copies of past reports and historical data are accessible through the Department of Labor's website.

Sources: Bernard Baumhol, *The Secrets of Economic Indicators*, 2d ed. (Upper Saddle River, NJ: Wharton School Publishing, 2008), 40–43; and U.S. Department of Labor, "Unemployment Insurance Chartbook," http://www.doleta.gov/unemploy/chartbook.cfm (accessed January 26, 2013).

MEASURES OF LABOR UTILIZATION

Knowledge of absolute labor market quantities like the number of long-term unemployed individuals is necessary but insufficient for regional analysis. Analysts therefore tend to favor relative quantities like the unemployment rate, because they illustrate the degree to which a region is utilizing the stock of available labor.

Labor utilization is relevant for a number of reasons. Because most individuals derive the bulk of their incomes from paid employment, the underutilization of labor may result in economic hardships such as reduced earnings and lack of health insurance. One study of the increase in underemployment that occurred between 2007 and 2009 in the United States concluded that excess underemployment caused $68 billion in lost annual earning, or $14,456 for every additional underemployed worker.[11] On a more abstract level, labor is a primary factor of production, so unused or underused labor is a waste of economic capacity. When a regional economy fails to maximize the use of its labor resources, it produces fewer goods and services than it is capable, which leads to reduced levels of prosperity and well-being.

Several measures of labor utilization regularly appear in regional analyses. No individual measure provides a comprehensive view of the degree to which a regional economy taps the potential of its human resources, but used together, such measures explain local labor market dynamics and can inform economic and workforce development policies. Five indicators are particularly important.

First, the *labor force participation rate* captures the share of the civilian noninstitutional population that is engaged in the civilian labor force. The participation rate shows what proportion of the population potentially available for work is working or actively seeking work. In 2011, North Carolina's labor force participation rate equaled 62.5 percent; in other words, slightly more than 6 of every 10 North Carolinians of working age were in the labor force. Of the remaining 37.5 percent of the civilian noninstitutional population, almost all—93.7 percent—were outside of the labor force by choice. Over time, labor force participation is an important driver of growth: the higher the share of the working-age population in the labor force, the more an economy can produce.

Second, the *employment-to-population ratio* measures the share of the civilian noninstitutional population that is working. The indicator shows the proportion of the working-age population engaged in an economically productive activity. In 2011, North Carolina's ratio averaged 55.9 percent, meaning that 55.9 percent of the working-age population held jobs that year. In general, the employment-to-population ratio points to an economy's ability to provide employment opportunities for its working-age population. The more favorable the ratio, the greater the share of the population engaged in the production of goods and services.

Third, the *employment rate* shows the share of the civilian labor force that is working, and the *unemployment rate* gauges the share of the civilian labor force that is jobless and actively seeking work. In 2011, the average employment rate in North Carolina equaled 89.5 percent, while the average unemployment rate was 10.5 percent. That extremely high unemployment rate was a sign of an unhealthy labor market caused by the 2007–2009 recession. In fact, the so-called Great Recession drove North Carolina's unemployment rate to the highest level recorded since the advent of modern state-level labor force statistics in the 1970s.

Fourth, the *long-term unemployment share* tracks the proportion of unemployed individuals who have been out of work for more than 26 weeks. Long spells of unemployment further raise an individual's odds of exhausting any savings and encountering financial hardships; the chances of finding work also drop the longer a person is unemployed. Some 46.5 percent of unemployed North Carolinians in 2011 had been jobless for more than 26 weeks. One alarming aspect of the recent recession was a spike in long-term unemployment. In fact, increasing durations of unemployment led the federal government to alter how it reports length of unemployment in early 2011, and the monthly national employment report now lists durations for periods lasting up to five years.[12]

Finally, the *underemployment rate* gauges the share of the adjusted labor force that is effectively jobless. The underemployment rate is the total number of unemployed workers, marginally attached workers, and individuals working part time for economic reasons divided by the sum of the civilian labor force and marginally attached workers. In 2011, North Carolina's underemployment rate equaled 17.9 percent. This disturbingly high figure was yet another consequence of the last recession and indicated that the state's labor market was not fully utilizing available labor.

When interpreting labor market indicators, civic leaders should remember that changes in rates of labor force utilization originate in structural and cyclical factors (see Box 7.2). Consider a structural development like population aging. All else equal, the labor force participation rate in an aging population should decline, as people above the customary retirement age elect not to work or become unable to work due to infirmity. Similarly, a structural change in the industrial composition of an economy might cause high levels of unemployment among workers in a declining industry. Cyclical forces also influence rates of labor utilization. Unemployment and underemployment normally rise during recessions, as firms terminate employees and freeze hiring due to a drop in the overall demand for goods and services.

Regional leaders must recognize that structural and cyclical factors influence the labor force experiences of different demographic groups in different ways. Hispanic and African American workers, for instance, typically record higher unemployment rates than white workers. That was so in North Carolina in 2011, a year in which 8.1 percent of white workers were unemployed, as opposed to 9.2 percent of Hispanic workers and 19 percent of African Americans. Along the same lines, the female labor force participation rate long has been below the corresponding male rate, though the gap has narrowed considerably since 1960. In 2011, North Carolina's female participation rate was 55.8 percent versus a male participation rate of 70 percent. Demographic differences are one reason why regional leaders should not limit their attention to overall indicators, as recognizing differences among groups is essential to ensuring that labor markets work on behalf of all residents.

Box 7.2 Types of Unemployment

In a dynamic economy, individuals regularly gain and lose jobs, so some share of the civilian labor force is always unemployed. When analyzing unemployment, it is necessary to differentiate among types of unemployment, as each one may require specific policy and programmatic responses.

Labor market economists commonly consider four types of unemployment.

1. Frictional Unemployment

Frictional unemployment is joblessness linked to short-term, often voluntary gaps in employment. Even when an economy is at full employment, some individuals will be jobless by choice (e.g., job changers) or because they are entering the labor market for the first time or reentering it after time away.

2. Seasonal Unemployment

Seasonal unemployment is joblessness originating in normal patterns of business activity. Seasonal unemployment is a common occurrence in industries such as construction, agriculture, leisure and hospitality services, and retail trade. Seasonal unemployment also may stem from temporary supply-side factors such as an influx of student workers to the labor market during the summer months.

3. Structural Unemployment

Structural unemployment is joblessness resulting from gaps between the skills supplied by the labor force and those demanded by employers. Structural unemployment generally is a local or regional phenomenon rooted in factors such as demand, technological advances, or changes in the size and composition of the labor force.

4. Cyclical Unemployment

Cyclical unemployment results when the overall level of economic demand in an economy is insufficient to support employment for everyone who desires work. Other names for the phenomenon include "demand-deficient" and "Keynesian" unemployment, the latter after the famous British economist John Maynard Keynes. Cyclical unemployment occurs when a drop in the aggregate level of demand in an economy leads firms to trim payrolls and reduce hiring in response. Because the short-term rigidity in wage rates prevents labor markets from settling at a new level of equilibrium, mass unemployment results.

Debates over the causes of unemployment are contentious, particularly because multiple forms of unemployment may exist simultaneously within an economy. In general, the most heated debates involve structural and cyclical unemployment. If unemployment fundamentally is structural, effective policy responses include providing retraining and encouraging workers to move to places where their skills are in demand. The policy response to cyclical unemployment is to boost overall levels of aggregate demand, which is a task the federal government can perform through temporary deficit spending.

State and regional leaders are more limited in how they can counter unemployment. The provision of job information and labor matching services can help minimize frictional and seasonal unemployment, while the funding of worker retraining initiatives can address structural unemployment. Remedying cyclical unemployment typically requires a federal response, because state and local governments are required to maintain balanced budgets and cyclical downturns are national in scope. Nevertheless, it is possible for state and local leaders to exacerbate a cyclical downturn by enacting budget reductions that offset federal efforts to stimulate the economy.

Source: Drawn from Edward Wolff, *Poverty and Income Distribution,* 2d ed. (Malden, MA: Wiley-Blackwell, 2009), 232–238.

SOURCES OF LABOR MARKET INFORMATION

As is the case with most statistical functions in the United States, multiple federal and state agencies share responsibility for collecting labor market information. Consider data about occupations, or "the type of work that a person does."[13] State Labor Market Information agencies and the U.S. Bureau of Labor Statistics jointly prepare estimates of employment levels and wage rates for individual occupations, while the Employment and Training Administration, a unit of the U.S. Department of Labor, sponsors a more expansive system of occupational information. The U.S. Office of Management and Budget, meanwhile, oversees the conceptual framework used to classify occupations. Such complexities result in a system that, as two noted analysts have quipped, "ain't always pretty, but it works."[14]

The federal labor-market information system is large and complex, but the core data products come from the U.S. Bureau of Labor Statistics (BLS). Established in 1884, the BLS collects "information upon the subject of labor, its relation to capital, the hours of labor and the earnings of laboring men and women, and the means of promoting their material, social, intellectual, and moral prosperity."[15] Prior to the 1930s, the BLS had limited funding and authority, but the mass unemployment that marked the Great Depression triggered the agency's evolution into a modern statistical organization. In 1959 the BLS became responsible for preparing monthly estimates of national labor force indicators.

Today, the BLS collaborates with multiple federal and state agencies. National labor force estimates come from the Current Population Survey, a representative monthly survey of 60,000 American households sponsored by the BLS and conducted by the U.S. Census Bureau.[16] State Labor Market Information (LMI) agencies, meanwhile, prepare state and local estimates under contract to the BLS. LMI offices, which typically are units within the state agencies responsible for administering the unemployment insurance program, receive funding from the BLS to assemble estimates according to federally prescribed methods. Each month, the BLS and LMI agencies prepare labor force estimates for more than 7,000 political and statistical geographies: census regions, census divisions, states, metropolitan statistical areas, micropolitan statistical areas, combined statistical areas, small labor market areas, counties and county equivalents, cities with 25,000 or more residents, and every city and town in the six states of New England.[17]

CORE CONCEPTS

The BLS and its state-level partners employ sophisticated statistical techniques to prepare accurate and reliable data that are consistent over time and comparable across geographies. To ensure the uniformity of data, the BLS has developed a standardized system of methods and concepts—a system that may differ from those used by other statistical agencies to measure similar phenomena. While a full discussion of BLS terminology and methods is beyond this chapter's scope, two sets of concepts require elaboration.

Persons and Jobs

Some BLS products measure *persons*: individual human beings, typically those who are age 16 and older. The monthly estimate of unemployment therefore reflects the total number of persons who meet a definition of unemployment. Other BLS products track *jobs*, or the positions on the payrolls of business establishments. There is not a 1-to-1 relationship between the number of employed persons and jobs. Think of a person who holds a full-time job during the day and a part-time job at night. A count of persons would report one employed person, but a tally of jobs would show two jobs. That explains why the number of employed persons in North Carolina in December 2011 totaled 4.2 million, but the tally of jobs in the state equaled 3.9 million.[18]

Place of Residence and Place of Work

BLS products that measure persons typically organize data according to *place of residence*, while those that track jobs normally tabulate data according to the *place of work* associated with a business establishment. This difference between counting people where they live and jobs where they are located is why payroll employment in the Winston-Salem, NC Metropolitan Statistical Area (MSA) equaled 207,100 in December 2011, but the number of employed persons was 220,328.[19] This is not anomalous; in fact, "the number of employed persons in a region usually will not match the number of jobs."[20]

DATA METHODS

Before exploring the core BLS data products, it is necessary to reflect on how the agency generates its numbers. Some BLS figures come from *statistical sampling*, which is a process by which analysts select and study a subset of a population. If chosen properly, the results from the sample will be representative of the whole population. Other products come from *enumerations* of every member of a population of interest, and still others rely on *administrative data*, such as unemployment insurance tax records. Data users further should note whether the figures contain adjustments for *seasonal effects* and avoid mixing unadjusted and adjusted figures. Finally, consumers of labor market information should ensure that comparisons drawn in a report involve comparable concepts and periods of time. (See chapter 4 for a full discussion of these concepts.)

Consumers of BLS data should remember that the estimates are subject to multiple revisions. When preparing data, the BLS must navigate a tension between timeliness and comprehensiveness. If the agency waited until every relevant piece of information became available, findings would not appear until well after the reference period, but a rapid publication schedule would cause findings to appear before all the facts were available. The BLS attempts to strike a balance by releasing preliminary data quickly and then revising as necessary. Each month the BLS publishes preliminary labor force data for the prior month and revised figures for the preceding two months.

The revisions sometimes are sizable, so a failure to check for revisions may result in the use of outdated data.

The BLS periodically benchmarks survey data. *Benchmarking* is a statistical process used to adjust survey estimates to a control population. An example of benchmarking occurs every March when state LMI agencies adjust state-level payroll employment totals derived from a survey of business establishments to match the counts found in unemployment insurance tax records. Benchmarking sometimes may result in significant revisions to published information: the benchmark change to North Carolina payroll data for 2011, for instance, changed totals from as far back as 2007.[21]

KEY DATA SOURCES

The BLS and state LMI agencies generate a wide array of national, state, and local labor market information. For the purposes of regional labor market analysis, four BLS products—the Current Population Survey, the Local Area Unemployment Survey, the Current Employment Statistics, and the Quarterly Census of Employment and Wages—provide much of the labor market information that underpins regional studies. All four sources produce static data that show specific phenomena at distinct moments in time.

Current Population Survey

Initiated in 1940 by the Works Progress Administration, the *Current Population Survey* (CPS) is "the primary source of labor force statistics for the population of the United States."[22] The BLS sponsors the survey's labor force component, but the U.S. Census Bureau conducts the study. The results are the foundation of the national monthly employment report and other important social indicators like the poverty rate.

Each month, the Census Bureau contacts a sample of 60,000 households randomly chosen as representative of the civilian noninstitutional population age 15 and older. The Census Bureau queries participating households eight times over an 18-month period: households sit for interviews in four consecutive months, followed by an eight-month pause, after which four more consecutive monthly interviews occur. Interviews occur during the week containing the 19th of the month and solicit information pertaining to the week containing the 12th of the month. Survey participation is voluntary, and the responses are confidential.[23]

The monthly CPS questionnaire contains a standard set of questions asked of all households, plus additional questions for "outgoing" households, or those in their fourth and eighth months of participation. Furthermore, the CPS program fields supplemental questionnaires about individual topics in some months; a few of the supplemental surveys are annual; others are less frequent. Two examples of regular supplements are the Displaced Workers Supplement, which is fielded every other January, and the Volunteer Supplement, which generally occurs in September of each year.[24]

The most important CPS supplement is the one fielded in March: the *Annual Social and Economic Supplement* (ASEC). For each household member age 15 and older, the ASEC asks about work experience, occupational type, industrial classification, hours worked, weeks worked, reasons for not working, total income, income sources, receipt of noncash employment benefits, and receipt of noncash public benefits. The ASEC further gathers data about common demographic characteristics.[25] Among other uses, the ASEC traditionally is the source used to determine the share of the population that lacks health insurance and is the official source of poverty estimates (see chapter 9).

Monthly CPS results are the foundation on which the BLS bases its national labor force estimates. As survey data, CPS estimates are prone to the types of sampling and nonsampling errors described in chapter 4. While the CPS is a rich information source, it yields reliable monthly labor force estimates only at the national level. That said, the CPS provides useful annual information for the nation, census regions, census divisions, states, the District of Columbia, the 50 most populous metropolitan areas, and certain central cities.[26]

Local Area Unemployment Statistics

A collaborative effort between the BLS and state LMI agencies, the *Local Area Unemployment Statistics* (LAUS) program is the source of monthly labor force estimates for states and localities. Like the CPS, the LAUS is a person-based study of the civilian noninstitutional population age 15 and older, though published data cover only persons age 16 and older. As with the CPS, the LAUS tabulates data by place of residence.[27]

The LAUS traces its roots to 1972, when responsibility for preparing state and local labor force estimates shifted to the BLS from another division of the U.S. Department of Labor. In 1973, the BLS unveiled a new estimation system that blended elements of the CPS with data derived from unemployment insurance records. The first monthly LAUS estimates for every census region and division, all 50 states, the District of Columbia, and Puerto Rico, and selected large metropolitan areas appeared in 1978; between 1978 and 1989, the BLS phased in estimates for other areas.[28] The BLS and state LMI agencies now prepare monthly labor force estimates for 7,300 geographic areas, with these estimates informing understanding of local labor market conditions and the annual awarding of some $61 billion in federal funding.[29]

LMI agencies prepare LAUS estimates for their respective states consistent with federal rules. Rather than conducting original and expensive statistical surveys, LMI agencies modify existing data sets—primarily the CPS, unemployment insurance wage and tax records, and payroll employment estimates—for state and local purposes. To produce state-level estimates, LMI agencies transform CPS data into valid labor force estimates. Local estimates originate in the application of different techniques to assorted data sets. As with the CPS, the LAUS reference week is the one that includes the 12th of the month. State data appear in seasonally adjusted and seasonally unadjusted formats, while local data exist in an unadjusted series.

The BLS releases national labor force estimates derived from the CPS as part of the monthly "Employment Situation Report" released at 8:30 a.m. on the first Friday of the month. State and local LAUS data appear later in the month. LMI agencies publish state data two weeks after the national report, with local estimates appearing 7 to 10 days later. Holidays and other factors like the annual benchmarking process may alter the release schedule. LMI agencies generally post an annual calendar of release dates on their websites.

The LAUS program produces two data series: the *Local Area Series* and the *Geographic Profile Series*. The Local Area Series is the normal monthly release of state and local labor force information mentioned earlier. Meanwhile, the Geographic Profile provides limited annual estimates of the demographic and economic characteristics of the labor forces of census regions and divisions, states, 50 large metropolitan statistical areas, and 17 central cities. Because the information in the Geographic Profile comes directly from the CPS, it is subject to multiple sources of sampling and nonsampling error. Despite its limitations, the Geographic Profile is the only source of detailed demographic characteristics about employed and unemployed persons.[30] Note that the totals in the two series may differ.

LAUS data are subject to various kinds of errors, including sampling and nonsampling errors, and errors resulting from the manipulation of data collected from other sources. LAUS data typically are valid at the 90 percent confidence level, meaning there is a 90 percent chance that the true value falls within a specified range. LAUS information is subject to the kinds of data revisions, seasonal adjustments, and benchmark corrections previously discussed.

Current Employment Statistics

A collaborative federal-state partnership launched in 1915, the *Current Employment Statistics* (CES) program—otherwise known as the "establishment survey"—is the main source of monthly information about business employment levels, wages, and hours.[31] Because the survey's focus is on jobs, the data reflect place of work, not place of residence.

Each month, the BLS draws from unemployment insurance tax records a sample of 145,000 private and public businesses spanning 557,000 individual nonagricultural worksites. The CES excludes establishments exempt from the unemployment insurance system, such as agricultural workplaces, domestic employers, and unincorporated small businesses. Prior to 2010, the CES only covered production and nonsupervisory positions, but the survey now covers all payroll positions. The CES questionnaire solicits information about the number of positions on the payrolls of individual business establishments for the week that includes the 12th of the month, as well as information about wages paid and hours worked. While the CES covers full- and part-time employment, the survey does not separate jobs by type. To capture employment changes in new and closing firms, the CES incorporates data from a statistical model developed by the BLS. The CES further arranges results by the industrial classification and ownership structure of business establishments. Participation in the CES is voluntary and responses are confidential, with public statistical agencies suppressing the release of any information that might permit the identification of an individual establishment.[32]

CES data inform the national monthly report on payroll growth, which is released as part of the *Employment Situation Report*. Payroll data appear in seasonally adjusted and seasonally unadjusted series. The joint release of LAUS and CES data is a regular source of confusion, particularly for months in which the two data products offer conflicting findings. Discrepancies appear because the two surveys measure different phenomena in different ways. The LAUS tracks individual employment through a survey of households, but the CES gauges payroll changes through a survey of business establishments. LAUS findings like the unemployment rate tend to attract popular and media attention, but analysts tend to favor the CES over the LAUS due to the kinds of information it provides, the associated level of detail, the ability to cross-reference the data against such comprehensive sources as unemployment insurance tax records, and the smaller margin of error (a national monthly change of +/–100,000 jobs is statistically significant in the CES compared to a change of +/–400,000 in the LAUS). Perhaps the most important monthly piece of CES data is the net change in payroll employment, which indicates whether the economy added more jobs than it lost or vice versa.[33]

To produce state-level estimates of payroll employment, LMI agencies process CES data in various ways to produce estimates for state and metropolitan areas. LMI agencies release state and local data at the same time they release LAUS findings. The joint release means that state and local data releases are subject to popular confusion similar to those at the national level.

As with the LAUS, the CES is prone to various types of errors, including sampling, nonsampling, and processing errors. The information further undergoes the kinds of data revisions, seasonal adjustments, and benchmark corrections discussed previously.

Quarterly Census of Employment and Wages

When the U.S. Congress established unemployment insurance under the Social Security Act of 1935, it mandated the collection of information needed to ensure state compliance with federal requirements. These administrative records are the basis of the *Quarterly Census of Employment Wages* (QCEW), known as the Covered Employment and Wages program or the ES-202 program, in reference to the identification number on an old reporting form.[34]

The QCEW effectively is a census of employment that covers "about 99.7% of all wage and salary civilian employment in the country."[35] The reason the QCEW is not a full census of civilian employment is its connection to the unemployment insurance program, which excludes business establishments exempt from the unemployment insurance system. As with the CES, the QCEW focuses on payroll jobs measured by place of work.

Because the QCEW originates in administrative tax records, business participation is mandatory, but there are no administrative tasks beyond those associated with paying unemployment insurance taxes. No data are released that would enable the identification of a specific business, and when it might be possible to identify an individual business from the data, the BLS and state LMI agencies suppress the information.

Each quarter, state LMI agencies aggregate employment and wage data from employer tax filings. QCEW reports contain information on total employment and wages during the quarter. The reference period for each month in the quarter is the week containing the 12th of the month. Recognize that the QCEW defines wages more broadly than the CES. The QCEW counts wages, paid leave time, overtime, bonuses, back pay, tips, in-kind payments, stock options, and, sometimes, employer contributions to defined benefit plans, but the CES only tracks wages, paid leave time, and overtime. Furthermore, the QCEW groups establishment data by place of work, industrial classification, employment size, and ownership structure.[36]

State LMI agencies release two kinds of QCEW data: quarterly reports appear 6 months after the end of a quarter, and the publication of annual data occurs 10 months after the end of the calendar year. Because the QCEW is a census, data exist at detailed industrial and geographic levels. LMI agencies prepare data for states, counties, metropolitan statistical areas, and state-specific geographies like economic development regions and workforce investment boards.

Given that the QCEW is a census, sampling error is not an issue, but nonsampling error may occur. Also, the information contained in the census is not subject to the kinds of data revisions, seasonal adjustments, and benchmark corrections discussed previously. While the QCEW provides more thorough information than the CES, the breadth comes at the expense of timeliness. Data users interested in the most current information therefore should consult the CES, but those desiring comprehensiveness should turn to the QCEW.

Other Data Sources

The CPS, LAUS, CES, and QCEW are not the only public sources of labor force and payroll information. The U.S. Bureau of Economic Analysis and U.S. Census Bureau prepare similar estimates. The American Community Survey, for one, collects LAUS-like labor market information from individuals of working age, while the Bureau of Economic Analysis compiles payroll employment and wage data that resemble, yet are broader than, the CES and QCEW. Along the same lines, many of the sources of business data introduced in chapter 6 contain information similar to that contained in the CES and LAUS. Other BLS products delve into certain topics in greater depth (e.g., mass layoffs and union membership). Numerous private, proprietary databases exist as well.

The selection of data hinges on the research questions under consideration, and in many circumstances no single source will provide everything. The hallmark of a good analysis therefore is the ability "to take employment data from various sources and figure out a way to work with them to develop one consistent story about the region's economy."[37]

OCCUPATIONAL STRUCTURE

Some analyses look beyond the general labor force data provided through surveys and enumerations and study the labor force in terms of shared characteristics such as race, gender, age, and educational attainment. One way to classify the labor force is in terms of occupation.

An *occupation* is "a category of jobs that are similar with respect to the work performed and the skills possessed by the incumbents."[38] Since 2000, federal agencies have classified occupations according to a common framework known as the *Standard Occupational Classification* (SOC) system. Developed by a task force coordinated by the U.S. Office of Management and Budget, the SOC "classifies all occupations in which work is performed for pay or profit."[39] The SOC framework is a hierarchy with four levels: the 840 detailed occupations contained within the system ultimately collapse into 23 major groups.[40] Table 7.1 lists the major groups

Table 7.1 Standard Occupational Classification (SOC) System, 2010

A. Listing of SOC Major Groups (Two-Digit Level)

SOC Code	Name	SOC Code	Name
11	Management Occupations	35	Food Preparation and Serving Related Occupations
13	Business and Financial Operations Occupations	37	Building and Grounds Cleaning and Maintenance Occupations
15	Computer and Mathematical Occupations	39	Personal Care and Service Occupations
17	Architecture and Engineering Occupations	41	Sales and Related Occupations
19	Life, Physical, and Social Sciences Occupations	43	Office and Administrative Support Occupations
21	Community and Social Service Occupations	45	Farming, Fishing, and Forestry Occupations
23	Legal Occupations	47	Construction and Extraction Occupations
25	Education, Training, and Library Occupations	49	Installation, Maintenance, and Repair Occupations
27	Arts, Design, Entertainment, Sports, and Media Occupations	51	Production Occupations
29	Health Care Practitioners and Technical Occupations	53	Transportation and Materials Moving Occupations
31	Health Care Support Occupations	55	Military Specific Occupations
33	Protective Service Occupations		

B. General SOC Hierarchy

Major Group (23 categories in total)
    Minor Group (97 categories in total)
        Broad Occupation (461 categories in total)
            Detailed Occupation (840 categories in total)

C. Examples of SOC Classifications

Motorcycle Mechanics		Fitness Trainers and Aerobics Instructors	
SOC Code	Title	SOC Code	Title
49–0000	Installation, Maintenance, and Repair Occupations	39–0000	Personal Care and Service Occupations
49–3000	Vehicle and Mobile Equipment Mechanics, Installers, and Repairers	39–9000	Other Personal Care and Service Workers
49–3050	Small Engine Mechanics	39–9030	Recreation and Fitness Workers
49–3052	Motorcycle Mechanics	39–9031	Fitness Trainers and Aerobics Instructors

Source: U.S. Office of Management and Budget, *Standard Occupational Classification Manual,* 2010 (Washington, DC: U.S. Government Printing Office, 2010).

and demonstrates how the hierarchy applies to two occupations: motorcycle mechanics and fitness instructors.

First published in 1980, the SOC received little attention before 2000, when a greatly revised and expanded version was required for federal agencies and recommended for state and local governments and private businesses. The SOC categorizes occupations by the actual work performed or, in some cases, by the education and skills needed to perform competently the work. An update to the SOC appeared in 2010, with another scheduled for 2018 and every 10 years thereafter.[41]

At first glance, the SOC resembles the North American Industrial Classification System (NAICS), a hierarchical statistical framework introduced in chapter 6. A difference is that the NAICS classifies business establishments based on the similarities in their production processes, but the SOC categorizes individual workers according to the work performed. In some ways, the two systems are complementary. A business in a particular industry normally will employ workers in multiple occupations (e.g., managers, production staff, salespersons), just as someone in a specific occupation might work in any number of industries. An accountant, for one, could work at a professional accounting firm or as in-house accountant for a manufacturer or a hospital. The person would be an accountant in all three situations, but the industry in which the accountant works would change.

The SOC framework classifies occupations, but provides no information about the wage levels and educational and skill requirements associated with specific occupations (see Box 7.3). Analysts interested in such information should consult the Occupation Informational Network (O*NET) or the Occupational Employment Statistics Program.

Sponsored by the Employment and Training Administration and administered by North Carolina's LMI agency, O*NET is "a comprehensive database of occupational profiles."[42] O*NET researchers base their work on the SOC system and then collect more detailed information about each occupation. Specifically, O*NET compiles information about the tasks and work activities performed by each occupation; the processes used to perform the tasks; the required knowledge, skills, and abilities needed to perform the tasks; and the personal characteristics associated with success in the occupation. O*NET further provides information about wage and employment trends for each occupation, along with a discussion of related occupations.

All O*NET information is available on the internet.[43] Unlike other websites discussed in this book, the O*NET site is geared toward general users, as one of the program's goals is to provide accessible career planning information to individuals ranging from secondary students considering what to study to displaced workers weighing their next career moves. The database is searchable in multiple ways, such as by interests, work activities, educational requirements, and growth prospects; it also contains a thorough listing of "green jobs" (see Box 7.4). Bear in mind that O*NET data are national in scope, and the system is not explicitly designed for regional analysis.

The *Occupational Employment Statistics Program (OES)* is a more conventional data product. Sponsored by the BLS and fielded by state LMI agencies, the OES yields "occupational employment and wage rate information for the U.S. economy, as well

Box 7.3 Education and Training Classification Systems

Every occupation requires some combination of education, training, skill, and experience for initial entry and as a threshold for obtaining and maintaining competency. The U.S. Bureau of Labor Statistics (BLS) endeavors to measure the education and training requirements associated with individual occupations.

Between 1995 and 2010, the BLS maintained a classification system that aimed to assign every occupation to one of 11 educational and training categories according to the "most significant source" of education and training associated with the occupation; categories included Bachelor's Degree, Postsecondary Vocational Training, and Short-Term On-the-Job Training. Unfortunately, the typology proved extremely confusing because, among other reasons, it blended aspects of formal education, training, and work experience.

In 2011, the BLS finalized a new education and classification system that addresses many of the problems inherent in the previous model. The new system classifies occupations along three dimensions: the typical level of formal education needed to enter the occupation; the amount of work experience, if any, required for entry into an occupation or that is acceptable in place of formal education; and the type of on-the-job training necessary for achieving competency in the occupation. By classifying each occupation in three ways, the BLS hopes to provide a more nuanced view of "the education and training needed for entry into a given occupation and to become competent at performing the occupation." Below are the categories associated with each dimension in the new BLS system:

- *Entry-level education:* doctoral or professional degree; master's degree; bachelor's degree; associate's degree; postsecondary, non-degree award; some college, no degree; high school diploma or equivalent; and less than high school
- *Work experience in a related occupation:* more than five years, one to five years, less than one year, and none
- *Typical on-the-job training:* internship or residency, apprenticeship, long-term on-the-job training, moderate-term on-the-job training, short-term on-the-job training, and none

The BLS began using the new classification system as part of the 2010 Employment Projections Program, and the system gradually will enter use in other federal statistical programs and those conducted by state Labor Market Information agencies, such as state-level employment projections.

Sources: U.S. Bureau of Labor Statistics, "Definitions for the Education and Training Classification System," http://www.bls.gov/emp/ep_definitions_edtrain.pdf (accessed February 17, 2013); and U.S. Bureau of Labor Statistics, "Education and Training Classification System Update: Final System," last revised February 1, 2012, http://www.bls.gov/emp/ep_finaledtrain.htm.

---

as States, the District of Columbia, Guam, Puerto Rico, the U.S. Virgin Islands, and all metropolitan and nonmetropolitan areas in each State."[44]

OES data come from a semiannual mail survey administered to 1.2 million nonagricultural business establishments over a three-year period. The BLS oversees the survey, but state LMI agencies field the questionnaires and tabulate the state-level results. The BLS prepares national estimates for industries down to the five-digit NAICS level, and some state LMI agencies tabulate certain data by NAICS industry code. Moreover, the OES groups occupations according to the SOC framework.[45]

Like the CES, the OES survey focuses on payroll jobs by place of work. The semiannual survey questionnaire asks selected business establishments to provide payroll

Box 7.4 Green Jobs

Over the past several years, the concept of "green jobs" has assumed a prominent place in national policy debates, yet despite the considerable interest in the idea, it remains nebulous.

The appeal of green jobs lies in the notion that it may be possible to address simultaneously two vexing public problems: the degradation of the environment and a lack of adequate economic opportunities. In an ideal world, the processes associated with transitioning from fossil fuels to clean energy sources and with using energy more efficiently would create well-paying, career-track jobs open to workers with diverse skills and talents.

While intellectually straightforward, the idea of green jobs encounters difficulties once people begin discussing the details and attempting to operationalize the concept. That is because, at least in part, the industrial and occupational classification systems used in the United States contain no specific measures of green industries and occupations. Moreover, many so-called green jobs are not high tech, futuristic positions, but existing jobs that employ new production techniques or produce new kinds of goods and services.

Public statistical agencies in numerous countries have attempted to define green jobs precisely enough for the purposes of measurement and analysis. According to the Organization for Economic Cooperation and Development, an international policy forum to which most wealthy nations belong, the green economy typically is defined and measured either in relation to the output produced by specific business establishments or to the production processes used by individual establishments.

In 2010, the U.S. Bureau of Labor Statistics (BLS) developed two definitions of green jobs, one related to output and the other to process. Under the output definition, green jobs are "jobs in businesses that produce goods or provide services that benefit the environment or conserve natural resources." Specifically, green goods and services fall into five categories: energy from renewable sources energy efficiency; pollution reduction and removal; natural resources conservation; and environmental compliance, education and training, and public awareness.

The process definition conceptualizes green jobs as "jobs in which workers' duties involve making their establishment's production processes more environmentally friendly or use fewer natural resources." Such processes separate into four types: energy from renewable sources; energy efficiency; pollution reduction and removal, greenhouse gas reduction, and recycling and reuse; and natural resources conversation.

Both definitions are used in various BLS data products, such as the Quarterly Census of Employment and Wages. The definitions are not mutually exclusive, meaning that some jobs might be counted twice, yet the use of a single definition likely would yield an undercount of green jobs. Over time, the BLS hopes to generate regular estimates of the number of green jobs, the industrial and occupation distribution of the jobs, the geographic location of the jobs, and the wages associated with the jobs, though recent budget developments have called that hope into question. Nevertheless, preliminary estimates consistent with the output definition appeared in 2012, and, according to the BLS, 2.4 percent of all the payroll jobs that exited in the United States in 2010 were associated with the production of green jobs and services. Of the estimated 3.1 million green jobs that existed, 2.3 million were in the private sector.

Sources: Van Jones, *The Green Collar Economy* (New York: HarperCollins, 2008), 9; OECD, *Entrepreneurship at a Glance 2011* (Paris: OECD Publishing, 2011), 24–35; U.S. Bureau of Labor Statistics, "The BLS Green Jobs Definition," http://www.bls.gov/green/green_definition.htm (accessed January 26, 2013); and U.S. Bureau of Labor Statistics, "Employment in Green Goods and Services: 2010," news release, March 22, 2012, 1–2, http://www.bls.gov/news.release/pdf/ggqcew.pdf.

information for the pay period spanning the 12th of the survey month (May or November). As with the CES, the OES samples businesses subject to the unemployment insurance system. Survey participation is voluntary and responses are confidential. The statistical agencies suppress the release of any information that would allow the identification of individual establishments.

The OES inquires specifically about employment levels and wages. For employment, the survey asks about full- and part-time payroll employment, but the results are not disaggregated by employment type. Wages refer to "straight-time, gross pay, exclusive of premium pay."[46] In other words, the OES measures wages rather than total compensation. Another BLS product—the National Compensation Survey—collects information about total compensation, but it covers relatively few geographical units, which makes the OES program a more geographically comprehensive source of data (see chapter 8).

Both the BLS and state LMI agencies provide access to OES data. The data product contains information about payroll employment levels, mean and median annual and hourly wages, and annual hourly wages for the 10th, 25th, 75th, and 90th percentiles. State and local estimates date from 1997, though national information dates from 1971, the survey's first year. Technical issues further limit the usefulness of OES data in time-series analysis: the three-year survey window requires historical comparisons to be based on findings from every fourth year.

Figure 7.2 compares OES employment and wage data for accountants and auditors in North Carolina and the Durham-Chapel Hill, NC MSA in May 2011. At that time, nonfarm businesses in North Carolina employed an estimated 27,500 accountants and auditors at an average hourly wage of $32.10. Half of those positions paid more than $28.86 per hour, half less than that. Hourly wages ranged from $19.44 (the 10th percentile) to $47.19 (the 90th percentile). In the Durham-Chapel Hill MSA, employers had 2,140 accounting and auditing positions that paid a median hourly wage of $31.65. Not only was the median hourly wage greater in Durham than in the state as a whole, but hourly wages also were higher at every point in the wage distribution. The 10th percentile wage in Durham was 8.4 percent greater than the statewide figure, the 90th percentile wage 10.2 percent higher.[47]

When interpreting values from the OES, data users must remember the figures are subject to nonsampling and sampling errors, with sampling error being particularly pronounced for OES data. Because the OES frequently works with small sample sizes, it is important to consider relative standard errors. In general, the smaller the relative standard error associated with a value, the more reliable the value is. OES estimates tend to be more precise for larger geographies like states than smaller ones like counties.

LABOR MARKET DYNAMICS

All of the data products discussed so far in this chapter capture static information, but labor markets are dynamic: people constantly find and lose jobs, just as business establishments regularly add and cut positions. Static data sets are unable to capture

Figure 7.2 Estimated Hourly Wages by Selected Percentiles for Accountants and Auditors (SOC Code #13-2011), North Carolina and the Durham-Chapel Hill, NC MSA, May 2011

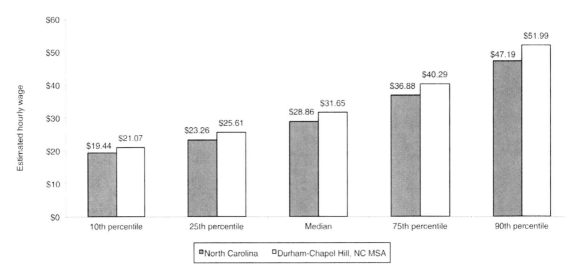

Source: U.S. Bureau of Labor Statistics, Occupational Employment Statistics, May 2011.

such churn, yet an appreciation of underlying labor market dynamics is essential to the formation of wise public policies.

Two factors complicate analyses of regional labor market dynamics. First, none of the data sets discussed previously in this chapter track both the supply and demand sides of the labor market. Some products, such the LAUS, measure aspects of labor supply, and others, such as the CES and QCEW, gauge aspects of labor demand, but none of them captures both functions.[48] Second, the few data products that attempt to measure supply and demand contain little information about states and regions. The lack of geographic detail is a longstanding weakness of America's labor market information system, albeit a weakness that the responsible agencies are trying to address. Despite the limitation, regional leaders seeking a dynamic view of the labor market can patch together elements of the story from three data products: Job Openings and Labor Turnover Survey, Business Employment Dynamics, and Local Employment Dynamics.

JOB OPENINGS AND LABOR TURNOVER SURVEY

Launched in 2000, the *Job Openings and Labor Turnover Survey* (JOLTS) is a monthly BLS survey of business demand for labor. Each month, the BLS fields a telephone survey to a sample of 16,000 business establishments drawn from those included in the QCEW. This means the survey covers nonagricultural business establishments subject to the unemployment insurance system. Participation is voluntary, and no information is released that would permit the identification of an individual establishment.[49]

The JOLTS questionnaire requests information about three topics: total payroll employment during the week that contains the 12th of the month; the total number of hires, quits, layoffs, discharges, and other separations that occurred during the calendar month; and the total number of job openings available as of the last day of the calendar month. Data are broken out by industry and not by any other criteria like occupation or establishment size. Some data appear in seasonally adjusted formats, others in unadjusted series.[50]

JOLTS data offer a monthly view of shifts in business demand for labor and flows of workers into and out of jobs. The job openings rate indicates how much demand for labor exists: the higher the rate, the higher the demand. Similarly, when combined with other information, JOLTS data offer insights into the reemployment prospects of unemployed workers. In December 2012, JOLTS data suggested that there were 3.4 unemployed workers for every available job opening—a ratio indicative of depressed demand for labor and bleak prospects for job seekers.[51] While such information is useful, it unfortunately is available only for the nation and the four census regions. The ratio of unemployed workers to job openings in the South in December 2012, for instance, was 3.1-to-1, which was slightly below the national rate.[52]

BUSINESS EMPLOYMENT DYNAMICS

In contrast to JOLTS, which measures worker flows, the *Business Employment Dynamics* (BED) program tracks job flows within individual business establishments. This BLS product is a longitudinal dataset derived from QCEW records. The BED tabulates changes in the employment levels of private, nonagricultural business establishments subject to the unemployment insurance system from one quarter to another. Records date from 1992.

To compute net quarterly changes in payroll levels, the BLS matches payroll records from individual establishments. The reference period is the pay period containing the 12th of the month, and quarterly changes represent the differences between the third months in pairs of calendar quarters. Net change is the difference between the sum of payroll positions added in new and expanding establishments, less the sum of positions eliminated by closing and contracting establishments.[53] A positive value indicates that more jobs were gained than lost; a negative value suggests the opposite.

Data appear eight months after the close of a quarter, and annual data are part of the first quarter report. The BLS collects BED information in seasonally adjusted and unadjusted formats. Data may be broken out by broad industry category, business establishment size, type of establishment (opening and closing or expanding and contracting), state, and year. Local or regional data currently are unavailable, but BLS has indicated that it intends to release information for counties and metropolitan statistical areas in the future.

Figure 7.3 Quarterly Net Changes in Payroll Levels (Seasonally Adjusted) of Private-Sector Business Establishments, North Carolina, 2007.IV–2011.IV

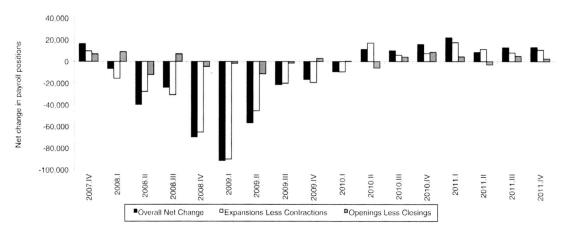

Sources: U.S. Bureau of Labor Statistics, Business Employment Dynamics.

Because the BLS prepares BED data from administrative records generated through the QCEW, participation is mandatory, but it involves no administrative tasks beyond those associated with paying unemployment insurance taxes. No information is released that would allow the identification of specific firms. As the BED originates in a virtual census of business establishments, the data are not prone to sampling error, though nonsampling errors may apply.

The strength of the BED is that it allows analysts to decompose changes in employment levels by multiple factors. Consider the experience of North Carolina during the first quarter of 2009, which was the worst quarter of job losses during the most recent recession. During that period, the state lost 87,778 more private-sector jobs than it gained, with contracting firms responsible for 98.3 percent of the net job losses. While net job loss abated in subsequent quarters and turned positive in the second quarter of 2010, thanks to hiring by existing establishments, the growth was insufficient to replace the positions previously lost (see Figure 7.3).[54]

Local Employment Dynamics

Unlike other data products explored in this chapter, the *Local Employment Dynamics* (LED) program is a project of the U.S. Census Bureau, not the BLS. The program's aim is to combine existing records about business establishments with census data about individuals. By marrying data about jobs and workers, the LED enables the analysis of worker and job flows at detailed levels of geography over time without the need to collect additional information from respondents. In essence, the LED is a "national longitudinal job frame."[55]

The LED is a voluntary partnership in which every state LMI agency participates.[56] State LMI agencies provide unemployment insurance information, such as employee wage records and QCEW data, to the Census Bureau, which matches those records with individual demographic variables. The result is a data set that blends information about workers and establishments. Because many states use a worker's Social Security number as an identifier for the purposes of unemployment insurance, it is possible to match wage and employment records to other data sets that contain Social Security numbers. Of course, the public statistical agencies hold all information in confidence and release nothing that would enable the identification of particular individuals or establishments.

The LED partnership produces several data products of which the most important is a set of *Quarterly Workforce Indicators* (QWI). The QWI compiles 30 workforce indicators—eight of which are publicly available—that gauge "trends in employment, hiring, job creation and destruction, and earnings, with unprecedented details of geography, age, gender, and industry going as far back as 1990."[57] Data appear nine months after the end of a quarter.

The QWI project is noteworthy in three respects. First, the QWI and its parent LED project are the only data products that integrate information about firms and workers. Second, the integrated data are available at extremely detailed levels of industry (three-digit NAICS code) and geography (down to the level of local workforce investment areas). Third, QWI data appear frequently, a fact that renders the information extremely useful to the development of economic policies and the operation of workforce development programs.

Nevertheless, the QWI and LED programs suffer from several limitations. One shortcoming is that the programs currently are unable to generate summary national statistics or follow workers who move across state lines. The relative youth of the programs means they enjoy less name recognition than more established programs like the CPS.

Consider the construction industry in the Asheville, NC MSA, a four-county region nestled in the Appalachian Mountains. Over the four-quarter period stretching from late 2008 through the middle of 2009, area construction establishments eliminated an average of 542 more payroll positions than they created, according to QWI data. During that time, an average of 2,327 individuals—1,567 of whom were men—went to work for construction establishments, while an average of 3,226 individuals—again, overwhelmingly men—separated from those employers. The monthly earnings of construction workers employed for an entire quarter averaged $3,027, while the earnings of new hires averaged $2,370.[58] Viewed in total, the data suggest that Asheville's construction industry contracted during the heart of the last recession and displaced predominately male workers with relatively high earnings.

A complementary product to QWI is *OnTheMap*, which is "a mapping and reporting tool showing employment and home location of workers with companion reports for user-defined areas."[59] In essence, OnTheMap is free, web-based mapping software that creates visual representations of QWI data. Other LED products include *Industry Focus*, which presents industry-specific workforce data, and *Community Economic Development Hot Reports*, which provide county-specific information of interest for the purposes of economic development. The LED partnership also has produced 42 state-level studies analyzing the characteristics of private-sector workers age 55 and older. All LED resources are available on the internet.[60]

LABOR FORCE PROJECTIONS

Projections of anticipated labor force conditions at a future point in time are the final kind of labor market information typically of interest to regional leaders. Insights into potential changes to a region's occupational structure, for example, might lead educational and workforce development institutions to alter or refine programs, just as an awareness of possible changes to an area's industrial structure might prompt shifts in economic development strategies. While forecasting is a messy business, credible projections aid policy makers and facilitate planning.

Unfortunately, the current labor-market information system fails to generate state and regional projections of the actual supply and demand for labor. The projections that exist generally are model-based and are somewhat removed from actual conditions, but as those projections are the best that are available, they are worth discussing in some detail.

Since the end of World War II, the BLS has maintained an *Employment Projections Program* (EPP) that assembles 10-year projections of "the future size and composition of the labor force, aggregate economic growth, detailed estimates of industry production, and industry and occupational employment."[61] EPP data appear every other year, with the current set covering the period 2010–2020. More specifically, the EPP produces four sets of interrelated projections: labor force projections, macroeconomic projections, industrial projections, and occupational projections.[62] Labor force projections forecast changes in the size of the civilian noninstitutional population and the civilian labor force, broken out by demographic characteristics like ethnicity. Similarly, occupational projections suggest the kinds of workers possibly needed by the industries projected to grow due to overall economic changes.

Releases of EPP data often attract media attention, but the findings are generally misinterpreted. The common mistake is to take EPP data as evidence that certain industries will be unable to find enough workers, even though the EPP does not measure labor surpluses or shortages; in fact, the model assumes a state of full employment. What the projections actually contain are separate counts of jobs at business establishments and individual members of the labor force, and the difference between the two is not an indicator of imbalances.[63] EPP data appear in two online BLS periodicals: the *Monthly Labor Review* and the *Occupational Outlook Quarterly*, which is a companion to the well-regarded *Occupational Outlook Handbook*, a biennial BLS publication popular with educators and career counselors.[64]

BLS forecasts are national in scope, but states prepare their own estimates through partnerships involving state LMI agencies, the BLS, and the Employment and Training Administration. As part of this partnership, which dates from the 1970s, states create detailed long-term (10-year) employment projections and less detailed short-term (two-year) forecasts.

Table 7.2 Ten Fastest Growing and Declining Occupations, Ranked by Numerical Change, Greensboro (Guilford County), North Carolina, 2008–2018

A. Fastest Growing Occupations

Rank	Occupation title	Numerical change	Percentage change
1	Home Health Aides	2,010	39.2
2	Combined Food Preparation and Serving Workers	1,510	22.8
3	Customer Service Representatives	940	14.9
4	Registered Nurses	920	19.9
5	Waiters and Waitresses	700	13.8
6	Personal and Home Care Aides	570	52.3
7	Truck Drivers, Heavy and Tractor-trailer	560	10.5
8	Landscaping and Groundskeeping Workers	490	16.8
9	Retail Salespersons	460	4.7
10	Elementary School Teachers, excluding Special Education	350	15.0

B. Fastest Declining Occupations

Rank	Occupation title	Numerical change	Percentage change
1	Laborers and Freight Stock and Material Movers, Hand	–310	–4.2
2	First-line Supervisors/Managers of Production	–260	–13.8
3	Team Assemblers	–210	–4.7
4	Sewing Machine Operators	–200	–23.0
5	Shipping, Receiving, and Traffic Clerks	–190	–9.8
6	General and Operations Managers	–180	–4.3
7	Textile Winding, Twisting, and Drawing Out Machine	–170	–31.5
8	Inspectors, Testers Sorters, Samplers, and Weighers	–160	–11.8
9	Machine Feeders and Offbearers	–150	–31.3
10	Upholsterers	–130	–18.3

Source: North Carolina Department of Commerce, Labor and Economic Analysis Division, North Carolina Occupational Trends 2008–2018, http://eslmi23.esc.state.nc.us/projections/index.asp.

Consistent with BLS methodologies described earlier, state estimates present separate forecasts of industrial and occupational employment, and the difference between the two is not an indicator of labor shortages or surpluses. Because states have discretion in how they prepare and present their projections, the most comprehensive information normally is available through the websites of state LMI agencies.[65]

Table 7.2 illustrates the kinds of occupational projections generated by states. The top panel lists the 10 occupations expected to add the most openings in Guilford County (Greensboro), North Carolina, between 2008 and 2018, while the bottom panel presents the 10 occupations expected to eliminate the most positions. The growing fields primarily are in health care, food service, and retail sales, and the declining occupations are related to manufacturing, mainly those tied to textile and furniture manufacturing. This pattern is consistent with the larger shift of the area's economy away from manufacturing and toward service and retail trade.[66]

LABOR MARKETS: A SUMMARY

For most Americans, the labor market is the most important part of the economy. When labor markets operate well and generate enough positions to accommodate all those who wish to work, individuals are able to provide for their families and build better futures. In the process, the increased output of goods and services resulting from efficient use of an area's human capital boosts regional prosperity.

Given the importance of the labor market, it is unsurprising that statistical agencies have honed advanced methods for measuring labor market conditions. Yet the United States' labor market information system, while sophisticated, is complex and fragmented. To raise awareness of the rich data collected by public statistical agencies, this chapter described the structure of the labor force, profiled key sources of data, explained occupational structures, discussed labor market dynamics, and introduced forecasts of labor market trends. With an appreciation of such concepts, regional leaders are better able to target policies and programs aimed at bolstering the labor market and ensuring that all workers can access meaningful employment opportunities—opportunities that manifest themselves in the wages and incomes earned by regional residents.

NOTES

1. Author's analysis of U.S. Census Bureau, American Community Survey, Five-Year Estimates, 2007–2011.

2. Lawrence Mishel, Jared Bernstein, and Heidi Shierholz, *The State of Working America,* 11th ed. (Ithaca, NY: Cornell University Press, 2009), 260–261.

3. Andrew Reamer, *Putting America to Work: The Essential Role of Federal Labor Market Statistics* (Washington, DC: Brookings Institution, 2010), 18, http://www.brookings.edu/~/media/Files/rc/papers/2010/1029_labor_reamer/1029_labor_reamer.pdf.

4. U.S. Census Bureau, "Estimates of the Resident Population by Selected Age Groups for the United States, States, and Puerto Rico: July 1, 2011 (SC-EST2011-01)," last revised May 2012, http://www.census.gov/popest/data/state/asrh/2011/index.html.

5. Author's analysis of U.S. Bureau of Labor Statistics, *Geographic Profile of Employment and Unemployment, 2011,* http://www.bls.gov/opub/gp/laugp.htm (accessed January 28, 2013); and U.S. Bureau of Labor Statistics, *Alternative Measures of Labor Underutilization for States: 2011 Annual Averages,* http://www.bls.gov/lau/stalt11q4.htm (accessed January 28, 2013).

6. Unless otherwise noted, the discussion of labor force concepts in this section and of measures of labor utilization in the next one is based on Mishel, Bernstein, and Shierholz, *The State of Working America*; U.S. Bureau of Labor Statistics, *Geographic Profile, 2011*; U.S. Bureau of Labor Statistics,

How the Government Measures Unemployment (Washington, DC: U.S. Department of Labor, 2009), http://www.bls.gov/cps/cps_htgm.pdf; and Edward Wolff, *Poverty and Income Distribution,* 2d ed. (Malden, MA: Wiley-Blackwell, 2009), 208–218.

7. Author's analysis of U.S. Bureau of Labor Statistics, Current Population Survey, 2011. For a more detailed discussion of the measurement of self-employment in the United States, see Steven Hipple, "Self-employment in the United States," *Monthly Labor Review*, September 2010, 17–32, http://www.bls.gov/opub/mlr/2010/09/art2full.pdf.

8. U.S. Department of Labor, "Unemployment Insurance Chartbook," http://www.doleta.gov/unemploy/chartbook.cfm (accessed January 26, 2013).

9. Alternate measures of labor underutilization for the United States are in Table A-15 of the monthly Employment Situation Report published by the U.S. Bureau of Labor Statistics. As of January 31, 2013, an archive of past copies of the Employment Situation Report was available at http://www.bls.gov/schedule/archives/empsit_nr.htm.

10. As of January 31, 2013, estimates from the Organization for Economic Development and Co-operation were available at http://stats.oecd.org/index.aspx?; estimates from the International Labour Organization were available at http://laborsta.ilo.org/; and international estimates prepared by the U.S. Bureau of Labor Statistics were available at http://bls.gov/fls/.

11. Andrew Sum and Ishwar Khatiwada, "The Nation's Underemployed in the 'Great Recession' of 2007–09," *Monthly Labor Review*, November 2010, 13, http://bls.gov/opub/mlr/2010/11/art1full.pdf.

12. As of January 31, 2013, an explanation of the changes to the measurement of the duration of unemployment was available at http://bls.gov/cps/duration.htm.

13. Alan Peters and Heather MacDonald, *Unlocking The Census with GIS* (Redlands, CA: ESRI, 2004), 137.

14. Joseph Cortright and Andrew Reamer, *Socioeconomic Data for Understanding Your Regional Economy* (Washington, DC: U.S. Department of Commerce, 1998), 13.

15. Joseph Goldberg and William Moye, *The First Hundred Years of The Bureau of Labor Statistics* (Washington, DC: U.S. Department of Labor, 1985), 4, http://www.bls.gov/opub/blsfirsthundred-years/100_years_of_bls.pdf.

16. U.S. Bureau of Labor Statistics, "Labor Force Data Derived from the Current Population Survey," in *BLS Handbook of Methods* (Washington, DC: U.S. Department of Labor, 1997), 2, http://bls.gov/opub/hom/pdf/homch1.pdf. Chapter revised online April 17, 2003.

17. U.S. Bureau of Labor Statistics, "Local Area Unemployment Statistics: Overview," last revised September 25, 2008, http://bls.gov/lau/lauov.htm.

18. Author's analysis of Current Employment Statistics and Local Area Unemployment Statistics, Seasonally adjusted data for North Carolina, December 2011.

19. Author's analysis of Current Employment Statistics and Local Area Unemployment Statistics, Winston-Salem, NC, Metropolitan Statistical Area, December 2011.

20. Cortright and Reamer, *Socioeconomic Data*, 28.

21. Lindsay Davis, Lyda Ghanbari, and Alice Ramey, *Revisions in State Establishment-based Employment Estimates Effective January 2012* (Washington, DC: U.S. Department of Labor, 2012), 1, http://www.bls.gov/sae/benchmark2012.pdf.

22. U.S. Census Bureau, "Current Population Survey: About," http://www.census.gov/cps/ (accessed February 9, 2013).

23. U.S. Bureau of Labor Statistics, "Labor Force Data Derived from the Current Population Survey," 1–2 and 7–8.

24. As of February 9, 2013, a listing of monthly CPS supplements was available at http://www.census.gov/cps/about/supplemental.html.

25. U.S. Census Bureau, "Current Population Survey: 2011 Annual Social and Economic (ASEC) Supplement," 1–1, http://www.census.gov/apsd/techdoc/cps/cpsmar11.pdf.

26. U.S. Bureau of Labor Statistics, "Labor Force Data Derived from the Current Population Survey," 10.

27. U.S. Bureau of Labor Statistics, "Local Area Unemployment Statistics: Frequently Asked Questions," last revised May 4, 2011, http://bls.gov/lau/laufaq.htm.

28. U.S. Bureau of Labor Statistics, "Measurement of Unemployment in States and Local Areas," in *BLS Handbook of Methods* (Washington, DC: U.S. Department of Labor, 1997), 1–2, http://www.bls.gov/opub/hom/pdf/homch4.pdf. Chapter revised online January 31, 2013.

29. U.S. Bureau of Labor Statistics, "Local Area Unemployment Statistics: Frequently Asked Questions."

30. U.S. Bureau of Labor Statistics, "Geographic Profile of Employment and Unemployment: Overview," last revised October 16, 2001, http://www.bls.gov/gps/gpsover.htm.

31. U.S. Bureau of Labor Statistics, "Employment, Hours, and Earnings from the Establishment Survey," in *BLS Handbook of Methods* (Washington, DC: U.S. Department of Labor, 1997), 1, http://bls.gov/opub/hom/pdf/homch2.pdf.

32. U.S. Bureau of Labor Statistics, "Current Employment Statistics: Frequently Asked Questions," last revised February 1, 2013, http://www.bls.gov/ces/cesfaq.htm.

33. Bernard Baumohl, *The Secrets of Economic Indicators: Hidden Clues to Future Economic Trends and Investment Opportunities*, 2d ed. (Upper Saddle River, NJ: Wharton School Publishing, 2008), 27–28; and U.S. Bureau of Labor Statistics, "Current Employment Statistics: Frequently Asked Questions."

34. U.S. Bureau of Labor Statistics, "Employment and Wages Covered by Unemployment Insurance," in *BLS Handbook of Methods* (Washington, DC: U.S. Department of Labor, 1997), 42, http://bls.gov/opub/hom/pdf/homch5.pdf.

35. U.S. Bureau of Labor Statistics, "Quarterly Census of Employment and Wages: Frequently Asked Questions," last revised June 27, 2012, http://www.bls.gov.cew/cewfaq.htm.

36. U.S. Bureau of Labor Statistics, "Quarterly Census of Employment and Wages: Frequently Asked Questions."

37. Cortright and Reamer, *Socioeconomic Data*, 28.

38. U.S. Office of Management and Budget, *Standard Occupational Classification Manual 2010* (Washington, DC: U.S. Government Printing Office, 2010), xxiii.

39. U.S. Office of Management and Budget, *Standard Occupational Classification Manual*, v.

40. Ibid., xvii.

41. Ibid., v–viii.

42. Ibid., xxvi.

43. As of February 9, 2013, the O*NET database was available at www.onetonline.org.

44. U.S. Bureau of Labor Statistics, "Occupational Employment Statistics: Frequently Asked Questions," last revised January 18, 2012, http://bls.gov/oes/oes_ques.htm.

45. U.S. Bureau of Labor Statistics, "Occupational Employment Statistics: Overview," last revised March 27, 2012, http://www.bls.gov/oes/oes_emp.htm.

46. U.S. Bureau of Labor Statistics, "Occupational Employment Statistics: Frequently Asked Questions."

47. Author's analysis of U.S. Bureau of Labor Statistics, Occupational Employment Statistics, May 2011.

48. The supply and demand functions of the labor market differ from those from other goods and services. For a discussion of a standard microeconomic explanation of the labor market, see N. Gregory Mankiw, *Principles of Microeconomics* (Fort Worth, TX: Dryden Press, 1998), 384–394.

49. U.S. Bureau of Labor Statistics, "Job Openings and Labor Turnover Survey: Frequently Asked Questions," last revised July 30, 2002, http://www.bls.gov/jlt/jltfaqs.htm.

50. Ibid.

51. Heidi Shierholz, *Job Openings and Hiring Dropped in December, and Have Not Increased Since Early 2012* (Washington, DC: Economic Policy Institute, 2013), http://www.epi.org/publication/job-seekers-ratio-february-2013/.

52. Author's analysis of U.S. Bureau of Labor Statistics, Job Openings and Labor Turnover Survey, Seasonally Adjusted Data, December 2012.

53. U.S. Bureau of Labor Statistics, "Business Employment Dynamics: Frequently Asked Questions," last revised January 6, 2004, http:///www.bls.gov/bdm/bdmover.html.

54. Author's analysis of U.S. Bureau of Labor Statistics, Business Employment Dynamics, 2007–2011.

55. Ron Jarmin, "Job-to-Job Flows: Sneak Peak at Upcoming Innovations from the Longitudinal Employer-Household Dynamics Program." Presentation to the Brookings Institution Roundtable on Putting America to Work: The Essential Role of Labor Market Statistics, Washington, DC, September 27, 2010, http://www.brookings.edu/~/media/Files/rc/speeches/2010/0927_labor_statistics_reamer/0927_labor_statistics_jarmin.pdf.

56. U.S. Census Bureau, "Local Employment Dynamics State Partners," http://lehd.did.census.gov/led/led/statepartners.html (accessed November 19, 2011).

57. U.S. Census Bureau, "Local Employment Dynamics: New Data from the States and the U.S. Census Bureau," http://lehd.did.census.gov/led/led/doc/LEDonepager_20110218.pdf (accessed March 22, 2011).

58. Author's analysis of U.S. Census Bureau, Quarterly Workforce Indicators, 2008–2009.

59. U.S. Census Bureau, "Local Employment Dynamics: New Data from the States and the U.S. Census Bureau."

60. As of February 13, 2013, LED data were available at http://lehd.did.census.gov.

61. U.S. Bureau of Labor Statistics, "Employment Projections," in *BLS Handbook of Methods* (Washington, DC: U.S. Department of Labor, 1997), http://www.bls.gov/opub/hom/pdf/homch13.pdf. Chapter revised online September 17, 2012.

62. For a discussion of the projection methodology behind the most recent set of projections, see Dixie Sommers and James Franklin, "Overview of Projections to 2020," *Monthly Labor Review,* January 2012, http://www.bls.gov/opub/mlr/2012/01/art1full.pdf.

63. U.S. Bureau of Labor Statistics, "Employment Projections: Frequently Asked Questions," last revised February 9, 2012, http://www.bls.gov/emp/ep_faq_001.htm.

64. As of February 13, 2013, the *Monthly Labor Review* was available at http://www.bls.gov/opub/mlr/; the *Occupational Outlook Quarterly* was available at http://www.bls.gov/ooq/; and the *Occupational Outlook Handbook* was available at http://www.bls.gov/oco/.

65. As of February 13, 2012, projection data for multiple states were available at http://www.projectionscentral.com.

66. Author's analysis of North Carolina Department of Commerce, Labor and Economic Analysis Division, North Carolina Occupational Trends 2008–2018, http://eslmi23.esc.state.nc.us/projections/index.asp.

8 Income, Wealth, and Living Standards

On a typical weekday in 2011, the average employed American spent eight hours at work.[1] Because people spend most of their waking hours on the job, they often look to their work for a sense of identity, accomplishment, and community. More practically, however, paid employment is the means by which individuals earn the money needed to support themselves.

For the vast majority of Americans, earnings from work are their primary source of income, which determines "the standard of living people can afford and the extent to which living standards vary from person to person."[2] Understanding trends related to income, its sources, its uses, and its distribution therefore is vital for assessing the material well-being of area residents and gauging whether regional living standards are rising or falling.

To inform analysis of regional income trends, this chapter and the following one discuss income and explain how income statistics help measure, albeit imperfectly, living standards. While the quality of human lives depends on more than money, the financial resources available to individuals enable them to satisfy immediate needs and save for the future. As the humorist Woody Allen has quipped, "Money is better than poverty, if only for financial reasons."[3] Taking income as a proxy for living standards is an established practice, partly because the data are readily available.

This chapter begins with two definitions of income and profiles of several rich data sources. Attention then shifts to individual income sources and the ways in which income is used. Finally, the chapter considers the related concept of wealth, which is an even better indicator of well-being than income. Chapter 9 broadens the discussion to include relative income measures like income distribution, inequality, and deprivation.

Despite its importance to well-being, income is difficult to define and measure. Key concepts vary greatly among public statistical agencies, and few statistical definitions are consistent with popular understandings. To illustrate when and how to apply the various income concepts and measures, chapters 8 and 9 present practical examples drawn from data for the Denver-Aurora-

Map 8.1 Principal Cities and Component Counties of Denver-Aurora-Broomfield, CO MSA, 2009 Delineation

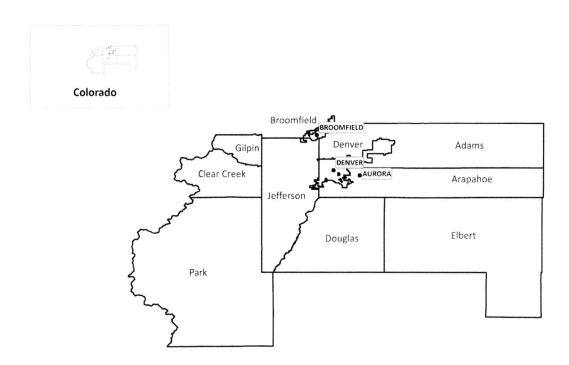

Source: U.S. Office of Management and Budget, "Update of Statistical Area Definitions and Guidance on Their Uses (OMB Bulletin No. 10-02)," December 1, 2009, http://www.whitehouse.gov/sites/default/files/omb/assets/bulletins/b10-02.pdf. Map prepared by William High.

Broomfield, CO Metropolitan Statistical Area (MSA), a 10-county region with 2.6 million residents in 2011 (see Map 8.1).[4]

Income Definitions and Data

Income is a flow of economic or financial resources received by an individual or household within a particular span of time. That flow of resources enables recipients to consume goods and services immediately, as happens when a person exchanges money for necessities, and at a later date, as when a person saves income for future use. It is precisely because the consumption and savings possibilities of individuals and households depend on their incomes that "more than any other type of data, income data tell us how we are doing economically."[5]

The relationship between income and living standards is simple: the more income an individual or household receives, the more it can consume today or in the future. Income is a dynamic flow influenced by factors such as wage gains and job losses. A worker may have a low income today, but if the worker's wages eventually rise, so will the worker's standard of living. The value of an income stream further depends on external factors. A household may have a high income presently, but if that income fails to keep pace with inflation, the household's living standards will erode. Similarly, judging whether an income is "high" or 'low" depends on a reference community. A household with $10,000 in annual income would be quite poor in the United States yet quite rich in many parts of the world.

Besides shining light on consumption and savings possibilities, income statistics offer perspectives into social equity. Because a regional economy's total output and total income should be equal, the distribution of income within an economy reflects the allocation of regional output. A shift in regional income from wages to corporate profits, for instance, indicates a redistribution of income away from workers and a drop in their living standards. Even if one were to assume that any given distribution of income within a community is inherently efficient, fairness matters, which is why perceived inequities often spark calls for such ameliorative public policies as the levying of higher corporate taxes or the funding of antipoverty initiatives.

DEFINING INCOME

The first step in any analysis of regional income is defining the term "income." Unfortunately, there is no standard definition. Statistical agencies instead conceptualize the term in ways consistent with their missions. As the country's economic accountant, the U.S. Bureau of Economic Analysis (BEA) views income in relation to economic output. The U.S. Census Bureau, in contrast, focuses on the cash money received by a person or household. While multiple definitions of income exist, those developed by the BEA and Census Bureau—more specifically, the concepts of *personal income* and *money income*—are appropriate for the purposes of regional analysis (see Box 8.1).

Personal Income

The official BEA measure, *personal income* is "the income that is received by all persons from all sources."[6] Personal income is "the sum of wage and salary disbursements, supplements to wages and salaries, proprietors' income with inventory valuation and capital consumption adjustments, rental income of persons with capital consumption adjustment, personal dividend income, personal interest income, and personal current transfer receipts, less contributions for government social insurance."[7] Four aspects of the BEA definition require elaboration.

First, the BEA calculates personal income for both physical persons and "quasi-individuals," such as certain nonprofit organizations. Second, personal income encompasses monetary resources, like cash wages, and nonmonetary ones, like Supplemental Nutrition Assistance benefits and the net rental value of owner-occupied housing. Third, the BEA definition subtracts the income required to pay taxes for social insurance programs. Fourth, the BEA computes personal income by place of residence, even though an individual may earn that income in a different community.[8]

Box 8.1 Adjusted Gross Income

As part of its work in administering the nation's tax laws, the Internal Revenue Service (IRS) compiles extensive income statistics. Yet for the purposes of regional analysis, the main IRS income concept—*adjusted gross income (AGI)*—is much less useful than the personal and money income measures compiled by the U.S. Bureau of Economic Analysis and U.S. Census Bureau.

AGI represents the income that individuals report on their tax forms before accounting for deductions and exemptions. In short, AGI is a measure of income subject to taxation. Forms of taxable income include wages and salaries, ordinary interest and dividends, capital gains, net business income, alimony, unemployment insurance benefits, and gambling winnings.

Imagine a single person who worked in 2009 for a firm and received a salary of $60,000, a total of $5,000 in employer-paid health insurance premiums, a $3,000 contribution to a firm-sponsored retirement account, and no other benefits. In reality, the person received $68,000 in resources, but because employer-paid health insurance premiums and retirement contributions are exempt from taxation, the amount reported as compensation would have been $60,000. If the person had contributed $10,000 to the firm's retirement plan, the salary reported to the IRS would have fallen to $50,000. When it came time to file taxes, the individual would have added other forms of taxable income, such as investment dividends, and subtracted allowable exclusions, such as student loan interest payments. If the hypothetical taxpayer earned $1,000 in dividends and paid $2,000 in student loan interest, the taxpayer's AGI would have equaled $49,000.

From that amount, the individual would have subtracted allowable deductions and exemptions. Assuming the person took the standard deduction and the exemption available to single persons in 2009 (worth $5,700 and $3,650, respectively), the amount subject to income tax would have been $39,650. The person therefore would have owed $6,106 in income tax. If the person had paid more than that amount via tax withholding during the year, a refund would have been due; if less, the balance would have been owed.

As the example illustrates, the income values reported on a person's tax forms are not indicators of the money or economic resources received during the year. While the hypothetical person described above actually received $61,000 in cash, the reported AGI captured only 80.3 percent of the sum. Similarly, AGI ignored the $8,000 received in nontaxable benefits, meaning that AGI reflected 71 percent of the taxpayer's total resources.

Another shortcoming of AGI is that it excludes low-income persons who have zero AGI. While not subject to the federal income tax, such persons still may have incomes. Also, the IRS tabulates AGI data for tax units, which are not identical to persons or households. A tax unit may have multiple persons, as in the case of a family, or a family might have multiple tax units, as when spouses file separately.

To illustrate the difference at the regional level, consider the Denver-Aurora-Broomfield, CO Metropolitan Statistical Area (MSA). In 2009, the last year with fully comparable data available at the time of writing, the region's 2.5 million residents received $115.2 billion in personal income, according to the U.S. Bureau of Economic Analysis. The U.S. Census Bureau, however, measured $79.2 billion in money income. Meanwhile, the 1 million tax units in the 10-county region reported a combined AGI of $65.1 billion, based on IRS data.

The Denver case shows that AGI data are more limited in scope than personal and money income and capture a narrower slice of the resources present in a community. Nevertheless, AGI data can complement analyses that employ more comprehensive income measures. The IRS provides free, online access to basic county-level tax information and offers the option to purchase additional data.

Sources: Ann Dunbar, "Alternative Measures of Household Income," *Regional Quarterly Report* (Washington, DC: U.S. Bureau of Economic Analysis, 2011), 138, http://www.bea.gov/scb/pdf/2011/10%20October/1011_regreport.pdf; Internal Revenue Service, *Form 1040: 2009 Instructions* (Washington, DC: U.S. Department of the Treasury, 2009), 12–13 and 81, http://www.irs.gov/pub/irs-prior/i1040--2009.pdf; and author's analysis of U.S. Bureau of Economic Analysis, "Table CA1-3: Personal Income Summary: Denver-Aurora-Broomfield, CO Metropolitan Statistical Area, 2009," last revised April 25, 2012; U.S. Census Bureau, American Community Survey, One-Year Estimates, 2009; and Internal Revenue Service, County Income Data: 2009, last revised August 20, 2012, http://www.irs.gov/uac/SOI-Tax-Stats---Free-County-Income-Data-Downloads.

A related statistic, *disposable personal income*, gauges the resources available to a person for voluntary spending. Disposable personal income is "total personal income minus personal current taxes."[9] Personal income, then, measures the resources available to someone after accounting for social insurance payments, while disposable personal income is the portion of personal income available for discretionary use once certain taxes are paid.

The BEA typically presents personal income as both an aggregate total and a per capita figure. To compute per capita personal income, the BEA estimates the personal income received by all residents of an area and then divides that figure by the resident population. Per capita personal income simply is an average (mean) value and is subject to all the limitations of that statistic, as explained in chapter 4. The presence of persons with extremely high incomes, for one, may distort the mean and make the average resident appear better off than is actually the case, which is why the median value often is a more relevant statistic.

Sources of Personal Income Data. Personal income statistics belong to the BEA's National Income and Product Accounts, with the main source of regional personal income statistics being the *State and Local Area Personal Income and Employment* series introduced in chapter 2. In review, the series measures the income and employment levels tied to an area's economic production and tracks changes in those values over time. Prepared on an industrial basis, this data series offers a comprehensive, consistent measure of the employment and income levels of area residents.[10]

At the state level, the BEA prepares quarterly and annual estimates of personal income. Quarterly estimates appear three months following the end of a quarter, annual estimates nine months after the end of the year. The annual series provides added detail about the components of personal income. At the regional level, the BEA releases annual estimates of personal income for every metropolitan statistical area, micropolitan area, and county some 15 months after the end of the reference year.

The BEA has state-level estimates of personal income dating from 1929 and local estimates since 1969.[11] An advantage of the personal income series is that it aggregates upward: substate values sum to a statewide total, which in turn contributes to the national figure. At the same time, the data have four limitations. First, substate data appear well after the end of the reference year. Second, less information is available for smaller geographies than for larger ones. Third, dollar values are nominal, not inflation-adjusted. Finally, per capita personal income figures illuminate just one dimension of regional well-being.

Money Income

The standard income measure of the U.S. Census Bureau, *money income* is the "income received (exclusive of certain money receipts such as capital gains) before payments for personal income taxes, social security, union dues, Medicare deductions, etc."[12] Three aspects of this definition require explanation.

First, money income is a narrower concept than personal income. While personal income estimates the total value of economic resources received over a span of time, money income includes only certain types of cash income. By excluding forms of income received disproportionately by affluent households, such as capital gains on assets, and certain in-kind benefits received predominately by low-income households, such as housing subsidies, money income often understates the incomes of the richest and poorest households. Second, as a pretax measure, money income is not an accurate assessment of the actual resources available for spending. Third, research has found that survey respondents normally underreport their incomes.

For such reasons, "there is no doubt that the money-only income concept underestimates available economic resources for families and individuals."[13] In recognition of this shortcoming, the Census Bureau has developed 15 alternate measures of income.[14] The standard definition, however, remains the official one and is the basis for associated measures like the poverty rate.

As the Census Bureau has an "interest in giving a sense of the standard living across households in an area," the agency typically reports median rather than average values.[15] As living standards vary by household type, it is necessary to consider household structure when reviewing income data. Median household income, for example, tends to be lower than median family income since the household universe includes more retirees and single people, while the family universe contains more working-age individuals and dual-earner households.

Sources of Money Income Data. The Census Bureau collects income data through several programs. At the national level, the most important source is the *Annual Social and Economic Supplement* (ASEC) to the Current Population Survey, first introduced in chapter 7. The ASEC survey, which occurs every March, covers 100,000 addresses. For each household member 15 years of age and older, the survey inquires about the amount of money income received from 18 sources during the preceding calendar year (see Table 8.1).[16] ASEC findings, which typically appear in the fall after the reference year, are "the most timely and most accurate cross-section data for the nation on income and poverty" and "the official source of national poverty estimates."[17] Furthermore, the ASEC is the principal source of national information about health insurance coverage and the uninsured (see Box 8.2).

The primary strength of the ASEC is that it "provides a consistent historical income time series, beginning in 1946, at the national level" along with consistent state data from 1984 onward.[18] A second benefit is that ASEC data may be cross-tabulated by demographic traits. Unfortunately, the ASEC is of limited use for regional analysis, as it contains little local data; even the state data are of limited use for less populous states unless multiyear averages are used.

For the purposes of regional analysis, the *American Community Survey* (ACS) is a richer data source (see chapter 5). The ACS generates income estimates for almost every level of geography. A "rolling sample" survey of approximately 3.5 million housing units, the ACS inquires about the income received by each household member age 15 and older during the preceding calendar year. Since 2010, the annual ACS release has involved three products: one-year estimates for geographies with at least 65,000 residents; three-year estimates for areas with 20,000 or more residents; and five-year estimates for all areas regardless of population size.

Box 8.2 Health Insurance Coverage

The *Annual Social and Economic Supplement* (ASEC) to the Current Population Survey has been the primary source of information about health insurance coverage and uninsured Americans. Since 1980, the survey program has asked responding households about their health insurance status in the prior calendar year, along with questions about the characteristics of that insurance. Strengths of ASEC estimates include their comprehensiveness and their suitability for cross-tabulation with other demographic and economic variables tracked in the study. Nevertheless, the estimates suffer from limitations. One perennial problem is that the survey appears to yield estimates of the number of Americans who are uninsured at one point in time rather than for the entire year. Another shortcoming is that the survey regularly underreports the number of individuals insured through the Medicare and Medicaid programs.

When it comes to regional analysis, the most important limitation of the ASEC is that estimates are unavailable for geographies smaller than states. Prompted in part by the rising cost of health insurance, a heightened awareness of the problems facing the uninsured, and the 2010 passage of national health insurance reform legislation, public statistical agencies have begun to collect substate information about health insurance coverage in a more systematic and regular fashion.

In 2008, the U.S. Census Bureau tested the inclusion of a question about health insurance coverage as part of the *American Community Survey* (ACS). The ACS questionnaire asked respondents to indicate whether each household member currently had insurance coverage from a list of eight possible public and private sources. In general, "insured" individuals had coverage from at least one of the listed sources, while "uninsured" individuals lacked coverage from any of the stated sources. When the 2008 test proved successful, the Census Bureau elected to add the question to all future versions of the ACS. The results, however, are subject to the various strengths and weaknesses of the survey (see chapter 5).

ACS data for 2010 suggest that an estimated 400,000 residents (15.8 percent) of the Denver-Aurora-Broomfield, CO Metropolitan Statistical Area (MSA) lacked health insurance coverage at the time they were surveyed. Some 83.8 percent of uninsured residents were between the ages of 18 and 64, and 15.8 percent were children; thanks to the Medicare program, just 0.4 percent of adults age 65 and older lacked insurance. Further analysis shows that 32 percent of uninsured individuals in the Denver MSA worked on a full-time, year-round basis, while 40.9 percent had completed at least some college. Half of all uninsured residents lived in households with annual incomes above $29,380.

To provide even more localized data about health insurance coverage, the Census Bureau began in 2011 to release annual health insurance estimates for states and counties. The *Small Area Health Insurance Estimates* (SAHIE) program is model-based and generates estimates by combining information from secondary data sources, such as the ACS and administrative data. The annual release contains state- and county-level estimates of people with and without health insurance coverage by age (with special attention paid to the child population), gender, income level, and—for states only—race and ethnicity. Limitations include the two-year lag between the reference year and the year of publication and the limited ability to cross-tabulate data by other socioeconomic characteristics.

Acknowledging that, the SAHIE program yields estimates for local areas that are not populous enough to have annual ACS estimates or that will not have available ACS data for a few more years. SAHIE data for 2010 in the 10 counties that are part of the Denver MSA indicate that the share of individuals under age 65 without health insurance ranged from 7.3 percent in Douglas County to 23 percent in Adams County. Among the low-income population (those with incomes below 138 percent of the Federal Poverty Level, or $30,793 for a four-person family), the proportion that was uninsured in 2010 ranged from 32.3 percent in Denver County to 41.4 percent in Park County.

Sources: Carmen DeNavas-Walt, Bernadette Proctor, and Jessica Smith, *Income, Poverty, and Health Insurance Coverage in the United States: 2011* (Washington, DC: U.S. Census Bureau, 2012), 21 and 63, http://www.census.gov/prod/2012pubs/p60–243.pdf; Joanna Turner, Michel Boudreaux, and Victoria Lynch, *A Preliminary Evaluation of Health Insurance Coverage in the 2008 American Community Survey* (Washington, DC: U.S. Census Bureau, 2009), 4–5 and 10, http://www.census.gov/hhes/www/hlthins/data/acs/2008/2008ACS_healthins.pdf; U.S. Census Bureau, *Small Area Health Insurance Estimates (SAHIE) 2010 Highlights* (Washington, DC: U.S. Census Bureau, 2012), 1, http://www.census.gov/did/www/sahie/data/2010/SAHIE_Highlights_2010.pdf; author's analysis of U.S. Census Bureau, American Community Survey, One-Year Estimates, 2010; and author's analysis of U.S. Census Bureau, Small Area Health Insurance Estimates, 2010.

Table 8.1 Sources of Money Income Tracked in Annual Social and Economic Supplement to the Current Population Survey, 2011

Earnings (wages/self-employment)
Unemployment compensation
Workers' compensation
Social security
Supplemental security income
Public assistance
Veterans' payments
Pension or retirement income
Survivor benefits
Disability benefits
Interest
Dividends
Rents, royalties, and estates and trusts
Educational assistance
Alimony
Child support
Financial assistance from outside of the household
Other income

Source: Carmen DeNavas-Walt, Bernadette Proctor, and Jessica Smith, *Income, Poverty, and Health Insurance Coverage in the United States: 2011* (Washington, DC: U.S. Census Bureau, 2012), 29, http://www.census.gov/prod/2012pubs/p60-243.pdf.

While the ACS provides income data for a broad range of geographies, the data are not as comprehensive as ASEC data. Besides employing a different sampling frame and methodology, the ACS tracks fewer income sources. Another weakness is that as a relatively new survey, the ACS is not suited for historical analysis, though the ACS gradually is evolving into the main source of local income data.[19]

Analysts seeking historical income data should turn to the *Decennial Census of Population and Housing*. The 1940 Census was the first to inquire about income. That year, enumerators asked all respondents age 14 and older about wage and salary income earned in 1939 and if they had received more than $50 in other income. In 1950, the Census Bureau began posing income questions to a subset of the household universe.[20] The 2000 Census was the last one to include income questions, and all future income data will come from the ACS.

The chief weakness of the decennial census is that it occurs once per decade, so the findings often become outdated before the next count. At the same time, the federal government allocates considerable funding to states and localities based on census data, so the use of outdated information may adversely affect the distribution of funds, particularly aid for public education. In 1994, Congress designated the *Small Area Income and Poverty* (SAIPE) program as the intercensal source of "updated estimates of income and poverty statistics for the administration of federal programs and the allocation of federal funds to local jurisdictions."[21]

The SAIPE program prepares "annual estimates of income and poverty statistics for all school districts, counties, and states."[22] Annual SAIPE data include state- and county-level estimates of median household income, poverty, and child poverty, along with school-district based estimates of the total population, child population (ages 5–17), and poverty counts for children between the ages of 5 and 17.[23] The Census Bureau tabulates SAIPE data annually and releases the findings in December of the year following the reference year.

Unlike the other Census Bureau products mentioned in this section, SAIPE is model-based, as opposed to survey-based. In short, the Census Bureau generates estimates from secondary data sources like the ACS. The advantage of this approach is that it permits SAIPE "to 'borrow strength' from multiple data sources, including administrative records and multiple household surveys, to produce estimates with lower variance than estimates from any one source."[24] Limitations include the long lag between the reference year and publication date and the inability to cross-tabulate data by demographic and economic characteristics.

A final source of income data is the *Survey of Income and Program Participation* (SIPP), "a longitudinal survey that collects information on topics such as income, participation in government transfer programs, employment, and health insurance coverage."[25] While other data products provide snapshots of income, the SIPP tracks shifts in the incomes of the same households over time. Thus, it is "useful mainly for understanding changes *for the same households* in income and poverty, that is the *dynamics* of income and poverty, over time (up to 3 or 4 years) and for examining the nature and frequency of poverty spells."[26]

The SIPP emerged from a set of studies undertaken in the 1970s and became a regular Census Bureau product in 1984. Due to budgetary fluctuations, the structure of the SIPP has varied over the years. The SIPP underwent one redesign in 1996, and another revamp began in 2013.[27]

The SIPP is a panel survey of groups of selected households interviewed at regular intervals (typically every four months) over several years. The 2008 SIPP began with a sample of 52,031 households, from which rotating subsamples were to participate in 13 interviews between 2008 and 2012.[28] At each interview, respondents answer a series of core questions and topical questions specific to that interview. The core questions pertain to employment and work earnings, income received from nonwork sources, income received from assets, health insurance coverage, educational factors, and participation in certain government social programs. Questions apply to every household member age 15 and older.[29]

Though the SIPP is an excellent source of detailed, dynamic income and program participation data, it is of limited use for regional analysis. SIPP estimates are not available for substate geographies. Moreover, the SIPP only began producing reliable state estimates as part of the 2004 panel, with estimates for only the 33 most populous states.[30]

PERSONAL AND MONEY INCOME IN THE DENVER MSA

One way to illustrate the differences between income concepts is to consider actual data from the Denver-Aurora-Broomfield, CO MSA.

According to the BEA, the residents of the Denver MSA received $119.7 billion in personal income in 2010 (all values are nominal, and 2010 was the most recent year of BEA data available at the time of writing), a total higher than that found in all but 18 other MSAs. On a per capita basis, the average Denver resident had a personal income of $46,871, which was 17.4 percent higher than the national figure.[31] The ACS, in contrast, reported lower income values for 2010 (ACS data for 2010 are used for consistency with available BEA estimates). According to the ACS, money income in the Denver MSA totaled $79.1 billion, and exceeded the income levels posted in all but 18 other MSAs. Per capita money income in Denver, meanwhile, averaged $30,852, a level 18.5 percent higher than the national one.[32]

To control for the distortion in the average caused by a handful of residents with extremely high incomes, the Census Bureau typically reports median values. In 2010, half of all Denver households had money incomes greater than of $58,732. Median income values also varied according to household type. Consider how the median income of family households was $36,371 higher than that of nonfamily households. Similarly, the median income of households headed by persons age 65 or older was $34,193 lower than that of households headed by individuals between ages 45 and 64.[33]

While not as comprehensive as personal income, money income is better suited for demographic analysis, as the Census Bureau collects the information needed to cross-tabulate income data by characteristics like race, education, and age. For example, in 2010 the median income of Denver households headed by white individuals ($62,200) was 56.1 percent higher than that of households headed by African-American individuals ($39,841). Similarly, households headed by non-Hispanic white persons recorded a median income 1.6 times greater than that of households led by individuals of Hispanic ethnicity ($65,733 vs. $40,951).[34]

Despite the apparent differences, personal and money income actually are complementary in nature. Personal income data compiled by the BEA capture a broader set of income sources and the flow of resources generated by regional economic production. Seen that way, Denver is one of the most productive MSAs in the country and has the ability to deliver a relatively high standard of living to its residents. At the same time, not all residents benefit equally from the region's income. Although narrower in scope, money income data from the Census Bureau illustrate the differences in living standards among population groups. For the purposes of regional analysis, then, the two sets of income measures illuminate distinct but connected aspects of regional well-being.

SOURCES OF INCOME

Regardless of the definition used, households and individuals derive all of their income from three sources: transfer payments, investment income, and earnings from work. Of the three, the earnings category is the largest: in 2010, earnings accounted for 84.3 percent of the money income received by Denver households.[35] Both the BEA and Census Bureau collect data on income components in ways consistent with each agency's definitions and methodologies.

Income Components

The smallest component of personal income, *transfer payments*, represents the income received from various benefit programs, mainly social insurance programs. Transfer payments come in two forms. First, there are government transfer payments, of which the most important "are social security payments, unemployment benefits, veterans' benefits, and family assistance payments."[36] In 2010, Americans received a combined $2.3 trillion in transfer receipts, of which $690.2 billion came from Social Security payments and $515.3 billion from Medicare benefits. Second, there are private transfer payments from businesses to individuals; most such payments are distributions from private pension plans. In 2010 private transfer payments totaled $47.4 billion.[37] Something to note about transfer payments is that most come from sources to which recipients have contributed, such as by paying payroll taxes or by contributing to pension plans.

Investment income, the next largest component of personal income, is the stream of resources generated from ownership of certain productive assets. Examples include the rent paid to property owners, the dividends paid to owners of corporate stocks, and the interest earned by holders of bank accounts, bonds, and other financial investments. In 2010, Americans received $1.6 trillion in investment income, of which $1 trillion came from personal interest income.[38]

The final and most important component of personal income is *earnings from work*, which has two components: labor earnings and proprietor's income. The BEA defines labor earnings as "the sum of not only wages and salaries received by employees but also of employer-paid fringe benefits, such as health insurance, life insurance, and pension contributions."[39] Seen that way, labor earnings are more like total compensation than total wages; the emphasis, in short, is on the total amount of economic resources received by workers, not simply the cash in their pay packets. Proprietor's income, meanwhile, is the income that self-employed individuals and owners of unincorporated businesses generate from their enterprises. In 2010, Americans received $8 trillion in labor earnings and $1.1 trillion in proprietor's income.[40]

Figure 8.1 breaks out the total personal income recorded in the Denver MSA in 2010 by source. That year, Denver residents received $119.7 billion in income. Net earnings from work accounted for 72.1 percent of the total, followed by investment income (16.3 percent) and transfer payments (11.6 percent). Upon closer inspection, the primary source of personal income was labor earnings. Of the $96.2 billion in earnings recorded before accounting for employee social insurance contributions, $82.5 billion (85.8 percent) went to the wages, salaries, and the employer-financed social insurance contributions of individuals working for pay at an organization.[41]

Data Sources

When it comes to analyzing the components of regional income, various BEA and Census Bureau data products provide estimates of transfer payments, investment income, and employment earnings. As with all income statistics, BEA and Census Bureau data are complementary in nature. BEA measures lend themselves to the analy-

Figure 8.1 Components of Personal Income in Denver-Aurora-Broomfield, CO MSA, 2010

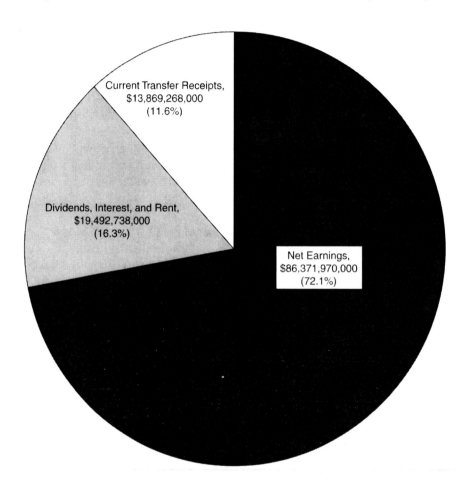

Source: U.S. Bureau of Economic Analysis, "Table CA04: Personal Income and Employment Summary, Denver, Aurora-Broomfield, Co, MSA," last revised April 25, 2012.

sis of economic output, while Census Bureau statistics are suited for demographic analyses. Consider receipt of Supplemental Nutrition Assistance Program (SNAP) benefits in 2010 in Denver. The BEA reported the total value of benefits received by regional residents ($334.3 million), while the Census Bureau's ACS program found that 20.8 percent of Denver households headed by African-American individuals received food assistance, compared to 5.3 percent of households headed by a white person.[42]

Regional leaders interested in transfer payments and investment income should consult the BEA's State and Local Area Personal Income and Employment series and various Census Bureau products, notably the ACS. When analyzing government transfer payments, additional information is available from administrative records. The Social Security Administration, for example, prepares an annual report on program beneficiaries for every state, county, and zip code in the country.[43] Some 319,070

Denver residents received $356.9 million in old age, survivors, and disability benefits in 2010.[44] Similar data are available from other agencies for programs like unemployment insurance, Temporary Assistance to Needy Families, and SNAP.

A limitation of income component data is their infrequent appearance. Data about labor earnings, however, are more readily available, so it is possible to track changes in the most important income component on a regular basis. Such data generally follow one of two things: employment earnings or hourly wages.

Employment Earnings

Compiled on an industrial basis, *employment earnings* are "the sum of three components of personal income—wage and salary disbursements, supplements to wages and salaries, and proprietors' income."[45] Many analyses report employment earnings as an aggregate total by place of work and as a net amount that excludes certain social insurance payments and is adjusted to place of residence. Analysts frequently will calculate *average earnings*, which is simply total earnings divided by estimated annual employment.

Earnings data shed light into the income generated through different kinds of economic activities and the relative productivity of different industries (see Box 8.3). Assuming firms pay workers their marginal product, average earnings serves as "a rough proxy for the value added per job."[46] Compare the differences between the information and retail trade industries in Denver. In 2010, the information industry had 53,496 jobs with average earnings of $97,069. Retail trade, in contrast, had 2.8 times as many jobs but average earnings of just $28,196—an amount 71 percent less than the average in the information industry.[47] One plausible explanation for this gap in earnings is that each information job adds more value than each retail job (see Box 8.4).

By subjecting data about employment earnings data to different analytical techniques, regional leaders can track changes in the local economy and better target economic development activities, policies, and programs. A sizable concentration of low-wage jobs, for example, might prompt regional leaders to require firms to meet certain wage standards as a condition of receiving tax subsidies.

Employment Earnings Data. Information about employment earnings is available from three data sources, all of which prior chapters have introduced. Perhaps the most comprehensive source is the BEA's *State and Local Area Personal Income and Employment* series. The main limitation is that the BEA publishes annual substate data well after the end of the reference year. A timelier source is the *Quarterly Census of Employment and Wages* (QCEW), which, as chapter 7 explained, is an enumeration of business establishments conducted by state labor market information agencies in conjunction with the U.S. Bureau of Labor Statistics (BLS). Series data come from unemployment insurance tax records and track the wages, paid leave time, overtime, bonuses, back pay, tips, in-kind payments, stock options, and, in some cases, employer contributions to defined compensation plans. QCEW reports appear six months after the quarter ends and annual reports occur 10 months after the fact. Finally, the Census Bureau's *County Business Patterns* program, which chapter 6 profiled, provides annual

Box 8.3 Labor Productivity

A key economic indicator that measures how much output employees produce for each hour worked, labor productivity is an important long-term driver of improvements in living standards. For most businesses, labor is the most important and expensive input, and the more productive their labor forces, the more goods and services the business can produce. Rising output allows firms to increase profits, which can lead to greater levels of business investment, higher returns to owners, increased employee compensation, or a combination thereof. Increasing productivity further allows for market demands to be met without outbreaks of shortages or price hikes.

The most accessible estimate of labor productivity is the quarterly *Productivity and Costs* report prepared by the U.S. Bureau of Labor Statistics. This report, which appears some five weeks after the end of a calendar quarter, tracks three key productivity-related measures for the entire nonfarm business sector, which generates roughly 75 percent of the nation's total economic output:

- *Output per hour of all persons* is the value of all goods and services produced during the quarter divided by the total number of hours worked to produce those goods and services. During calendar year 2010, output grew at an annualized, seasonally adjusted rate of 4.1 percent, meaning that employees produced more per hour worked than they did a year earlier.
- *Compensation per hour* is the average hourly compensation (e.g., wages, salaries, and employer-paid benefits) paid to workers in nonfarm businesses. The quarterly report shows real and nominal values. In 2010, hourly compensation grew by 2 percent before inflation and 0.4 percent after inflation.
- *Unit labor cost* is the cost of the labor required to produce one unit of output. The unit labor cost equals total labor costs divided by real output. In 2010, unit labor costs declined by 2 percent.

All together, the three measures provide complementary insights into how efficiently firms marshal labor to produce output. The 2010 data show that workers improved their productivity and were able to produce more during each hour worked. Because hourly output grew faster than compensation per hour, unit labor costs fell in 2010, meaning the labor costs associated with producing a single unit were lower than one year before.

Increases in hourly compensation that exceed those in output are signs of inflation. Rises in compensation that exceed improvements in output reduce the profitability of firms, which may cause them to raise prices in an attempt to maintain profitability. Higher prices, in turn, may lead workers in other firms to push for wage increases to keep pace with rising prices, thereby reducing the profitability of those firms, which then raise prices in response, causing the cycle to repeat.

At the same time, compensation increases are not necessarily negative, provided that output grows faster than compensation. Improved productivity on the part of workers should lead to increases in compensation and, by extension, living standards. That outcome is not automatic. In 2010, workers became more productive, but their inflation-adjusted hourly compensation remained essentially flat. That suggests that the benefits of an expanded economy accrued chiefly to business profits and firm owners and not to the individuals who labored to expand the economy.

Sources: Bernard Baumohl, *The Secrets of Economic Indicators: Hidden Clues to Future Economic Trends and Investment Opportunities*, 2d ed. (Upper Saddle River, NJ: Wharton School Publishing, 2008), 303–310; and U.S. Bureau of Labor Statistics, "Productivity and Costs: Second Quarter 2011, Revised," news release, September 1, 2011, 4 and 6, http://bls.gov/news.release/archives/prod2_09012011.pdf.

Box 8.4 Differences in Labor Earnings

Different jobs pay different wages. Even within the same occupation, wages may differ among workers performing the same job, as happens when someone working a night shift receives a higher wage than someone performing the same job during the day shift. While the fact that earnings differ among workers is obvious, the reasons for those differences are less so.

Neoclassical economic models hold that workers in competitive, profit-maximizing firms earn the value of their marginal product of labor. Consider a factory that employs one worker who earns $1,000 a week and produces 150 units that sell for $10 each. The value of the worker's output is $1,500, and the firm earns a marginal profit of $500 after paying the worker. If the firm brings on a second employee who earns a $1,000 a week and if that worker's efforts allow the firm to produce an extra 110 units that sell for $10 each, the worker produces $1,100 in extra value, with the firm earning an additional profit of $100. The hiring of a third worker who enables the production of 50 added units, however, would be unprofitable, as the worker's wage would exceed the $500 value of extra output.

When it comes to the pay received by individual workers, neoclassical theory holds that those who are more productive—meaning they generate higher marginal products of labor—will command higher wages. Differences in productivity may arise from such factors as education, experience, and ability. Perhaps the best-known extension of this idea is the human capital model developed by Nobel laureate Gary Becker. Under this model, individual workers decide how much schooling and training to pursue. While education and training can cause a worker to become more productive, and therefore better paid, it also carries costs in the form of time, money, and foregone opportunities. Individuals therefore must calculate whether the expected future benefits of education and training, discounted to their present values, will exceed the present costs. If the value is positive, the education and training is worthwhile.

Like the neoclassical model in which it is rooted, the human capital model rests upon certain assumptions that seldom hold in the real world. Also, this supply-side model views education strictly as an investment decision. Yet it is unclear whether education actually enhances a person's productivity or if it merely signals a high level of individual ability or class status and thus functions as a screening device. If so, education's social rate of return is lower than its individual one.

Other economic models emphasize the role of demand-side and institutional factors in the setting of wages. For example, unionization tends to lead to higher wage levels than exist in the absence of unions, though the wage effects differ by industry. Similarly, the segmentation of the labor market into a stable, well-paid primary market and a secondary, lower-paid, contingent market results in wage differences among workers in the various market segments. Another set of theories looks at wages as being determined by the internal labor markets that exist within firms. A final group of theories views wage differences as the results of shifts in occupational or industrial demand. A change in an economy's industrial composition—a shift from agriculture to industry, for example—may disadvantage workers in the shrinking industry relative to those in the growing one.

Each demand-side and institutional model possesses distinct strengths and weaknesses, yet they share a belief that wages do not occur "naturally"; instead, they are influenced by human choices and public policies. Policies that hinder workers from unionizing, for instance, likely will lower wages. Demand-side and institutional models therefore lend themselves to broad policy prescriptions.

Sources: N. Gregory Mankiw, *Principles of Microeconomics* (Fort Worth, TX: Dryden Press, 1998), 384–388; and Edward Wolff, *Poverty and Income Distribution*, 2d ed. (Malden, MA: Wiley-Blackwell, 2009), chapters 8 and 9.

earnings estimates for a broad range of places. This program's data, however, appear with a considerable lag and are not suited for certain kinds of analyses.

Hourly Wages

Hourly wages are the "remuneration (pay, wages) of a worker or group of workers for services performed during a specific period of time."[48] The definition of what is included as part of hourly wages varies by statistical program, but the focus normally is on the cash wages received by employees. Some data sets monitor gross or pretax wages, others after-tax wages. Similarly, some studies follow straight-time wages, which exclude supplements paid for overtime or shift differentials, and others capture all payments. When interpreting wage data, it is important to remember they reflect the wage payments reported by employers rather the wages received by individuals. The statistical basis, in short, is wages and hours per job, not per employed person.

Hourly Wage Data. Three sources of hourly wage information are well-suited for regional analysis. The first is the *Current Employment Statistics* (CES) program of the BLS (see chapter 7). Based on a survey of business establishments, the CES provides monthly estimates of the wages paid by covered establishments. The CES tracks the gross wages (regular and overtime) paid to all "production workers, construction workers, or nonsupervisory workers in the service sector."[49] The count excludes employer-paid benefits and noncash benefits. Hours reflect all those worked during the reference period, including overtime and paid leave.

The CES provides national wage and hour information for all major industry groups, but the state and local data are limited in scope. At the state and metropolitan levels, wage and hour estimates traditionally have been available just for production industries and the private sector in general. In 2010, the BLS expanded the availability of state and local estimates. Labor market information agencies now publish statewide CES data for all industries with adequate sample sizes and MSA-level data for the entire private sector.[50]

A second relevant data source is the *Occupational Employment Statistics Program* (OES) first mentioned in chapter 7. OES data come from a semiannual mail survey of business establishments subject to the unemployment insurance system. Unlike the CES, the OES compiles data on the basis of occupation rather than industry. The OES tracks payroll employment levels, mean and median wages (hourly and annual), and average hourly wages paid to workers at the 10th, 25th, 75th, and 90th percentiles of the wage distribution. State and local estimates are available from 1997 onward, though time-series comparisons require careful consideration since only OES data from every fourth year are comparable.

The final source of wage information is the *National Compensation Survey* (NCS). Established in 1996 from the merger of three BLS programs, the NCS is "an establishment-based survey that provides comprehensive measures of occupational earnings, employer costs of employee compensation, compensation trends, wages in one geographic area relative to other geographic areas, the incidence of employer-provided benefits among workers, and provisions of employer-provided benefit plans."[51]

These data provide the foundation for four BLS products: the *Survey of Wages*, the *Employment Cost Index*, the *Employer Costs for Employee Compensation* series, and the *Employee Benefits Survey*.

NCS data originate in an establishment-based survey of the civilian workforce, defined as all workers in private industry or state and local government. Excluded from the survey are federal employees, military personnel, agricultural workers, domestic workers, the self-employed, unpaid volunteers, Americans working abroad, and individuals on long-term disability. The BLS selects business establishments through a three-step process. Individual private establishments rotate through the survey over a five-year period, while state and local government establishments cycle through over a 10-year period. Some establishments provide wage and benefit data annually, others quarterly.[52] The BLS organizes information by occupational group and produces estimates for the nation, the nine census divisions, some 80 MSAs, and a few nonmetropolitan areas.[53]

An annual data product, the *Survey of Wages* is quite useful for regional analysis. While the NCS resembles the OES, it is a smaller survey that covers fewer occupations and geographies but provides more information about the occupations and places that are included. This happens because the BLS collects the data through on-site observations at business establishments. A second NCS strength is that it classifies workers into occupations "on the basis of the work performed and the skills required in each occupation."[54] To that end, the BLS uses a standardized process to group workers according to their actual tasks and responsibilities. This enables an analyst to differentiate between the wages received by an attorney supervising a large case and those earned by an attorney tasked with a small part of the case. A final advantage is that the BLS adjusts NCS data in a way that permits the drawing of meaningful geographic comparisons. For such reasons, the NCS is superior to the OES for the comparison of wage rates.

To illustrate the usefulness of the NCS, consider July 2010 data for the Denver MSA. That month, the area's civilian workers earned an average of $24.38 per hour in straight-time pay. The typical private-sector worker received $23.95 per hour, the average state and local government worker $27.44. Within the private sector, half of all workers earned less than $19 per hour, while a quarter earned less than $12.61. Management occupations had the highest median wage ($40.26 per hour), food preparation and serving related occupations the lowest ($8.30).[55]

When analyzing wage data, it is important to remember that factors not apparent in the data influence wage rates. The exclusion of tips from the wage data, for example, likely understates the wages associated with food preparation and serving occupations. Similarly, wage rates tend to be higher for workers who possess higher levels of formal education, belong to a union, or work for larger establishments. A failure to consider such factors may lead to erroneous conclusions. For example, the comparatively high wage levels found among state and local government workers often are a product of the relatively high level of education possessed by government workers and the high degree of unionization common to the sector.

While the Survey of Wages is of greatest benefit to regional analysis, the other NCS components are also informative. The catch is that those tools contain limited information for geographies smaller than census divisions. Nevertheless, they are helpful in that they provide a regular, consistent source of information about employment costs and benefits.

Established in 1975 to track wage growth during an era of high inflation, the *Employment Cost Index* (ECI) is "a measure of the change in the cost of labor, free from the influence of employment shifts among occupations and industry categories."[56] The ECI focuses on civilian workers and measures changes in wages, salaries, and employer costs for paid leave time, supplemental pay, nonproduction bonuses, insurance benefits, retirement and savings plans, and mandated benefits like Social Security. The ECI presents index values relative to December 2005. Each quarterly report presents seasonally adjusted and unadjusted values for the reference period and percentage changes in the index between the current and previous quarters and between the current quarter and the same quarter in the prior year. Separate estimates exist for civilian workers broken out by industry type (private or state and local government), occupational group, union status, census region, census division, and metropolitan status.[57] While the quarterly data are nominal values, an online series with inflation-adjusted values exists.[58] The BLS historically had not released ECI data for geographies smaller than census divisions, but in 2008 the agency began releasing estimates for 14—later 15—metropolitan areas.[59] Values for those places are included in the data releases that occur each January, April, July, and October.

Because the ECI only presents index values, analysts seeking to measure the cash value of employer costs for wages and benefits must turn to a related quarterly data series, *Employer Costs for Employee Compensation* (ECEC). The ECEC measures "the average cost to employers for wages and salaries, and for benefits, per employee hour worked" and covers the same kinds of workers, occupations, geographies, and benefits as the ECI, though the two surveys differ in how they track changes over time.[60] Released two months following the end of the reference quarter, the ECEC reports costs per hour worked as nominal dollar amounts and as shares of total compensation. In the second quarter of 2012, national private-sector compensation costs equaled $28.80 per hour (see Figure 8.2). Wages and salaries were the largest expense ($20.27), followed by mandated benefits ($2.37), insurance benefits ($2.34), paid leave ($1.97), retirement benefits ($1.02), and supplemental pay ($0.82).[61]

The final NCS element, the *Employee Benefits Survey* (EBS), is an annual product covering "the incidence of employer-provided benefits and on the provisions (terms) of employee benefit plans, for civilian workers (as defined by the NCS), workers in private industry, and State and local government workers."[62] The EBS focuses on seven broad benefit categories: health care, retirement, life and disability insurance, paid leave, health promotion benefits, pretax benefits, and quality of life benefits. Special attention is afforded to retirement and health insurance benefits.

For each benefit, the EBS reports the number of workers offered the benefit, the provisions of the benefit, the number of workers with access to the benefit, the number of workers participating in the benefit, and the share of covered workers utilizing the benefit. Estimates exist for all civilian workers broken out by sector, occupation, union status, wage group, establishment size, census region, and census division. EBS data normally appear in July of the reference year.

Figure 8.2 Average Hourly Employer Costs for Employee Compensation, United States, Second Quarter of 2012

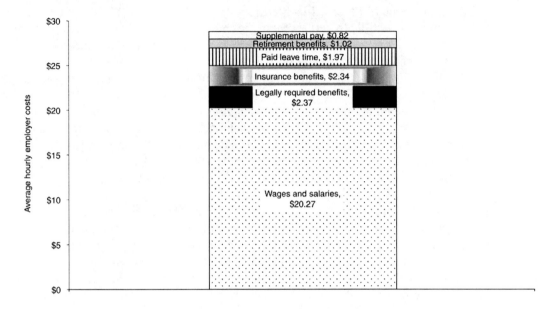

Sources: U.S. Bureau of Labor Statistics, "Employer Costs for Employee Compensation: June 2012," news release, September 11, 2012, http://www.bls.gov/schedule/archives/ecec_nr.htm.

A shortcoming of the EBS is a lack of state and local estimates. Nevertheless, the EBS sheds light on regional concerns. Consider health insurance data from March 2012 for the Mountain census division, the one that encompasses the Denver MSA. According to the EBS, 68 percent of private-sector employees in the Mountain division had access to employer-sponsored medical plan; of employees with access, 70 percent enrolled in the benefit. Private-sector employers offering medical plans paid an average of 79 percent of the premiums for individual coverage and 68 percent of family premiums.[63] The data further indicate that low-wage workers are less likely than higher-paid workers to have access to or make use of medical benefits. Access and take-up rates further vary by occupation, establishment size, and union status.

As with any survey-based study, the four components of the NCS are prone to sampling and nonsampling errors. Sampling error is particularly important to the NCS, so it is necessary to remember that the reported values are estimates with a true value that likely falls somewhere within a specified range. Take the previously mentioned NCS finding that the average civilian worker in July 2010 in the Denver MSA earned $24.38 per hour in straight-time pay. In actuality, there exists a 90-percent chance that the true hourly value falls between $22.66 and $26.10.[64] NCS data also are subject to various kinds of data adjustments and corrections.

USES OF INCOME

The importance of income lies not in money itself but in its ability to enable individuals and households to satisfy their preferences for consumption and savings. A full appreciation of income therefore requires an understanding of the ways in which households and individuals expend it.

The most comprehensive source of information about the use of income is the *Consumer Expenditure Survey* (CE), a BLS program that relies on data collected by the Census Bureau. While the BLS has collected data about consumer expenditures since 1888, the modern CE came into existence in 1979 as a tool for updating the Consumer Price Index (see chapter 2) and for generating "timely and detailed information on the spending patterns of different types of families."[65]

Designed to yield information representative of the entire civilian noninstitutional population, the CE encompasses two surveys, both of which focus on *consumer units*, which resemble, but are not identical to, households. The first CE survey, the *Interview Survey*, involves a sample of 14,000 consumer units. Each consumer unit participates in one 65-minute interview per calendar quarter for five consecutive quarters; by design, 20 percent of the sample turns over each quarter. The interviews normally occur in person and involve questions about the dollar amounts spent on specified items during the reference period; interviews also solicit information about the consumer unit's socioeconomic characteristics. According to the BLS, the interview survey captures between 60 and 70 percent of total expenditures, typically larger purchases, while a set of global estimates provide values for another 20 to 25 percent of total spending. To document smaller purchases, the CE fields a second survey, the *Diary Survey*, to a sample of 12,000 consumer units. Selected consumer units prepare diaries logging all expenses incurred during two consecutive one-week periods; respondents also provide socioeconomic information.[66]

The BLS releases CE data in two formats. Each October, the BLS publishes an *Annual Report* containing a set of 10 tables with data for the previous calendar year. Annual tables list average expenditure and income data broken out by income quintile; pretax income; size and composition of consumer units; the number of earners in consumer units; the age, race, educational attainment, and Hispanic ethnicity status of the head of the consumer unit; housing tenure; and census region.[67] Unfortunately, the annual release contains no local data, but a second periodic publication, the *Biennial Report*, contains the information found in the Annual Report plus detailed information for 18 metropolitan areas.[68] When using MSA data, it is important to remember that they account for neither inflation nor differences in living costs.

The strength of the CE is "that it allows data users to relate the expenditures and income of consumers to the characteristics of those consumers."[69] This information provides important perspectives into the well being of different population segments even when detailed geographic information is unavailable. Consider how 2011 CE data indicated that the share of pretax income devoted to food expenditures fell as income rose. Households in the bottom fifth of the income distribution—those with average pretax incomes of $9,805—devoted an average of 16.1 percent of their spending to food, while the top fifth of households—those with average pretax incomes of \$161,292—devoted an average of 11.6 percent.[70] An awareness of that fact might persuade, a locality not to impose a sales tax on groceries due to the levy's disproportionate impact on low-income households.

Remember that the CE is a survey, so the data are prone to various kinds of errors, including sampling and nonsampling errors. Users of CE data should keep in mind that the data are estimates and that the true value of any variable likely falls within a specified range.

WEALTH

In any given period, the incomes and expenditures of a household or individual might not be equal. When a household spends less than it receives in income, the surplus funds may be set aside for future consumption. Conversely, if a household spends more than it receives in income, it must cover the gap by drawing down savings or borrowing. The stock of savings to which a household adds and subtracts represents *wealth*. For most households and individuals, the primary way in which they build wealth over time is by saving portions of their incomes.

Wealth is an important determinant of long-term economic well-being.[71] Wealth matters for reasons beyond the income that some forms generate. First, some types of wealth provide services directly to the owners. When a household lives in a house that it owns, for instance, it benefits from the shelter provided by the structure. Second, the ability to tap the value of wealth—either by selling an asset or borrowing against it—permits households to finance consumption in excess of their incomes; in emergency situations, this aspect of wealth provides a degree of economic security. Third, wealth provides a means for financing investments with short-term costs but potential long-term benefits, such as higher education and entrepreneurship. Fourth, the generation of income from wealth requires no trade-off between labor and leisure, as is the case with paid work. Lastly, wealth often confers social prestige, economic influence, and political power.[72]

The standard definition of wealth is the one used in the *Survey of Consumer Finances* (SCF), which is "a triennial interview survey of U.S. families sponsored by the Board of Governors of the Federal Reserve System with the cooperation of the U.S. Department of the Treasury."[73] A survey of 6,492 families designed to be representative of all American families (defined similarly to the Census Bureau's concept of "households"), the SCF defines household wealth as "assets and liabilities that have a current market value and that are directly or indirectly marketable."[74] The emphasis, then, is on items with values that owners may readily tap for consumption purposes. Seen that way, *net worth* is the difference between the total market value of assets owned and that of debts owed.

The SCF collects information about 10 asset classes: the gross value of owner-occupied housing, other real estate, cash and checking accounts, savings accounts, bonds and securities, the cash surrender value of life insurance plans, the cash surrender value of pension plans, corporate stock and mutual funds, net equity in unincorporated businesses, and equity in trust funds. The SCF further collects data about three types of liabilities: mortgage debt, consumer debt, and other debt.

Figure 8.3 Median Family Net Worth by Income Quintile, United States, 2010

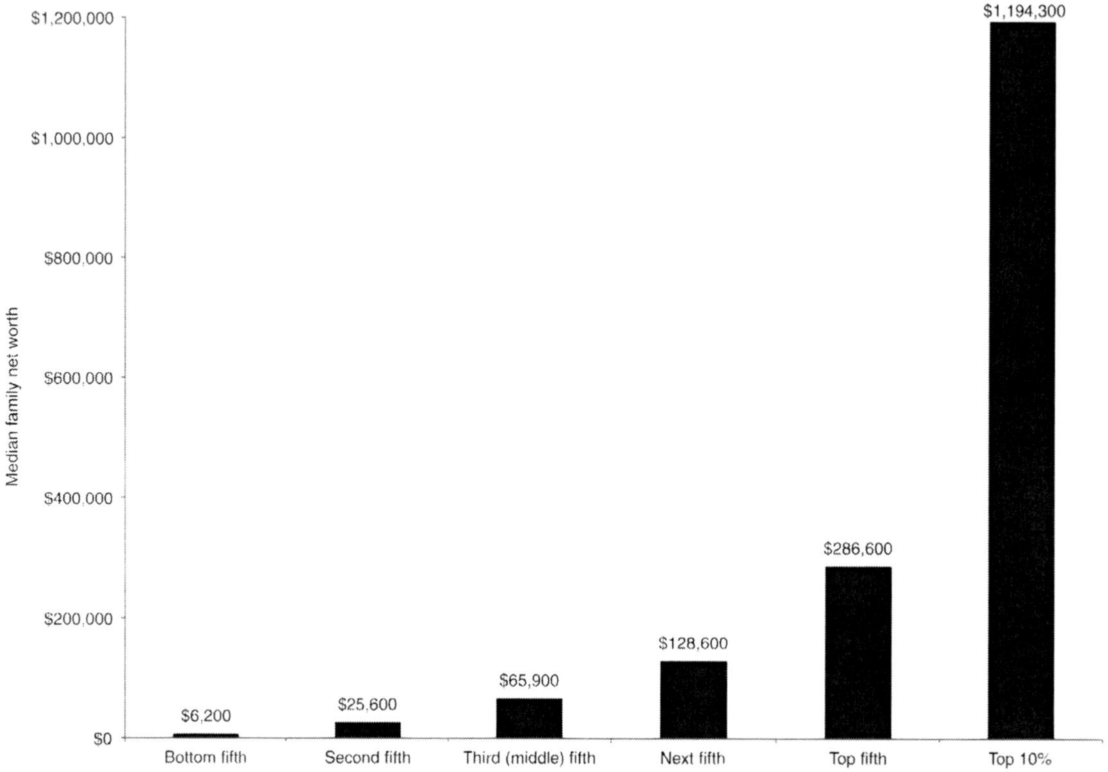

Source: Jesse Bricker et al., *Changes in U.S. Family Finances from 2007 to 2010: Evidence from the Survey of Consumer Finances* (Washington, DC: Board of Governors of the Federal Reserve System, 2012), 17, http://www .federalreserve.gov/pubs/bulletin/2012/pdf/scf12.pdf.

In 2010, the latest year for which SCF results were available at the time of writing, half of all American families had a net worth greater than $77,300, and half had less than that amount (all values are nominal). The median figure, however, masks great differences in family net worth. For families in the bottom fifth of the income distribution, half had a net worth of less than $6,200, while half of all families in the top tenth of the income distribution had a net worth of more than $1.2 million (see Figure 8.3). Families in the middle of the income distribution (third quintile) had a median net worth of $65,900.[75] Similar patterns appear when viewing wealth in conjunction with socioeconomic traits like family structure, education, race, ethnicity, employment status, and occupation.

As with income statistics, it is necessary to understand the components of wealth. For the vast majority of American families, their homes are their single largest asset and represent the bulk of their net worth. Nonfinancial assets, including real estate, accounted for 62.1 percent of all assets owned by American families in 2010; of this

Figure 8.4 Distribution of Marketable Net Worth by Percentile Group, United States, 1983–2010

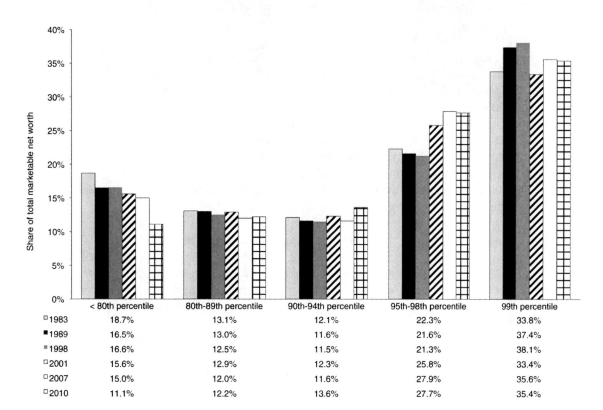

	< 80th percentile	80th-89th percentile	90th-94th percentile	95th-98th percentile	99th percentile
□1983	18.7%	13.1%	12.1%	22.3%	33.8%
■1989	16.5%	13.0%	11.6%	21.6%	37.4%
▦1998	16.6%	12.5%	11.5%	21.3%	38.1%
▨2001	15.6%	12.9%	12.3%	25.8%	33.4%
□2007	15.0%	12.0%	11.6%	27.9%	35.6%
▦2010	11.1%	12.2%	13.6%	27.7%	35.4%

Source: J. Lawrence Mishel, Josh Bivens, Elise Gould, and Heidi Shierholz, *The State of Working America*, 12th ed. (Ithaca, NY: Cornell University Press, 2012), 380.

amount, nearly half was in the form of ownership of a primary residence.[76] Contrary to popular perceptions, most American families own few stocks, either directly or indirectly through tax-advantaged retirement accounts, and most of those who own shares control modest portfolios. In 2010, only 49.9 percent of families held any stock, with half of those families owning portfolios worth less than $29,000. Half of all middle-income families (third quintile) had no more than $12,000 in shares.[77]

While a full explanation is beyond the scope of this volume, it is important to acknowledge the highly skewed distribution of wealth found in the United States—a distribution even more unequal than that of income (see chapter 9) and one that has increased sharply since the early 1980s. One analysis by the Economic Policy Institute, a nonprofit research organization in the District of Columbia, found that the top fifth of American families possessed 88.9 percent of the nation's net wealth in 2010, up from 81.3 percent in 1983. Furthermore, the top 1 percent of families—those with average wealth of $16.4 million—controlled 35.4 percent of America's wealth, up from 33.8 percent in 1983 (see Figure 8.4). The study found that 38.3 percent of the total increase in net wealth over that period accrued to the top 1 percent of families, while a mere 4.3 percent went to the bottom 80 percent; in fact, none of the gain went to the bottom 60 percent of American families, which instead experienced declines in average wealth.[78]

Despite the importance of wealth data, very little information is available for states and regions. The SCF contains no information for geographies smaller than census regions, and other data sources cover individual pieces of wealth but not all of those needed to fashion a comprehensive picture. Because homes are the most significant asset owned by most households, regional leaders can gain insights into this asset class by analyzing the housing data in the Census Bureau's ACS. For owner-occupied housing units, the ACS asks respondents to provide an estimate of their unit's value, their monthly housing costs, including real estate taxes, their mortgage status, and their mortgage payments, if any. The questionnaire also asks about the physical characteristics of housing units, such as the number of bedrooms.

Using data collected in 2010 for the Denver MSA reveals that the region contained some 648,718 owner-occupied homes with a median value of $245,900. Of Denver's owner-occupied housing units, 79 had outstanding mortgages, and half of all owners with a mortgage paid more than $1,679 in monthly housing costs. Additionally, 27 percent of all homeowners with a mortgage in the Denver MSA spent more than 35 percent of their annual incomes on housing costs, which suggests that a lack of affordable housing may trouble the region.[79]

Private, academic, and nonprofit organizations also prepare reports containing state and local information pertaining to wealth. One of the more useful sources is the *Assets & Opportunity Scorecard,* a regular report prepared by CFED, a nonprofit organization in the District of Columbia.[80] The report provides "the most comprehensive look available at Americans' financial security today and their opportunities to create a more prosperous future" and compiles data indicators and inventories public policies related to five topics: financial assets and income, businesses and jobs, housing and homeownership, health care, and education.[81] As part of the report, CFED calculates the extent of "asset poverty" in each state. In 2011, some 28.9 percent of all Colorado families lacked enough net worth to maintain themselves at the federal poverty level for three months if they lost their incomes; among households headed by someone belonging to a racial or ethnic minority group, 49.7 percent were asset poor, compared to 23.7 percent of households headed by a non-Hispanic white person.[82]

INCOME, WEALTH, AND LIVING STANDARDS: A SUMMARY

Income is a stream of resources originating in labor earnings, investment returns, and transfer payments. Those resources enable individuals, households, and families to provide for themselves, immediately and over time. The degree to which households satisfy their needs and preferences is an important component of individual and regional well-being. Simply put, the more income a household possesses, the more it can consume or save, while the greater the amount of income present in a community, the higher the standard of living its residents potentially can enjoy.

Because income is difficult to define and measure, regional leaders interested in using income data as proxy measures of well-being require a basic familiarity with income concepts, components, and uses, along with the related subject of wealth. Yet an appreciation of absolute measures of income is insufficient for understanding economic living standards: the relative distribution of income within a region must also be taken into account. After all, individuals judge their well-being not simply in terms of how much income they receive but also by how their income compares to that of a larger community. The relative dimension of income is the focus of the next chapter.

Notes

1. U.S. Bureau of Labor Statistics, "American Time Use Survey: 2011 Results," news release, June 22, 2012, 15, http://www.bls.gov/news.release/pdf/atus.pdf.

2. Joseph Cortright and Andrew Reamer, *Socioeconomic Data for Understanding Your Regional Economy* (Washington, DC: U.S. Department of Commerce, 1998), 35.

3. Woody Allen, *The Complete Prose of Woody Allen* (New York: Wings Books, 1992), 63.

4. U.S. Census Bureau, "Annual Estimates of the Population of Metropolitan and Micropolitan Statistical Areas: April 1, 2010 to July 1, 2011 (CBSA-EST2011–01)," last revised April 2012, http://www.census.gov/popest/data/metro/totals/2011/tables/CBSA-EST2011-01.xls.

5. Cortright and Reamer, *Socioeconomic Data*, 35.

6. U.S. Bureau of Economic Analysis, "Regional Definitions: Personal Income," last revised May 3, 2011, http://bea.gov/regional/definitions/nextpage.cfm?key=Personal%20income.

7. Ibid.

8. Chapter 2 provides a full discussion of personal income.

9. U.S. Bureau of Economic Analysis, "Regional Definitions: Disposable Personal Income," last revised May 3, 2011, http://bea.gov/regional/definitions/nextpage.cfm?key=Disposable%20personal%20income.

10. Robert Brown, "BEA's State and Local Area Personal Income." Presentation to Pacific Northwest Regional Economic Analysis Project, Reno, NV, September 29, 2009, http://workshops.reaproject.org/2009/Reno-Nevada/presentations/Brown-BEA-Income.ppt.

11. While relevant data have been collected for decades, the various data series are not necessarily continuous.

12. Carmen DeNavas-Walt, Bernadette Proctor, and Jessica Smith, *Income, Poverty, and Health Insurance Coverage in the United States: 2011* (Washington, DC: U.S. Census Bureau, 2012), 29, http://www.census.gov/prod/2012pubs/p60-243.pdf.

13. Constance Citro, "Income and Poverty Measures," in *Encyclopedia of the U.S. Census,* ed. Margo Anderson (Washington, DC: CQ Press, 2000), 261–262.

14. U.S. Census Bureau, "Alternative Measures of Income Definitions," last revised September 12, 2012, http://www.census.gov/hhes/www/income/data/historical/measures/redefs.html.

15. Cortright and Reamer, *Socioeconomic Data,* 36.

16. DeNavas-Walt, *Income, Poverty, and Health Insurance Coverage,* 29. The 18 income sources tracked in the Annual Social and Economic Supplement are earnings (wages/self-employment); unemployment compensation; workers' compensation; social security; supplemental security income; public assistance; veterans' payments; pension or retirement income; survivor benefits; disability benefits; interest; dividends; rents, royalties, and estates and trusts; educational assistance; alimony; child support; financial assistance from outside of the household; and other income.

17. U.S. Census Bureau, "Guidance about Income Sources," last revised November 1, 2011, http://www.census.gov/hhes/www/income/method/guidance/index.html.

18. U.S. Census Bureau, "Guidance on Survey Differences in Income and Poverty Estimates: Highlights," last revised September 13, 2011, http://www.census.gov/hhes/www/income/method/guidance/highlights.html.

19. U.S. Census Bureau, "Guidance on Survey Differences in Income and Poverty Estimates: Background," last revised September 13, 2011, http://www.census.gov/hhes/www/income/method/guidance/background.html.

20. Citro, "Income and Poverty Measures," 260–261.

21. U.S. Census Bureau, "Guidance on Survey Differences in Income and Poverty Estimates: Background."

22. U.S. Census Bureau, "About SAIPE," last revised November 29, 2011, http://www.census.gov/did/www/saipe/about/index.html.

23. U.S. Census Bureau, "Small Area Income and Poverty Estimates: Release Highlights of 2010," last revised November 29, 2011, http://www.census.gov/did/www/saipe/data/highlights/2010.html.

24. U.S. Census Bureau, "Guidance on Survey Differences in Income and Poverty Estimates: Background."

25. U.S. Census Bureau, "SIPP User's Guide (2009 Revisions): Chapter 2," 1, http://www.census.gov/sipp/usrguide/ch2_nov20.pdf.

26. U.S. Census Bureau, "Guidance on Survey Differences in Income and Poverty Estimates: Highlights"; emphasis in original.

27. U.S. Census Bureau, "Evolution and History of SIPP," accessed October 15, 2011, http://www.census.gov/sipp/evol.html; and U.S. Census Bureau, "SIPP User's Guide: Chapter 2," 2.

28. U.S. Census Bureau, "SIPP User's Guide (2008 Revisions): Chapter 3," 3.2–3.4, http://www.census.gov/sipp/usrguide/ch3may4.pdf.

29. U.S. Census Bureau, "SIPP User's Guide: Chapter 3," 3.3.

30. U.S. Census Bureau, "SIPP User's Guide (2008 Revisions): Chapter 11," 11.31–11.32, http://www.census.gov/sipp/usrguide/chap11rev2008.pdf.

31. Author's analysis of U.S. Bureau of Economic Analysis, "Table CA 1-3. Personal Income Summary: 2010," last revised April 25, 2012.

32. Author's analysis of U.S. Census Bureau, American Community Survey, One-Year Estimates, 2010.

33. Ibid.

34. Ibid.

35. Ibid.

36. Edward Wolff, *Poverty and Income Distribution*, 2d ed. (Malden, MA: Wiley-Blackwell, 2009), 22.

37. Author's analysis of U.S. Bureau of Economic Analysis, "Table 2.1: Personal Income and Its Disposition, 2010," last revised October 26, 2012.

38. Ibid.

39. Wolff, *Poverty and Income Distribution*, 22.

40. Author's analysis of U.S. Bureau of Economic Analysis, "Table 2.1: Personal Income and Its Disposition, 2010."

41. Author's analysis of U.S. Bureau of Economic Analysis, "Table CA04: Personal Income and Employment Summary, Denver-Aurora-Broomfield, CO Metropolitan Statistical Area, 2010," last revised April 25, 2012.

42. Author's analysis of U.S. Bureau of Economic Analysis, "Table CA35: Personal Current Transfer Receipts, Denver-Aurora-Broomfield, CO Metropolitan Statistical Area, 2010," last revised April 25, 2012; and author's analysis of U.S. Census Bureau, American Community Survey, One-Year Estimates, 2010.

43. As of November 10, 2012, compilations of Social Security data were available at http://www.ssa.gov/policy/docs/statcomps/index.html.

44. Author's analysis of Social Security Administration, "OASDI Beneficiaries by State and County: 2010," http://www.ssa.gov/policy/docs/statcomps/oasdi_sc/2010/index.html.

45. U.S. Bureau of Economic Analysis, "Regional Definitions: Earnings," last revised May 3, 1011, http://www.bea.gov/regional/definitions/nextpage.cfm?key=Earnings.

46. Cortright and Reamer, *Socioeconomic Data,* 39.

47. Author's analysis of U.S. Bureau of Economic Analysis, "Table CA25N: Total Full-Time and Part-Time Employment by NAICS Industry, Denver-Aurora-Broomfield, CO Metropolitan Statistical Area, 2010," last revised April 25, 2012; and "Table CA06N: Compensation of Employees by NAICS Industry, Denver-Aurora-Broomfield, CO Metropolitan Statistical Area, 2010," last revised December 14, 2011.

48. U.S. Bureau of Labor Statistics, "Glossary: Earnings," http://bls.gov/bls/glossary.htm#earnings (accessed November 10, 2012).

49. U.S. Bureau of Labor Statistics, "State and Metro Area Employment, Hours, and Earnings: Frequently Asked Questions, last revised September 6, 2012, http://bls.gov/sae/790faq2.htm.

50. Employment and Training Administration, *Guide to State and Local Workforce Data for Analysis and Informed Decision Making: Version 2* (Washington, DC: U.S. Department of Labor, 2012), 12, https://winwin.workforce3one.org/view/2001212365477234753/info.

51. U.S. Bureau of Labor Statistics, "National Compensation Measures" in *BLS Handbook of Methods* (Washington, DC: U.S. Department of Labor, 1997), 1, http://bls.gov/opub/hom/pdf/homch8.pdf (accessed September 28, 2011).

52. U.S. Bureau of Labor Statistics, "National Compensation Measures," 1–5.

53. As of November 10, 2012, a listing of covered geographies was available at http://www.bls.gov/ncs/ocs/compub.htm.

54. U.S. Bureau of Labor Statistics, "National Compensation Measures," 5.

55. U.S. Bureau of Labor Statistics, *Denver-Aurora-Boulder, CO, National Compensation Survey: July 2010* (Washington, DC: U.S. Department of Labor, 2011), 3 and 23, http://www.bls.gov/ncs/ocs/sp/ncbl1631.pdf.

56. U.S. Bureau of Labor Statistics, "National Compensation Measures," 10.

57. Ibid., 10–14.

58. As of October 31, 2012, the inflation-adjusted data series was available online at http://www.bls.gov/web/eci/ecconstnaics.pdf.

59. As of November 12, 2012, the 15 areas with quarterly ECI estimates are the following: Atlanta-Sandy Springs-Gainesville, GA-AL, CSA; Boston-Worcester-Manchester, MA-NH, CSA; Chicago-Naperville-Michigan City, IL-IN-WI, CSA; Dallas-Fort Worth, TX, CSA; Detroit-Warren-Flint, MI, CSA; Houston-Baytown-Huntsville, TX, CSA; Los Angeles-Long Beach-Riverside, CA, CSA; Miami-Fort Lauderdale-Pompano Beach, FL, MSA; Minneapolis-St. Paul-St. Cloud, MN-WI, CSA; New York-Newark-Bridgeport, NY-NJ-CT-PA, CSA; Philadelphia-Camden-Vineland, PA-NJ-DE-MD, CSA; Phoenix-Mesa-Scottsdale, AZ, MSA; San Jose-San Francisco-Oakland, CA, CSA; Seattle-Tacoma-Olympia, WA, CSA; and Washington-Baltimore-Northern Virginia, DC-MD-VA-WV, CSA.

60. U.S. Bureau of Labor Statistics, "National Compensation Measures," 15.

61. U.S. Bureau of Labor Statistics, "Employer Costs for Employee Compensation: June 2012," news release, September 11, 2012, 10, http://www.bls.gov/news.release/pdf/ecec.pdf.

62. U.S. Bureau of Labor Statistics, "National Compensation Measures," 19.

63. U.S. Bureau of Labor Statistics, "Employee Benefits in the United States: March 2012," news release, July 11, 2012, 9, http://www.bls.gov/news.release/pdf/ebs2.pdf.

64. Author's analysis of data from U.S. Bureau of Labor Statistics, *Denver-Aurora-Boulder, CO, National Compensation Survey: July 2010.*

65. U.S. Bureau of Labor Statistics, "Consumer Expenditures and Income" in *BLS Handbook of Methods* (Washington, DC: U.S. Department of Labor, 1997), 2, accessed September 28, 2011, http://bls.gov/opub/hom/pdf/homch16.pdf.

66. U.S. Bureau of Labor Statistics, "Consumer Expenditures and Income," 2–5.

67. U.S. Bureau of Labor Statistics, "Frequently Asked Questions: Consumer Expenditure Survey," http://www.bls.gov/cex/csxfaqs.htm (accessed November 10, 2012).

68. In the 2009–2010 version of the survey, the 18 metropolitan areas were Atlanta, Baltimore, Boston, Chicago, Cleveland, Dallas-Fort Worth, Detroit, Houston, Los Angeles, Miami, Minneapolis-St. Paul, San Diego, San Francisco, Seattle, New York, Philadelphia, Phoenix, and Washington, DC. As of November 12, 2012, a listing of metropolitan areas for which estimates exist was available at http://bls.gov/cex/csxmsa.htm.

69. U.S. Bureau of Labor Statistics, "Consumer Expenditures and Income," 7.

70. Author's analysis of U.S. Bureau of Labor Statistics, "Table 1: Quintiles of Income before Taxes: Average Annual Expenditures and Characteristics, Consumer Expenditure Survey, 2011," http://www.bls.gov/cex/2011/Standard/quintile.pdf.

71. Wolff, *Poverty and Income Distribution,* 134.

72. Ibid., 135–136.

73. Jesse Bricker et al., *Changes in U.S. Family Finances from 2007 to 2010: Evidence from the Survey of Consumer Finances* (Washington, DC: Board of Governors of the Federal Reserve System, 2012), 3, http://www.federalreserve.gov/pubs/bulletin/2012/pdf/scf12.pdf.

74. Wolff, *Poverty and Income Distribution,* 136.

75. Bricker, *Changes in U.S. Family Finances*, 17.

76. Ibid., 42.

77. Ibid., 41.

78. Lawrence Mishel, Josh Bivens, Elise Gould, and Heidi Shierholz, *The State of Working America,* 12th ed. (Ithaca, NY: Cornell University Press, 2012), 380–382.

79. Author's analysis of U.S. Census Bureau, American Community Survey, One-Year Estimates, 2010.

80. As of November 12, 2012, data from the 2012 version of the Assets and Opportunity Scorecard were available at http://assetsandopportunity.org/scorecard/about/main_findings/.

81. Jennifer Brooks and Kasey Wiedrich, *Assets & Opportunity Scorecard: A Portrait of Financial Insecurity and Policies to Rebuild Prosperity in America* (Washington, DC: CFED, 2012), 4, http://assetsandopportunity.org/assets/2012_scorecard.pdf.

82. CFED, "State Profile: Colorado" from 2012 Assets & Opportunity Scorecard, http://scorecard.assetsandopportunity.org/2012/state/co (accessed November 12, 2012).

9 | Income Distribution, Inequality, and Deprivation

Income is an instrumental good and therefore lacks any intrinsic value. The worth of income instead lies entirely in its usefulness in achieving other ends. Think about television programs focused on the lives of the rich. What these shows celebrate is not the absolute size of a person's income, but the comparatively sumptuous lifestyle the money affords. If the show featured an affluent person who lived modestly, it would not be entertaining. Even for people of ordinary means, income matters for what it allows them to do, like buying a home. Perhaps the best description of income's instrumental value comes from the philosopher Aristotle who observed, "The life of money-making is one undertaken under compulsion, and wealth is evidently not the good we are seeking; for it is merely useful for the sake of something else."[1]

The degree to which income enables individuals to achieve desired ends is relative to the distribution of income within a larger community. An annual household income of $50,000, say, would be an above-average income in many parts of rural Colorado but below average in metropolitan Denver. Interpreting income statistics therefore requires a familiarity with absolute and relative measures of income. The relative nature of income matters because individuals tend to judge their well-being in relation to the specific communities in which they live, work, and socialize rather than against a fixed standard.

This chapter moves beyond the absolute income measures detailed in chapter 8 to explore the relative nature of income and the role that relative measures of income can play in analyzing regional living standards. While relative wealth differences might be a better indicator of well-being, income is a more practical proxy measure because the relevant data appear on a more regular basis, in more formats, and for more units of geography. Nevertheless, one could apply the basic techniques covered in this chapter to wealth data or any monetary distribution.

The discussion proceeds in four parts. The first section explains the idea of a regional income distribution, and the second section introduces the concept of income inequality. The third section addresses income deprivation—what

Americans call "poverty"—and ways of measuring it. The final section introduces the American Human Development Index, an emerging approach for measuring living standards in a multidimensional way that accounts for factors besides income. Because relative and absolute income measures are related, chapter 9 again offers practical examples drawn from data for the Denver-Aurora-Broomfield, CO Metropolitan Statistical Area (MSA), a 10-county region that was home to 2.6 million residents in 2011.[2]

INCOME DISTRIBUTION

Regardless of whether one is measuring personal or money income (see chapter 8), the allocation of income within a regional economy varies among units of consumption, be they persons, households, or families. The first step in illuminating relative differences in living standards therefore is to document the distribution of income within a region of interest.

Table 9.1 illustrates those differences by using American Community Survey (ACS) money income data for 2011 to divide Denver's roughly 1 million households into five equally sized groups (quintiles) of 201,404 households each. That year, one-fifth of Denver households had annual incomes below $25,550, while one-fifth had incomes in excess of $115,341 (column 1). To provide added detail on the area's richest households, the table decomposes the top quintile into two smaller groups: households with incomes between the 80th and 95th percentiles and those in the top 5 percent of the income distribution. In 2011, the richest Denver households had at least $204,309 in annual income. The table also presents the average annual incomes of the households in each group (column 2). For households in the lowest quintile the average annual income was $13,882, while the average income of the top 5 percent of households equaled $338,585. The average income for the middle fifth of households (third quintile) was $59,556.[3]

Familiarity with a region's income distribution is essential for any analysis of social welfare. Consider the distribution of aggregate money income in the Denver MSA. As the third and fourth columns of Table 9.1 show, households in the two lowest income quintiles received disproportionately little of Denver's total money income. Despite accounting for 40 percent of all households, the bottom two quintiles received just 12.6 percent of the region's money income. The top quintile, in contrast, received 49.3 percent of all income, with the top 5 percent of households—some 50,351 households in all—collecting 21.2 percent of the regional total.[4] Additionally, by using other data from the ACS, a regional analyst could cross-tabulate income statistics for the Denver population by many of the demographic variables described in chapter 5.

An awareness of a region's income distribution can also foster a more realistic and nuanced discussion of social problems and the potential effects of public policies. Take, for instance, the common claim that a proposed policy will benefit the "middle class." While the idea of the middle class resonates with Americans, the concept lacks a fixed definition. Viewed through the lens of relative income statistics, a Denver household at the middle of the income distribution would have an average annual

Table 9.1 Household Money Income in the Denver-Aurora-Broomfield, CO MSA, by Quintile, 2011

	Income range	Average income	Total income	Share of total income
	(1)	(2)	(3)	(4)
Lowest fifth	$0–$25,549	$13,882	$2,795,832,177	3.5%
Second fifth	$25,550–$47,231	$36,260	$7,302,906,464	9.1%
Middle fifth	$47,232–$73,528	$59,556	$11,994,762,761	14.9%
Next fifth	$73,529–$115,341	$92,465	$18,622,813,182	23.2%
Top fifth	$115,342+	$196,777	$39,631,724,516	49.3%
Next 15%	$115,342–$204,308	$149,507	$22,583,575,434	28.1%
Top 5%	$204,309+	$338,585	$17,048,149,082	21.2%

Source: Author's analysis of U.S. Census Bureau, American Community Survey, One-Year Estimates, 2011.

income of $59,556, with the range of middle-income households spanning all those earning $47,232 to $73,528 in income. Yet when people cite the middle class as a policy rationale, they typically are envisioning households with much higher incomes. In effect, they are defining the middle class not in terms of income, but by class and wealth markers like advanced education, professional occupation, and homeownership.

A good example of the misunderstandings that may result from flawed analysis of the income distribution was the long-running policy debate over whether to raise the top marginal federal income tax rate—the rate levied on the last dollar of income received—from 35 percent, the rate set by the U.S. Congress in the early 2000s, to 39.6 percent, the rate levied from 1993 to 2001.[5] For much of the period, the debate hinged on whether to raise the rate paid by married households with $250,000 or more in taxable income ($200,000 or more for single persons). Opponents claimed the change would harm the middle class. Raising the top tax rate may have been undesirable, but the claim that it would harm the middle class was untrue, if by middle class one meant households in the middle of the income distribution. Congress ultimately resolved the debate by restoring the old marginal tax rate for married couples with $450,000 or more in taxable income ($400,000 or more for single persons)—a decision estimated to effect 0.8 percent of taxpayers, all of whom fall well above the middle of the income distribution.[6]

INCOME INEQUALITY

Two tools useful for understanding the dispersion of income within a community are the concentration ratio and the Gini coefficient, both of which relate to the larger concepts of income inequality and economic mobility. Remember that while this section focuses on income data, the same techniques for analyzing inequality are applicable to any monetary distribution, such as hourly wages, weekly earnings, and household wealth.

CONCENTRATION RATIO

A *concentration ratio* is "the simplest summary statistic on income inequality," and compares the share of total income possessed by one income group—typically the richest—to that of another group—typically the poorest.[7] If the income distribution in a community were fully equal, each segment of the distribution would receive the same share of the total. Returning to Table 9.1, if income had been distributed perfectly equally within the Denver MSA in 2011, each quintile would have received $16.1 billion in total income. If that income had been distributed perfectly equally within each quintile, each household would have had an annual income of $79,780. As shown in the third and fourth columns of Table 9.1, Denver's actual income distribution was not so equal. The top 20 percent of households received 49.3 percent of total income, while the bottom 40 percent of households shared 12.6 percent of all income in the region. Households in the middle of the income distribution fared better, but even then they only received 14.9 percent of all the money income in the Denver region.[8]

Another way of using concentration ratios is to compare the magnitude of differences among groups. In practice, studies of income typically emphasize three gaps: the gap between the richest and poorest units, the gap between the richest and middle-income units, and the gap between middle-income and the poorest units. Applying concentration ratios to 2011 income data for the Denver metro reveals that the top quintile received 14.2 times as much income as the bottom quintile and 3.3 times as much as the middle quintile. Similarly, the collective income of the top 5 percent of households was 6.1 times greater than that of the lowest fifth of households and 1.4 times greater than that of the middle fifth. The income of the middle quintile, in turn, was 4.3 times greater than that of the lowest quintile and 1.6 times greater than that of the second quintile.[9]

The popularity of concentration ratios stems from their simplicity. A shortcoming is that studies typically use ratios exclusively to compare the richest units within a distribution—normally those in the top 20 percent, top 10 percent, and top 1 percent—to the poorest units within a distribution. This is important, but a single-minded focus on gaps between the top and the bottom obscures other changes, such as a shifting of income from the middle to the bottom or an increasing concentration within the top income bracket, like a shift from the top 10 percent to the top 5 percent. Analysts therefore should not focus exclusively on the gap between the richest and poorest units, or they may lose sight of the entire distribution.

GINI COEFFICIENT

Named for its creator, Italian economist Corrado Gini, the *Gini coefficient* is a statistical technique for measuring the inequality present in a distribution. Though the measure's actual computation is beyond this book's scope, the calculation yields a value ranging between the numbers zero and one (sometimes zero to 100). A zero value indicates a perfectly equal distribution of income, while a score of one reflects a completely unequal distribution in which one entity receives all the income.[10] As part of the ACS, the Census Bureau computes Gini scores for every covered level of geography. In 2011, the United States had a Gini score of 0.475, Colorado a score of 0.459, and Denver a score of 0.457.[11] These readings suggest that the country had a relatively unequal distribution of income with income distributed somewhat more equally in Colorado than in the nation and slightly more equally in Denver than in the state.

Compared to concentration ratios, Gini coefficients are less intuitive and more difficult to compute. At the same time, Gini coefficients are more sensitive to changes in the middle of the income distribution than to those at the top or bottom ends; in other words, the coefficients better capture changes within the broad middle of the income distribution. Gini scores also are immune to external changes to the income distribution, as happens when all incomes rise proportionally due to inflation. The measure further captures changes brought about by redistributions in income. Gini coefficients become more unequal when income shifts from the poor to the rich and more equitable when income flows in the other direction.[12]

A final strength of the Gini coefficient is that it permits the drawing of meaningful comparisons across time and place. That explains why Gini scores feature in international studies of income inequality—studies in which the United States normally fares poorly compared to other advanced industrial nations and even some less-advanced ones. According to the United Nations Development Program, the 0.408 Gini coefficient recorded in 2010 in the United States ranked behind that of every other advanced economy and equaled the score of Tunisia.[13] Similarly, a 2011 study by the Organization for Economic Cooperation and Development concluded that income inequality in the United States, as measured by the Gini coefficient, was greater than all but three of the world's 34 richest counties: Turkey, Mexico, and Chile.[14]

ECONOMIC MOBILITY

The comparatively high level of income inequality found in the United States is a contested political matter. Observers concerned about inequality argue that, besides being unfair, it prevents people from achieving their full potential; fosters an unhealthy concentration of political, economic, and social power; and retards economic growth.[15] Moreover, so the argument runs, inequality is not a natural phenomenon but one brought about by structural conditions that public policies can ameliorate. For proof, proponents of the this interpretation point to the experience of the United States between the late 1940s and early 1970s, an era in which living standards rose and inequality declined due to policy choices intended to bring about "the sharp reduction in the gap between the rich and the working class, and the reduction in wage differentials among workers."[16]

On the other side of the debate are claims that inequality is an essential feature of a market economy—a feature that provides people with incentives to work. Enhanced work effort, runs the argument, will expand the absolute size of the economy, which will cause everyone to enjoy a higher absolute income level even if their relative places in the income distribution hold constant. Some adherents of this view further posit that inequality is not a problem in the United States owing to the existence of an exceptionally high degree of *economic mobility*, defined as "the ability of people to move up or down the economic ladder within a lifetime or from one generation to the next."[17]

Viewed that way, inequality is not a problem in the United States because people who work hard have exceptional opportunities to advance over their lifetimes, just as their children enjoy good odds of surpassing their parents. Proponents of this view further argue that the correct emphasis of public policy should be on the promotion of equality of opportunities rather than on equality of outcomes.

Unfortunately, a variety of studies suggest "there is less economic mobility in the United States than has long been presumed."[18] Not only does America have less *relative mobility*—a concept that refers to changes in a person's position in the income distribution—than other wealthy nations, but *absolute mobility*—a concept that refers to an overall amount of income that a person receives—also has decreased. Americans consequently appear less likely to move up the income ladder during their lifetimes than once was the case. Even more disturbingly, American children seem less likely to have higher incomes than their parents. A recent report sponsored by the Pew Charitable Trusts, a national philanthropic organization, found that the median income among the generation of men in their thirties in 2004 was 12 percent lower than that of the generation of men in their thirties in the early 1970s, a finding that suggests a troubling decline in *intergenerational mobility*.[19]

Apart from being prone to methodological complexities and concerns, studies into economic mobility normally take the nation, not the state or region, as the unit of analysis, so little regional information consequently is available. That said, civic leaders interested in the topic would benefit from consulting the reports of the Economic Mobility Project, a research program sponsored by the Pew Charitable Trusts.[20] Even when detailed regional information is unavailable, public leaders should not ignore the fundamental links between economic inequality, mobility, and well-being.

INCOME DEPRIVATION

A final set of income statistics measures income deprivation, which is the lack of resources adequate to satisfy basic needs. If analyses of income distribution and inequality focus on the living standards of a population as a whole, deprivation measures assess the conditions of population segments that fall short of a specified income level.

Analysts typically measure deprivation in one of two ways: *Direct deprivation measures* attempt to gauge the extent to which segments of the population actually lack basic material goods like food and shelter. An example is the annual food insecurity measure prepared by the U.S. Department of Agriculture. The statistic captures the share of households that "were, at times, unable to acquire enough food for one or more household members because they had insufficient money and other resources for food."[21] Between 2009 and 2011, an average of 13.4 percent of all Colorado households experienced a period of food insecurity.[22] *Indirect deprivation measures*, in contrast, use another variable, normally income, as a proxy for the ability of a family, household, or person to meet its material needs. In the United States, the main deprivation measure—the Federal Poverty Level—is an indirect one that takes income as a proxy for the ability of a person, household, or family to satisfy certain material needs.

THE FEDERAL POVERTY LEVEL

A statistic crafted in 1965 by Mollie Orshansky, an analyst at the Social Security Administration, the *Federal Poverty Level* (FPL) is the primary deprivation measure used in the United States.[23] Orshansky's original purpose was "to specify in dollar terms what a minimally 'decent' level of consumption or 'needs' would be for families of different types."[24] To answer the question, Orshansky took survey data showing that three-person families spent about one-third of their incomes on food and trebled the number. She then adjusted the total by household size to control for economies of consumption. Finally, Orshansky compared the money income received by households to the corresponding income threshold. Poor households were those with incomes below the income threshold for their household size.

By Orshansky's own admission, the measure's purpose was not to establish an adequate income level, but to suggest a floor under which a household could not survive. Nevertheless, in 1969 the Nixon administration designated Orshansky's thresholds, adjusted annually for changes in the Consumer Price Index, as the nation's official measure of poverty.[25] In 2011, the poverty threshold for a four-person family equaled $23,021.[26] Table 9.2 lists the average poverty thresholds for families of different sizes, along with multiples of the poverty thresholds regularly encountered in regional analyses.

The adoption of the poverty threshold was unique in two regards. First, while other nations track poverty, no other country has an "official" statistical measure.[27] Second, responsibility for defining the measure rests not with a statistical agency, but with the U.S. Office of Management and Budget, a division of the Executive Office of the President.[28] This has helped to turn the FPL into a politicized measure that has proven virtually immune to refinement; in effect, the 1969 decision to fix the poverty level served to "freeze the poverty line despite changes in buying habits and changes in acceptable living standards."[29]

Responsibility for tabulating poverty statistics rests with the Census Bureau. The official count is the one derived from the Annual Social and Economic Supplement to the Current Population Survey (see chapter 8). A limitation of that measure is that it is a lagging indicator. For instance, the Census Bureau did not collect official poverty data for 2011 until March 2012 and did not publish the results until September 2012. To fill the information gap between annual updates to the official count, the U.S. Department of Health and Human Services issues interim poverty guidelines, but those guidelines are a management tool, not an official statistic.[30]

POVERTY IN THE DENVER MSA

Though the Annual Social and Economic Supplement to the Current Population Survey is the official source of poverty information, it contains relatively little substate data. For the purposes of regional analysis, the ACS is a richer source of information.

Table 9.2 Federal Poverty Thresholds (Weighted Averages) and Selected Poverty Level Threshold Ratios, by Size of Family Unit, 2011

Family Size	Poverty Threshold	50% of Poverty Threshold[a]	130% of Poverty Threshold[b]	150% of Poverty Threshold[c]	200% of Poverty Threshold[d]
One person	$11,484	$5,742	$14,929	$17,226	$22,968
Two persons	$14,657	$7,329	$19,054	$21,986	$29,314
Three persons	$17,916	$8,958	$23,291	$26,874	$35,832
Four persons	$23,021	$11,511	$29,927	$34,532	$46,042
Five persons	$27,251	$13,626	$35,426	$40,877	$54,502
Six persons	$30,847	$15,424	$40,101	$46,271	$61,694
Seven persons	$35,085	$17,543	$45,611	$52,628	$70,170
Eight persons	$39,064	$19,532	$50,783	$58,596	$78,128
Nine or more persons	$46,572	$23,286	$60,544	$69,858	$93,144

Source: Carmen DeNavas-Walt, Bernadette Proctor, and Jessica Smith, *Income, Poverty, and Health Insurance Coverage in the United States: 2011* (Washington, DC: U.S. Census Bureau, 2012), 49, http://www.census.gov/prod/2012pubs/p60-243.pdf.
[a]A poverty level threshold ratio used to indicate "deep" poverty.
[b]A poverty level threshold ratio used in determining eligibility for the Supplemental Nutrition Assistance Program.
[c]A poverty level threshold ratio often used to determine eligibility for various assistance programs.
[d]A poverty level threshold ratio commonly used to designate the "working poor."

In particular, the ACS provides poverty estimates cross-tabulated by numerous demographic and economic characteristics, along with estimates of the depth of poverty, or the poverty gap, which reflects "the additional income necessary to boost an income unit up to the poverty line."[31]

According to the ACS, an average of 328,306 Denver residents—12.8 percent of the regional population—fell below the poverty level in 2011.[32] This overall poverty rate, however, masks important differences among population groups. White residents of Denver in 2011 had a poverty rate much lower than that of other racial groups: some 10.5 percent of the white population had incomes below the poverty threshold, compared to 11.7 percent of the Asian population and 27.8 percent of the African-American population. Similarly, 7.8 percent of non-Hispanic whites fell below the FPL, as opposed to 23.5 percent of Denver's Hispanic residents. And 17.8 percent of the region's children lived in poverty, as did 7.9 percent of the population age 65 and older.[33]

ACS data also allow for an analysis of the depth of poverty present in a community. As Figure 9.1 indicates, 40.9 percent of Denver's poor residents in 2011 experienced "deep" poverty, meaning their incomes were below 50 percent of the FPL, or $11,511 for a family of four. Another 27.9 percent of poor residents had incomes between 50 and 74 percent of the poverty level, and the remaining 31.2 percent of poor residents had incomes between 75 percent of the poverty threshold and the poverty line.[34]

Figure 9.1 Distribution of Persons by Ratio of Income to the Federal Poverty Level (FPL), Denver-Aurora-Broomfield, CO MSA, 2011

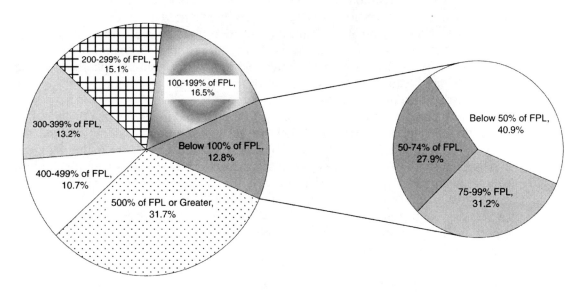

Source: U.S. Census Bureau, American Community Survey, One-Year Estimates, 2011.

Of course, economic hardships are not limited to those individuals with incomes below the FPL; in fact, persons with incomes above the line also may struggle to make ends meet. According to ACS data, not only were 12.8 percent of Denver's residents poor in 2011, but an additional 16.5 percent of the local population had incomes between 100 and 200 percent of the poverty level, a range commonly used as a proxy measure for the income of the "working poor," or people who earn low incomes despite working for much of the year.[35] Viewed that way, 29.3 percent of Denver's inhabitants were poor or nearly poor in 2011.

One dimension of poverty not captured in ACS data is the duration of poverty. While widely thought of as a static phenomenon, poverty actually is dynamic in that people regularly cycle above and below the poverty threshold. Sometimes the total time spent below the poverty line is brief, such as when a low-wage worker loses a job before quickly finding a new one; but in other instances the spell is long, as when a worker becomes disabled and can no longer hold a job. Long durations may trigger a spiral of downward mobility, as happens when a prolonged job loss leads a person to default on a mortgage and become homeless. The best information on poverty duration comes from longitudinal studies, and while studies vary in their conclusions, the general consensus is that the poverty population constantly churns, meaning that the number of people who experience a bout of poverty over a span of time differs from the actual number who fall below the FPL at any given moment.

LIMITATIONS OF THE FEDERAL POVERTY LEVEL

Despite its age and ubiquity, the FPL is a flawed statistic that no longer accurately measures income deprivation. Among its flaws, the poverty level ignores geographical variations in living costs, overstates the share of income spent on food, excludes important expenses like child care, fails to account for taxes, and omits the value of noncash transfer payments.[36] Observers on the right of the political spectrum say the measure's flaws lead to an overstatement of the incidence of poverty; critics on the left argue that they produce an understatement.

The most comprehensive critique of the FPL appeared in 1995 when the National Academy of Sciences (NAS) published the results of a congressionally mandated review.[37] Among its 25 recommendations, the NAS study called for including more expenses in the poverty measure, estimating costs based on consumer expenditure data, adjusting expenses for variations in living costs, including certain near-cash transfer payments in the calculation of available resources, and subtracting medical and tax payments from the resource total. Though well regarded by scholars, the NAS report did not prompt changes in the official measure.

As an outgrowth of the NAS process, the Census Bureau began preparing a set of experimental poverty measures reflecting different NAS recommendations. These alternative calculations generally yield poverty rates somewhat higher than the official one. Had the primary NAS measure been in effect in 2010, the national poverty rate would have equaled 15.5 percent versus an official rate of 15.1 percent. By extension, 1.1 million more Americans would have lived in poverty, which would have brought the total poverty count to 47.5 million.[38]

The Supplemental Poverty Measure

The Obama administration recently has taken steps toward advancing an NAS-style measure as a supplement to the official poverty statistic.[39] First released in November 2011, the *Supplemental Poverty Measure*, a joint research product of the Census Bureau and U.S. Bureau of Labor Statistics, moves "beyond consideration of money income to estimate the value of such in-kind transfers as food stamps, net taxes paid to the government (taxes paid less the value of tax credits received), and medical and work-related expenses (such as child-care and commuting costs). It also employs a new standard of need, linked to what low-income families actually spend."[40] When applied to 2011 data, the supplemental measure yields a poverty rate of 16.1 percent, compared to the official rate of 15.1 percent. This means that an additional 3.1 million Americans were poor, which brought the total number of poor Americans to 49.7 million.[41]

Because the supplemental measure accounts for the receipt of certain transfer payments and the payment of medical expenses, it shows that a statistically significant smaller share of the child population experienced poverty in 2011 than was captured in the official measure (18.1 percent versus 22.3 percent), while a larger share of older adults experienced poverty (15.1 percent versus 8.7 percent).[42] These differences occurred because children are the main beneficiaries of many of the income transfer payments included in the supplemental measure and typically incur few medical expenses. Older adults, in contrast, have fewer income sources that were not already included in the poverty measure, but they are more likely to have high out-of-pocket medical expenses of the kind accounted for in the supplemental measure. The new statistic also uses a higher income threshold for older households.

The main advantage of the supplemental measure is that it allows researchers to gauge the effects of policy interventions on poverty. The lower child poverty rate suggests that initiatives like the Supplemental Nutrition Assistance Program and Earned Income Tax Credit indeed alleviate economic hardship. Unfortunately, the supplemental measure suffers from many of the same limitations of the FPL, including "the most fundamental problem with the official poverty measure—the extent to which it has 'defined deprivation' down over the last several decades because it has not kept pace with changes in typical living standards in the United States."[43] Though useful, the supplemental measure currently is a research effort and not a replacement for the FPL, which remains the official statistic used by the federal government.

Other Poverty Measures

Frustration with the official poverty statistic has prompted analysts to construct alternate poverty measures. The Office of Economic Opportunity of the City of New York has developed its own set of NAS-style estimates that indicated that 21 percent of city residents were poor in 2010, compared to an official poverty rate of 18.8 percent.[44] A second approach is to calculate how much income certain household types would need to afford the market prices of a basket of core goods and services in a manner broadly similar to that of the U.S. Department of Labor's Family Budgets Program, a long-standing initiative discontinued in 1981.[45] In North Carolina, for instance, the Budget and Tax Center, a nonprofit organization in Raleigh, estimated that a "family of two adults and four children must earn \$48,814 annually—an amount equal to 221 percent of the federal poverty level—to afford the actual costs of seven essential expenses" in 2010.[46] Finally, some analysts simply double the FPL and take that amount as a proxy for economic hardship; seen that way, four-person families with less than \$46,042 in income would have been income deprived in 2011.

All of these alternate methods suffer from limitations. Critics of NAS-style measures claim they suffer the same basic problems as the official poverty statistic: the thresholds are set too low, and the definition of poverty is too narrow. The family budgets approach, meanwhile, is not standardized and is seldom suited for geographic or time-series comparisons.[47] And the 200 percent of FPL measure is a rough guideline that works well in some situations but not in others.

ALTERNATE METHODS FOR MEASURING INCOME DEPRIVATION

Many of the problems with the FPL and derivative measures stem from its nature as an *absolute measure* that defines poverty in binary terms in relation to an exact income threshold. A person below that income level, even by \$1, is poor, just as a person above that income level, even by \$1, is not.[48] Moreover, the cutoff point used in the United States effectively is an assessment of how much income a three-person American family requires to purchase sustain "a minimally nutritionally sound diet" based on standards from the 1950s.[49] However, the determinants of a sound diet have evolved in response to social trends. It would be possible, after all, for someone to obtain all needed calories solely by eating potatoes and raw vegetables, but Americans generally consider some level of meat consumption to be part of a sound diet. Similarly, living standards change over time. In the 1950s, food cost more than it does today and claimed a greater share of household budgets, but child-care bills—a significant cost for many families today—were less common. Yet the FPL ignores both the drop in food costs as a share of household income and the rise in child-care costs.

Another problem with absolute measures is that they erode over time, which is why the official poverty statistic "now excludes the majority of low-income Americans who experience food insecurity, including the most severe form of food insecurity, and majorities or near-majorities of Americans experiencing various other forms of economic hardship."[50] Consider how, according to one recent analysis, 63.7 percent of all households facing "food insecurity" in 2008 had incomes above the poverty level.[51] This suggests that the FPL is losing its ability to measure deprivation, which Mollie Orshansky herself often warned might be the case.

These limitations are why most analysts prefer relative measures of poverty, which are rooted in the idea that "a person's needs are relative to what others in their society have."[52] Scholars Ron Haskins and Isabel Sawhill of the Brookings Institution explain, "Relative poverty is a better measure of individual well-being than absolute poverty, because social context and community norms about what it means to be poor change over time, implying that the poverty line should be adjusted as economic growth makes everyone better off."[53]

Relative Measures

Relative poverty measures, which are common in European countries, tie income deprivation to the real standard of living, such as by setting the deprivation threshold at a level equal to 60 percent of median income.[54] The Republic of Ireland, for example, computes two core measures of poverty as part of the regular *Survey on Income and Living Conditions* conducted by the country's Central Statistics Office. The first measure, the "at-risk-of-poverty" rate, is relative and gauges "the proportion of individuals who are considered to be at risk of experiencing poverty based on the level of their current income and taking into account their household composition."[55] Persons at risk of poverty are those with equalized annual incomes below 60 percent of the national median income. In 2010, an income of €10,831 ($14,363 at official annual exchange rates) equaled 60 percent of national median income; that year, 15.8 percent of thc Irish population fell below the at-risk of poverty threshold.[56] The second measure that the statistical agency computes is a "consistent poverty" rate that estimates the share of people who are at risk of poverty and who experienced at least two forms of material depravation, such as an inability to heat a home or buy new clothes, due to a lack of money. In 2010, some 6.2 percent of the Irish population met both criteria and were consistently poor.[57]

The main advantage of a relative poverty measure like the at-risk-of-poverty rate is that it tracks whether periods of economic prosperity produce income gains for all members of society. At the same time, it is harder to reduce relative poverty rates since median income typically rises, especially during economic expansions. Additionally, by combining the at-risk-of-poverty rate with the consistent poverty measure, the Irish statistical agency is better able to identify not just residents who have low incomes but also those facing the greatest material hardships—knowledge that could foster more effective policy interventions. The American poverty measure, in contrast, captures none of those nuances.

Subjective Measures

A second alternative method of gauging income deprivation is through subjective measures based on community perceptions. By using polling and related statistical tools, analysts have developed techniques "to discover the minimum amount of income or consumption that individuals require to maintain what they consider to be an adequate standard of living."[58] In the United States, the Gallup Organization, a research firm, asks survey respondents to indicate the minimum weekly income that a four-person family needs to "get along." In 2007, respondents reported an average "get-along income" of $52,087—an amount 2.4 times greater than the FPL. Interestingly, the gap between the two measures has widened over time. Upon its creation, the FPL equaled 72 percent of the reported get-along income, but in 2007, it amounted to 41 percent of the cited value. Had the FPL maintained its original relationship to the get-along value, the poverty threshold for a four-person family in 2007 would have totaled $37,500, an amount 74.4 percent greater than the actual threshold of $21,500.[59]

Capability Deprivation

All of the concepts discussed so far in this chapter gauge deprivation in relation to one variable: income. While income "may be the most prominent means for a good life without deprivation," it is only one determinant of a person's quality of life.[60] If poverty is defined not as a lack of an adequate income but as "the lack of the capability to live a minimally decent life," then factors other than income limit what persons can do and can become.[61] In other words, deprivation is the product of multiple factors that prevent individuals from engaging in important life activities they otherwise would wish to undertake.

Consider the difference between hunger caused by fasting and hunger caused by a lack of food. In both cases, a person is consuming too few calories, but in the first instance, the choice is voluntary, so the person is not deprived. The second situation is one of deprivation because the person would prefer to have more food. Moreover, factors other than a lack of money could prevent an individual from accessing food. A person might have the money to buy food yet be unable to purchase it because political factors limit the access of the person's ethnic group to the food market. Similarly, a person might lack the money to buy food because of institutional barriers that prevent the person from participating in the labor market. In such situations,

Box 9.1 Social Inclusion

The definition of deprivation has a direct influence on the formation and implementation of public policy. When deprivation is associated with just one variable, the resulting policy debates and responses revolve around that factor. This is clearly the case in the United States, where the primary deprivation measure tracks income and the major policy interventions focus on raising income levels relative to a specified threshold.

The capability approach, in contrast, conceptualizes deprivation as stemming from multiple, intertwined factors that hinder individuals from engaging in important endeavors they otherwise would wish to pursue. The emphasis is on the multidimensional nature of deprivation and the relationships among various factors. For example, if legal barriers in a society hinder immigrants from participating in the labor market, the inability of an immigrant to earn a living may cause the person to become homeless, which in turn may lead to other ills like malnourishment or substance abuse. Altogether, this set of factors results in a state of deprivation that a simple boost in income will not rectify.

Beginning in the late 1970s, researchers and policy makers in France and then in other European countries, became progressively more interested in understanding what the economist Amartya Sen describes as "the multidimensional nature of deprivation as well as the importance of casual—and often dynamic—connections." This research led to the development of the idea of *social inclusion* as a coherent system for organizing public responses to complex, intertwined problems of deprivation, such as those stemming from persistent long-term unemployment. Simply put, social inclusion is, as a team of American analysts has written, "an overarching framework for addressing a myriad of social policy issues, including income inequality, skill levels, education, health inequalities, housing affordability, and work-life balance."

One recent application of a social inclusion framework occurred in the United Kingdom, which used the approach to organize a response to the problem of child poverty. Child poverty began to rise steadily in the United Kingdom starting in the 1970s, and by the mid-1990s some 25 percent of British children were poor, as measured against a relative poverty standard. Due to an increased awareness of the extent of the problem and the toll that poverty exacts from children, the Labor government then in office undertook an effort to halve child poverty within 10 years and eliminate it by 2020.

The British response involved three broad strategies. First, because many poor children lived in households in which no adult worked, policy makers promoted work participation on the part of parents by offering a variety of programs and by making work more remunerative through the adoption of a minimum wage and a generous set of work-based tax credits. Second, officials reformed tax credit and benefit programs in an effort to boost the incomes of *all* families with children. Finally, the government expanded public investments in services for children, such as universal preschool, and strengthened parental leave rights to help adults balance their work and family obligations (e.g., longer paid maternity leaves).

What is interesting about the British approach is the extent to which a strategy to reduce child poverty focused on adults rather than poor children. That is precisely because the problems facing children and their parents are interconnected. Such interventions proved successful. Between 1998–1999 and 2007–2008, the child poverty rate fell to 22.5 percent from 26.7 percent, when measured against a relative poverty standard. If the United Kingdom measured poverty in a manner similar to the United States, the child poverty rate would have dropped by half, falling from 26 percent to 13 percent.

Sources: Heather Boushey, Shawn Fremstad, Rachel Gragg, and Margy Waller, *Social Inclusion for the United States* (Washington, DC: Center for Economic and Policy Research, 2007); Amartya Sen, *Social Exclusion: Concept, Application, and Scrutiny* (Manila: Asian Development Bank, 2000); and Jane Waldfogel, *Britain's War on Poverty* (New York: Russell Sage Foundation, 2010).

deprivation results not simply from a lack of money but from active exclusion from aspects of social and economic life (see Box 9.1).

THE AMERICAN HUMAN DEVELOPMENT INDEX

The use of income statistics as a proxy for living standards is an accepted technique with a long pedigree. As this chapter has noted, income merits consideration because of its instrumental value in enabling individuals, households, and families to meet their needs and satisfy their preferences. Furthermore, income data lend themselves to analysis due to their intuitive simplicity, their easy accessibility, and their frequent tabulation. At the same time, income measures offer a one-dimensional view of human life—a view in which money is the sole measure of everything. Yet as the father of economics, Adam Smith, wrote in *The Wealth of Nations*, "It is not for its own sake that men desire money, but for the sake of what they can purchase with it."[62]

The overarching limitation of an income-centered approach to measuring well-being is its exclusion of other ends that people value, such as education, health, longevity, security, and opportunity. The exclusion, in short, of what Nobel laureate economist Amartya Sen calls "the basic development ideal: namely, advancing the richness of human life, rather than the richness of the economy in which human beings live, which is only a part of it."[63]

Contemporary efforts to better measure human development are rooted in the work of Mahbub ul Haq, an economist and former finance minister of Pakistan who agreed with the notion that "existing measures of human progress failed to account for the true purpose of development—to improve people's lives."[64] To better measure developmental ends the United Nations Development Program prepared and published its first *Human Development Report* in 1990.[65] The central feature of this annual study is the *Human Development Index* (HDI), which is "a numerical index that combines GDP per capita, life expectancy at birth, and literacy."[66]

"The process of enlarging people's freedoms and opportunities and improving their well-being," the human development approach attempts to measure the process through which individuals develop their capabilities and expand the opportunities available to them over time.[67] For practical reasons, the model emphasizes three dimensions of human development: a long and healthy life (health), access to knowledge (education), and a decent standard of living (income). The framework employs a variety of statistical indicators to measure each dimension—both for entire populations and assorted geographic, gender, racial and ethnic subgroups—in some 187 countries. Furthermore, the study computes a total HDI score for each country. Scores range from zero to one, and the higher the score, the higher the level of development.

The 2011 edition of the *Human Development Report* found that Norway had the highest HDI score in the world, and the Democratic Republic of the Congo had the lowest. The United States possessed the world's fourth-highest HDI score, but it actually performed well below the average values recorded in other developed countries on a number of indicators. American life expectancy (78.5 years at birth), for example, was lower than that of most Western European and Nordic countries, not to mention Israel, Singapore, Korea, Malta, Slovenia, and Chile.[68]

Table 9.3 U.S. States and District of Columbia Ranked by Composite American Human Development Index Score, 2008

Rank (1 = highest)	State	Composite score	Rank (1 = highest)	State	Composite score
1	Connecticut	6.30	27	Oregon	5.03
2	Massachusetts	6.24	28	Michigan	4.99
3	District of Columbia	6.21	29	North Dakota	4.92
4	New Jersey	6.16	30	Maine	4.89
5	Maryland	5.96	31	Ohio	4.87
6	New York	5.77	32	Georgia	4.86
7	Minnesota	5.74	33	South Dakota	4.82
8	New Hampshire	5.73	34	Wyoming	4.80
9	Hawaii	5.73	35	Nevada	4.78
10	Colorado	5.65	36	Indiana	4.74
11	Rhode Island	5.56	37	Missouri	4.68
12	California	5.56	38	Texas	4.67
13	Virginia	5.53	39	Idaho	4.65
14	Washington	5.53	40	North Carolina	4.64
15	Illinois	5.39	41	New Mexico	4.56
16	Delaware	5.33	42	Montana	4.49
17	Alaska	5.27	43	South Carolina	4.36
18	Vermont	5.27	44	Tennessee	4.33
19	Wisconsin	5.23	45	Kentucky	4.23
20	Pennsylvania	5.12	46	Oklahoma	4.15
21	Arizona	5.11	47	Alabama	4.09
22	Utah	5.08	48	Louisiana	4.07
23	Florida	5.07	49	Mississippi	3.93
24	Iowa	5.06	50	Arkansas	3.87
25	Kansas	5.06	51	West Virginia	3.85
26	Nebraska	5.05			

Source: Kristen Lewis and Sarah Budd-Sharps, *The Measure of America: American Human Development Report, 2010–2011* (New York: New York University Press), 45.

Although the HDI enjoys considerable name recognition in many parts of the world, it received little notice in the United States prior to 2008, when the American Human Development Project, an initiative of the Social Science Research Council, a research organization in New York City, released the first *American Human Development Report*. That report and a subsequent edition applied a modified human development framework to the United States and computed American HDI scores for each state and congressional district, selected metropolitan areas, and specific population group.[69] Table 9.3 ranks the states in order of their HDI scores for 2008, the most recent year for which data were available at the time of writing. Connecticut posted the highest American HDI score, and West Virginia recorded the lowest. The report found that the average Connecticut resident lived five years longer than did the typical resident of West Virginia, earned 50.1 percent more, and was more than twice as likely to have earned at least a bachelor's degree. The overall level of human development in West Virginia was slightly below the national level recorded in 1990.[70]

So far, the report series only has computed HDI scores for a few of the largest metropolitan areas, but the existing breakdowns by congressional districts are useful for regional analysis. Community leaders in Denver, for instance, could look to the American HDI and see that a number of western states posted comparatively high American HDI scores in 2008, with Colorado logging the nation's tenth-highest score. When ranked by congressional district, however, the performance of the Denver area is mixed. In 2008, one of the area's congressional districts (CO-6) had the nation's eighteenth-highest HDI score, while three others (CO-2, CO-5, and CO-1) ranked lower though still within the top 35 percent of the distribution. The remaining district (CO-7) ranked in the bottom half of all American congressional districts. Of the five Denver districts, residents of CO-6, which spans the metro's southern tier, lived longer, were better educated, and earned higher incomes than the residents of the other districts. Moreover, an analysis of data for congressional districts reveals that three local districts (CO-2, CO-5, and CO-6) outperformed the nation in the areas of education and health.[71]

As time passes, the human development framework should increase in prominence. Since the publication of the first index, the project has released state level reports for California, Louisiana, and Mississippi, as well as an online calculator containing both state- and county-level information pertaining to education.[72] It also would be possible for ambitious regional analysts to compute their own versions of HDI scores consistent with the project's methodologies. Even if a region did not compute its own HDI score, it is feasible to obtain a sense of regional performance by looking at multiple indicators contained in the ACS and related data products. The fundamental point is to recognize that well-being involves more than income.

The main advantages of the HDI are its recognition of the multidimensional nature of prosperity and its capability to produce a single composite score that captures performance in several dimensions of regional well-being in a form comparable across time and place. On the other hand, the HDI model suffers from various methodological challenges and limitations. For example, the index is only as reliable and the scores only as comparable as are the underlying statistics, which can be difficult to obtain in regions at lower developmental levels.

Some critics on the left of the political spectrum, meanwhile, fault the approach for ignoring issues of environmental sustainability, while critics on the right dislike the degree to which the measure deemphasizes per capita measures of income and Gross Domestic Product.[73] Some conservatives also deride the whole endeavor as a value-driven exercise that "is basically a measure of how Scandinavian your country is."[74] Nevertheless, since 1990, the HDI model has emerged, at least outside of the United States, as the best-known alternative to one-dimensional, income-based assessments of living standards.

INCOME DISTRIBUTION, INEQUALITY, AND DEPRIVATION: A SUMMARY

Income matters not as an ends in itself, but as a means for satisfying needs and preferences. This instrumental dimension of income renders it an important determinant of living standards; at the same time, it is not simply absolute income levels that matter for regional analysis. Because individuals normally judge their well-being in relation to particular reference communities, relative measures of income are essential to studies of regional living standards. To grasp the relationship, it is necessary to consider the distribution of income within a region, the degree to which income is concentrated within segments of the population, and the proportion of the population deprived of a certain level of resources. An awareness of such factors facilitates the adoption of public policies and actions aimed at ensuring that regional economic growth translates into broadly shared improvements in living standards, not just in terms of income; but rather, in all of the dimensions that make human life worthwhile.

NOTES

1. Aristotle, *Nicomachean Ethics*, 1.5.1096a5-10.
2. U.S. Census Bureau, "Annual Estimates of the Population of Metropolitan and Micropolitan Statistical Areas: April 1, 2010 to July 1, 2011 (CBSA-EST2011-01)," last revised April 2012, http://www.census.gov/popest/data/metro/totals/2011/tables/CBSA-EST2011-01.xls.
3. Author's analysis of U.S. Census Bureau, American Community Survey, One-Year Estimates, 2011.
4. Ibid.
5. Edward Wolff, *Poverty and Income Distribution,* 2d ed. (Malden, MA: Wiley-Blackwell, 2009), 589.
6. Tax Policy Center, "Table T13-0015—The American Taxpayer Relief Act as Passed by the Senate; High Income Rates, Pease, and PEP; Distribution of Federal Tax Change by Cash Income Level, 2013," last revised January 7, 2013, http://www.taxpolicycenter.org/numbers/displayatab.cfm?DocID=3771.
7. Wolff, *Poverty and Income Distribution,* 61.
8. Author's analysis of U.S. Census Bureau, American Community Survey, One-Year Estimates, 2011.
9. Ibid.
10. Wolff, *Poverty and Income Distribution,* 64–65. This source also explains the calculation of Gini coefficients.
11. Author's analysis of U.S. Census Bureau, American Community Survey, One-Year Estimates, 2011.
12. Wolff, *Poverty and Income Distribution,* 60–61 and 65–66.
13. United Nations Human Development Program, *Human Development Report 2011: Sustainability*

and Equity: A Better Future for All (New York: Palgrave-Macmillan, 2011),135–138, http://hdr.undp.org/en/media/HDR_2011_EN_Complete.pdf.

14. Organization for Economic Cooperation and Development, *Divided We Stand: Why Inequality Keeps Rising* (Paris: OECD Publishing, 2011), 45.

15. Mike Konczal, "Occupy Wall Street and the Diversity of Objections to Inequality," Rortybomb (blog), October 17, 2011, http://rortybomb.wordpress.com/2011/10/17/occupy-wall-street-and-the-diversity-of-objections-to-inequality/.

16. Paul Krugman, *The Conscience of a Liberal* (New York: Norton, 2007), 38.

17. Isabel Sawhill and John Morton, *Economic Mobility: Is the American Dream Alive and Well?* (Washington, DC: Pew Charitable Trusts, 2007), 4, http://www.economicmobility.org/assets/pdfs/EMP%20American%20Dream%20Report.pdf.

18. Sawhill and Morton, *Economic Mobility,* 1.

19. Ibid., 10–12.

20. As of October 25, 2012, all of the Economic Mobility Project's reports were available at http://www.economicmobility.org.

21. Alisha Coleman-Jensen, Mark Nord, Margaret Andrews, and Steven Carlson, *Household Food Security in the United States in 2011* (Washington, DC: U.S. Department of Agriculture, 2012), 5, http://www.ers.usda.gov/media/884525/err141.pdf.

22. Coleman-Jensen, *Household Food Security,* 17.

23. For a detailed history of the poverty measure, see Gordon Fisher, *The Development of the Orshansky Thresholds and Their Subsequent History as the Official U.S. Poverty Measure* (Washington, DC: U.S. Census Bureau, 1992), revised September 2007, http://census.gov/hhes/poverty/povmeas/papers/orshansky.html.

24. Wolff, *Poverty and Income Distribution,* 94.

25. Shawn Fremstad, A Modern Framework for Measuring Poverty and Basic Economic Security (Washington, DC: Center for Economic and Policy Research, 2010), 18–19, http://www.cepr.net/documents/publications/poverty-2010-04.pdf.

26. U.S. Census Bureau, "Poverty Thresholds 2011," http://www.census.gov/hhes/www/poverty/data/threshld/thresh11.xls (accessed October 24, 2012).

27. Wolff, *Poverty and Income Distribution,* 93.

28. For the basic definition, see U.S. Office of Management and Budget, "OMB Statistical Policy Directive No. 14," May 1978, http://www.census.gov/hhes/povmeas/methodology/ombdir14.html.

29. Fisher, *Development of the Orshansky Thresholds.*

30. As of October 23, 2012, the U.S. Department of Health and Human Services poverty guidelines for 2012 were available at http://aspe.hhs.gov/poverty/12poverty.shtml.

31. Mary Edwards, *Regional and Urban Economics and Economic Development* (Boca Raton, FL: Auerbach Publications, 2007), 589.

32. Author's analysis of U.S. Census Bureau, American Community Survey, One-Year Estimates, 2011.

33. Ibid.

34. Ibid.

35. The Working Poor Families Project, a national public policy initiative, considers a "working family" one in which "all family members age 15 and older either have a combined work effort if 39 weeks or more in the prior 12 months, or all family members age 15 and over have a combined work effort of 26 to 39 weeks in the prior 12 months and one currently unemployed parent looked for work in the prior 4 weeks." A "low-income working family" is one with an annual income below 200 percent of the federal poverty level. For more information, see http://www.workingpoorfamilies.org/indicators.html (site active as of October 25, 2012).

36. John Quinterno, *Making Ends Meet on Low Wages: The 2008 North Carolina Living Income Standard* (Raleigh, NC: North Carolina Budget & Tax Center, 2008), 4, http://www.ncjustice.org/assets/library/1169_2008lisreportmar.pdf.

37. For full details of the review, see Constance Citro and Robert Michael, eds., *Measuring Poverty: A New Approach* (Washington, DC: National Academy Press, 1995).

38. Author's analysis of U.S. Census Bureau, "Table. Official and National Academy of Sciences (NAS) Based Poverty Rates: 1999 to 2010," http://www.census.gov/hhes/povmeas/data/nas/tables/2010/web_tab4_nas_measures_historical_1999_2010.xls (accessed October 25, 2012); and Carmen DeNavas-Walt, Bernadette Proctor, and Jessica Smith, *Income, Poverty, and Health Insurance Coverage in the United States: 2011* (Washington, DC: U.S. Census Bureau, 2012), 14, http://www.census.gov/prod/2012pubs/p60-243.pdf.

39. For additional information, see http://www.census.gov/hhes/povmeas/methodology/supplemental/research.html (site active as of October 24, 2012).

40. Nancy Folbre, "What Percentage Lives in Poverty?" Economix (blog), November 14, 2011, http://economix.blogs.nytimes.com/2011/11/14/what-percentage-lives-in-poverty/.

41. Kathleen Short, *The Research Supplemental Poverty Measure: 2011* (Washington, DC: U.S. Census Bureau, 2012), 6, http://www.census.gov/prod/2012pubs/p60-244.pdf.

42. Short, *Research Supplemental Poverty Measure*, 6.

43. Shawn Fremstad, "The New Supplemental Poverty Numbers," Poverty Byte (blog), http://www.cepr.net/index.php/data-bytes/poverty-bytes/is-child-poverty-less-of-a-problem-than-we-thought.

44. Office of Economic Opportunity, *The CEO Poverty Measure, 2005–2010* (New York: City of New York, 2012), iii, http://www.nyc.gov/html/ceo/downloads/pdf/CEO_Poverty_Measure_April_16.pdf.

45. Fremstad, *A Modern Framework*, 4–5.

46. Alexandra Forter Sirota and Edward McLenaghan, *Making Ends Meet after the Great Recession: The 2010 Living Income Standard for North Carolina* (Raleigh, NC: North Carolina Budget and Tax Center, 2011), 3, http://www.ncjustice.org/?q=making-ends-meet-after-great-recession-2010-living-income-standard-north-carolina.

47. As of October 24, 2012, a listing of states with self-sufficiency budgets prepared according to a methodology developed by Wider Opportunities for Women, a nonprofit organization in the District of Columbia, was available at http://www.wowonline.org/ourprograms/fess/index.asp.

48. Though often described as an absolute measure of poverty, the FPL is not a purely absolute measure. This is because the statistic is rooted in a study of actual consumption patterns, albeit a study from some 60 years ago. In many ways, the American poverty measure is an "abstracted" one that "has no relationship to actual, contemporary living standards." In the same manner, the term "relative" poverty suggests a measure that has little basis in objective reality. The term "actual" poverty therefore may better capture the idea of measuring "poverty and deprivation as things connected to real-word living standards, social context, and community norms." While the distinction between abstract and actual poverty is intriguing, this volume relies on the traditional distinction between absolute and relative poverty measures. For a fuller discussion of abstract and actual poverty, see Fremstad, *A Modern Framework*, 24.

49. Wolff, *Poverty and Income Distribution*, 95.

50. Fremstad, *A Modern Framework*, 27–28.

51. Ibid., 28.

52. Edwards, *Regional and Urban Economics*, 582.

53. Ron Haskins and Isabel Sawhill, *Creating an Opportunity Society* (Washington, DC: Brookings Institution Press, 2009), 37.

54. Eurostat, the statistical agency of the European Union, defines "people at risk of poverty or social exclusion" as those with "an equivalised disposable income below 60% of the national median equivalised disposable income after social transfers." In 2010, an estimated 23.4 percent of the combined population of the European Union's 27 member states was at risk of poverty or social exclusion. Estimated shares ranged from a high of 41.6 percent in Bulgaria to a low of 14.4 percent in the Czech Republic. A description of the Eurostat measure is available in Mélina Antuofermo and Emilio Di Meglio, *23% of EU Citizens Were at Risk of Poverty and Social Exclusion in 2010* (Luxembourg: Eurostat, 2012), 7, http://epp.eurostat.ec.europa.eu/cache/ITY_OFFPUB/KS-SF-12-009/EN/KS-SF-12-009-EN.PDF.

55. Central Statistics Office, *Survey on Income and Living Conditions, 2010* (Dublin: Government of Ireland, 2012), 25, http://www.cso.ie/en/media/csoie/releasespublications/documents/silc/2010/silc_2010.pdf.

56. Central Statistics Office, *Survey on Income and Living Conditions*, 25; and Federal Reserve System, "Table G.5A. Foreign Exchange Rates (Annual)," http://www.federalreserve.gov/releases/g5a/current/ (accessed October 25, 2012).

57. Central Statistics Office, *Survey on Income and Living Conditions*, 61.

58. Wolff, *Poverty and Income Distribution*, 96–97.

59. Fremstad, *A Modern Framework,* 3–4.

60. Amartya Sen, *Social Exclusion: Concept, Application, and Scrutiny* (Manila: Asian Development Bank, 2000), 3, http://housingforall.org/Social_exclusion.pdf.

61. Ibid., 4.

62. Adam Smith, *The Wealth of Nations* (1776), IV.1.

63. Sarah Burd-Sharps, Kristen Lewis, and Eduardo Borges Martins, *The Measure of America: American Human Development Report 2008–2009* (New York: Columbia University Press, 2008), 10.

64. Ibid.

65. As of October 25, 2012, all past versions of the *Human Development Report* were available at http://hdr.undp.org/en/reports/.

66. Partha Dasgupta, *Economics: A Very Short Introduction* (New York: Oxford University Press, 2007), 18.

67. Burd-Sharps, *The Measure of America 2008–2009*, 14–15.

68. United Nations Human Development Program, *Human Development Report 2011*, 127–130.

69. The first edition of the report also contained data for census regions and divisions.

70. Kristen Lewis and Sarah Burd-Sharps, *The Measure of America: American Human Development Report 2010–2011* (New York: New York University Press, 2010), 41 and 45.

71. Lewis, *The Measure of America 2009–2010,* 219–227. Note that the composition of congressional districts changed following the 2010 Census.

72. As of October 25, 2012, the online education calculator was available at http://measureofamerica.org/forecaster.

73. See, for instance, Dasgupta, *Economics,* chapter 7.

74. Bryan Caplan, "Against the Human Development Index," EconLog (blog), May 22, 2009, http://econlog.econlib.org/archives/2009/05/against_the_hum.html.

10 | Conclusion

Running the Numbers

When two strangers meet, one of the first questions they often ask of each other is, "Where do you live?" The logic underlying the question is that knowing the place that someone calls home offers insights into the person's background and experiences. Sometimes this assumption leads people into the realm of stereotyping: not every New Yorker is an overbearing jerk nor is every Minnesotan the personification of nice. Nevertheless, the basic idea has merit since humans are social creatures inclined to define themselves in relation to the places where they live and work.

Despite the importance of place, standard approaches to economic and social analysis often ignore the concept, either by assuming it away or by focusing solely on larger geographies, such as nations. While interesting to know, say, how unemployment rates in the United States compare to those in Austria or Australia, what matters for most people is joblessness in their community. Yet studies often omit this local dimension, thereby depriving regional leaders of insights that could help address local concerns.

The central conviction of this book is that thoughtful analyses of economic and social phenomena can help regional leaders better their communities. A related conviction is that the ability to locate, analyze, and interpret socioeconomic data is not limited to experts; expertise is valuable, but the core concepts and techniques are within the comprehension of any curious individual able to overcome common fears of quantitative information. Once regional leaders set aside such fears, they will discover that economic and social analysis is a powerful tool for enriching their communities.

This book's purpose is to fill the gap in the popular discussion of regional affairs by describing fundamental data concepts, sources, and methods and demonstrating their applicability to practical matters with which regional leaders frequently wrestle. The book therefore explains the strengths and weaknesses of data sources compiled by public statistical agencies like the U.S. Bureau of Economic Analysis (BEA), the U.S. Bureau of Labor Statistics (BLS), and the U.S. Census Bureau. Possessed of a familiarity with such sources, regional leaders can function as sophisticated consumers of information capable of identifying salient facts, adjudicating competing claims, and acting upon the findings of research reports and studies.

If readers recall nothing else from this volume, they hopefully will remember two things. First, no one should grant quantitative analysis more credit than it deserves, for at the end of the day it simply is a means for representing, organizing, and expressing complex phenomena in forms that limited, fallible human minds can grasp. Second, no one should expect any analysis, no matter how sophisticated, to yield a single correct answer; analysis simply is a systematic framework for documenting regional realities, understanding underlying dynamics, identifying potential responses, and making rational decisions. The critical task, therefore, is interpretation. To bring order out of seemingly chaotic flows of quantitative information, regional leaders should cultivate seven habits of the mind that can inform the design, evaluation, interpretation, and implementation of economic and social studies.

Habit 1. Know What Needs to Be Known and Why

Regional leaders typically turn to economic and social analysis in reaction to a specific trigger, such as a complaint from an influential community group or an unfavorable media story. Commissioning a study often is the first step in a response, as it is difficult to address a problem without understanding its contours.

When it comes to regional affairs, most questions of interest to community leaders involve four subjects: persons, jobs, businesses, and output. Each topic is measurable at a moment in time or over a span of time. While the four topics overlap, different public statistical agencies are responsible for tracking each one. The Census Bureau, for instance, is the major source of information about persons, just as the BEA is the leading provider of data about economic output. Even when different agencies track the same topic, they typically define and measure the concept in particular ways. For example, the Census Bureau tracks money income while the BEA tracks personal income.

To ensure the relevance of an analysis, it is necessary at the outset to identify what needs to be known and why. Imagine an inquiry into how many regional residents have low incomes. If the goal were to document how many people currently have low incomes to better target human service programs, a study built on Census Bureau data related to persons would be appropriate. If the real purpose were to ascertain if low incomes stemmed from changes in a region's economic structure, different data would be required.

This in no way implies that regional leaders must work out all their questions in advance. Such refinement can occur during project design and in partnership with the responsible analysts. Nevertheless, regional leaders should have a general sense of what they wish to know and, more importantly, why they wish to know it. Simply saying that "we need a study" or that "we need numbers" raises the odds that an analysis will prove unresponsive to the matters of concern and result in a waste of time and money, to say nothing of the chance to learn something.

Habit 2. Learn Regional Geography

Place matters when discussing regional economic and social affairs. While people intuitively grasp the concept's importance, defining a region precisely enough for analytical purposes is more complex. Scholars, developers, planners, and politicians frequently invoke "regions" and "regionalism" as justifications for policy changes and public investments without clearly delimiting their region of interest. Is a region a territory that specific physical features bound, a collection of places that share a common economy, or an area over which unified political governance applies? The answer to that question provides the foundation of any regional economic and social analysis. If a study defines a region too narrowly, it will exclude relevant data, but if a study defines a region too broadly, it will capture extraneous information.

Compounding the difficulties is the fact that regional leaders tend to think in terms of political geography—a problem especially acute among leaders elected from geographic constituencies. Yet social and economic phenomena rarely follow political lines. In a regional economy spanning multiple counties, a county government cannot influence the entire economy, but in the absence of a formal regional government, there is no entity with the authority to act on behalf of the entire region. Conflating regions with political units is a recipe for conflict and ineffectiveness.

The first chapter of this book outlines the powerful but confusing geographical framework developed by the Census Bureau. While it would be unreasonable to expect regional leaders to master the framework in all its complexity, it is necessary for local leaders to understand a few key concepts, notably the core-based statistical areas of metropolitan statistical areas, combined statistical areas, and micropolitan statistical areas. Such statistical geographies represent coherent, functional regions that are large enough to capture the extent and diversity of the relationships among individuals, households, firms, and communities, but are small enough to be distinct places. As a rule of thumb, core-based statistical areas should be the starting point for regional economic and social analysis.

Communities outside core-based statistical areas face different analytical challenges. Leaders in such places should therefore familiarize themselves with the definitions of "rural" and "urban" developed by the Census Bureau and the classification typologies of the Economic Research Service of the U.S. Department of Agriculture. These frameworks facilitate the study of nonmetropolitan places in nuanced ways reflective of population sizes and interregional ties.

Local leaders should establish logical coherence as the minimum standard when defining a region for the purposes of economic and social analysis. A region at the least should represent an economically functional area, as economic growth typically is the most pressing concern of individual citizens and a common driver of social issues.

Habit 3. Befriend Essential Data Sources

Unlike most industrialized countries, the United States lacks a centralized national statistical organization and instead relies on a fragmented system involving multiple federal and state agencies. The intricacy of the system often frustrates new users of public data—a frustration with which anyone who has spent five minutes attempting to navigate the Census Bureau's American FactFinder website can attest.

America's public statistical system, though sometimes maddening, annually produces vast amounts of economic and social data, much of which is available for free on the internet. For the purposes of regional analysis, three agencies—the Census Bureau, BEA, and BLS—generate the most useful information. The Census Bureau collects demographic information about individual persons, the BEA statistics related to economic output, and the BLS data about employment. All three agencies gather information about businesses in different ways, but the products prepared by the Census Bureau's Economic Directorate are the most comprehensive, particularly those that originate in the quinquennial Economic Census, an enumeration comparable in importance to the better known Decennial Census of Population and Housing.

At the risk of oversimplification, regional leaders should consult the Census Bureau for data about individual persons and businesses, the BEA for information about economic output and production, and the BLS for insights into jobs and employment. Moreover, the following four data products, all of which this book explains in depth, can help answer many of the most common questions that regional leaders tend to ask:

- The *Regional Accounts* system of the BEA provides a comprehensive and consistent picture of economic activity for states and metropolitan areas; the gross domestic product by state and metropolitan areas series, and the state and local area personal income and employment series are particularly useful for regional analysis (see chapter 2).
- The *American Community Survey* (ACS) is an annual Census Bureau product that has become the nation's primary source of demographic information for local communities; the ACS produces one-year, three-year, and five-year community estimates (see chapter 5).
- The *Economic Census*, a project of the Census Bureau, collects data about the location of business establishments, their employment levels, their payroll sizes, and their sales volumes; the census occurs every five years, but derivative programs like the *County Business Patterns* series provide annual estimates of related topics (see chapter 6).
- The *Local Area Unemployment Statistics* (LAUS), the *Current Employment Statistics* (CES) series, and the *Quarterly Census of Employment and Wages* (QCEW), regular products of the BLS and state labor market information agencies, are key sources of data about employment, jobs, wages, and hours (see chapter 7).

Regional leaders can improve their understanding of important data products simply by exploring websites like the Census Bureau's American FactFinder. Another option is to cultivate ties to local experts like those employed by state labor market information agencies, State Data Centers, and Business and Industry Data Centers (see appendices 3 and 4). Lastly, regional leaders could seek the expertise housed in various applied research centers located at local colleges and universities.

HABIT 4. BRUSH UP ON BASIC MATH AND STATISTICS

The writer Mark Twain supposedly remarked, "There are three kinds of lies: lies, damned lies, and statistics." Statistics and other forms of quantitative information hold the power to illuminate regional problems, but they also have the potential to cloud understanding. On one level, this is due to the imperfect nature of statistics; even the best measures are fuzzy approximations of reality subject to multiple caveats and limitations. On another level, people sometimes try to massage or manipulate statistics precisely because many individuals fear quantitative data—a fear that leads them to avoid numbers altogether or accept them too readily. When it comes to data, regional leaders should mind another saying, "Fool me once, shame on you; fool me twice, shame on me."

Chapter 4 attempts to demystify quantitative analysis by explaining common data concepts and statistical techniques. A basic awareness of the differences between absolute and relative quantities, the dynamics of change and growth, the importance of time effects, and the consequences of shifts in price levels can help regional leaders avoid basic errors of interpretation. More complex statistical analyses require regional leaders to understand how descriptive and inferential statistics differ and to ask themselves four basic questions:

- What are the analytical problems, definitions, and measures?
- Which kinds of data does a study use?
- Which statistical tools are being used?
- What is the purpose of the analysis?

Brushing up on basic math and statistics, by itself, will not turn occasional consumers of regional data into subject matter experts, but it will prevent them from feeling intimidated by quantitative information and being led astray, while equipping community leaders to ask direct questions capable of cutting to the heart of a matter.

HABIT 5. APPRECIATE THE ART OF "SATISFICING"

In reviewing regional economic and social studies, community leaders should recognize the common problems with which analysts grapple. One problem is when a break in a data series occurs, as transpired with BEA data when the North American Industrial Classification System replaced the Standard Industrial Classification typology; data from older years therefore are not comparable to information from recent ones. Additionally, statistical definitions sometimes change, as happened when the Census Bureau altered its racial categories between the censuses conducted in 1990 and 2000, thereby rendering the counts from the two years not strictly comparable. Similar difficulties arise whenever the U.S. Office of Management Budget revises the boundaries of core-based statistical areas.

Other significant problems include time lags and the trade-off between accuracy and completeness. None of the data sets described in this volume appear in real time, making all of them lagging or retrospective sources of information. With some data products, such as the LAUS and CES, the gap between the time when events are measured and findings become available is about a month; other products follow longer production schedules and may not appear until several years later. The tension between data timeliness and completeness is one with no ideal resolution. Err on the side of completeness, and information may not appear until well after the fact, though it is apt to be definitive in nature. Lean toward timeliness, however, and information appears sooner but is subject to multiple, frequently significant revisions.

Regional leaders attempting to steer policy by socioeconomic data resemble motorists attempting to drive by staring in the rearview mirror. Because there is no way to eliminate the problems, regional leaders must become comfortable in dealing with uncertainty. Making the best out of the limited, imperfect data that are available, or "satisficing," to borrow from the late Nobel laureate Herbert Simon, often is the only strategy. Learning how to satisfice is an essential skill that can help civic leaders avoid "analysis paralysis," limit personal frustrations, and extract maximum value from available information.

HABIT 6. TAP THE INNER LIBERAL ARTS STUDENT

Regional studies abound with numbers, mathematical techniques, and statistical methods, yet the fundamental task is one of finding meaning in a forest of facts and figures—a task that shares much in common with the liberal arts. Like any good literature, philosophy, or history student, a consumer of regional analyses must engage an issue of importance, ask questions, reflect on the answers, consider multiple perspectives, synthesize the information, communicate the resulting insights, and revisit conclusions in response to feedback and new information.

This is not to say that technical skills are unimportant, just that they are insufficient to resolve an issue. To the perpetual consternation of schools of public affairs, technocratic analysis seldom resolves policy arguments. This is partly because, as noted throughout this book, regions are complex and human understanding is imperfect. At the same time, many of the issues of interest to communities—issues of poverty and opportunity, growth and development, individual betterment and social progress—are political in the broad sense of the word: they affect individual community members but only joint action can address them. Moreover, such issues often involve competing conceptions of shared values and the common good, the very concerns that stand at the heart of the liberal arts disciplines.

Understood that way, the overarching purpose of regional analysis is less a matter of finding the right solution to a problem and more about documenting, understanding, interpreting, and addressing regional realities for the benefit of a community. Regional leaders who approach economic and social analysis as students of the liberal arts might be able to view situations more fully and imagine a broader range of possible responses—responses that account for the needs and values of the community as a whole.

HABIT 7. REMEMBER THE PUBLIC PURPOSE

Debates about economic and social policy frequently grow heated due to clashes of differing values and interests. The involvement of money and prospects of economic gain or loss only exacerbate the tensions. Despite long-standing rhetoric alleging that public policy and government are unimportant and ineffective, they matter greatly. The public sector has the capability to influence the distribution of resources and to create winners and losers. For instance, the provision of a tax incentive to a relocating firm may come at the expense of a local firm, just as the elimination of an environmental regulation may boost an individual firm's profitability yet degrade a community's ecosystem.

Only the public sector is responsible for considering the needs of an entire community. Weighing issues of social inclusion and exclusion, private benefits and socialized costs, and short-term growth and long-term development are responsibilities properly entrusted to the public sector. Regional leaders, especially elected and appointed ones, must not forget their mandate to represent all segments of society and to "promote the general welfare," as it states in the preamble to the U.S. Constitution. Whenever regional leaders allow questions related to the common good to pass in silence, they fail in their duties. Market concerns and private interests matter, but so do nonmarket concerns. The challenge is in striking balances that represent the diversity of opinions, values, and experiences that are present in a community.

A FINAL WORD

Regional economic and social analysis is a way of understanding and improving the lives of the individuals who call a community home. There is no point in undertaking such analyses for their own sake, and the standard against which to judge any such study is its usefulness in expanding the opportunities available to local residents and improving the quality of their lives. For when all is said is done, that is the only reason why civic leaders should ever bother to run the numbers.

Appendix 1

U.S. Census 2010 Questionnaire

U.S. DEPARTMENT OF COMMERCE
Economics and Statistics Administration
U.S. CENSUS BUREAU

United States Census 2010

This is the official form for all the people at this address. It is quick and easy, and your answers are protected by law.

Use a blue or black pen.

Start here

The Census must count every person living in the United States on April 1, 2010.

Before you answer Question 1, count the people living in this house, apartment, or mobile home using our guidelines.

- Count all people, including babies, who live and sleep here most of the time.

The Census Bureau also conducts counts in institutions and other places, so:

- Do not count anyone living away either at college or in the Armed Forces.
- Do not count anyone in a nursing home, jail, prison, detention facility, etc., on April 1, 2010.
- Leave these people off your form, even if they will return to live here after they leave college, the nursing home, the military, jail, etc. Otherwise, they may be counted twice.

The Census must also include people without a permanent place to stay, so:

- If someone who has no permanent place to stay is staying here on April 1, 2010, count that person. Otherwise, he or she may be missed in the census.

1. How many people were living or staying in this house, apartment, or mobile home on April 1, 2010?

Number of people = _____

2. Were there any additional people staying here April 1, 2010 that you did not include in Question 1?
Mark ☒ all that apply.

- ☐ Children, such as newborn babies or foster children
- ☐ Relatives, such as adult children, cousins, or in-laws
- ☐ Nonrelatives, such as roommates or live-in baby sitters
- ☐ People staying here temporarily
- ☐ No additional people

3. Is this house, apartment, or mobile home —
Mark ☒ ONE box.

- ☐ Owned by you or someone in this household with a mortgage or loan? Include home equity loans.
- ☐ Owned by you or someone in this household free and clear (without a mortgage or loan)?
- ☐ Rented?
- ☐ Occupied without payment of rent?

4. What is your telephone number? We may call if we don't understand an answer.

Area Code + Number
_____ - _____ - _____

OMB No. 0607-0919-C; Approval Expires 12/31/2011.

Form **D-61** (1-15-2009)

USCENSUSBUREAU

5. Please provide information for each person living here. Start with a person living here who owns or rents this house, apartment, or mobile home. If the owner or renter lives somewhere else, start with any adult living here. This will be Person 1.
What is Person 1's name? Print name below.

Last Name _____

First Name _____   MI ___

6. What is Person 1's sex? Mark ☒ ONE box.

☐ Male   ☐ Female

7. What is Person 1's age and what is Person 1's date of birth?
Please report babies as age 0 when the child is less than 1 year old.
Print numbers in boxes.

Age on April 1, 2010	Month	Day	Year of birth

→ NOTE: Please answer BOTH Question 8 about Hispanic origin and Question 9 about race. For this census, Hispanic origins are not races.

8. Is Person 1 of Hispanic, Latino, or Spanish origin?

- ☐ No, not of Hispanic, Latino, or Spanish origin
- ☐ Yes, Mexican, Mexican Am., Chicano
- ☐ Yes, Puerto Rican
- ☐ Yes, Cuban
- ☐ Yes, another Hispanic, Latino, or Spanish origin — Print origin, for example, Argentinean, Colombian, Dominican, Nicaraguan, Salvadoran, Spaniard, and so on. ⟋

_____

9. What is Person 1's race? Mark ☒ one or more boxes.

- ☐ White
- ☐ Black, African Am., or Negro
- ☐ American Indian or Alaska Native — Print name of enrolled or principal tribe. ⟋

_____

- ☐ Asian Indian
- ☐ Chinese
- ☐ Filipino
- ☐ Japanese
- ☐ Korean
- ☐ Vietnamese
- ☐ Native Hawaiian
- ☐ Guamanian or Chamorro
- ☐ Samoan
- ☐ Other Asian — Print race, for example, Hmong, Laotian, Thai, Pakistani, Cambodian, and so on. ⟋
- ☐ Other Pacific Islander — Print race, for example, Fijian, Tongan, and so on. ⟋

_____

- ☐ Some other race — Print race. ⟋

_____

10. Does Person 1 sometimes live or stay somewhere else?

☐ No   ☐ Yes — Mark ☒ all that apply.

- ☐ In college housing
- ☐ In the military
- ☐ At a seasonal or second residence
- ☐ For child custody
- ☐ In jail or prison
- ☐ In a nursing home
- ☐ For another reason

→ If more people were counted in Question 1, continue with Person 2.

1. Print name of **Person 2**

Last Name

First Name   MI

2. **How is this person related to Person 1?** *Mark X ONE box.*

☐ Husband or wife   ☐ Parent-in-law
☐ Biological son or daughter   ☐ Son-in-law or daughter-in-law
☐ Adopted son or daughter   ☐ Other relative
☐ Stepson or stepdaughter   ☐ Roomer or boarder
☐ Brother or sister   ☐ Housemate or roommate
☐ Father or mother   ☐ Unmarried partner
☐ Grandchild   ☐ Other nonrelative

3. **What is this person's sex?** *Mark X ONE box.*

☐ Male ☐ Female

4. **What is this person's age and what is this person's date of birth?**
Please report babies as age 0 when the child is less than 1 year old.
Print numbers in boxes.

Age on April 1, 2010   Month   Day   Year of birth

→ NOTE: Please answer BOTH Question 5 about Hispanic origin and
Question 6 about race. For this census, Hispanic origins are not races.

5. **Is this person of Hispanic, Latino, or Spanish origin?**

☐ **No,** not of Hispanic, Latino, or Spanish origin
☐ Yes, Mexican, Mexican Am., Chicano
☐ Yes, Puerto Rican
☐ Yes, Cuban
☐ Yes, another Hispanic, Latino, or Spanish origin — *Print origin, for example,
Argentinean, Colombian, Dominican, Nicaraguan, Salvadoran, Spaniard, and so on.*

6. **What is this person's race?** *Mark X one or more boxes.*

☐ White
☐ Black, African Am., or Negro
☐ American Indian or Alaska Native — *Print name of enrolled or principal tribe.*

☐ Asian Indian   ☐ Japanese   ☐ Native Hawaiian
☐ Chinese   ☐ Korean   ☐ Guamanian or Chamorro
☐ Filipino   ☐ Vietnamese   ☐ Samoan
☐ Other Asian — *Print race, for   ☐ Other Pacific Islander — *Print
example, Hmong, Laotian, Thai,   race, for example, Fijian, Tongan,
Pakistani, Cambodian, and so on.*   and so on.*

☐ Some other race — *Print race.*

7. **Does this person sometimes live or stay somewhere else?**

☐ No ☐ Yes — *Mark X all that apply.*

☐ In college housing   ☐ For child custody
☐ In the military   ☐ In jail or prison
☐ At a seasonal   ☐ In a nursing home
  or second residence   ☐ For another reason

→ If more people were counted in Question 1 on the front page,
continue with Person 3.

1. Print name of **Person 3**

Last Name

First Name   MI

2. **How is this person related to Person 1?** *Mark X ONE box.*

☐ Husband or wife   ☐ Parent-in-law
☐ Biological son or daughter   ☐ Son-in-law or daughter-in-law
☐ Adopted son or daughter   ☐ Other relative
☐ Stepson or stepdaughter   ☐ Roomer or boarder
☐ Brother or sister   ☐ Housemate or roommate
☐ Father or mother   ☐ Unmarried partner
☐ Grandchild   ☐ Other nonrelative

3. **What is this person's sex?** *Mark X ONE box.*

☐ Male ☐ Female

4. **What is this person's age and what is this person's date of birth?**
Please report babies as age 0 when the child is less than 1 year old.
Print numbers in boxes.

Age on April 1, 2010   Month   Day   Year of birth

→ NOTE: Please answer BOTH Question 5 about Hispanic origin and
Question 6 about race. For this census, Hispanic origins are not races.

5. **Is this person of Hispanic, Latino, or Spanish origin?**

☐ **No,** not of Hispanic, Latino, or Spanish origin
☐ Yes, Mexican, Mexican Am., Chicano
☐ Yes, Puerto Rican
☐ Yes, Cuban
☐ Yes, another Hispanic, Latino, or Spanish origin — *Print origin, for example,
Argentinean, Colombian, Dominican, Nicaraguan, Salvadoran, Spaniard, and so on.*

6. **What is this person's race?** *Mark X one or more boxes.*

☐ White
☐ Black, African Am., or Negro
☐ American Indian or Alaska Native — *Print name of enrolled or principal tribe.*

☐ Asian Indian   ☐ Japanese   ☐ Native Hawaiian
☐ Chinese   ☐ Korean   ☐ Guamanian or Chamorro
☐ Filipino   ☐ Vietnamese   ☐ Samoan
☐ Other Asian — *Print race, for   ☐ Other Pacific Islander — *Print
example, Hmong, Laotian, Thai,   race, for example, Fijian, Tongan,
Pakistani, Cambodian, and so on.*   and so on.*

☐ Some other race — *Print race.*

7. **Does this person sometimes live or stay somewhere else?**

☐ No ☐ Yes — *Mark X all that apply.*

☐ In college housing   ☐ For child custody
☐ In the military   ☐ In jail or prison
☐ At a seasonal   ☐ In a nursing home
  or second residence   ☐ For another reason

→ If more people were counted in Question 1 on the front page,
continue with Person 4.

1. Print name of **Person 4**

Last Name

First Name   MI

2. How is this person related to Person 1? *Mark* X *ONE box.*

☐ Husband or wife   ☐ Parent-in-law
☐ Biological son or daughter   ☐ Son-in-law or daughter-in-law
☐ Adopted son or daughter   ☐ Other relative
☐ Stepson or stepdaughter   ☐ Roomer or boarder
☐ Brother or sister   ☐ Housemate or roommate
☐ Father or mother   ☐ Unmarried partner
☐ Grandchild   ☐ Other nonrelative

3. What is this person's sex? *Mark* X *ONE box.*

☐ Male   ☐ Female

4. What is this person's age and what is this person's date of birth?
Please report babies as age 0 when the child is less than 1 year old.
Print numbers in boxes.

Age on April 1, 2010   Month   Day   Year of birth

→ NOTE: Please answer BOTH Question 5 about Hispanic origin and
Question 6 about race. For this census, Hispanic origins are not races.

5. Is this person of Hispanic, Latino, or Spanish origin?

☐ **No,** not of Hispanic, Latino, or Spanish origin
☐ Yes, Mexican, Mexican Am., Chicano
☐ Yes, Puerto Rican
☐ Yes, Cuban
☐ Yes, another Hispanic, Latino, or Spanish origin — *Print origin, for example,*
Argentinean, Colombian, Dominican, Nicaraguan, Salvadoran, Spaniard, and so on. ↘

6. What is this person's race? *Mark* X *one or more boxes.*

☐ White
☐ Black, African Am., or Negro
☐ American Indian or Alaska Native — *Print name of enrolled or principal tribe.* ↘

☐ Asian Indian   ☐ Japanese   ☐ Native Hawaiian
☐ Chinese   ☐ Korean   ☐ Guamanian or Chamorro
☐ Filipino   ☐ Vietnamese   ☐ Samoan
☐ Other Asian — *Print race, for*   ☐ Other Pacific Islander — *Print*
example, Hmong, Laotian, Thai,   *race, for example, Fijian, Tongan,*
Pakistani, Cambodian, and so on. ↘   *and so on.* ↘

☐ Some other race — *Print race.* ↘

7. Does this person sometimes live or stay somewhere else?

☐ No   ☐ Yes — *Mark* X *all that apply.*

☐ In college housing   ☐ For child custody
☐ In the military   ☐ In jail or prison
☐ At a seasonal   ☐ In a nursing home
   or second residence   ☐ For another reason

→ If more people were counted in Question 1 on the front page,
continue with Person 5.

---

1. Print name of **Person 5**

Last Name

First Name   MI

2. How is this person related to Person 1? *Mark* X *ONE box.*

☐ Husband or wife   ☐ Parent-in-law
☐ Biological son or daughter   ☐ Son-in-law or daughter-in-law
☐ Adopted son or daughter   ☐ Other relative
☐ Stepson or stepdaughter   ☐ Roomer or boarder
☐ Brother or sister   ☐ Housemate or roommate
☐ Father or mother   ☐ Unmarried partner
☐ Grandchild   ☐ Other nonrelative

3. What is this person's sex? *Mark* X *ONE box.*

☐ Male   ☐ Female

4. What is this person's age and what is this person's date of birth?
Please report babies as age 0 when the child is less than 1 year old.
Print numbers in boxes.

Age on April 1, 2010   Month   Day   Year of birth

→ NOTE: Please answer BOTH Question 5 about Hispanic origin and
Question 6 about race. For this census, Hispanic origins are not races.

5. Is this person of Hispanic, Latino, or Spanish origin?

☐ **No,** not of Hispanic, Latino, or Spanish origin
☐ Yes, Mexican, Mexican Am., Chicano
☐ Yes, Puerto Rican
☐ Yes, Cuban
☐ Yes, another Hispanic, Latino, or Spanish origin — *Print origin, for example,*
Argentinean, Colombian, Dominican, Nicaraguan, Salvadoran, Spaniard, and so on. ↘

6. What is this person's race? *Mark* X *one or more boxes.*

☐ White
☐ Black, African Am., or Negro
☐ American Indian or Alaska Native — *Print name of enrolled or principal tribe.* ↘

☐ Asian Indian   ☐ Japanese   ☐ Native Hawaiian
☐ Chinese   ☐ Korean   ☐ Guamanian or Chamorro
☐ Filipino   ☐ Vietnamese   ☐ Samoan
☐ Other Asian — *Print race, for*   ☐ Other Pacific Islander — *Print*
example, Hmong, Laotian, Thai,   *race, for example, Fijian, Tongan,*
Pakistani, Cambodian, and so on. ↘   *and so on.* ↘

☐ Some other race — *Print race.* ↘

7. Does this person sometimes live or stay somewhere else?

☐ No   ☐ Yes — *Mark* X *all that apply.*

☐ In college housing   ☐ For child custody
☐ In the military   ☐ In jail or prison
☐ At a seasonal   ☐ In a nursing home
   or second residence   ☐ For another reason

→ If more people were counted in Question 1 on the front page,
continue with Person 6.

1. Print name of **Person 6**

   Last Name

   First Name   MI

2. **How is this person related to Person 1?** *Mark X ONE box.*

   ☐ Husband or wife
   ☐ Biological son or daughter
   ☐ Adopted son or daughter
   ☐ Stepson or stepdaughter
   ☐ Brother or sister
   ☐ Father or mother
   ☐ Grandchild

   ☐ Parent-in-law
   ☐ Son-in-law or daughter-in-law
   ☐ Other relative
   ☐ Roomer or boarder
   ☐ Housemate or roommate
   ☐ Unmarried partner
   ☐ Other nonrelative

3. **What is this person's sex?** *Mark X ONE box.*

   ☐ Male   ☐ Female

4. **What is this person's age and what is this person's date of birth?**
   Please report babies as age 0 when the child is less than 1 year old.
   Print numbers in boxes.

   Age on April 1, 2010   Month   Day   Year of birth

   → NOTE: Please answer BOTH Question 5 about Hispanic origin and Question 6 about race. For this census, Hispanic origins are not races.

5. **Is this person of Hispanic, Latino, or Spanish origin?**

   ☐ **No,** not of Hispanic, Latino, or Spanish origin
   ☐ Yes, Mexican, Mexican Am., Chicano
   ☐ Yes, Puerto Rican
   ☐ Yes, Cuban
   ☐ Yes, another Hispanic, Latino, or Spanish origin — *Print origin, for example, Argentinean, Colombian, Dominican, Nicaraguan, Salvadoran, Spaniard, and so on.* ↘

6. **What is this person's race?** *Mark X one or more boxes.*

   ☐ White
   ☐ Black, African Am., or Negro
   ☐ American Indian or Alaska Native — *Print name of enrolled or principal tribe.* ↘

   ☐ Asian Indian   ☐ Japanese   ☐ Native Hawaiian
   ☐ Chinese   ☐ Korean   ☐ Guamanian or Chamorro
   ☐ Filipino   ☐ Vietnamese   ☐ Samoan
   ☐ Other Asian — *Print race, for example, Hmong, Laotian, Thai, Pakistani, Cambodian, and so on.* ↘   ☐ Other Pacific Islander — *Print race, for example, Fijian, Tongan, and so on.* ↘

   ☐ Some other race — *Print race.* ↘

7. **Does this person sometimes live or stay somewhere else?**

   ☐ No   ☐ Yes — *Mark X all that apply.*

   ☐ In college housing   ☐ For child custody
   ☐ In the military   ☐ In jail or prison
   ☐ At a seasonal or second residence   ☐ In a nursing home
   ☐ For another reason

   → If more than six people were counted in Question 1 on the front page, turn the page and continue.

→ *If more people live here, turn the page and continue.*

Form D-61 (1-15-2009)

Use this section to complete information for the rest of the people you counted in Question 1 on the front page. *We may call for additional information about them.*

Person 7

Last Name

First Name

MI

Sex
☐ Male
☐ Female

Age on April 1, 2010

Date of Birth
Month Day Year

Related to Person 1?
☐ Yes
☐ No

Person 8

Last Name

First Name

MI

Sex
☐ Male
☐ Female

Age on April 1, 2010

Date of Birth
Month Day Year

Related to Person 1?
☐ Yes
☐ No

Person 9

Last Name

First Name

MI

Sex
☐ Male
☐ Female

Age on April 1, 2010

Date of Birth
Month Day Year

Related to Person 1?
☐ Yes
☐ No

Person 10

Last Name

First Name

MI

Sex
☐ Male
☐ Female

Age on April 1, 2010

Date of Birth
Month Day Year

Related to Person 1?
☐ Yes
☐ No

Person 11

Last Name

First Name

MI

Sex
☐ Male
☐ Female

Age on April 1, 2010

Date of Birth
Month Day Year

Related to Person 1?
☐ Yes
☐ No

Person 12

Last Name

First Name

MI

Sex
☐ Male
☐ Female

Age on April 1, 2010

Date of Birth
Month Day Year

Related to Person 1?
☐ Yes
☐ No

Thank you for completing your official 2010 Census form.

FOR OFFICIAL USE ONLY

JIC1 JIC2

If your enclosed postage-paid envelope is missing, *please mail your completed form to:*

U.S. Census Bureau
National Processing Center
1201 East 10th Street
Jeffersonville, IN 47132

If you need help completing this form, *call 1-866-872-6868 between 8:00 a.m. and 9:00 p.m., 7 days a week. The telephone call is free.*

TDD — *Telephone display device for the hearing impaired. Call 1-866-783-2010 between 8:00 a.m. and 9:00 p.m., 7 days a week. The telephone call is free.*

¿NECESITA AYUDA? *Si usted necesita ayuda para completar este cuestionario, llame al 1-866-928-2010 entre las 8:00 a.m. y 9:00 p.m., 7 días a la semana. La llamada telefónica es gratis.*

The U.S. Census Bureau estimates that, for the average household, this form will take about 10 minutes to complete, including the time for reviewing the instructions and answers. Send comments regarding this burden estimate or any other aspect of this burden to: Paperwork Reduction Project 0607-0919-C, U.S. Census Bureau, AMSD-3K138, 4600 Silver Hill Road, Washington, DC 20233. You may e-mail comments to <Paperwork@census.gov>; use "Paperwork Project 0607-0919-C" as the subject.

Respondents are not required to respond to any information collection unless it displays a valid approval number from the Office of Management and Budget.

Source: U.S. Census Bureau, "Census 2010 Questionnaire," http://www.census.gov/2010census/pdf/2010_Questionnaire_Info.pdf.

Appendix 2

The American Community Survey 2011 Questionnaire

U.S. DEPARTMENT OF COMMERCE
Economics and Statistics Administration
U.S. CENSUS BUREAU

THE American Community Survey

This booklet shows the content of the American Community Survey questionnaire.

Please complete this form and return it as soon as possible after receiving it in the mail.

This form asks for information about the people who are living or staying at the address on the mailing label and about the house, apartment, or mobile home located at the address on the mailing label.

If you need help or have questions about completing this form, please call **1-800-354-7271.** The telephone call is free.

Telephone Device for the Deaf (TDD): Call 1-800-582-8330. The telephone call is free.

¿NECESITA AYUDA? Si usted habla español y necesita ayuda para completar su cuestionario, llame sin cargo alguno al **1-877-833-5625.** Usted también puede pedir un cuestionario en español o completar su entrevista por teléfono con un entrevistador que habla español.

For more information about the American Community Survey, visit our web site at: http://www.census.gov/acs/www/

USCENSUSBUREAU

Start Here

➡ **Please print today's date.**
Month   Day   Year

➡ **Please print the name and telephone number of the person who is filling out this form.** We may contact you if there is a question.
Last Name

First Name   MI

Area Code + Number

➡ **How many people are living or staying at this address?**
• **INCLUDE** everyone who is living or staying here for more than 2 months.
• **INCLUDE** yourself if you are living here for more than 2 months.
• **INCLUDE** anyone else staying here who does not have another place to stay, even if they are here for 2 months or less.
• **DO NOT INCLUDE** anyone who is living somewhere else for more than 2 months, such as a college student living away or someone in the Armed Forces on deployment.
Number of people

➡ Fill out pages 2, 3, and 4 for everyone, including yourself, who is living or staying at this address for more than 2 months. Then complete the rest of the form.

FORM **ACS-1(INFO)(2011)KFI**
(06-14-2010)   OMB No. 0607-0810

Person 1

(Person 1 is the person living or staying here in whose name this house or apartment is owned, being bought, or rented. If there is no such person, start with the name of any adult living or staying here.)

1 What is Person 1's name?
Last Name *(Please print)*   First Name   MI

2 How is this person related to Person 1?
☒ Person 1

3 What is Person 1's sex? *Mark (X) ONE box.*
☐ Male   ☐ Female

4 What is Person 1's age and what is Person 1's date of birth?
Please report babies as age 0 when the child is less than 1 year old.
Print numbers in boxes.
Age (in years)   Month   Day   Year of birth

→ **NOTE:** Please answer BOTH Question 5 about Hispanic origin and Question 6 about race. For this survey, Hispanic origins are not races.

5 Is Person 1 of Hispanic, Latino, or Spanish origin?
☐ **No,** not of Hispanic, Latino, or Spanish origin
☐ Yes, Mexican, Mexican Am., Chicano
☐ Yes, Puerto Rican
☐ Yes, Cuban
☐ Yes, another Hispanic, Latino, or Spanish origin – *Print origin, for example, Argentinean, Colombian, Dominican, Nicaraguan, Salvadoran, Spaniard, and so on.* ↘

6 What is Person 1's race? *Mark (X) one or more boxes.*
☐ White
☐ Black, African Am., or Negro
☐ American Indian or Alaska Native – *Print name of enrolled or principal tribe.* ↘

☐ Asian Indian   ☐ Japanese   ☐ Native Hawaiian
☐ Chinese   ☐ Korean   ☐ Guamanian or Chamorro
☐ Filipino   ☐ Vietnamese   ☐ Samoan
☐ Other Asian – *Print race, for example, Hmong, Laotian, Thai, Pakistani, Cambodian, and so on.* ↘   ☐ Other Pacific Islander – *Print race, for example, Fijian, Tongan, and so on.* ↘

☐ Some other race – *Print race.* ↘

Person 2

1 What is Person 2's name?
Last Name *(Please print)*   First Name   MI

2 How is this person related to Person 1? *Mark (X) ONE box.*
☐ Husband or wife
☐ Biological son or daughter
☐ Adopted son or daughter
☐ Stepson or stepdaughter
☐ Brother or sister
☐ Father or mother
☐ Grandchild
☐ Parent-in-law
☐ Son-in-law or daughter-in-law
☐ Other relative
☐ Roomer or boarder
☐ Housemate or roommate
☐ Unmarried partner
☐ Foster child
☐ Other nonrelative

3 What is Person 2's sex? *Mark (X) ONE box.*
☐ Male   ☐ Female

4 What is Person 2's age and what is Person 2's date of birth?
Please report babies as age 0 when the child is less than 1 year old.
Print numbers in boxes.
Age (in years)   Month   Day   Year of birth

→ **NOTE:** Please answer BOTH Question 5 about Hispanic origin and Question 6 about race. For this survey, Hispanic origins are not races.

5 Is Person 2 of Hispanic, Latino, or Spanish origin?
☐ **No,** not of Hispanic, Latino, or Spanish origin
☐ Yes, Mexican, Mexican Am., Chicano
☐ Yes, Puerto Rican
☐ Yes, Cuban
☐ Yes, another Hispanic, Latino, or Spanish origin – *Print origin, for example, Argentinean, Colombian, Dominican, Nicaraguan, Salvadoran, Spaniard, and so on.* ↘

6 What is Person 2's race? *Mark (X) one or more boxes.*
☐ White
☐ Black, African Am., or Negro
☐ American Indian or Alaska Native – *Print name of enrolled or principal tribe.* ↘

☐ Asian Indian   ☐ Japanese   ☐ Native Hawaiian
☐ Chinese   ☐ Korean   ☐ Guamanian or Chamorro
☐ Filipino   ☐ Vietnamese   ☐ Samoan
☐ Other Asian – *Print race, for example, Hmong, Laotian, Thai, Pakistani, Cambodian, and so on.* ↘   ☐ Other Pacific Islander – *Print race, for example, Fijian, Tongan, and so on.* ↘

☐ Some other race – *Print race.* ↘

Person 3

1 **What is Person 3's name?**

Last Name *(Please print)* | First Name | MI

2 **How is this person related to Person 1?** *Mark (X) ONE box.*

☐ Husband or wife
☐ Biological son or daughter
☐ Adopted son or daughter
☐ Stepson or stepdaughter
☐ Brother or sister
☐ Father or mother
☐ Grandchild
☐ Parent-in-law

☐ Son-in-law or daughter-in-law
☐ Other relative
☐ Roomer or boarder
☐ Housemate or roommate
☐ Unmarried partner
☐ Foster child
☐ Other nonrelative

3 **What is Person 3's sex?** *Mark (X) ONE box.*

☐ Male ☐ Female

4 **What is Person 3's age and what is Person 3's date of birth?**
Please report babies as age 0 when the child is less than 1 year old.
Print numbers in boxes.

Age (in years) | Month | Day | Year of birth

→ NOTE: **Please answer BOTH Question 5 about Hispanic origin and Question 6 about race. For this survey, Hispanic origins are not races.**

5 **Is Person 3 of Hispanic, Latino, or Spanish origin?**

☐ **No,** not of Hispanic, Latino, or Spanish origin
☐ Yes, Mexican, Mexican Am., Chicano
☐ Yes, Puerto Rican
☐ Yes, Cuban
☐ Yes, another Hispanic, Latino, or Spanish origin – *Print origin, for example, Argentinean, Colombian, Dominican, Nicaraguan, Salvadoran, Spaniard, and so on.* ⬐

6 **What is Person 3's race?** *Mark (X) one or more boxes.*

☐ White
☐ Black, African Am., or Negro
☐ American Indian or Alaska Native — *Print name of enrolled or principal tribe.* ⬐

☐ Asian Indian ☐ Japanese ☐ Native Hawaiian
☐ Chinese ☐ Korean ☐ Guamanian or Chamorro
☐ Filipino ☐ Vietnamese ☐ Samoan
☐ Other Asian – *Print race, for example, Hmong, Laotian, Thai, Pakistani, Cambodian, and so on.* ⬐
☐ Other Pacific Islander – *Print race, for example, Fijian, Tongan, and so on.* ⬐

☐ Some other race – *Print race.* ⬐

Person 4

1 **What is Person 4's name?**

Last Name *(Please print)* | First Name | MI

2 **How is this person related to Person 1?** *Mark (X) ONE box.*

☐ Husband or wife
☐ Biological son or daughter
☐ Adopted son or daughter
☐ Stepson or stepdaughter
☐ Brother or sister
☐ Father or mother
☐ Grandchild
☐ Parent-in-law

☐ Son-in-law or daughter-in-law
☐ Other relative
☐ Roomer or boarder
☐ Housemate or roommate
☐ Unmarried partner
☐ Foster child
☐ Other nonrelative

3 **What is Person 4's sex?** *Mark (X) ONE box.*

☐ Male ☐ Female

4 **What is Person 4's age and what is Person 4's date of birth?**
Please report babies as age 0 when the child is less than 1 year old.
Print numbers in boxes.

Age (in years) | Month | Day | Year of birth

→ NOTE: **Please answer BOTH Question 5 about Hispanic origin and Question 6 about race. For this survey, Hispanic origins are not races.**

5 **Is Person 4 of Hispanic, Latino, or Spanish origin?**

☐ **No,** not of Hispanic, Latino, or Spanish origin
☐ Yes, Mexican, Mexican Am., Chicano
☐ Yes, Puerto Rican
☐ Yes, Cuban
☐ Yes, another Hispanic, Latino, or Spanish origin – *Print origin, for example, Argentinean, Colombian, Dominican, Nicaraguan, Salvadoran, Spaniard, and so on.* ⬐

6 **What is Person 4's race?** *Mark (X) one or more boxes.*

☐ White
☐ Black, African Am., or Negro
☐ American Indian or Alaska Native — *Print name of enrolled or principal tribe.* ⬐

☐ Asian Indian ☐ Japanese ☐ Native Hawaiian
☐ Chinese ☐ Korean ☐ Guamanian or Chamorro
☐ Filipino ☐ Vietnamese ☐ Samoan
☐ Other Asian – *Print race, for example, Hmong, Laotian, Thai, Pakistani, Cambodian, and so on.* ⬐
☐ Other Pacific Islander – *Print race, for example, Fijian, Tongan, and so on.* ⬐

☐ Some other race – *Print race.* ⬐

Person 5

1 What is Person 5's name?

Last Name (Please print)   First Name   MI

2 How is this person related to Person 1? Mark (X) ONE box.

☐ Husband or wife
☐ Biological son or daughter
☐ Adopted son or daughter
☐ Stepson or stepdaughter
☐ Brother or sister
☐ Father or mother
☐ Grandchild
☐ Parent-in-law

☐ Son-in-law or daughter-in-law
☐ Other relative
☐ Roomer or boarder
☐ Housemate or roommate
☐ Unmarried partner
☐ Foster child
☐ Other nonrelative

3 What is Person 5's sex? Mark (X) ONE box.

☐ Male   ☐ Female

4 What is Person 5's age and what is Person 5's date of birth?
Please report babies as age 0 when the child is less than 1 year old.
Print numbers in boxes.

Age (in years)   Month   Day   Year of birth

→ **NOTE: Please answer BOTH Question 5 about Hispanic origin and Question 6 about race. For this survey, Hispanic origins are not races.**

5 Is Person 5 of Hispanic, Latino, or Spanish origin?

☐ **No,** not of Hispanic, Latino, or Spanish origin
☐ Yes, Mexican, Mexican Am., Chicano
☐ Yes, Puerto Rican
☐ Yes, Cuban
☐ Yes, another Hispanic, Latino, or Spanish origin – Print origin, for example, Argentinean, Colombian, Dominican, Nicaraguan, Salvadoran, Spaniard, and so on.

6 What is Person 5's race? Mark (X) one or more boxes.

☐ White
☐ Black, African Am., or Negro
☐ American Indian or Alaska Native — Print name of enrolled or principal tribe.

☐ Asian Indian   ☐ Japanese   ☐ Native Hawaiian
☐ Chinese   ☐ Korean   ☐ Guamanian or Chamorro
☐ Filipino   ☐ Vietnamese   ☐ Samoan
☐ Other Asian – Print race, for example, Hmong, Laotian, Thai, Pakistani, Cambodian, and so on.   ☐ Other Pacific Islander – Print race, for example, Fijian, Tongan, and so on.

☐ Some other race – Print race.

→ If there are more than five people living or staying here, print their names in the spaces for Person 6 through Person 12. We may call you for more information about them.

Person 6

Last Name (Please print)   First Name   MI

Sex ☐ Male ☐ Female   **Age (in years)**

Person 7

Last Name (Please print)   First Name   MI

Sex ☐ Male ☐ Female   **Age (in years)**

Person 8

Last Name (Please print)   First Name   MI

Sex ☐ Male ☐ Female   **Age (in years)**

Person 9

Last Name (Please print)   First Name   MI

Sex ☐ Male ☐ Female   **Age (in years)**

Person 10

Last Name (Please print)   First Name   MI

Sex ☐ Male ☐ Female   **Age (in years)**

Person 11

Last Name (Please print)   First Name   MI

Sex ☐ Male ☐ Female   **Age (in years)**

Person 12

Last Name (Please print)   First Name   MI

Sex ☐ Male ☐ Female   **Age (in years)**

Housing

➡ **Please answer the following questions about the house, apartment, or mobile home at the address on the mailing label.**

1 Which best describes this building?
Include all apartments, flats, etc., even if vacant.

- ☐ A mobile home
- ☐ A one-family house detached from any other house
- ☐ A one-family house attached to one or more houses
- ☐ A building with 2 apartments
- ☐ A building with 3 or 4 apartments
- ☐ A building with 5 to 9 apartments
- ☐ A building with 10 to 19 apartments
- ☐ A building with 20 to 49 apartments
- ☐ A building with 50 or more apartments
- ☐ Boat, RV, van, etc.

2 About when was this building first built?
- ☐ 2000 or later – *Specify year*

  [   ]

- ☐ 1990 to 1999
- ☐ 1980 to 1989
- ☐ 1970 to 1979
- ☐ 1960 to 1969
- ☐ 1950 to 1959
- ☐ 1940 to 1949
- ☐ 1939 or earlier

3 When did PERSON 1 (listed on page 2) move into this house, apartment, or mobile home?

Month   Year

[   ]   [   ]

A *Answer questions 4 – 6 if this is a HOUSE OR A MOBILE HOME; otherwise, SKIP to question 7a.*

4 How many acres is this house or mobile home on?
- ☐ Less than 1 acre → *SKIP to question 6*
- ☐ 1 to 9.9 acres
- ☐ 10 or more acres

5 IN THE PAST 12 MONTHS, what were the actual sales of all agricultural products from this property?
- ☐ None
- ☐ $1 to $999
- ☐ $1,000 to $2,499
- ☐ $2,500 to $4,999
- ☐ $5,000 to $9,999
- ☐ $10,000 or more

6 Is there a business (such as a store or barber shop) or a medical office on this property?
- ☑ Yes
- ☑ No

7 a. How many separate rooms are in this house, apartment, or mobile home?
Rooms must be separated by built-in archways or walls that extend out at least 6 inches and go from floor to ceiling.

- • INCLUDE bedrooms, kitchens, etc.
- • EXCLUDE bathrooms, porches, balconies, foyers, halls, or unfinished basements.

Number of rooms

[   ]

b. How many of these rooms are bedrooms?
Count as bedrooms those rooms you would list if this house, apartment, or mobile home were for sale or rent. If this is an efficiency/studio apartment, print "0".

Number of bedrooms

[   ]

---

8 Does this house, apartment, or mobile home have –

	Yes	No
a. hot and cold running water?	☐	☐
b. a flush toilet?	☐	☐
c. a bathtub or shower?	☐	☐
d. a sink with a faucet?	☐	☐
e. a stove or range?	☐	☐
f. a refrigerator?	☐	☐
g. telephone service from which you can both make and receive calls? *Include cell phones.*	☐	☐

9 How many automobiles, vans, and trucks of one-ton capacity or less are kept at home for use by members of this household?
- ☐ None
- ☐ 1
- ☐ 2
- ☐ 3
- ☐ 4
- ☐ 5
- ☐ 6 or more

10 Which FUEL is used MOST for heating this house, apartment, or mobile home?
- ☐ Gas: from underground pipes serving the neighborhood
- ☐ Gas: bottled, tank, or LP
- ☐ Electricity
- ☐ Fuel oil, kerosene, etc.
- ☐ Coal or coke
- ☐ Wood
- ☐ Solar energy
- ☐ Other fuel
- ☐ No fuel used

Housing (continued)

11 a. LAST MONTH, what was the cost of electricity for this house, apartment, or mobile home?

Last month's cost – *Dollars*

[ ]

OR

☐ Included in rent or condominium fee
☐ No charge or electricity not used

b. LAST MONTH, what was the cost of gas for this house, apartment, or mobile home?

Last month's cost – *Dollars*

[ ]

OR

☐ Included in rent or condominium fee
☐ Included in electricity payment entered above
☐ No charge or gas not used

c. IN THE PAST 12 MONTHS, what was the cost of water and sewer for this house, apartment, or mobile home? *If you have lived here less than 12 months, estimate the cost.*

Past 12 months' cost – *Dollars*

[ ]

OR

☐ Included in rent or condominium fee
☐ No charge

d. IN THE PAST 12 MONTHS, what was the cost of oil, coal, kerosene, wood, etc., for this house, apartment, or mobile home? *If you have lived here less than 12 months, estimate the cost.*

Past 12 months' cost – *Dollars*

[ ]

OR

☐ Included in rent or condominium fee
☐ No charge or these fuels not used

12 IN THE PAST 12 MONTHS, did anyone in this household receive Food Stamps or a Food Stamp benefit card? *Include government benefits from the Supplemental Nutrition Assistance Program (SNAP). Do NOT include WIC or the National School Lunch Program.*

☐ Yes
☐ No

13 Is this house, apartment, or mobile home part of a condominium?

☐ Yes → **What is the monthly condominium fee?** *For renters, answer only if you pay the condominium fee in addition to your rent; otherwise, mark the "None" box.*

Monthly amount – *Dollars*

[ ]

OR

☐ None

☐ No

14 Is this house, apartment, or mobile home – *Mark (X) ONE box.*

☐ Owned by you or someone in this household with a mortgage or loan? *Include home equity loans.*
☐ Owned by you or someone in this household free and clear (without a mortgage or loan)?
☐ Rented?
☐ Occupied without payment of rent? → SKIP to **C**

B *Answer questions 15a and b if this house, apartment, or mobile home is RENTED. Otherwise, SKIP to question 16.*

15 a. What is the monthly rent for this house, apartment, or mobile home?

Monthly amount – *Dollars*

[ ]

b. Does the monthly rent include any meals?

☐ Yes
☐ No

C *Answer questions 16 – 20 if you or someone else in this household OWNS or IS BUYING this house, apartment, or mobile home. Otherwise, SKIP to* **E** *on the next page.*

16 About how much do you think this house and lot, apartment, or mobile home (and lot, if owned) would sell for if it were for sale?

Amount – *Dollars*

[ ]

17 What are the annual real estate taxes on THIS property?

Annual amount – *Dollars*

[ ]

OR

☐ None

18 What is the annual payment for fire, hazard, and flood insurance on THIS property?

Annual amount – *Dollars*

[ ]

OR

☐ None

Housing (continued)

19 **a. Do you or any member of this household have a mortgage, deed of trust, contract to purchase, or similar debt on THIS property?**

- ☐ Yes, mortgage, deed of trust, or similar debt
- ☐ Yes, contract to purchase
- ☐ No → *SKIP to question 20a*

b. How much is the regular monthly mortgage payment on THIS property?
Include payment only on FIRST mortgage or contract to purchase.

Monthly amount – *Dollars*

$ _____ .00

OR

- ☐ No regular payment required → *SKIP to question 20a*

c. Does the regular monthly mortgage payment include payments for real estate taxes on THIS property?

- ☐ Yes, taxes included in mortgage payment
- ☐ No, taxes paid separately or taxes not required

d. Does the regular monthly mortgage payment include payments for fire, hazard, or flood insurance on THIS property?

- ☐ Yes, insurance included in mortgage payment
- ☐ No, insurance paid separately or no insurance

20 **a. Do you or any member of this household have a second mortgage or a home equity loan on THIS property?**

- ☐ Yes, home equity loan
- ☐ Yes, second mortgage
- ☐ Yes, second mortgage and home equity loan
- ☐ No → *SKIP to* **D**

b. How much is the regular monthly payment on all second or junior mortgages and all home equity loans on THIS property?

Monthly amount – *Dollars*

$ _____ .00

OR

- ☐ No regular payment required

D *Answer question 21 if this is a MOBILE HOME. Otherwise, SKIP to* **E** *.*

21 **What are the total annual costs for personal property taxes, site rent, registration fees, and license fees on THIS mobile home and its site?**
Exclude real estate taxes.

Annual costs – *Dollars*

$ _____ .00

E *Answer questions about PERSON 1 on the next page if you listed at least one person on page 2. Otherwise, SKIP to page 28 for the mailing instructions.*

Person 1

➡ Please copy the name of Person 1 from page 2, then continue answering questions below.

Last Name

First Name   MI

7 Where was this person born?

☐ In the United States – Print name of state.

☐ Outside the United States – Print name of foreign country, or Puerto Rico, Guam, etc.

8 Is this person a citizen of the United States?

☐ Yes, born in the United States → SKIP to 10a

☐ Yes, born in Puerto Rico, Guam, the U.S. Virgin Islands, or Northern Marianas

☐ Yes, born abroad of U.S. citizen parent or parents

☐ Yes, U.S. citizen by naturalization – Print year of naturalization

☐ No, not a U.S. citizen

9 When did this person come to live in the United States? Print numbers in boxes.

Year

10 a. At any time IN THE LAST 3 MONTHS, has this person attended school or college? Include only nursery or preschool, kindergarten, elementary school, home school, and schooling which leads to a high school diploma or a college degree.

☐ No, has not attended in the last 3 months → SKIP to question 11

☐ Yes, public school, public college

☐ Yes, private school, private college, home school

b. What grade or level was this person attending? Mark (X) ONE box.

☐ Nursery school, preschool

☐ Kindergarten

☐ Grade 1 through 12 – Specify grade 1 – 12

☐ College undergraduate years (freshman to senior)

☐ Graduate or professional school beyond a bachelor's degree (for example: MA or PhD program, or medical or law school)

11 What is the highest degree or level of school this person has COMPLETED? Mark (X) ONE box. If currently enrolled, mark the previous grade or highest degree received.

NO SCHOOLING COMPLETED

☐ No schooling completed

NURSERY OR PRESCHOOL THROUGH GRADE 12

☐ Nursery school

☐ Kindergarten

☐ Grade 1 through 11 – Specify grade 1 – 11

☐ 12th grade - **NO DIPLOMA**

HIGH SCHOOL GRADUATE

☐ Regular high school diploma

☐ GED or alternative credential

COLLEGE OR SOME COLLEGE

☐ Some college credit, but less than 1 year of college credit

☐ 1 or more years of college credit, no degree

☐ Associate's degree (for example: AA, AS)

☐ Bachelor's degree (for example: BA, BS)

AFTER BACHELOR'S DEGREE

☐ Master's degree (for example: MA, MS, MEng, MEd, MSW, MBA)

☐ Professional degree beyond a bachelor's degree (for example: MD, DDS, DVM, LLB, JD)

☐ Doctorate degree (for example: PhD, EdD)

F Answer question 12 if this person has a bachelor's degree or higher. Otherwise, SKIP to question 13.

12 This question focuses on this person's BACHELOR'S DEGREE. Please print below the specific major(s) of any BACHELOR'S DEGREES this person has received. (For example: chemical engineering, elementary teacher education, organizational psychology)

13 What is this person's ancestry or ethnic origin?

(For example: Italian, Jamaican, African Am., Cambodian, Cape Verdean, Norwegian, Dominican, French Canadian, Haitian, Korean, Lebanese, Polish, Nigerian, Mexican, Taiwanese, Ukrainian, and so on.)

14 a. Does this person speak a language other than English at home?

☐ Yes

☐ No → SKIP to question 15a

b. What is this language?

For example: Korean, Italian, Spanish, Vietnamese

c. How well does this person speak English?

☐ Very well

☐ Well

☐ Not well

☐ Not at all

15 a. Did this person live in this house or apartment 1 year ago?

☐ Person is under 1 year old → SKIP to question 16

☐ Yes, this house → SKIP to question 16

☐ No, outside the United States and Puerto Rico – Print name of foreign country, or U.S. Virgin Islands, Guam, etc., below; then SKIP to question 16

☐ No, different house in the United States or Puerto Rico

b. Where did this person live 1 year ago?

Address (Number and street name)

Name of city, town, or post office

Name of U.S. county or municipio in Puerto Rico

Name of U.S. state or Puerto Rico   ZIP Code

Person 1 (continued)

16 Is this person CURRENTLY covered by any of the following types of health insurance or health coverage plans? *Mark "Yes" or "No" for EACH type of coverage in items a – h.*

	Yes	No
a. Insurance through a current or former employer or union (of this person or another family member)	☐	☐
b. Insurance purchased directly from an insurance company (by this person or another family member)	☐	☐
c. Medicare, for people 65 and older, or people with certain disabilities	☐	☐
d. Medicaid, Medical Assistance, or any kind of government-assistance plan for those with low incomes or a disability	☐	☐
e. TRICARE or other military health care	☐	☐
f. VA (including those who have ever used or enrolled for VA health care)	☐	☐
g. Indian Health Service	☐	☐
h. Any other type of health insurance or health coverage plan – *Specify*	☐	☐

17 a. Is this person deaf or does he/she have serious difficulty hearing?

☐ Yes
☐ No

b. Is this person blind or does he/she have serious difficulty seeing even when wearing glasses?

☐ Yes
☐ No

G *Answer question 18a – c if this person is 5 years old or over. Otherwise, SKIP to the questions for Person 2 on page 12.*

18 a. Because of a physical, mental, or emotional condition, does this person have serious difficulty concentrating, remembering, or making decisions?

☐ Yes
☐ No

b. Does this person have serious difficulty walking or climbing stairs?

☐ Yes
☐ No

c. Does this person have difficulty dressing or bathing?

☐ Yes
☐ No

H *Answer question 19 if this person is 15 years old or over. Otherwise, SKIP to the questions for Person 2 on page 12.*

19 Because of a physical, mental, or emotional condition, does this person have difficulty doing errands alone such as visiting a doctor's office or shopping?

☐ Yes
☐ No

20 What is this person's marital status?

☐ Now married
☐ Widowed
☐ Divorced
☐ Separated
☐ Never married → *SKIP to* **I**

21 In the PAST 12 MONTHS did this person get –

	Yes	No
a. Married?	☐	☐
b. Widowed?	☐	☐
c. Divorced?	☐	☐

22 How many times has this person been married?

☐ Once
☐ Two times
☐ Three or more times

23 In what year did this person last get married?

Year

I *Answer question 24 if this person is female and 15 – 50 years old. Otherwise, SKIP to question 25a.*

24 Has this person given birth to any children in the past 12 months?

☐ Yes
☐ No

25 a. Does this person have any of his/her own grandchildren under the age of 18 living in this house or apartment?

☐ Yes
☐ No → *SKIP to question 26*

b. Is this grandparent currently responsible for most of the basic needs of any grandchildren under the age of 18 who lives in this house or apartment?

☐ Yes
☐ No → *SKIP to question 26*

c. How long has this grandparent been responsible for these grandchildren? *If the grandparent is financially responsible for more than one grandchild, answer the question for the grandchild for whom the grandparent has been responsible for the longest period of time.*

☐ Less than 6 months
☐ 6 to 11 months
☐ 1 or 2 years
☐ 3 or 4 years
☐ 5 or more years

26 Has this person ever served on active duty in the U.S. Armed Forces, military Reserves, or National Guard? *Active duty does not include training for the Reserves or National Guard, but DOES include activation, for example, for the Persian Gulf War.*

☐ Yes, now on active duty
☐ Yes, on active duty during the last 12 months, but not now
☐ Yes, on active duty in the past, but not during the last 12 months
☐ No, training for Reserves or National Guard only → *SKIP to question 28a*
☐ No, never served in the military → *SKIP to question 29a*

27 When did this person serve on active duty in the U.S. Armed Forces? *Mark (X) a box for EACH period in which this person served, even if just for part of the period.*

☐ September 2001 or later
☐ August 1990 to August 2001 (including Persian Gulf War)
☐ September 1980 to July 1990
☐ May 1975 to August 1980
☐ Vietnam era (August 1964 to April 1975)
☐ March 1961 to July 1964
☐ February 1955 to February 1961
☐ Korean War (July 1950 to January 1955)
☐ January 1947 to June 1950
☐ World War II (December 1941 to December 1946)
☐ November 1941 or earlier

28 a. Does this person have a VA service-connected disability rating?

☐ Yes (such as 0%, 10%, 20%, ... , 100%)
☐ No → *SKIP to question 29a*

b. What is this person's service-connected disability rating?

☐ 0 percent
☐ 10 or 20 percent
☐ 30 or 40 percent
☐ 50 or 60 percent
☐ 70 percent or higher

Person 1 (continued)

29 **a. LAST WEEK, did this person work for pay at a job (or business)?**

☐ Yes → SKIP to question 30
☐ No – Did not work (or retired)

b. LAST WEEK, did this person do ANY work for pay, even for as little as one hour?

☐ Yes
☐ No → SKIP to question 35a

30 **At what location did this person work LAST WEEK?** If this person worked at more than one location, print where he or she worked most last week.

a. Address (Number and street name)

_____

If the exact address is not known, give a description of the location such as the building name or the nearest street or intersection.

b. Name of city, town, or post office

_____

c. Is the work location inside the limits of that city or town?

☐ Yes
☐ No, outside the city/town limits

d. Name of county

_____

e. Name of U.S. state or foreign country

_____

f. ZIP Code

[   ]

31 **How did this person usually get to work LAST WEEK?** If this person usually used more than one method of transportation during the trip, mark (X) the box of the one used for most of the distance.

☐ Car, truck, or van
☐ Bus or trolley bus
☐ Streetcar or trolley car
☐ Subway or elevated
☐ Railroad
☐ Ferryboat
☐ Taxicab
☐ Motorcycle
☐ Bicycle
☐ Walked
☐ Worked at home → SKIP to question 39a
☐ Other method

J Answer question 32 if you marked "Car, truck, or van" in question 31. Otherwise, SKIP to question 33.

32 **How many people, including this person, usually rode to work in the car, truck, or van LAST WEEK?**
Person(s)

[   ]

33 **What time did this person usually leave home to go to work LAST WEEK?**

Hour   Minute
[   ] : [   ]   ☐ a.m.
☐ p.m.

34 **How many minutes did it usually take this person to get from home to work LAST WEEK?**
Minutes

[   ]

K Answer questions 35 – 38 if this person did NOT work last week. Otherwise, SKIP to question 39a.

35 **a. LAST WEEK, was this person on layoff from a job?**

☒ Yes → SKIP to question 35c
☐ No

b. LAST WEEK, was this person TEMPORARILY absent from a job or business?

☐ Yes, on vacation, temporary illness, maternity leave, other family/personal reasons, bad weather, etc. → SKIP to question 38
☐ No → SKIP to question 36

c. Has this person been informed that he or she will be recalled to work within the next 6 months OR been given a date to return to work?

☐ Yes → SKIP to question 37
☐ No

36 **During the LAST 4 WEEKS, has this person been ACTIVELY looking for work?**

☐ Yes
☐ No → SKIP to question 38

37 **LAST WEEK, could this person have started a job if offered one, or returned to work if recalled?**

☐ Yes, could have gone to work
☐ No, because of own temporary illness
☐ No, because of all other reasons (in school, etc.)

38 **When did this person last work, even for a few days?**

☐ Within the past 12 months
☐ 1 to 5 years ago → SKIP to **L**
☐ Over 5 years ago or never worked → SKIP to question 47

39 **a. During the PAST 12 MONTHS (52 weeks), did this person work 50 or more weeks? Count paid time off as work.**

☐ Yes → SKIP to question 40
☐ No

b. How many weeks DID this person work, even for a few hours, including paid vacation, paid sick leave, and military service?

☐ 50 to 52 weeks
☐ 48 to 49 weeks
☐ 40 to 47 weeks
☐ 27 to 39 weeks
☐ 14 to 26 weeks
☐ 13 weeks or less

40 **During the PAST 12 MONTHS, in the WEEKS WORKED, how many hours did this person usually work each WEEK?**

Usual hours worked each WEEK

[   ]

Person 1 (continued)

L *Answer questions 41 – 46 if this person worked in the past 5 years. Otherwise, SKIP to question 47.*

41 – 46 CURRENT OR MOST RECENT JOB ACTIVITY. *Describe clearly this person's chief job activity or business last week. If this person had more than one job, describe the one at which this person worked the most hours. If this person had no job or business last week, give information for his/her last job or business.*

41 Was this person –
Mark (X) ONE box.

☐ an employee of a PRIVATE FOR-PROFIT company or business, or of an individual, for wages, salary, or commissions?

☐ an employee of a PRIVATE NOT-FOR-PROFIT, tax-exempt, or charitable organization?

☐ a local GOVERNMENT employee (city, county, etc.)?

☐ a state GOVERNMENT employee?

☐ a Federal GOVERNMENT employee?

☐ SELF-EMPLOYED in own NOT INCORPORATED business, professional practice, or farm?

☐ SELF-EMPLOYED in own INCORPORATED business, professional practice, or farm?

☐ working WITHOUT PAY in family business or farm?

42 For whom did this person work?

If now on active duty in the Armed Forces, mark (X) this box → ☐ *and print the branch of the Armed Forces.*

Name of company, business, or other employer

[   ]

43 What kind of business or industry was this?
Describe the activity at the location where employed. (For example: hospital, newspaper publishing, mail order house, auto engine manufacturing, bank)

[   ]

44 Is this mainly – *Mark (X) ONE box.*

☐ manufacturing?

☐ wholesale trade?

☐ retail trade?

☐ other (agriculture, construction, service, government, etc.)?

45 What kind of work was this person doing?
(For example: registered nurse, personnel manager, supervisor of order department, secretary, accountant)

[   ]

46 What were this person's most important activities or duties? *(For example: patient care, directing hiring policies, supervising order clerks, typing and filing, reconciling financial records)*

[   ]

47 INCOME IN THE PAST 12 MONTHS

Mark (X) the "Yes" box for each type of income this person received, and give your best estimate of the TOTAL AMOUNT during the PAST 12 MONTHS. (NOTE: The "past 12 months" is the period from today's date one year ago up through today.)

Mark (X) the "No" box to show types of income NOT received.

If net income was a loss, mark the "Loss" box to the right of the dollar amount.

For income received jointly, report the appropriate share for each person – or, if that's not possible, report the whole amount for only one person and mark the "No" box for the other person.

a. Wages, salary, commissions, bonuses, or tips from all jobs. *Report amount before deductions for taxes, bonds, dues, or other items.*

☐ Yes → $ [   ] .00
☐ No
TOTAL AMOUNT for past 12 months

b. Self-employment income from own nonfarm businesses or farm businesses, including proprietorships and partnerships. *Report NET income after business expenses.*

☐ Yes → $ [   ] .00   ☐ Loss
☐ No
TOTAL AMOUNT for past 12 months

c. Interest, dividends, net rental income, royalty income, or income from estates and trusts. *Report even small amounts credited to an account.*

☐ Yes → $ [   ] .00   ☐ Loss
☐ No
TOTAL AMOUNT for past 12 months

d. Social Security or Railroad Retirement.

☐ Yes → $ [   ] .00
☐ No
TOTAL AMOUNT for past 12 months

e. Supplemental Security Income (SSI).

☐ Yes → $ [   ] .00
☐ No
TOTAL AMOUNT for past 12 months

f. Any public assistance or welfare payments from the state or local welfare office.

☐ Yes → $ [   ] .00
☐ No
TOTAL AMOUNT for past 12 months

g. Retirement, survivor, or disability pensions. *Do NOT include Social Security.*

☐ Yes → $ [   ] .00
☐ No
TOTAL AMOUNT for past 12 months

h. Any other sources of income received regularly such as Veterans' (VA) payments, unemployment compensation, child support or alimony. *Do NOT include lump sum payments such as money from an inheritance or the sale of a home.*

☐ Yes → $ [   ] .00
☐ No
TOTAL AMOUNT for past 12 months

48 What was this person's total income during the PAST 12 MONTHS? *Add entries in questions 47a to 47h; subtract any losses. If net income was a loss, enter the amount and mark (X) the "Loss" box next to the dollar amount.*

☐ None OR $ [   ] .00   ☐ Loss
TOTAL AMOUNT for past 12 months

→ Continue with the questions for Person 2 on the next page. If no one is listed as person 2 on page 2, SKIP to page 28 for mailing instructions.

Person 1 (continued)

16 Is this person CURRENTLY covered by any of the following types of health insurance or health coverage plans? *Mark "Yes" or "No" for EACH type of coverage in items a – h.*

	Yes	No
a. Insurance through a current or former employer or union (of this person or another family member)	☐	☐
b. Insurance purchased directly from an insurance company (by this person or another family member)	☐	☐
c. Medicare, for people 65 and older, or people with certain disabilities	☐	☐
d. Medicaid, Medical Assistance, or any kind of government-assistance plan for those with low incomes or a disability	☐	☐
e. TRICARE or other military health care	☐	☐
f. VA (including those who have ever used or enrolled for VA health care)	☐	☐
g. Indian Health Service	☐	☐
h. Any other type of health insurance or health coverage plan – *Specify*	☐	☐

17 **a. Is this person deaf or does he/she have serious difficulty hearing?**

☐ Yes
☐ No

b. Is this person blind or does he/she have serious difficulty seeing even when wearing glasses?

☐ Yes
☐ No

G *Answer question 18a – c if this person is 5 years old or over. Otherwise, SKIP to the questions for Person 2 on page 12.*

18 **a. Because of a physical, mental, or emotional condition, does this person have serious difficulty concentrating, remembering, or making decisions?**

☐ Yes
☐ No

b. Does this person have serious difficulty walking or climbing stairs?

☐ Yes
☐ No

c. Does this person have difficulty dressing or bathing?

☐ Yes
☐ No

H *Answer question 19 if this person is 15 years old or over. Otherwise, SKIP to the questions for Person 2 on page 12.*

19 **Because of a physical, mental, or emotional condition, does this person have difficulty doing errands alone such as visiting a doctor's office or shopping?**

☐ Yes
☐ No

20 **What is this person's marital status?**

☐ Now married
☐ Widowed
☐ Divorced
☐ Separated
☐ Never married → *SKIP to* ▮

21 **In the PAST 12 MONTHS did this person get –**

	Yes	No
a. Married?	☐	☐
b. Widowed?	☐	☐
c. Divorced?	☐	☐

22 **How many times has this person been married?**

☐ Once
☐ Two times
☐ Three or more times

23 **In what year did this person last get married?**

Year

Answer question 24 if this person is female and 15 – 50 years old. Otherwise, SKIP to question 25a.

24 **Has this person given birth to any children in the past 12 months?**

☐ Yes
☐ No

25 **a. Does this person have any of his/her own grandchildren under the age of 18 living in this house or apartment?**

☐ Yes
☐ No → *SKIP to question 26*

b. Is this grandparent currently responsible for most of the basic needs of any grandchildren under the age of 18 who lives in this house or apartment?

☐ Yes
☐ No → *SKIP to question 26*

c. How long has this grandparent been responsible for these grandchildren? *If the grandparent is financially responsible for more than one grandchild, answer the question for the grandchild for whom the grandparent has been responsible for the longest period of time.*

☐ Less than 6 months
☐ 6 to 11 months
☐ 1 or 2 years
☐ 3 or 4 years
☐ 5 or more years

26 **Has this person ever served on active duty in the U.S. Armed Forces, military Reserves, or National Guard?** *Active duty does not include training for the Reserves or National Guard, but DOES include activation, for example, for the Persian Gulf War.*

☐ Yes, now on active duty
☐ Yes, on active duty during the last 12 months, but not now
☐ Yes, on active duty in the past, but not during the last 12 months
☐ No, training for Reserves or National Guard only → *SKIP to question 28a*
☐ No, never served in the military → *SKIP to question 29a*

27 **When did this person serve on active duty in the U.S. Armed Forces?** *Mark (X) a box for EACH period in which this person served, even if just for part of the period.*

☐ September 2001 or later
☐ August 1990 to August 2001 (including Persian Gulf War)
☐ September 1980 to July 1990
☐ May 1975 to August 1980
☐ Vietnam era (August 1964 to April 1975)
☐ March 1961 to July 1964
☐ February 1955 to February 1961
☐ Korean War (July 1950 to January 1955)
☐ January 1947 to June 1950
☐ World War II (December 1941 to December 1946)
☐ November 1941 or earlier

28 **a. Does this person have a VA service-connected disability rating?**

☐ Yes (such as 0%, 10%, 20%, ... , 100%)
☐ No → *SKIP to question 29a*

b. What is this person's service-connected disability rating?

☐ 0 percent
☐ 10 or 20 percent
☐ 30 or 40 percent
☐ 50 or 60 percent
☐ 70 percent or higher

Person 2

The balance of the questionnaire has questions for Person 2, Person 3, Person 4, and Person 5. The questions are the same as the questions for Person 1.

Mailing Instructions

➔ **Please make sure you have...**

- listed all names and answered the questions on pages 2, 3, and 4

- answered all Housing questions

- answered all Person questions for each person.

➔ **Then...**

- put the completed questionnaire into the postage-paid return envelope. If the envelope has been misplaced, please mail the questionnaire to:

  U.S. Census Bureau
  P.O. Box 5240
  Jeffersonville, IN 47199-5240

- make sure the barcode above your address shows in the window of the return envelope.

Thank you for participating in the American Community Survey.

INFORMATIONAL COPY

The Census Bureau estimates that, for the average household, this form will take 38 minutes to complete, including the time for reviewing the instructions and answers. Send comments regarding this burden estimate or any other aspect of this collection of information, including suggestions for reducing this burden, to: Paperwork Project 0607-0810, U.S. Census Bureau, 4600 Silver Hill Road, AMSD – 3K138, Washington, D.C. 20233. You may e-mail comments to Paperwork@census.gov; use "Paperwork Project 0607-0810" as the subject. Please DO NOT RETURN your questionnaire to this address. Use the enclosed preaddressed envelope to return your completed questionnaire.

Respondents are not required to respond to any information collection unless it displays a valid approval number from the Office of Management and Budget. This 8-digit number appears in the bottom right on the front cover of this form.

Form ACS-1(INFO)(2011)KFI (06-14-2010)

For Census Bureau Use

POP	EDIT	PHONE		JIC1	JIC2
EDIT CLERK		TELEPHONE CLERK		JIC3	JIC4

Source: U.S. Census Bureau, "American Community Survey 2011 Questionnaire," http://www.census.gov/acs/www/Downloads/questionnaires/2011/Quest11.pdf.

Appendix 3

State Labor Market Information Agencies

Alabama
Alabama Department of Industrial
  Relations
Labor Market Information Division
Room 4427
649 Monroe Street
Montgomery, AL 36131-2280
Phone: (334) 242-8859
http://www2.dir.state.al.us

Alaska
Alaska Department of Labor and
  Workforce Development
Research and Analysis Section
1111 West 8th Street
Juneau, AK 99801
Phone: (907) 465-6040
http://almis.labor.state.ak.us

Arizona
Arizona Department of Administration
Budget and Resource Planning
Suite 440
100 N. 15th Avenue
Phoenix, AZ 85007
Phone: (602) 542-1510
http://www.workforce.az.gov/

Arkansas
Arkansas Department of Workforce
  Services
Administrative Services
1501 S. Main Street

Little Rock, AR 72201
Phone: (501) 371-1027
http://www.discoverarkansas.net/

California
Employment Development Department
Labor Market Information Division
Building 1100
7000 Franklin Boulevard
Sacramento, CA 95823
Phone: (916) 262-2602
http://www.labormarketinfo.edd.ca.gov

Colorado
Colorado Department of Labor &
  Employment
Office of Government, Policy, and
  Public Relations
Suite 600
633 17th Street
Denver, CO 80202-2117
Phone: (303) 318-8850
http://lmigateway.coworkforce.com/
  lmigateway/

Connecticut
Connecticut Department of Labor
Office of Research
200 Folly Brook Boulevard
Wethersfield, CT 06109-1114
Phone: (860) 263-6255
http://www.ctdol.state.ct.us/lmi/index.htm

Appendix 3

Delaware
Delaware Department of Labor
Office of Occupational and Labor Market
    Information
4425 North Market Street
Wilmington, DE 19802
Phone: (302) 761-8060
http://www.delawareworks.com/oolmi/welcome.
    shtml

District of Columbia
DC Department of Employment Services
Office of Labor Market Research and
    Information
Suite 5600
4058 Minnesota Ave. NE
Washington, DC 20019
Phone: (202) 698-4215
http://does.dc.gov/does/

Florida
Department of Economic Opportunity
Labor Market Statistics Center
MSC G-020
107 East Madison Street
Tallahassee, FL 32399-4111
Phone: (850) 245-7257
http://www.labormarketinfo.com

Georgia
Georgia Department of Labor
Workforce Statistics & Economic Research
Suite 300
223 Courtland Street NE
Atlanta, GA 30303-1751
Phone: (404) 232-3875
http://www.dol.state.ga.us/em/get_labor_market_
    information.htm

Hawaii
Department of Labor and Industrial Relations
Research and Statistics Office
#304
830 Punchbowl Street
Honolulu, HI 96813

Phone: (808) 586-9013
http://www.hiwi.org

Idaho
Idaho Department of Labor
Research and Analysis Bureau
3rd Floor
317 West Main Street
Boise, ID 83735-0670
Phone: (208) 332-3570 x3217
http://lmi.idaho.gov

Illinois
Illinois Department of Economic Security
Division of Economic Information and Analysis
9th Floor
33 South State St
Chicago, IL 60603-2802
Phone: (312) 793-2316
http://lmi.ides.state.il.us

Indiana
Indiana Department of Workforce
    Development
Research and Analysis
10 North Senate Avenue
Indianapolis, IN 46204-2277
Phone: (317) 234-4295
http://www.hoosierdata.in.gov

Iowa
Iowa Department of Workforce Development
Labor Market Information Division
1000 East Grand Avenue
Des Moines, IA 50319-0209
Phone: (515) 281-5193
http://www.iowaworkforce.org/lmi/

Kansas
Kansas Department of Labor
LMI Information Services
401 SW Topeka Boulevard
Topeka, KS 66603-3182
Phone: (785) 296-5070
http://klic.dol.ks.gov

Kentucky
Office of Employment and Training
Department for Workforce Investment
Research and Statistics Branch
275 East Main Street
Frankfort, KY 40621
Phone: (502) 564-7976
http://www.workforcekentucky.ky.gov

Louisiana
Louisiana Workforce Commission
Information Technology
1001 North 23rd Street
Baton Rouge, LA 70804-4094
Phone: (225) 342-3222
http://www.laworks.net

Maine
Maine Department of Labor
Center for Workforce Research and
    Information
118 State House Station
Augusta, ME 04333-0118
Phone: (207) 621-5186
http://www.state.me.us/labor/cwri/

Maryland
Department of Labor, Licensing and Regulation
Office of Workforce Information and
    Performance
Room 316
1100 North Eutaw Street
Baltimore, MD 21201-2206
Phone: (410) 767-2953
http://www.dllr.state.md.us/lmi/index.htm

Massachusetts
Massachusetts Division of Unemployment
    Assistance
Research
2nd floor
19 Staniford Street
Boston, MA 02114
Phone: (617) 626-6556
http://www.detma.org/LMIdataprog.htm

Michigan
Department of Technology, Management and
    Budget
Bureau of LMI and Strategic Initiatives
Suite 9-100
3032 W. Grand Boulevard
Detroit, MI 48202-3105
Phone: (313) 456-3105
http://www.milmi.org

Minnesota
Minnesota Department of Employment and
    Economic Development
BLS Cooperative Programs
Suite E-200
332 Minnesota Street
St Paul, MN 55101-1351
Phone: (651) 259-7396
http://www.deed.state.mn.us

Mississippi
Mississippi Department of Employment Security
Labor Market Information
1235 Echelon Pkwy
Jackson, MS 39213
Phone: (601) 321-6260
http://mdes.ms.gov

Missouri
Missouri Department of Economic Development
Missouri Economic Research and Information
    Center
Room 580
301 West High Street
Jefferson City, MO 65101
Phone: (573) 751-3637
http://www.missourieconomy.org

Montana
Department of Labor and Industry
Research and Analysis
1st Floor
840 Helena Avenue
Helena, MT 59601
Phone: (406) 444-3293
http://ourfactsyourfuture.org

Nebraska
Nebraska Department of Labor
550 South 16th Street
Lincoln, NE 68508
Phone: (402) 471-9964
http://www.dol.nebraska.gov

Nevada
Department of Employment, Training and
    Rehabilitation
Research and Analysis Bureau
500 East Third Street
Carson City, NV 89713
Phone: (775) 684-0387
http://www.detr.state.nv.us/lmi/index.htm

New Hampshire
New Hampshire Department of Employment
    Security
Economic and Labor Market Information Bureau
32 South Main Street
Concord, NH 03301-4587
Phone: (603) 228-4126
http://www.nhes.state.nh.us/elmi/index.html

New Jersey
New Jersey Department of Labor and Workforce
    Development
Labor Market and Demographic Research
P.O. Box 388
1 John Fitch Plaza, 5th Floor
Trenton, NJ 08625-0388
Phone: (609) 984-6925
http://lwd.dol.state.nj.us/labor/lpa/LMI_index.
    html

New Mexico
New Mexico Department of Workforce
    Solutions
Economic Research and Analysis
Suites 2000 and 2200
121 Tijeras NE
Albuquerque, NM 87102
Phone: (505) 383-2722
http://www.dws.state.nm.us/dws-lmi.html

New York
New York State Department of Labor
Labor Statistics, Division of Research and
    Statistics
Building 12 (Rm. 400)
State Office Campus
Albany, NY 12240-0020
Phone: (518) 485-7990
http://www.labor.state.ny.us

North Carolina
North Carolina Department of Commerce
Labor and Economic Analysis Division
P.O. Box 25903
Raleigh, NC 27611
Phone: (919) 733-3454
http://www.ncesc.com

North Dakota
Job Service North Dakota
Research and Statistics
1000 East Divide Avenue
Bismarck, ND 58501
Phone: (701) 328-2888
http://www.ndworkforceintelligence.com

Ohio
Ohio Department of Job and Family
    Services
Labor Market Information Division
4020 East Fifth Avenue
Columbus, OH 43219
Phone: (614) 466-9820
http://ohioLMI.com

Oklahoma
Oklahoma Employment Security
    Commission
Economic Research and Analysis
Room 310
2401 North Lincoln Boulevard
Oklahoma City, OK 73105
Phone: (405) 557-7221
http://www.ok.gov/oesc_web/Services/Find_
    Labor_Market_Statistics/index.html

Oregon
Oregon Employment Department
Workforce and Economic Research
Room 207
875 Union Street NE
Salem, OR 97311-9986
Phone: (503) 947-1212
http://www.qualityinfo.org/olmisj/OlmisZine

Pennsylvania
Center for Workforce Information and
 Analysis
Pennsylvania Department of Labor and
 Industry
Room 220
651 Boas Street
Harrisburg, PA 17121
Phone: (717) 787-3266 / (717) 787-6507
http://www.paworkstats.state.pa.us

Rhode Island
Rhode Island Department of Labor and
 Training
Labor Market Information
1511 Pontiac Ave
Cranston, RI 02920-4407
Phone: (401) 462-8767
http://www.dlt.ri.gov/lmi/

South Carolina
South Carolina Department of Employment and
 Workforce
Labor Market Information Division
Room 510
1550 Gadsden Street
Columbia, SC 29201
Mailing Address:
P.O. Box 995
Columbia, SC 29202
Phone: (803) 737-2660
http://www.sces.org/lmi/index.asp

South Dakota
South Dakota Department of Labor and Regulation

Labor Market Information Center
420 South Roosevelt Street
Aberdeen, SD 57401-5131
Phone: (605) 626-2314
http://dol.sd.gov/lmic/

Tennessee
Department of Labor and Workforce
 Development
Research and Statistics/LMI
Suite 3A
220 French Landing Drive
Nashville, TN 37243-1002
Phone: (615) 253-6922
http://www.state.tn.us/labor-wfd/lmi.htm

Texas
Texas Workforce Commission
Labor Market Information
Suite 0252
101 E. 15th Street
Austin, TX 78778-0001
Phone: (512) 936-3105
http://www.tracer2.com

Utah
Utah Department of Workforce
 Services
Research and Analysis
140 East 300 South
P.O. Box 45249
Salt Lake City, UT 84111
Phone: (801) 526-9719
http://jobs.utah.gov/wi/

Vermont
Vermont Department of Labor
Economic and Labor Market Information
 Section
P.O. Box 488
5 Green Mountain Drive
Montpelier, VT 05601-0488
Phone: (802) 828-4153
http://www.vtlmi.info/

Virginia
Virginia Employment Commission
Economic Information Services Division
P.O. Box 1358
Room 327
703 East Main Street
Richmond, VA 23219-1358
Phone: (804) 786-7496 / (804) 786-5670
http://www.vawc.virginia.gov/altentry.
   asp?action=lmiguest

Washington
Washington Employment Security Department
Labor Market and Economic Analysis
2nd Floor
604 Woodland Square Loop SE
Lacey, WA 98503
Phone: (360) 407-4531
http://www.workforceexplorer.com

West Virginia
WORKFORCE West Virginia
Research, Information and Analysis Division

Room 209
112 California Avenue
Charleston, WV 25305-0112
Phone: (304) 558-2658
http;//workforcewv.org/lmi/

Wisconsin
Wisconsin Department of Workforce
   Development
Bureau of Workforce Training
201 East Washington Avenue
Madison, WI 53702
Phone: (608) 266-2930
http://worknet.wisconsin.gov/worknet/

Wyoming
Wyoming Department of Workforce Services
Research and Planning
2nd Floor
246 South Center Street, 2nd floor
Casper, WY 82602
Phone: (307) 473-3801
http://wydoe.state.wy.us

Source: U.S. Bureau of Labor Statistics, "State Labor Market Information Contact List," http://www.bls.gov/bls/ofolist.htm (accessed May 2012).

Appendix 4

State Data Center Agencies

Alabama
Center for Business and Economic
    Research
Box 870221
149 Bidgood Hall
Tuscaloosa, AL 35487-0221
(205) 348-6191
http://cber.cba.ua.edu

Alabama Department of Economic and
    Community Affairs
P.O. Box 5690
Suite 338
401 Adams Avenue
Montgomery, AL 36104-5690
(334) 242-5525
Fax: (334) 242-5515

Alaska
Census and Geographic Information
    Network
Research and Analysis
Alaska Department of Labor
P.O. Box 115501
1111 W 8th Street
 Juneau, AK 99811-5504
(907) 465-6029
http://almis.labor.state.ak.us

Alaska Department of Community and
    Economic Development
Division of Community and Business
    Development
150 3rd Street
Anchorage, AK 99508
(907) 465-8249

Alaska State Library
Government Publications/Technical
    Services
P.O. Box 110571
Juneau, AK 99811-0571
(907) 465-2927

University of Alaska–Anchorage
Institute of Social and Economic Research
3211 Providence Drive
Anchorage, AK 99508
(907) 786-1377

Arizona
Arizona Department of Administration
Office of Employment and Population
    Statistics
Room 440
100 N. 15th Avenue
Phoenix, AZ 85007
(602) 771-1155
http://www.workforce.az.gov

Arizona State Library, Archives, and Public
  Records
3rd Floor
1700 West Washington
Phoenix, AZ 85007
(602) 926-3870
(602) 926-3873

Arizona State University
L. William Seidman Research Institute
W.P. Carey School of Business
P.O. Box 87401
Tempe, AZ 85287-4011
(480) 965-3961

Economic and Business Research Program
Eller College of Management
P.O. Box 210108
The University of Arizona
Tucson, AZ 85721-0108
(520) 621-2109

Northern Arizona University
Arizona Rural Policy Institute
P.O. Box 15066
Flagstaff, AZ 86011-5066
(928) 523-7313

Arkansas
University of Arkansas–Little Rock
2801 South University
Little Rock, AR 72204
(501) 569-8530
http://www.aiea.ualr.edu/census/default.html

Arkansas State Library
900 West Capitol
Little Rock, AR 72201-1049
(501) 682-2053

Department of Workforce Services Labor Market
  Information and Analysis
P.O. Box 2981
Little Rock, AR 72203-2981
(501) 682-3121

California
State Census Data Center
Department of Finance
8th Floor
915 L Street
Sacramento, CA 95814-3706
http://www.dof.ca.gov/html/Demograp
  /druhpar.htm

Association of Bay Area
  Governments
P.O. Box 2050
101 Eighth Street
Oakland, CA 94604-2050
(510) 464-7966

Sacramento Area COG
Suite 300
1415 L Street
Sacramento, CA 95814
(916) 321-9000

San Diego Association of
  Governments
Wells Fargo Plaza
Suite 800
401 B Street
San Diego, CA 92101
(619) 699-6918

Southern California Association of
  Governments
12th Floor
818 West 7th Street
Los Angeles, CA 90017
(213) 236-1893

University of California–Berkeley
UC Data Archive and Technical
  Assistance
#5670
2420 Bowditch Street
Berkeley, CA 94720-5100
(510) 642-6571

Colorado
Division of Local Government
Colorado Department of Local Affairs
Room 521
1313 Sherman Street
Denver, CO 80203
(303) 866-3120
http://dola.colorado.gov/dlg/demog/index.html

Connecticut
Connecticut State Data Center
Map and Geographic Information Center
   (MAGIC)
University of Connecticut Libraries
Unit 2005M
369 Mansfield Road, Unit
Storrs, CT 06269-2005
860-486-4589
http://ctsdc.uconn.edu

Delaware
Delaware Office of Management and Budget
Suite 301
122 William Penn Street
Dover, DE 19901
(302) 739-3090
http://stateplanning.delaware.gov/census_data_
   center/

College of Urban Affairs and Public Policy
University of Delaware
Room 286
Graham Hall
Academy Street
Newark, DE 19716
(302) 831-8406

District of Columbia
Data Services Division
DC Office of Planning
State Data Center
Suite E650
1100 4th Street SW
Washington, DC 20024
(202) 442-7630
http://www.planning.dc.gov

DC Department of Health
Research and Analysis Division
Suite 2100
825 North Capitol Street NE
Washington, DC 20002
(202) 442-9032

Martin Luther King Memorial Library
Washingtonian Division
Room 307
901 G Street NW
Washington, DC 20001-4531
(202) 727-1213

Metropolitan Washington Council of
   Governments
Suite 300
777 North Capitol Street NE
Washington, DC 20002-4201
(202) 962-3200

Florida
Florida Department of Economic Opportunity
Labor Market Statistics
State Census Data Center
MSC G-020
107 East Madison Street
Tallahassee, FL 32399-4111
(850) 245-7258
http://www.labormarketinfo.com/library/census.
   htm

Office of Economic and Demographic Research
The Florida Legislature
Suite 574
111 West Madison Street
Tallahassee, FL 32399-6588
(850) 487-1402

State Library of Florida
Government Documents Reference
R.A. Gray Building
500 S. Bonough Street
Tallahassee, FL 32399-0250
(850) 245-6668

Georgia
Planning Research and Evaluation Division
Office of Planning and Budget
270 Washington Street SW
Atlanta, GA 30334
(404) 656-4445
http://opb.georgia.gov/00/channel_
 modifieddate/0,2096,161890977_
 161891591,00.html

Carl Vinson Institute of Government
201 N. Milledge Avenue
University of Georgia
Athens, GA 30602-5482
(706) 542-0383

Office of Decision Support Systems
Planning and Environmental
 Management Division
60 Executive Park South NE
Atlanta, GA 30329
(404) 679-4946

Reference Library and Information
 Department
Georgia Institute of Technology
704 Cherry Street NW
Atlanta, GA 30332-0900
(404) 894-1389

University of Georgia Libraries
Government Documents Department
2nd Floor
320 S. Jackson Street
Athens, GA 30602
(706) 542-3472

Hawaii
Hawaii State Data Center
Department of Business, Economic Development,
 and Tourism
4th Floor
250 South Hotel Street
Honolulu, HI 96813
(808) 586-2493

http://www.hawaii.gov/dbedt/info/economic/
 census/

Hawaii State Library
Federal Documents Section
478 South King Street
Honolulu, HI 96813-2994
(808) 586-3477

Idaho
Idaho Department of Labor
317 Main Street
Boise, ID 83735
(208) 332-3570 x3220
http://labor.idaho.gov/dnn/Default.
 aspx?alias=labor.idaho.gov/dnn/idl

Illinois
Illinois Department of Commerce and Economic
 Opportunity
Office of Information Management
500 East Monroe Street
Springfield, IL 62701-1643
Phone (217) 524-0187 or (217) 782-1381
http://www.illinoisbiz.biz/dceo/

Chicago Metropolitan Agency for
 Planning
233 South Wacker Drive
Suite 800
Sears Tower
Chicago, IL 60606
General Phone: (312) 454-0400

Illinois Department of Commerce and Economic
 Opportunity (BIDC)
Office of Information Management
500 East Monroe Street
Springfield, IL 62701
(217) 785-6117

Regional Development Institute
Northern Illinois University
DeKalb, IL 60115
(815) 753-0934

University of Illinois at Chicago
Richard J. Daley Library
801 South Morgan Street
Chicago, IL 60607
(312) 996-5277

Urban Data Visualization Lab
College of Urban Planning and Public Affairs
University of Illinois at Chicago
412 South Peoria Street
Chicago, IL 60607
(312) 413-8435

Indiana
Indiana State Library
Indiana State Data Center
140 North Senate Avenue
Indianapolis, IN 46204
(317) 232-3732
http://www.in.gov/library/isdc.htm

Indiana Business Research Center (BIDC)
Suite 210
777 Indiana Avenue
Indianapolis, IN 46202-5151
(317) 274-2205

Indiana Business Research Center
Suite 240
100 S. College Avenue
Bloomington, IN 47404
(812) 855-5507

Indiana Department of Workforce
  Development
Research and Analysis
Indiana Government Center South,
  SE211
10 North Senate Avenue
Indianapolis, IN 46204
(317) 233-2697

Indiana Geographic Information
  Council
Indiana State Library, GIS

140 N. Senate Avenue
Indianapolis, IN 46204
(317) 234-2924

Iowa
State Library of Iowa
Miller Building
1112 East Grand Avenue
Des Moines, IA 50319-0232
(515) 281-4350
http://www.iowadatacenter.org

Department of Sociology
The University of Iowa
W140 Seashore Hall
Iowa City, IA 52242-1401
(319) 335-2887

Regional Economic Capacity Analysis
  Program (RECAP)
Iowa State University
17 East Hall
Ames, IA 50011-1070
(515) 294-9903

Center for Social and Behavioral
  Research
University of Northern Iowa
Cedar Falls, IA 50614
(319) 273-2105

Kansas
State Library of Kansas
300 SW 10th Street
Topeka, KS 66612-1593
(785) 296-3296
http://kslib.info/sdc/

Center for Economic Development and Business
  Research
Box 121
1845 Fairmount Street
Wichita State University
Wichita, KS 67260-0121
(316) 978-3225

The Docking Institute of Public Affairs
Fort Hays State University
600 Park Street
Hays, KS 67601
(785) 628-4509

Institute for Policy and Social Research
Suite 607
1541 Lilac Lane
The University of Kansas
Lawrence, KS 66044-3177
(785) 864-9111

Kentucky
Urban Studies Institute, College of Arts and
    Science
426 West Bloom Street
University of Louisville
Louisville, KY 40208
(502) 852-8918
http://ksdc.louisville.edu

Louisiana
Louisiana State Census Data Center
Office of Information Technology
P.O. Box 94095 70804
Suite 2-130
1201 N 3rd Street
Baton Rouge, LA 70802
(225) 219-5987
http://www.louisiana.gov/Explore/
    Demographics_and_Geography/

Center for Business and Economic Research
University of Louisiana at Monroe
Monroe, LA 71209-0101
(318) 342-1151

Louisiana Section
State Library of Louisiana
P.O. Box 131
Baton Rouge, LA 70821-0131
(225) 342-2791

Louisiana State University A&M
Department of Sociology
126 Stubbs Hall
Baton Rouge, LA 70803
(225) 578-1115

Maine
Maine State Planning Office
38 State House Station
Augusta, ME 04333-0038
(207) 624-7660
http://www.state.me.us/spo/economics/
    census/

Maryland
Maryland Department of Planning
Maryland State Data Center
301 West Preston Street
Baltimore, MD 21201
(410) 767-4450
http://www.mdp.state.md.us/msdc/

Minnesota
State Demographic Center
Minnesota Department of Administration
300 Centennial Office Building
658 Cedar Street
St. Paul, MN 55155
(651) 201-2473
http://www.demography.state.mn.us

Metropolitan Council
390 Robert Street North
Saint Paul, MN 55101
(651) 602-1322
Fax (651) 602-1674

Minnesota Population Center
University of Minnesota
50 Willey Hall
225 19th Avenue South
Minneapolis, MN 55455
(612) 624-4389

Wilder Research Center
451 Lexington Parkway North
St. Paul, MN 55104
(651) 280-2675

Mississippi
Center for Population Studies
Room 301
Leavell Hall
University of Mississippi
University, MS 38677-1848
(662) 915-7288
http://www.olemiss.edu/depts/population
_studies

Center for Policy Research and Planning
3825 Ridgewood Road
Jackson, MS 39211

Missouri
Missouri State Data Center
Missouri State Library
P.O. Box 387
Jefferson City, MO 65102-0387
600 West Main Street
Jefferson City, MO 65101
(573) 526-1087
http://mcdc2.missouri.edu

City of St. Louis Planning and Urban Design
   Agency
Suite 1100
1015 Locust Street
St. Louis, MO 63101
(314) 622-3400

East-West Gateway Council of
   Governments
Suite 1600
One Memorial Drive
St. Louis, MO 63102
(314) 421-4220 or (618) 274-2750

Geographic Resources Center
104 Stewart Hall
University of Missouri–Columbia
Columbia, MO 65211
(573) 882-1356

Missouri Economic Research and Information
   Center
Missouri Department of Economic
   Development
301 W High Street
Jefferson City, MO 65101
(573) 751-3637

Missouri Office of Administration
Division of Budget and Planning
Room 124
State Capitol Building
Jefferson City, MO 65102
(573) 751-9318

Office of Social and Economic Data Analysis
602 Clark Hall
University of Missouri–Columbia
Columbia, MO 65211
(573) 884-2727; (573) 882-7397

Montana
Census and Economic Information Center
Montana Department of Commerce
P.O. Box 200505
301 South Park Avenue
Helena, MT 59620-0505
(406) 841-2739
http://ceic.mt.gov

Bureau of Business and Economic Research
Gallagher Business Building
32 Campus Drive, 36840
University of Montana
Missoula, MT 59812-2086
(406) 243-5113

Montana State Library
P.O. Box 201800
1515 East 6th Avenue
Helena, MT 59620-1800
(406) 444-5432

Research Analysis Bureau
Montana Department of Labor and Industry
P.O. Box 1728
Helena, MT 59624
(406) 444-2430

Nebraska
Center for Public Affairs Research
Nebraska State Data Center
University of Nebraska at Omaha
6001 Dodge Street CB108
Omaha, NE 68182-0059
(402) 554-2134
http://www.unomaha.edu/~cpar

Nebraska Department of Labor
Labor Market Information
P.O. Box 94600
550 South 16th Street
Lincoln, NE 68509-4600
(402) 471-2600

Nebraska Department of Natural Resources
P.O. Box 94676
301 Centennial Mall South
Lincoln, NE 68509-4676
(402) 471-1767

Nebraska Library Commission
Federal Documents Librarian
The Atrium
Suite 120
1200 North Street
Lincoln, NE 68508-2006
(402) 471-2045

Nevada
Nevada State Data Center
Nevada State Library and Archives

100 N Stewart Street
Carson City, NV 89710-4285
(775) 684-3324
http://nevadaculture.org

New Hampshire
New Hampshire Office of Energy and
    Planning
Johnson Hall, 3rd Floor
107 Pleasant Street
Concord, NH 03301
(603) 271-2155
http://www.nh.gov/oep/index.htm

New Jersey
New Jersey State Data Center
Division of Labor Market and Demographic
    Research
New Jersey Department of Labor
One John Fitch Plaza—Labor Building, 5th Floor
Trenton, NJ 08625-0388
(609) 984-2595
http://lwd.dol.state.nj.us/labor/lpa/content/njsdc_
    index.html

Data and Statistical Services
Social Science Reference Center
Firestone Library, Princeton University
1 Washington Road
Princeton, NJ 08544
(609) 258-3211

New Jersey State Library
U.S. Documents Office
P.O. Box 520
185 West State Street
Trenton, NJ 08625-0520
(609) 278-2240

Rutgers Regional Report
Rutgers University
Suite 300
33 Livingston Avenue
New Brunswick, NJ 08901-1981
(732) 932-5475

Rutgers University–Alexander Library
169 College Avenue
New Brunswick, NJ 08901-1981
(732) 932-5475

New Mexico
New Mexico Economic Development Department
New Mexico State Data Center
P.O. Box 20003
1100 St. Francis Drive
Santa Fe, NM 87504-5003
(505) 827-2486 or (505) 827-0333
http://www.edd.state.nm.us

Bureau of Business and Economic Research
Business and Industrial Data Center
MSCO6 3510
1 University of New Mexico
Albuquerque, NM 87131-0001
(505) 277-8300

Bureau of Business and Economic Research
State Data Center
MSCO6 3510
1 University of New Mexico
(505) 277-3038

Department of Economics/3CQ
New Mexico State University
Box 30001
Las Cruces, NM 88003-0001
(505) 646-4905

New Mexico State Library
1209 Camino Carlos Rey
Santa Fe, NM 87507
(505) 476-9710

New York
New York State Data Center
Empire State Development
30 South Pearl Street
Albany, NY 12245
(518) 292-5300
http://esd.ny.gov/NYSDataCenter.html

Cornell Program on Applied Demographics
2nd Floor
Beebe Hall
Cornell University
Ithaca, NY 14853
(607) 255-8399
(607) 254-2903

New York State Library
Cultural Education Center
6th Floor
Empire State Plaza
Albany, NY 12230
(518) 474-5355

North Carolina
Office of State Budget and Management
20320 Mail Service Center
Raleigh, NC 27699-0320
(919) 807-4781
http://www.osbm.state.nc.us/ncosbm/facts_and_
    figures/state_data_center.shtm

Center for Geographic Information and Analysis
Department of Environmental and Natural
    Resources
20322 Mail Service Center
Raleigh NC 27699-0322
(919) 733-2090

Odum Institute for Research in Social Science
Manning Hall CB 3355
University of North Carolina
Chapel Hill, NC 27599-3355
(919) 962-0512

State Library of North Carolina
4641 Mail Service Center
Raleigh, NC 27699-4641
(919) 807-7458

North Dakota
North Dakota Department of Commerce
P.O. Box 2057
1600 East Century Avenue

Bismarck, ND 58502
(701) 328-4499
http://www.commerce.nd.gov

Department of Geography
University of North Dakota
P.O. Box 9020
221 Centennial Drive
Grand Forks, ND 58202-9020
(701) 777-4587

North Dakota State Library
Liberty Memorial Building
604 East Boulevard Avenue
Bismarck, ND 58505-0800
(701) 328-4622

Office of Intergovernmental Assistance
North Dakota Division of Community Services
North Dakota Department of Commerce
Suite 2
1600 East Century Avenue
Bismarck, ND 58505-2057
(701) 328-5300

Ohio
Policy Research and Strategic Planning
Ohio Department of Development
P.O. Box 1001
Columbus, OH 43266-0101
27th Floor
77 South High Street
Columbus, OH 43215
(614) 466-2116
http://www.odod.state.oh.us/research

Buckeye Hills–Hocking Valley Regional
   Development District
P.O. Box 520
Reno, OH 45773-0520
(740) 374-9436

Northern Ohio Data and Information
   Services (NODIS)
2121 Euclid Avenue, UR 32

Cleveland State University
Cleveland, OH 44115-2114
(216) 687-2209

ODJFS/Labor Market Information
Bureau Research, Assessment and Accountability
P.O. Box 1618
4300 Kimberly Parkway
Columbus, OH 43216-1618
(614) 466-9842

State Library of Ohio
Government Information
   Services
274 East First Avenue
Columbus, OH 43201
(614) 995-0033

Oklahoma
Oklahoma Census Data Center
Oklahoma Department of Commerce
900 North Stiles Avenue
Oklahoma City, OK 73104
(405) 815-5182
http://www.okcommerce.gov

Center for Economic and Management Research
Suite 4
307 West Brooks
The University of Oklahoma
Norman, OK 73019-0450
(405) 325-2931

Oklahoma Department of Libraries
200 NE 18th Street
Oklahoma City, OK 73105-3298
(405) 521-2502

Oregon
Population Research Center
506 SW Mill
Portland State University
Portland, OR 97207-0751
(503) 725-5157
http://www.pdx.edu/prc/

Documents Center
University of Oregon Library
1501 Kincaid Street
Eugene, OR 97403-1299
(541) 346-1970

Office of Economic Analysis
U20
155 Cottage Street NE
Salem, OR 97310-3966
(503) 378-4967

Oregon Employment Department
875 Union Street NE
Salem, OR 97311
(541) 947-3098
Oregon State Library
250 Winter Street NE
Salem, OR 97310-0640
(503) 378-5020

Pennsylvania
Pennsylvania State Data Center
Institute of State and Regional Affairs
777 West Harrisburg Pike
Penn State Harrisburg
Middletown, PA 17057-4898
(717) 948-6336
http://pasdc.hbg.psu.edu/index.html

PA SDC Institute of State and Regional Affairs
777 West Harrisburg Pike
Harrisburg, PA 17105
(717) 948-6690

Pennsylvania State Library
Room 219
Forum Building
333 Market Street
Harrisburg, PA 17057
(717) 787-2327

Pennsylvania State Data Center
State Capital Office
Room 357

Forum Building
Harrisburg, PA 17120
Mailing Address:
777 West Harrisburg Pike
Middletown, PA 17057
(717) 772-2710

Rhode Island
Rhode Island Department of Administration
Statewide Planning Program
One Capitol Hill
Providence, RI 02908-5872
(401) 222-1234
http://www.planning.ri.gov/census/ri2000.htm

Brown University
Scholarly Resources Librarian
Social Sciences Data
John D. Rockefeller Library
Box A
Providence, RI 02912-A
(401) 863-7978

RI Department of Administration
  (RIGIS)
One Capitol Hill
Providence, RI 02908
(401) 222-7978

Rhode Island Economic Development
  Corporation
Suite 101
315 Iron Horse Way
Providence, RI 02908
(401) 278-9100

South Carolina
Office of Research and Statistics
South Carolina Budget and Control
  Board
Room 425
1000 Assembly Street
Columbia, SC 29201
(803) 734-3780
http://www.ors.state.sc.us

South Carolina State Library
P.O. Box 11469
Columbia, SC 29211
(803) 734-7625

South Dakota
South Dakota State Data Center
Extension Sociologist
South Dakota State University
Brookings, SD 57007
(605) 688-4899 or 4901
http://www.sdstate.edu/soc/rlcdc/index.cfm

South Dakota State Library
Government Publications
800 Governors Drive
Pierre, SD 57501-2294
(605) 773-5075

Labor Market Information Center
South Dakota Department of Labor
Box 4730
420 South Roosevelt Street
Aberdeen, SD 57401-4730
(605) 626-2314

South Dakota Department of Health
Data, Statistics and Vital Records
600 East Capitol Avenue
Pierre, SD 57501-2536
(605) 773-5303

Rural Life Census Data Center
P.O. Box 504
Scobey Hall 226,
South Dakota State University
Brookings, SD 57007-1296
(605) 688-4899

Tennessee
Center for Business and Economic Research
University of Tennessee
713 Stokely Management Center
Knoxville, TN 37996-0570
(865) 974-6070
http://cber.bus.utk.edu

Texas
Texas State Data Center
Institute for Demographic and Socioeconomic
    Research (IDSER)
501 W. Cesar E. Chavez Boulevard
University of Texas at San Antonio
San Antonio, TX 78207-4415
(210) 458-6543
http://txsdc.utsa.edu

Office of the State Demographer
Stephen F. Austin Building
Suite 220W
1700 North Congress Avenue
Austin, TX 78701
(512) 936-3542

Texas Natural Resources Information System
    (TNRIS)
P.O. Box 13231
Austin, TX 78711
(512) 463-8337

Texas State Library
P.O. Box 12927
Lorenzo de Zavala Building
Austin, TX 78711-2927
(512) 463-5455

Utah
Governor's Office of Planning and Budget
P.O. Box 142210
Suite 150
Utah State Capitol Complex
Salt Lake City, UT 84114-2210
(801) 537-9013
http://www.governor.utah.gov/dea/

Bureau of Economic and Business
    Research
Room 401
1645 East Campus Center Drive
University of Utah
Salt Lake City, UT 84112
(801) 581-3358

Governor's Office of Economic
Development
Suite 500
324 South State Street
Salt Lake City, UT 84111
(801) 538-8700

Workforce Development and
Information
140 East 300 South
Salt Lake City, UT 84111
(801) 526-9987
Fax (801) 526-9238

Vermont
Center for Rural Studies
206 Morrill Hall
University of Vermont
Burlington, VT 05405
(802) 656-0864
http://crs.uvm.edu/census/

Vermont Department of Libraries
109 State Street
Montpelier, VT 05609
(802) 828-3265

Virginia
Virginia Employment Commission
703 East Main Street
Richmond, VA 23219
(804) 786-8624
http://www.vec.virginia.gov

Libraries of Virginia
Documents Section
800 East Broad Street
Richmond, VA 23219-3491
(804) 692-3552

Weldon Cooper Center for Public Service
2400 Old Ivy Road
University of Virginia
Charlottesville, VA 22903
(434) 982-5581

Washington
Office of Financial Management
Forecasting Division
P.O. Box 43113
210 11th Avenue, SW
Olympia, WA 98504-3113
(360) 902-0535
http://www.ofm.wa.gov

Center for Social Science
Computation and Research
Box 353345
145 Savery Hall
University of Washington
Seattle, WA 98195-3345
(206) 543-8110

Central Washington University
Brooks Library—MS 7548
400 East University Way
Ellensburg, WA 98926
(509) 963-1960

Employment Security
Department Labor Market and Economic
Analysis
P.O. Box 9046
Suite 15
5411 East Mill Plain Blvd
Vancouver, WA 98661
(360) 735-5093

Puget Sound Regional Council
Suite 500
1011 Western Avenue
Seattle, WA 98104-1035
(206) 971-3602

University of Washington
Suzzallo Library
Government Publications Division
Box 352900
Seattle, WA 98195-2900
(206) 685-3130

Washington State Library
P.O. Box 42460
Olympia, WA 98504-2460
(360) 704-527

Holland and Terrell Libraries
P.O. Box 645610
Washington State University
Pullman, WA 99164-5610
(360) 867-2153

Western Washington University
Department of Sociology—CSSI
516 High Street, MS-9081
Bellingham, WA 98225-9081
(360) 650-3176

West Virginia
West Virginia Development Office
Capitol Complex
Charleston, WV 25305-0311
(304) 957-2033
http://www.wvdo.org/business/statedatacenter.html

Bureau of Business and Economic Research
P.O. Box 6025
West Virginia University
Morgantown, WV 26506-6025
(304) 293-1801

Reference Library
West Virginia State Library Commission
Science and Cultural Center
Capitol Complex
Charleston, WV 25305
(304) 558-2045

Wisconsin
Department of Administration
Demographic Services Center
P.O. Box 8944
9th Floor
101 E. Wilson Street
Madison, WI 53708-8944
(608) 266-1927
http://www.doa.state.wi.us/dir

Applied Population Laboratory
Department of Rural Sociology
316E Ag Hall
1450 Linden Drive
University of Wisconsin, Madison
Madison, WI 53706-1522
(608) 265-9545

Wyoming
Department of Administration and
  Information
Economic Analysis Division
2800 Central Avenue
Cheyenne, WY 82002
(307) 777-7161
http://eadiv.state.wy.us

Wyoming Survey and Analysis Center
2nd Floor
UW Office Annex
406 South 21st Street
Laramie, WY 82071
Mailing Address:
1000 E University Ave
Laramie, WY 82071
(307) 766-2189

Source: U.S. Census Bureau, "State Data Center Network," http://www.census.gov/sdc/network.html
(accessed May 2012).

Selected Bibliography

This selected bibliography lists the published books, articles, and reports used in the preparation of this volume, as well as many of the online resources consulted. However, it excludes some online resources due to the lack of a standardized way of cataloguing those resources.

A complication often encountered when undertaking research into regional economic and social affairs is that much statistical information exists not in fixed, printed forms but in online databases that users may query to tabulate their own reports from packaged data. Such databases provided the information used in many of the specific regional analyses featured throughout the book. Citations for the data sets used in regional-specific calculations appear in the chapter notes rather than this bibliography.

The URLs found in the chapter notes and in this bibliography were active on the date stated in the citation or at the time of final manuscript preparation but are subject to change at any time.

Acemoglu, Daron, and James Robinson. *Why Nations Fail: The Origins of Power, Prosperity, and Poverty.* New York: Crown Publishing, 2012.

Acs, Zoltan, Ed Glaeser, Robert Litan, Lee Fleming, Stephen Goetx, William Kerr, Steven Klepper, Stuart Rosenthal, Olav Sorenson, and William Strange. *Entrepreneurship and Urban Success: Toward a Policy Consensus.* Kansas City, MO: Ewing Marion Kauffman Foundation, 2008. http://sites.kauffman.org/pdf/state_local_roadmap_022608.pdf.

Acs, Zoltan, Brian Headd, and Hezekiah Agwara. *Nonemployer Start-up Puzzle.* Washington, DC: U.S. Small Business Administration, 2009. http://archive.sba.gov/advo/research/rs354tot.pdf.

Allegretto, Sylvia. *The State of Working America's Wealth, 2011.* Washington, DC: Economic Policy Institute, 2011. http://www.epi.org/page/-/BriefingPaper292.pdf.

Ambargis, Zoë. "Regional Input-Output Modeling System." Presentation at the Pacific Northwest Regional Economic Analysis Project, Reno, NV, September 29, 2009. http://workshops.reaproject.org/2009/Reno-Nevada/presentations/Ambargis-RIMS.ppt.

Anderson, Margo. *The American Census: A Social History*. New Haven, CT: Yale University Press, 1988.

Andreski, Patricia, April Beaule, Mary Dascola, Denise Duffy, Eva Leissou, Katherine McGonagle, Jay Schlegel, and Robert Schoeni. *Panel Survey of Income Dynamics Main Interview User Manual: Release 2011.1*. Anne Arbor, MI: Institute for Social Research, 2011. http://psidonline.isr.umich.edu/data/Documentation/UserGuide2009.pdf.

Antuofermo, Mélina, and Emilio Di Meglio. "23% of EU Citizens Were at Risk of Poverty and Social Exclusion in 2010." *Eurostat: Statistics in Focus*, 9/2012. http://epp.eurostat.ec.europa.eu/cache/ITY_OFFPUB/KS-SF-12-009/EN/KS-SF-12-009-EN.PDF.

Arias, Elizabeth. "United States Life Tables, 2008." *National Vital Statistics Report*, September 24, 2012. http://www.cdc.gov/nchs/data/nvsr/nvsr61/nvsr61_03.pdf.

Baker, Dean. *Debt, Deficits, and Demographics: Why We Can Afford the Social Contract*. Washington, DC: New America Foundation, 2012. http://nsc.newamerica.net/sites/newamerica.net/files/policydocs/Baker_Dean_DebtDeficitsDemographics_November2012.pdf.

Bartsch, Kristina. "The Employment Projections for 2008–18." *Monthly Labor Review*, November 2009, 3–9. http://www.bls.gov/opub/mlr/2009/11/art1full.pdf.

Baumohl, Bernard. *The Secrets of Economic Indicators: Hidden Clues to Future Economic Trends and Investment Opportunities*. 2d ed. Upper Saddle River, NJ: Wharton School Publishing, 2008.

Bennett, Claudette. "Race: Questions and Classifications." In *Encyclopedia of the U.S. Census*, ed. Margo Anderson, 313–317. Washington, DC: CQ Press, 2000.

Berner, Maureen. *Statistics for Public Administration: Practical Uses for Better Decision Making*. Washington, DC: ICMA Press, 2010.

Bess, Rebecca, and Zoë Ambargis. "Input-Output for Impact Analysis: Suggestions for Practitioners Using RIMS II Multipliers." Presentation to the Southern Regional Association Conference, New Orleans, LA, March 2011. http://www.bea.gov/papers/pdf/WP_IOMIA_RIMSII_020612.pdf.

Blair, John. *Local Economic Development: Analysis and Practice*. Thousand Oaks, CA: Sage Publications, 1995.

Blakely, Edward, and Ted Bradshaw. *Planning Local Economic Development: Theory and Practice*. 3d ed. Thousand Oaks, CA: Sage Publications, 2002.

Boettcher, Jennifer, and Leonard Gaines. *Industry Research Using The Economic Census: How to Find It, How to Use It*. Westport, CT: Greenwood Press, 2004.

Boslaugh, Sarah, and Paul Andrew Watters. *Statistics in a Nutshell*. Sebastopol, CA: O'Reilly, 2008.

Bosworth, Brian. "Regional Economic Analysis to Support Job Development Strategies." In *Jobs and Economic Development: Strategies and Practice*, ed. Robert Giloth, 85–104. Thousand Oaks, CA: Sage Publications, 1998.

Boushey, Heather, Shawn Fremstad, Rachel Gragg, and Margy Waller. *Social Inclusion for the United States*. Washington, DC: Center for Economic and Policy Research. http://inclusionist.org/files/socialinclusionusa.pdf.

Bricker, Jesse, Arthur Kennickell, Kevin Moore, and John Sabelhaus. *Changes in U.S. Family Finances from 2007 to 2010: Evidence from the Survey of Consumer Finances*.

Washington, DC: Board of Governors of the Federal Reserve Board, 2012. http://www.federalreserve.gov/pubs/bulletin/2012/pdf/scf12.pdf.

Brooks, Jennifer, and Kasey Wiedrich. *Assets & Opportunity Scorecard: A Portrait of Financial Insecurity and Policies to Rebuild Prosperity in America*. Washington, DC: CFED, 2012. http://assetsandopportunity.org/assets/2012_scorecard.pdf.

Brown, Robert. "BEA's State and Local Area Personal Income." Presentation at the Pacific Northwest Regional Economic Analysis Project, Reno, NV, September 29, 2009. http://workshops.reaproject.org/2009/Reno-Nevada/presentations/Brown-BEA-Income.ppt.

Burd-Sharps, Sarah, Kristen Lewis, and Eduardo Borges Martins. *The Measure of America: American Human Development Report, 2008–2009*. New York: Columbia University Press, 2008.

Caplan, Bryan. "Against the Human Development Index." EconLog (blog), May 22, 2009. http://econlog.econlib.org/archives/2009/05/against_the_hum.html.

Carlton, David, and Peter Coclanis. "Introduction." In *Confronting Southern Poverty in the Great Depression*, ed. David Carlton and Peter Coclanis, 1–37. Boston: Bedford Books, 1996.

Cassidy, John. *How Markets Fail: The Logic of Economic Calamities*. New York: Farrar, Strauss and Giroux, 2009.

Census Department. *Population Census 2011: Preliminary Data*. Budapest: Hungarian Central Statistical Office, 2012. http://www.ksh.hu/docs/eng/xftp/idoszaki/nepsz2011/enepszelo2011.pdf.

Central Statistics Office. *Survey on Income and Living Conditions, 2010*. Dublin: Government of Ireland, 2012. http://www.cso.ie/en/media/csoie/releasespublications/documents/silc/2010/silc_2010.pdf.

CFED. "State Profile: Colorado." In *2012 Assets and Opportunity Scorecard*. Washington, DC: CFED, 2012. http://scorecard.assetsandopportunity.org/2012/state/co (accessed November 12, 2012).

Chapa, Jorge. "Hispanic/Latino Ethnicity and Identifiers." In *Encyclopedia of the U.S. Census*, ed. Margo Anderson, 243–246. Washington, DC: CQ Press, 2000.

Citro, Constance. "Income and Poverty Measures." In *Encyclopedia of the U.S. Census*, ed. Margo Anderson. Washington, DC: CQ Press, 2000.

Citro, Constance, and Robert Michael, eds. *Measuring Poverty: A New Approach*. Washington, DC: National Academies Press, 1995.

CNN Money.com. "2009 Fortune 1000." http://money.cnn.com/magazines/fortune/fortune500/2009/full_list/ (accessed January 6, 2012)

———. "2011 Global 500." *Fortune*. http://money.cnn.com/magazines/fortune/global500/2011/full_list/index.html (accessed February 15, 2013).

Cobb, James. *The Selling of the South: The Southern Crusade for Industrial Development*. Baton Rouge: Louisiana State University Press, 1982.

Coleman-Jensen, Alisha, Mark Nord, Margaret Andrews, and Steven Carlson. *Household Food Security in the United States in 2011*. Washington, DC: U.S. Department of Agriculture, 2012. http://www.ers.usda.gov/media/884525/err141.pdf.

Commission of the European Communities. *GDP and Beyond: Measuring Progress in a Changing World*. Brussels: European Union, 2009. http://eur-lex.europa.eu/LexUriServ/LexUriServ.do?uri=COM:2009:0433:FIN:EN:PDF.

Congressional Budget Office. *The Budget and Economic Outlook: Fiscal Years 2010 to 2020.* Washington, DC: Congress of the United States, 2010. http://cbo.gov/ftpdocs/108xx/doc10871/01-26-Outlook.pdf.

———. *Taxing Businesses through the Individual Income Tax.* Washington, DC: Congress of the United States, 2012. http://www.cbo.gov/sites/default/files/cbofiles/attachments/43750-TaxingBusinesses2.pdf.

Cortright, Joseph, and Andrew Reamer. *Socioeconomic Data for Understanding Your Regional Economy.* Washington, DC: U.S. Department of Commerce, 1998. http://www.econdata.net/pdf/uguide.pdf.

Daly, Lew, and Stephen Posner. *Beyond GDP: New Measures for a New Economy.* New York: Demos, 2011. http://www.demos.org/publication/beyond-gdp-new-measures-new-economy.

Dasgupta, Partha. *Economics: A Very Short Introduction.* New York: Oxford University Press, 2007.

Davis, Lindsay, Lyda Ghanbari, and Alice Ramey. *Revisions in State Establishment-based Employment Estimates Effective January 2012.* Washington, DC: U.S. Department of Labor, 2012. http://www.bls.gov/sae/benchmark2012.pdf.

DeNavas-Walt, Carmen, Bernadette Proctor, and Jessica Smith. *Income, Poverty, and Health Insurance Coverage in the United States: 2011.* Washington, DC: U.S. Census Bureau, 2012. http://www.census.gov/prod/2012pubs/p60-243.pdf.

Division of Employment Security. "North Carolina Economic Development Regions and Workforce Development Boards, 2010." Last revised February 2012. http://www.ncesc1.com/lmi/publications/maps/Economic_Development_Regions_&_Workforce_Development_Board_Areas.pdf.

Dolan, Edwin, and Kevin Klein. *Survey of Economics.* 4th ed. Redding, CA: BVT Publishing, 2010.

Donegan, Mary, Joshua Drucker, Harvey Goldstein, Nichola Lowe, and Emil Malizia. "Which Indicators Explain Metropolitan Performance Best?" *Journal of the American Planning Association* 74, no. 2 (2008): 180–195.

Downey, George. *Gross Domestic Product by State Estimation Methodology.* Washington, DC: U.S. Bureau of Economic Analysis, 2006. http://www.bea.gov/regional/gsp/help/.

Doyle, Pat. "Federal Household Surveys." In *Encyclopedia of the U.S. Census,* ed. Margo Anderson, 218–227. Washington, DC: CQ Press, 2000.

Dunbar, Ann. "Alternative Measures of Household Income." *Regional Quarterly Report,* October 2011, 138. http://www.bea.gov/scb/pdf/2011/10%20October/1011_regreport.pdf.

Economic Research Service. "Farm Labor: Background." http://www.ers.usda.gov/topics/farm-economy/farm-labor/background.aspx#Numbers (accessed February 17, 2013).

———. "Rural Classification: Overview." http://www.ers.usda.gov/topics/rural-economy-population/rural-classifications.aspx (accessed January 19, 2013).

———. "Rural Classification: What Is Rural?" http://www.ers.usda.gov/topics/rural-economy-population/rural-classifications/what-is-rural.aspx (accessed January 19, 2013).

———. "Rural-Urban Continuum Codes: Documentation." http://www.ers.usda.gov/data-products/rural-urban-continuum-codes/documentation.aspx (accessed January 19, 2013).

———. "Urban Influence Codes: Documentation." http://www.ers.usda.gov/data-prod-ucts/urban-influence-codes.aspx (accessed January 19, 2013).

Economist. *Guide to Economic Indicators: Making Sense of Economics*. 6th ed. New York: Bloomberg Press, 2006.

Edwards, Mary. *Regional and Urban Economic and Economic Development*. Boca Raton, FL: Auerbach Publications, 2007.

Eisinger, Peter. *The Rise of the Entrepreneurial State*. Madison: University of Wisconsin Press, 1988.

Employment and Training Administration. *Guide to State and Local Workforce Data for Analysis and Informed Decision Making: Version 2*. Washington, DC: U.S. Department of Labor, 2012. https://winwin.workforce3one.org/view/2001212365477234753/info.

Fisher, Gordon. *The Development of the Orshansky Thresholds and Their Subsequent History as the Official U.S. Poverty Measure*. Washington, DC: U.S. Census Bureau, 1992. Last revised September 2007. http://census.gov/hhes/poverty/povmeas/papers/orshansky.html.

Florida, Richard. *The Rise of the Creative Class*. New York: Basic Books, 2002.

Folbre, Nancy. "What Percentage Lives in Poverty?" Economix (blog), November 14, 2011. http://economix.blogs.nytimes.com/2011/11/14/what-percentage-lives-in-poverty/.

Fremstad, Shawn. *A Modern Framework for Measuring Poverty and Basic Economic Security*. Washington, DC: Center for Economic and Policy Research, 2010. http://www.cepr.net/documents/publications/poverty-2010-04.pdf.

———. *The New Supplemental Poverty Numbers: Do They Paint an Accurate Picture of Poverty Today?* Washington, DC: Center for Economic and Policy Research, November 2011. http://www.cepr.net/index.php/data-bytes/poverty-bytes/is-child-poverty-less-of-a-problem-than-we-thought.

Frey, William, Jill Wilson, Alan Berube, and Audrey Singer. *Tracking Metropolitan America into the 21st Century: A Field Guide to the New Metropolitan and Micro-politan Definitions*. Washington, DC: Brookings Institution Press, 2004. http://www.psc.isr.umich.edu/dis/census/freybrookings.pdf.

Friedland, Robert, and Laura Summer. *Demography Is Not Destiny*. Washington, DC: National Academy on an Aging Society, 1999. http://www.agingsociety.org/agingso-ciety/pdf/destiny1.pdf.

Gans, Judith. *Illegal Immigration to the United States: Causes and Policy Solutions*. Tucson, AZ: Udall Center for Studies in Public Policy, 2007. http://udallcenter.arizona.edu/immigration/publications/fact_sheet_no_3_illegal_immigration.pdf.

Gauthier, Jason. *Measuring America: The Decennial Censuses from 1790 to 2000*. Washington, DC: U.S. Census Bureau, 2002. http://www.census.gov/prod/2002pubs/pol02marv.pdf.

Giventer, Lawrence. *Statistical Analysis for Public Administration*. 2d ed. Sudbury, MA: Jones and Bartlett, 2008.

Goldberg, Joseph, and William Moye. *The First Hundred Years of the Bureau of Labor Statistics*. Washington, DC: U.S. Department of Labor, 1985. http://www.bls.gov/opub/blsfirsthundredyears/100_years_of_bls.pdf.

Groves, Robert. "A Future Without Key Social and Economic Statistics for the Country." U.S. Census Bureau Director's Blog (blog), May 11, 2012. http://directorsblog.blogs. census.gov/2012/05/11/a-future-without-key-social-and-economic-statistics-for-the-country/.

Harris, Jennifer. "BLS Establishment Estimates Revised to Incorporate March 2010 Benchmarks." Washington DC: U.S. Bureau of Labor Statistics, February 2011.

Haskins, Ron, and Isabel Sawhill. *Creating an Opportunity Society*. Washington, DC: Brookings Institution Press, 2009.

Haupt, Arthur, and Thomas Kane. *Population Handbook*. 5th ed. Washington, DC: Population Reference Bureau, 2004.

Headd, Brian. *An Analysis of Small Business and Jobs*. Washington, DC: U.S. Small Business Administration, 2010. http://www.sba.gov/sites/default/files/files/an%20 analysis%20of%20small%20business%20and%20jobs(1).pdf.

Headd, Brian, and Radwan Saade. *Do Small Business Definition Decisions Distort Small Business Research Results?* Washington, DC: U.S. Small Business Administration, 2008. http://ftp.sbaonline.sba.gov/advo/research/rs330tot.pdf.

Hipple, Steven. "Self-Employment in the United States." *Monthly Labor Review*, September 2010, 17–32. http://www.bls.gov/opub/mlr/2010/09/art2full.pdf.

Horovitz, Bruce. "After Gen X, Millennials, What Should Next Generation Be?" *USA Today,* May 4, 2012. http://usatoday30.usatoday.com/money/advertising/story/2012-05-03/naming-the-next-generation/54737518/1.

Internal Revenue Service. *Form 1040: 2009 Instructions.* Washington, DC: U.S. Department of the Treasury, 2009. http://www.irs.gov/pub/irs-prior/i1040-2009.pdf.

Jarmin, Ron. "Job-to-Job Flows: Sneak Peak at Upcoming Innovations from the Longitudinal Employer-Household Dynamics Program." Presentation to the Brookings Institution Roundtable on Putting America to Work: The Essential Role of Labor Market Statistics, Washington, DC, September 27, 2010. http://www.brookings. edu/~/media/Files/rc/speeches/2010/0927_labor_statistics_reamer/0927_labor_ statistics_jarmin.pdf.

Jones, Van. *The Green Collar Economy*. New York: HarperCollins, 2008.

Jurjevich, Jason, and Greg Schrock. *Is Portland Really the Place Where Young People Go to Retire? Migration Patterns of Portland's Young and College-Educated, 1980–2010.* Portland, OR: Portland State University, 2012. http://mkn.research.pdx.edu/wp-content/ uploads/2012/09/JurjevichSchrockMigrationReport1.pdf.

Kennedy, Robert. Remarks at the University of Kansas, March 18, 1968, John F. Kennedy Presidential Museum and Library. http://www.jfklibrary.org/Research/Ready-Reference/RFK-Speeches/Remarks-of-Robert-F-Kennedy-at-the-university-of-Kansas-March-18-1968.aspx, accessed August 31, 2011.

Kenney, Caitlin. "BLS Changes Survey to Record Longer Periods of Unemployment." National Public Radio, December 28, 2010. http://m.npr.org/news/front/132411278.

Konoczal, Mike. "Occupy Wall Street and the Diversity of Objections to Inequality." Rortybomb (blog), November 14, 2011. http://rortybomb.wordpress.com/2011/10/17/ occupy-wall-street-and-the-diversity-of-objections-to- inequality/.

Krugman, Paul. *The Conscience of a Liberal*. New York: Norton, 2007.

Landefeld, J. Steven, Brent Moulton, Joel Platt, and Shaunda Villones. "GDP and Beyond: Measuring Economic Progress and Sustainability." *Survey of Current Business*, April 2010, 12–25. http://www.bea.gov/scb/pdf/2010/04%20April/0410_gpd-beyond.pdf.

Lewis, Kristen, and Sarah Burd-Sharps. *The Measure of America: American Human Development Report, 2010–2011.* New York: New York University Press, 2010.

Liner, Charles D. "Introduction." In *State and Local Government Relations in North Carolina: Their Evolution and Current Status*, ed. Charles D. Liner. 2d ed. Chapel Hill, NC: Institute of Government, 1995.

Luttrell, Kelly, Patrice Treubert, and Michael Parisi. "Integrated Business Data, 2003." *Statistics of Income Bulletin*, Fall 2006. http://www.irs.gov/pub/irs-soi/03intbus.pdf.

MacDonald, Heather, and Alan Peters. *Urban Policy and the Census.* Redlands, CA: Esri Press, 2011.

Malizia, Emil, and Edward Feser. *Understanding Local Economic Development.* Rutgers, NJ: Center for Urban Policy Research, 1999.

Mankiw, N. Gregory. *Principles of Microeconomics.* Fort Worth, TX: Dryden Press, 1998.

Marcuss, Rosemary, and Richard Kane. "U.S. National Income and Product Accounts: Born of the Great Depression and World War II." *Survey of Current Business*, February 2007, 32–46. http://www.bea.gov/scb/pdf/2007/02%20February/0207_history_article.pdf.

Markusen, Ann. *Regions: The Economics and Politics of Territory.* Totowa, NJ: Rowman & Littlefield, 1987.

———. "Urban Development and the Politics of the Creative Class: Evidence from a Study of Artists." *Environment and Planning A* 38 (2006): 1921–1940.

Markusen, Ann, and Greg Schrock. "The Artistic Dividend: Urban Artistic Specialization and Economic Development Implications." *Urban Studies* 43, no. 10 (2006): 1661–1686.

———. "Consumption-Driven Urban Development." *Urban Geography* 30, no. 4 (2009): 344–367.

Martin, Ron, and Peter Sunley. "Deconstructing Clusters: Chaotic Concept or Policy Panacea?" *Journal of Economic Geography* 3 (2003): 5–35.

McCulla, Stephanie, and Charles Ian Mead. *An Introduction to the National Income and Product Accounts.* Washington, DC: U.S. Bureau of Economic Analysis, 2007. http://bea.gov/scb/pdf/national/nipa/methpap/mpi1_0907.pdf.

McCulla, Stephanie, and Shelly Smith. *Measuring the Economy: A Primer on GDP and the National Income and Product Accounts.* Washington, DC: U.S. Bureau of Economic Analysis, 2007. http://bea.gov/national/pdf/nipa_primer.pdf.

McFalls, Joseph. *Population: A Lively Introduction.* 5th ed. Washington, DC: Population Reference Bureau, 2007. http://www.prb.org/pdf07/62.1LivelyIntroduction.pdf.

McLean, Mary, and Kenneth Voytek. *Understanding Your Economy: Using Analysis to Guide Local Strategic Planning.* 2d ed. Chicago: APA Planners Press, 1992.

Meier, Kenneth, Jeffrey Brudney, and John Bohte. *Applied Statistics for Public and Nonprofit Administration.* 7th ed. Belmont, CA: Thomson Wadsworth, 2009.

Mishel, Lawrence, Jared Bernstein, and Heidi Shierholz. *The State of Working America, 2008/2009.* Ithaca, NY: Cornell University Press, 2009.

Mishel, Lawrence, Josh Bivens, Elise Gould, and Heidi Shierholz. *The State of Working America.* 12th ed. Ithaca, NY: Cornell University Press, 2012.

Mitchell, John. "Change of Heartland: The Great Plains." *National Geographic*, May 2004. http://ngm.nationalgeographic.com/ngm/0405/feature1/fulltext.html.

Morgan, Jonathan. "Clusters and Competitive Advantage: Finding a Niche in the New Economy." *Popular Government*, Spring/Summer 2004, 43–54. http://ncinfo.iog.unc.edu/pubs/electronicversions/pg/pgspsm04/article6.pdf.

Moss, David. *A Concise Guide to Macroeconomics: What Managers, Executives, and Students Need to Know.* Boston: Harvard Business School Press, 2007.

Murdock, Steve, Chris Kelley, Jeffrey Jordan, Beverly Pecotte, and Alvin Luedke. *Demographics: A Guide to Methods and Data Sources for Media, Business, and Government.* Boulder, CO: Paradigm Publishers, 2006.

National Agricultural Statistics Service. *2007 Census of Agriculture.* Vol. 1, *United States Summary and State Data.* Washington, DC: U.S. Department of Agriculture, 2009. http://www.agcensus.usda.gov/Publications/2007/Full_Report/Volume_1,_Chapter_1_US/usv1.pdf.

———. "Farm Labor Survey." http://www.nass.usda.gov/Surveys/Guide_to_NASS_Surveys/Farm_Labor/index.asp (accessed February 17, 2013).

———. *USDA's National Agricultural Statistics Service: An Evolving Statistical Service for American Agriculture.* Washington, DC: U.S. Department of Agriculture, 2005. http://www.nass.usda.gov/About_NASS/evolving_nass.pdf.

National Emergency Council. "Report on Economic Conditions of the South." In *Confronting Poverty in the Great Depression,* eds. David Carlton and Peter Coclanis, 41–80. Boston: Bedford Books, 1996.

National Research Council. *Using the American Community Survey: Benefits and Challenges*, eds. Constance Citro and Graham Kalton. Washington, DC: National Academies Press, 2007.

North, Douglass. "Location Theory and Regional Economic Growth." *Journal of Political Economy* 63, no. 3 (1955): 243–258.

Obama, Barack. Presidential Proclamation: Small Business Week. Washington, DC: White House, 2011. http://www.whitehouse.gov/the-press-office/2011/05/12/presidential-proclamation- small-business-week (accessed January 6, 2012).

OECD. *Divided We Stand: Why Inequality Keeps Rising.* Paris: OECD Publishing, 2011.

———. *Entrepreneurship at a Glance 2011.* Paris: OECD Publishing, 2011.

———. *How's Life? Measuring Well-Being.* Paris: OECD Publishing, 2011.

Office of Economic Opportunity. *The CEO Poverty Measure, 2005–2010.* New York: City of New York, 2012. http://www.nyc.gov/html/ceo/downloads/pdf/CEO_Poverty_Measure_April_16.pdf.

O'Keefe, Ed. "2010 Census Was $1.6 Billion under Budget." Federal Eye (blog), August 10, 2012. http://voices.washingtonpost.com/federaleye/2010/08/2010_census_was_16_billion_und.html.

Panek, Sharon, Slavea Assenova, Jake Hinso, and Ralph Rodriguez. "Gross Domestic Product by Metropolitan Area: Advance Statistics for 2010 and Revised Statistics for 2007–2009." *Survey of Current Business*, October 2011, 93–98. http://www.bea.gov/scb/pdf/2011/10%20October/1011_gdp_metro_text.pdf.

Panek, Sharon, Frank Baumgardner, and Matthew McCormick. "Introducing New Measures of the Metropolitan Economy." *Survey of Current Business*, November 2007, 79–114. http://bea.gov/scb/pdf/2007/11%20November/1107_gdpmetro.pdf.

Paulos, John Allen. *Innumeracy: Mathematical Illiteracy and Its Consequences*. New York: Hill and Wang, 2001.

Peck, Jamie. "Struggling with the Creative Class." *International Journal of Urban and Regional Research* 29, no. 4 (2005): 740–770.

Peters, Alan, and Heather MacDonald. *Unlocking the Census with GIS*. Redlands, CA: Esri Press, 2004.

Porter, Michael. "Location, Competition, and Economic Development: Local Clusters in a Global Economy." *Economic Development Quarterly* 14, no. 15 (2000): 15–34.

Potter, Jonathan. "Policy Issues in Clusters, Innovation, and Entrepreneurship." In *Clusters, Innovation, and Entrepreneurship*, eds. Jonathan Potter and Gabriela Miranda, 21–41. Paris: OECD Publishing, 2009.

Powell, William. *North Carolina: A History*. Chapel Hill: University of North Carolina Press, 1988.

Quinterno, John. "Community Colleges in North Carolina: What History Can Tell Us about Our Future." *North Carolina Insight*, May 2008, 58–77.

———. "The Demographics of Aging in North Carolina." *North Carolina Insight*, June 2009, 1–47.

———. *Making Ends Meet on Low Wages: The 2008 North Carolina Living Income Standard*. Raleigh: North Carolina Budget and Tax Center, 2008. http://www.ncjustice.org/assets/library/1169_2008lisreportmar.pdf.

———. *Strengthening State Economic Development Systems: A Framework for Change*. Chevy Chase, MD: Working Poor Families Project, 2010. http://www.workingpoor-families.org/pdfs/WPFP_policybrief_winter2010.pdf.

———. *When Any Job Isn't Enough: Jobs-Centered Development in the American South*. Winston-Salem, NC: Mary Reynolds Babcock Foundation, 2009. http://www.sbnstrategies.com/2009/10/02/jobs-centered- development-in-the-american-south/.

———. *Where Do National Employment Numbers Come From?* Chapel Hill, NC: South by North Strategies, 2012. http://www.sbnstrategies.com/archives/12139.

Rampell, Catherine. "The Beginning of the End of the Census?" *New York Times*, May 19, 2012. http://www.nytimes.com/2012/05/20/sunday-review/the-debate-over-the-american-community-survey.html.

Reamer, Andrew. *Putting America to Work: The Essential Role of Federal Labor Market Statistics*. Washington, DC: Brookings Institution, 2010. http://www.brookings.edu/~/media/Files/rc/papers/2010/1029_labor_reamer/1029_labor_reamer.pdf.

———. *Surveying for Dollars: The Role of the American Community Survey in the Geographic Distribution of Federal Funds*. Washington, DC: Brooking Institution, 2010. http://www.brookings.edu/~/media/Files/rc/reports/2010/0726_acs_reamer/0726_acs_reamer.pdf.

Regional Technology Strategies, Mt. Auburn Associates, Arkansas Arts Council, Arkansas Science and Technology Authority, and Arkansas Association of Two-Year Colleges. *Creativity in the Natural State: Growing Arkansas's Creative Economy*.

Carrboro, NC: Regional Technology Strategies, 2007. http://rtsinc.org/publications/pdf/Arkansas_final.pdf.

Richardson, Harry. *Regional and Urban Economics.* New York: Penguin, 1978.

Saulny, Susan. "Census Data Presents Rise in Multiracial Population of Youths." *New York Times,* March 24, 2011. http://www.nytimes.com/2011/03/25/us/25race.html.

Sawhill, Isabel, and John Morton. *Economic Mobility: Is the American Dream Alive and Well?* Washington, DC: Pew Charitable Trusts, 2007. http://www.economicmobility.org/assets/pdfs/EMP%20American%20Dream%20Report.pdf.

Saxon, John. *Social Services in North Carolina.* Chapel Hill: University of North Carolina School of Government, 2008.

Schrock, Greg, and Jason Jurjevich. *Is Portland Really the Place Where Young People Go to Retire? Analyzing Labor Market Outcomes for Portland's Young and College-Educated.* Portland, OR: Portland State University, 2012. http://mkn.research.pdx.edu/wp-content/uploads/2012/09/SchrockJurjevich_YCELaborMarket_Full1.pdf.

Sen, Amartya. *Social Exclusion: Concept, Application, and Scrutiny.* Manila: Asian Development Bank, 2000. http://housingforall.org/Social_exclusion.pdf.

Shierholz, Heidi. *Job Openings and Hiring Dropped in December, and Have Not Increased Since Early 2012.* Washington, DC: Economic Policy Institute, 2013. http://www.epi.org/publication/job-seekers-ratio-february-2013/.

Short, Kathleen. *The Research Supplemental Poverty Measure: 2011.* Washington, DC: U.S. Census Bureau, 2012. http://www.census.gov/prod/2012pubs/p60-244.pdf.

Shrestha, Laura. *Life Expectancy in the United States.* Washington, DC: Congressional Research Service, 2006. http://aging.senate.gov/crs/aging1.pdf.

Sirota, Alexandra Forter, and Edward McLenaghan. *Making Ends Meet after the Great Recession: The 2010 Living Income Standard for North Carolina.* Raleigh: North Carolina Budget and Tax Center, 2011. http://www.ncjustice.org/sites/default/files/LIVING%20INCOME%20Standard%20-%202010.pdf.

Skidelsky, Robert. *Keynes: The Return of the Master.* New York: Public Affairs, 2009.

Snyder, Thomas, and Sally Dillow. *Digest of Education Statistics 2011.* Washington, DC: U.S. Department of Education, 2012. http://nces.ed.gov/pubs2012/2012001.pdf.

Sommers, Dixie, and James Franklin. "Overview of Projections to 2020." *Monthly Labor Review,* January 2012, 3–20. http://www.bls.gov/opub/mlr/2012/01/art1full.pdf

State of Maryland. "Maryland's Genuine Progress Indicator: An Index for Sustainable Prosperity." http://www.green.maryland.gov/mdgpi/index.asp (accessed December 28, 2012).

Stiglitz, Joseph. "The Great GDP Swindle." *Guardian,* September 13, 2009. http://www.guardian.co.uk/commentisfree/2009/sep/13/economics-economic-growth-and-recession-global-economy.

Stiglitz, Joseph, Amartya Sen, and Jean-Paul Fitoussi. *Mismeasuring Our Lives: Why GDP Doesn't Add Up.* New York: New Press, 2010. Google Play e-book.

Strauss, William, and Neil Howe. *Generations: The History of America's Future.* New York: Morrow, 1991.

Streitfeld, David. "An Effort to Save Flint, Mich., by Shrinking It." *New York Times,* April 22, 2009. http://www.nytimes.com/2009/04/22/business/22flint.html.

Sugden, Robert, and Alan Williams. *The Principles of Practical Cost-Benefit Analysis*. New York: Oxford University Press, 1978.

Sum, Andrew, and Ishwar Khatiwada. "The Nation's Underemployed in the 'Great Recession' of 2007-09." *Monthly Labor Review*, November 2010, 3–15. http://bls.gov/opub/mlr/2010/11/art1full.pdf.

Tavernise, Sabrina. "Married Couples Are No Longer a Majority, Census Finds." *New York Times*, May 26, 2011. http://www.nytimes.com/2011/05/26/us/26marry.html.

Tax Policy Center. "The American Taxpayer Relief Act as Passed by the Senate; High Income Rates, Pease, and Pep; Distribution of Federal Tax Change by Cash Income Level, 2013." Last revised January 7, 2013. http://www.taxpolicycenter.org/numbers/displayatab.cfm?DocID=3771.

Tiebout, Charles. "Exports and Regional Economic Growth." *Journal of Political Economy* 64, no. 2 (1956): 160–164.

Turner, Joanna, Michel Boudreaux, and Victoria Lynch. *A Preliminary Evaluation of Health Insurance Coverage in the 2008 American Community Survey*. Washington, DC: U.S. Census Bureau, 2009. http://www.census.gov/hhes/www/hlthins/data/acs/2008/2008ACS_healthins.pdf.

United Nations Human Development Program. *Human Development Report 2011: Sustainability and Equity: A Better Future for All*. New York: Palgrave-Macmillan, 2011. http://hdr.undp.org/en/media/HDR_2011_EN_Complete.pdf.

U.S. Bureau of Economic Analysis. "2012 Release Schedule." News release. http://bea.gov/newsreleases/2012rd.htm (accessed October 26, 2012).

———. *Local Area Personal Income and Employment Methodology*. Washington, DC: U.S. Department of Commerce, 2012. http://bea.gov/regional/docs/lapi2010/.

———. "Note on Future Regional Statistical Releases." News release, August 1, 2012. http://www.bea.gov/regional/docs/releasenote.cfm.

———. "Regional Definitions: Disposable Personal Income." Last revised May 3, 2011. http://bea.gov/regional/definitions/nextpage.cfm?key=Disposable%20personal%20income.

———. "Regional Definitions: Earnings." Last revised May 2, 2011. http://www.bea.gov/regional/definitions/nextpage.cfm?key=Earnings.

———. "Regional Definitions: Personal Income." Last revised May 3, 2011. http://bea.gov/regional/definitions/nextpage.cfm?key=Personal%20income.

———. "Regional Economic Accounts Overview." http://www.bea.gov/regional/pdf/overview/regional_intro.pdf (accessed September 4, 2011).

———. *RIMS II: An Essential Tool for Regional Developers and Planners*. Washington, DC: U.S. Department of Commerce, 2012. http://www/bea.gov/regional/pdf/rims/RIMSII_User_Guide.pdf.

———. "Widespread Economic Growth Across States in 2011." News release, June 5, 2012. http://www.bea.gov/newsreleases/regional/gdp_state/gsp_highlights.pdf.

U.S. Bureau of Labor Statistics. "2012 Release Calendar." News release. Last revised September 20, 2012 http://www.bls.gov/schedule/news_release/2012_sched.htm.

———. "American Time Use Survey: 2011 Results." News release, June 22, 2012. http://www.bls.gov/news.release/pdf/atus.pdf.

————. "Business Employment Dynamics: Frequently Asked Questions." Last revised January 6, 2004. http:///www.bls.gov/bdm/bdmover.html.

————. "Consumer Expenditure Survey: Frequently Asked Questions." Last revised September 6, 2012. http://www.bls.gov/cex/csxfaqs.htm.

————. "Consumer Expenditures and Income." In *BLS Handbook of Methods*. Washington, DC: U.S. Department of Labor, 1997. Last revised September 28, 2011. http://bls.gov/opub/hom/pdf/homch16.pdf.

————. "Consumer Price Index." In *BLS Handbook of Methods*. Washington, DC: U.S. Department of Labor, 1997. Last revised June 2007. http://bls.gov/opub/hom/pdf/homch17.pdf.

————. "Current Employment Statistics: Frequently Asked Questions." Last revised February 1, 2013. http://www.bls.gov/ces/cesfaq.htm.

————. "Definitions for the Education and Training Classification System." http://www.bls.gov/emp/ep_definitions_edtrain.pdf (accessed February 17, 2013).

————. "Earnings." http://bls.gov/bls/glossary.htm#earnings (accessed May 3, 2011).

————. "Education and Training Classification System Update: Final System." Last revised February 1, 2012. http://www.bls.gov/emp/ep_finaledtrain.htm.

————. "Employee Benefits in the United States: March 2012." News release, July 11, 2012. http://www.bls.gov/news.release/pdf/ebs2.pdf.

————. "Employer Costs for Employee Compensation: June 2012." News release, September 11, 2012. http://www.bls.gov/news.release/pdf/ecec.pdf.

————. "Employment and Wages Covered by Unemployment Insurance." In *BLS Handbook of Methods*. Washington, DC: U.S. Department of Labor, 1997. http://bls.gov/opub/hom/pdf/homch5.pdf.

————. "Employment, Hours, and Earnings from the Establishment Survey." In *BLS Handbook of Methods*. Washington, DC: U.S. Department of Labor, 2010. http://bls.gov/opub/hom/pdf/homch2.pdf.

————. "Employment in Green Goods and Services: 2010." News release, March 22, 2012. http://www.bls.gov/news.release/pdf/ggqcew.pdf.

————. "Employment Projections." In *BLS Handbook of Methods*. Washington, DC: U.S. Department of Labor, 1997. Chapter revised online September 17, 2012. http://www.bls.gov/opub/hom/pdf/homch13.pdf.

————. "Employment Projections: Frequently Asked Questions." Last revised February 9, 2012. http://www.bls.gov/emp/ep_faq_001.htm.

————. "Employment Situation, September 2012." News release, October 5, 2012. http://www.bls.gov/news.release/archives/empsit_10052012.pdf.

————. "Geographic Profile of Employment and Unemployment: Overview." Last revised October 16, 2001. http://www.bls.gov/gps/gpsover.htm.

————. *How the Government Measures Unemployment*. Washington, DC: U.S. Department of Labor, 2009. http://www.bls.gov/cps/cps_htgm.pdf.

————. "Job Openings and Labor Turnover Survey: Frequently Asked Questions." Last revised July 30, 2002. http://www.bls.gov/jlt/jltfaqs.htm.

————. "Labor Force Data Derived from the Current Population Survey." In *BLS Handbook of Methods*. Washington, DC: U.S. Department of Labor, 1997. Chapter revised online April 17, 2003. http://bls.gov/opub/hom/pdf/homch1.pdf.

————. "Local Area Unemployment Statistics: Frequently Asked Questions." Revised May 4, 2011. http://bls.gov/lau/laufaq.htm.

————. "Local Area Unemployment Statistics: Overview." Revised September 25, 2008. http://bls.gov/lau/luov.html.

————. "Measurement of Unemployment in States and Local Areas." In *BLS Handbook of Methods*. Washington, DC: U.S. Department of Labor, 1997. Chapter revised online January 31, 2013. http://bls.gov/opub/hom/pdf/homch4.pdf.

————. "National Compensation Measures." In *BLS Handbook of Methods*. Washington, DC: U.S. Department of Labor, 1997. Last revised September 28, 2011. http://bls.gov/opub/hom/pdf/homch8.pdf.

————. "Occupational Employment Statistics: Frequently Asked Questions." Last revised January 18, 2012. http://bls.gov/oes/oes_ques.htm.

————. "Occupational Employment Statistics: Overview." Last revised March 27, 2012. http://www.bls.gov/oes/oes_emp.htm.

————. "Productivity and Costs: Second Quarter 2011, Revised." News release, September 1, 2011. http://bls.gov/news.release/archives/prod2_09012011.pdf.

————. "Quarterly Census of Employment and Wages: Frequently Asked Questions." Last revised June 27, 2012. http://www.bls.gov.cew/cewfaq.htm.

————. "State and Metro Area Employment, Hours, and Earnings: Frequently Asked Questions." http://bls.gov/sae/790faq2.htm.

————. "The BLS Green Jobs Definition." http://www.bls.gov/green/green_definition.htm (accessed January 26, 2013).

U.S. Census Bureau. *2007 Economic Census User Guide*. Washington, DC: U.S. Census Bureau, 2009. http://www.census.gov/econ/census07/pdf/econ_user_guide.pdf.

————. *2008 Redistricting Data Prototype Summary File*. Washington, DC: 2009. http://www.census.gov/geo/www/geoareas/GTC_08.pdf.

————. "2010 Census Data Products: United States, at a Glance, Version 2.2." http://www.census.gov/population/www.cen2010/glance/ (accessed October 26, 2012).

————. *The 2012 Statistical Abstract: The National Data Book*. 131st ed. Washington, DC: U.S. Department of Commerce, 2011. http://www.census.gov/compendia/statab/ http://www.census.gov/compendia/statab/2012edition.html.

————."About Population Projections." http://www/census.gov/population/projections/about (accessed January 2, 2013).

————. "About SAIPE." Last revised November 29, 2011. http://www.census.gov/did/www/saipe/about/index.html.

————. "Alternative Measures of Income Definitions." Last revised September 12, 2012. http://www.census.gov/hhes/www/income/data/historical/measures/redefs.html.

————. American Community Survey: Design and Methodology. Washington, DC: U.S. Department of Commerce, 2006. http://www.census.gov/history/pdf/ACSHistory.pdf.

————. "American Community Survey and Puerto Rico Community Survey 2011 Subject Definitions." http://www.census.gov/acs/www/Downloads/data_documentation/SubjectDefinitions/2011_ACSSubjectDefinitions.pdf (accessed January 17, 2013).

————. "American Community Survey: When to Use 1-Year, 3-Year, or 5-Year Estimates." http://www.census.gov/acs/www/guidance_for_data_users/estimates/ (accessed January 2, 2013).

————. "American National Standards Institute (ANSI) Codes." Last revised December 1, 2011. http://www.census.gov/geo/www/ansi/ansi.html.

————. "Appendix A: Geographic Terms and Concepts." In *2010 Redistricting Data (Public Law 94–171) Summary File.* Washington, DC: U.S. Department of Commerce, 2011. https://www.census.gov/prod/cen2010/doc/pl94-171.pdf.

————. "Apportionment Population and Number of Representatives, by State: 2010 Census." http://2010.census.gov/news/pdf/apport2010_table1.pdf (accessed September 17, 2011)

————. "Business Dynamics Statistics: Overview." http://www.ces.census.gov/ces/dataproducts/bds/overview.html (accessed February 15, 2013).

————. "Chapter 5: Geographic Shapefiles Concepts Overview." In *TIGER/Line Files: Technical Documentation.* Washington, DC: U.S. Department of Commerce, 2012. http://www.census.gov/geo/www/tiger/tgrshp2012/TGRSHP2012_TechDoc_Ch5.pdf.

————. "Census 2010 Questionnaire." http://2010.census.gov/2010census/pdf/2010_Questionnaire_Info.pdf (accessed September 17, 2011).

————. "Census of Governments: About the Survey." http://www.census.gov/govs/cog2012/about_the_data.html (accessed February 15, 2013).

————. *A Compass for Understanding and Using American Community Survey Data: What General Data Users Need to Know.* Washington, DC: U.S. Department of Commerce, 2008. http://www.census.gov/acs/www/Downloads/handbooks/ACSGeneral-Handbook.pdf.

————. *A Compass for Understanding and Using American Community Survey Data: What PUMS Data Users Need to Know.* Washington, DC: U.S. Department of Commerce, 2009. http://www.census.gov/acs/www/Downloads/handbooks/ACSPUMS.pdf.

————. "County Business Patterns: About the Data." http://www.census.gov/econ/cbp/overview.htm (accessed February 15, 2013).

————. "County Business Patterns: Coverage and Methodology." http://www.census.gov/econ/cbp/methodology.htm (accessed February 15, 2013).

————. *County and City Data Book: 2007.* 14th ed. Washington, DC: U.S. Department of Commerce, 2010. http://www.census.gov/compendia/databooks/pdf_version.html.

————. "Current Population Survey: About." http://www.census.gov/cps/about/faq.html (accessed February 9, 2013).

————. "Current Population Survey: Frequently Asked Questions." http://www.census.gov/cps/about/faq.html (accessed January 2, 2013).

————. "Current Population Survey: Methodology." http://www.census.gov/cps/methodology (accessed January 2, 2013).

————. "Current Population Survey: Supplemental Surveys." http://www.census.gov/cps/about/supplemental.html (accessed January 2, 2013).

————. "Design and Methodology: American Community Survey." Washington, DC: U.S. Department of Commerce, 2009. http://www.census.gov/acs/www/Downloads/survey_methodology/acs_design_methodology.pdf.

————. "Evolution and History of SIPP." http://www.census.gov/sipp/evol.html (accessed October 15, 2011).

————. "Federal-State Cooperative for Population Estimates: Overview." http://www.census.gov/popest/fscpe/overview.html (accessed January 2, 2013).

———. "Frequently Asked Questions about NAPCS." http://www.census.gov/eos/www/napcs/faqs.html (accessed February 15, 2013).

———. "Guidance About Income Sources." Last revised November 1, 2011. http://www.census.gov/hhes/www/income/method/guidance/index.html.

———. "Guidance on Survey Differences in Income and Poverty Estimates: Background." Last revised September 13, 2011. http://www.census.gov/hhes/www/income/method/guidance/background.html.

———. "Local Employment Dynamics: New Data from the States and the U.S. Census Bureau." http://lehd.did.census.gov/led/led/doc/LEDonepager_20110218.pdf (accessed March 22, 2011).

———. "Local Employment Dynamics State Partners." http://lehd.did.census.gov/led/led/statepartners.html (accessed November 19, 2011).

———. "Mission Statement." Accessed September 2, 2011. http://www.census.gov/aboutus/#.

———. "Nonemployer Statistics: Definitions." http://www.census.gov/nonemployer/definitions.htm (accessed February 15, 2013).

———. "Nonemployer Statistics: About the Data." http://www.census.gov/econ/nonemployer/overview.htm (accessed February 5, 2013).

———. "Nonemployer Statistics: How the Data Are Collected." http://www.census.gov/econ/nonemployer/methodology.htm (accessed February 5, 2013).

———. "Population Estimates: Geographic Terms and Coverage." http://www.census.gov/popest/about/geo/terms.html (accessed January 2, 2013).

———. "Residence Rules and Residence Situations for the 2010 Census." http://www.census.gov/population/www/cen2010/resid_rules/resid_rules.html (accessed January 2, 2013).

———. "SIPP User's Guide." http://www.census.gov/sipp/usrguide.html (accessed November 12, 2012).

———. *Small Area Health Insurance Estimates (SAHIE) 2010 Highlights.* Washington, DC: U.S. Department of Commerce, 2012. http://www.census.gov/did/www/sahie/data/2010/SAHIE_Highlights_2010.pdf.

———. "Small Area Income and Poverty Estimates: Release Highlights of 2010." Last revised November 29, 2011. http://www.census.gov/did/www/saipe/data/highlights/2010.html.

———. "Statistics of U.S. Businesses: About the Data." http://www.census.gov/econ/susb/about_the_data.html (accessed February 15, 2013).

———. "Statistics of U.S. Businesses: Definitions." http://www.census.gov/econ/susb/definitions.html (accessed February 15, 2013).

———. *State and Metropolitan Area Data Book: 2010.* 7th ed. Washington, DC: U.S. Department of Commerce, 2010. http://www.census.gov/compendia/databooks/pdf_version.html.

———. "State Data Centers: Program Overview." http://www.census.gov/sdc/index.html (accessed January 2, 2013).

———. "Survey of Business Owners: About the Survey." http://www.census.gov/econ/sbo/about.html (accessed February 15, 2013).

———. "Survey of Business Owners: How the Data Are Collected." http://www.census.gov/econ/sbo/methodology.html (accessed February 15, 2013).

————. *TIGER/Line Files: Technical Documentation*. Washington, DC: December 2006. http://www.census.gov/geo/www/tiger/tiger2006fe/TGR06FE.pdf.

————. "2007 Economic Census: Definitions." Last revised April 13, 2011. http://www.census.gov/econ/census07/www/definitions.html.

U.S. Department of Commerce. *Fiscal Year 2013: Budget in Brief*. Washington, DC: U.S. Department of Commerce, n.d. http://www.osec.doc.gov/bmi/budget/FY13BIB/fy2013bib_final.pdf (accessed October 26, 2012).

U.S. Department of Housing and Urban Development. *Investing in People and Places: FY 2011 Budget*. Washington, DC: U.S. Department of Housing and Urban Development, 2010. http://hud.gov/budgetsummary2011/full-budget-2011.pdf.

U.S. Department of Labor. *Fiscal Year 2013: Budget in Brief*. Washington, DC: U.S. Department of Labor, n.d. http://www.dol.gov/dol/budget/2013/PDF/FY2013BIB.pdf (accessed October 26, 2012).

————. "National Agricultural Workers Survey." http://www.doleta.gov/agworker/naws.cfm (accessed February 17, 2013).

————. "Unemployment Insurance Chartbook." http://www.doleta.gov/unemploy/charbook.cfm (accessed January 26, 2013).

U.S. Government Accountability Office. *Quantitative Data Analysis: An Introduction*. Washington, DC: U.S. Government Accountability Office, 1992.

————. *Tax Gap Actions Needed to Address Noncompliance with S Corporation Tax Rules*. Washington, DC: U.S. Government Accountability Organization, 2009. http://www.gao.gov/new.items/d10195.pdf.

————. *Using Statistical Sampling*. Washington, DC: U.S. Government Accountability Office, 1992.

U.S. Office of Management and Budget. *North American Industry Classification System: United States, 2007*. Lanham, MD: Bernan, 2007.

————. "Revised Delineations of Metropolitan Statistical Areas, Micropolitan Statistical Areas, and Combined Statistical Areas, and Guidance on Uses of the Delineations of These Areas (OMB Bulletin No. 13-01)." February 28, 2013. http://www.whitehouse.gov/sites/default/files/omb/bulletins/2013/b-13-01.pdf.

————. *Standard Occupational Classification Manual 2010*. Washington, DC: U.S. Government Printing Office, 2010.

————. "Statistical Policy Directive No. 14." May 1978. http://www.census.gov/hhes/povmeas/methodology/ombdir14.html.

————. "Update of Statistical Area Definitions and Guidance on Their Uses (OMB Bulletin No. 10-02)." December 1, 2009. http://www.whitehouse.gov/sites/default/files/omb/assets/bulletins/b10-02.pdf.

U.S. Small Business Administration. "Mission Statement." http://www.sba.gov/content/mission-statement-0 (accessed February 15, 2013).

Vincent, Grayson, and Victoria Velkoff. *The Next Four Decades: The Older Population in the United States: 2010–2050*. Washington, DC: U.S. Census Bureau, 2010. http://www.census.gov/prod/2010pubs/p25-1138.pdf.

White, Jesse. "Economic Development in North Carolina: Moving toward Innovation." *Popular Government*, Spring/Summer 2004, 2–13. http://ncinfo.iog.unc.edu/pubs/electronicversions/pg/pgspsm04/article1.pdf.

Wilson, Steven. *Population Dynamics of the Great Plains: 1950–2007.* Washington, DC: U.S. Census Bureau, 2009. http://www.census.gov/prod/2009pubs/p25-1137.pdf.

Wolff, Edward. *Poverty and Income Distribution.* 2d ed. Malden, MA: Wiley-Blackwell, 2009.

Yaukey, David. *Demography: The Study of Human Population.* New York: St. Martin's Press, 1985.

Zeisset, Paul. "Economic Census." In *Encyclopedia of the U.S. Census,* ed. Margo Anderson. Washington, DC: CQ Press, 2000.

Index

Italic page references indicate charts, graphs, and boxed text.

About the Author

John Quinterno is the founder and principal of South by North Strategies, Ltd., a research consultancy specializing in economic and social policy. Over the course of his career, Quinterno has directed multiple applied research projects into matters of labor economics, workforce development, regional policy, social insurance, and postsecondary education. Quinterno's writings on policy subjects have appeared in numerous publications and he has served on a variety of civic boards and commissions. A graduate of the University of Notre Dame and the University of North Carolina at Chapel Hill, Quinterno resides in Chapel Hill.